# Blood Is Thicker Than Alcohol



Tracey Ford

**First Published in 2025 by Tracey Ford**
**Written by Tracey Ford**
**Editing by Beverley Ward**
**Formatted and proofread by Anne Grange**
**Cover Design by MA Rehman**


**ISBN: 978-1-0369-3276-3**

# About the Author

Tracey Ford is a rebellious storyteller, recovery advocate, and unapologetic voice for women who've lived through it.

Born and bred in Sheffield, she's walked the long road from teenage mum and addiction to award-winning filmmaker and public speaker. Her work disrupts shame, challenges systems, and builds spaces where lived experience leads.

Tracey sits on the national CLERO board (College of Lived Experience Recovery Organisations) and actively participates in Sheffield's and the National Inclusive Recovery Cities Movement, championing trauma-informed, inclusive approaches that centre community and compassion.

Founder of the SWIPE Women's Network and invited speaker at the United Nations, Tracey blends Northern humour with raw honesty to empower others to reclaim their stories. She runs bespoke Have a Word with Yourself workshops for women ready to prioritise themselves, alongside a free downloadable workbook of the same name.

You can learn more about her work and writing at:

www.haveawordwithyourself.co.uk

# Dedications

**For Frank Ford**

You always claimed you 'didn't give a flying fuck', but I know deep-down that you did. I'm not gonna sugarcoat it though! You could be a bastard at times, but you were *my* bastard, and I wouldn't trade anything we went through for the world. Because had I not gone through it, I wouldn't be the woman I am today.

**To Mum**

Thank you for the strength I didn't realise I'd inherited until I needed it most.

**To Ada**

Thank you for stepping up when my dad stepped down, for picking up the pieces, and for putting me back together again.

**To Sarah**

My ride or die, the one who's seen every version of me and never flinched and held me together when I couldn't.

**For Danielle and Lauren**

My heartbeat, my hope, my reason. You are living proof that cycles can be broken.

**For Pat Betts**

Thank you for validating that tough love rules were made to be broken.

**And for all the families still navigating life alongside alcoholism or any addiction**

Your love, grit, and quiet endurance deserve to be seen and, more importantly, *heard*.

**For those navigating recovery**

And those still finding their way, every scar, every relapse, every time you got back up, that's ***your*** proof, not of failure, but of fight. You're still here. That's everything.

For every woman who's ever had to *have a word with herself* — this one's for you.

# Foreword

***'Blood Is Thicker Than Alcohol is an amazing and enlightening insight into recovery as an emblem of human potential.'***

Tracey Ford has been a power for good in Sheffield for as many years as I have known her – a champion for recovery and for communities, whose drive and determination has shaped local responses not only to drug and alcohol treatment and recovery but to community growth and wellbeing and providing a voice for lived experience. It is also wonderful to observe as that authentic voice for action and social justice has been heard on both a national and international stage.

It is for this reason it gives me great personal pride and pleasure to provide a foreword to *Blood Is Thicker Than Alcohol*. Tracey has been a supporter of my work, a personal source of support and inspiration and a fellow advocate and champion for both recovery communities and for the families impacted by both addiction and by recovery.

And that is what makes this book so special and unique. There are many accounts out there of recovery journeys that chronicle the multiple adversities people experience and the incredible story of resilience, growth and human flourishing that are inspiring and moving. All that is in this book, described in characteristic depth and intensity by Tracey, but this is so much more. While Tracey does indeed describe her own decline and rebirth, there are two stories – Tracey's story and that of her dad, Frank, whose story does not have such a happy ending.

Yet this is a love story of a daughter for a father who never escapes the shackles of alcoholism and the painful physical decline that results from it. Yet against that background, an unrequited love is realised after a fashion.

This story is intertwined with Tracey's own story of challenges with drugs and mental health and their impact on her identity and relationships.

So the book ultimately is a life journey with disappointment, with distress, with death but ultimately this is an incredible story of not just survival but of thriving. Tracey writes powerful of themes of love and loss, despair and grief, but all in the backdrop of what is an incredible story of human flourishing and overcoming adversity.

No two recovery stories are the same and what this book offers is a powerful, unique and honest insight into one woman's journey from lost to found, alone to connected and from powerless to empowered. *Blood is thicker than alcohol* is an amazing and enlightening insight into recovery as an emblem of human potential.

*By David Best: Director, Recovery Outcomes Institute, US Director, STAR Recovery, UK; Honorary Professor of the Australian National University; Honorary Associate Professor, Monash University; Australia Affiliate Senior Scientist, Public Health Institute, USA.*

# Contents

# 1: June 2002 – The Phone Call

I'd taken an impromptu day off work and was just getting down to my cleaning routine when I was interrupted by the phone shrilling in the living room. A sales call? I didn't recognise the number...

'Hello?'

'Hi-ya, shugs, how are you doing?'

Wow! It was Dad, a blast from the past. I'd not heard from him for ages, but it was nice to hear his voice.

'I'm sound, thanks, Dad. Just doing some housework. How's you?'

'I'm doing just great. Listen, I'm calling off a mate's phone, so just a quickie. I'm coming over to Sheffield later today and was wondering if I can stay over at yours?'

I was taken aback. The last time he'd stayed over at mine was years ago, when he was wooing this wealthy bird from Cornwall; the cheeky git had me playing gooseberry so his then partner didn't find out he was cheating. As usual, I found myself saying yes, when really, I was screaming NOOOOO! But Dad didn't like being refused. He was a man who was used to getting his own way.

'Yeah, Dad. Sure. What time are you thinking of getting here?"

'Should be there about four-ish. Are you sure you don't mind?'

'Of course not, Dad.' Anxiety started brewing in the pit of my stomach.

'Nice one. It won't be for long, a couple of days maybe, just until I find my own place.'

And before I could reply, the phone was dead.

*Shit, shit, shit!* Now my stomach was doing friggin' summersaults...Where was he going to stay? I didn't have a spare bed. And how long was he planning on staying? Getting a place of his own wasn't going to be easy. And how was he going to get one? He hadn't even got a fucking job. Then I thought about Pat. What the FUCK was I going to tell him? He was at work and had no idea I'd just agreed for my dad to move in with us. I hadn't even discussed it with him.

*Shit, shit, shit!*

I thought about calling Dad back but what would I say?

'Hi, Dad, sorry I've changed my mind. You're not welcome at my home?' Nah, I couldn't do that. I was nervous calling Pat, but it was easier than saying no to Dad. I knew he'd be busy at work, but I had to call him.

'Or reyt, what's up?

He was obviously in a good mood. Little did he know I was about to piss on his bonfire.

'Pat. Listen, I've just come off the phone to Dad.'

'And?'

'Weeell, he's coming up to Sheffield and asked if he could stay over at ours for a couple of days.'

The pause at the other end of the phone was a little too long for my liking.

'I don't see why not? It's only for a couple of days, isn't it?'

I was surprised at his reaction. After all, he wasn't Dad's biggest fan.

'Well he says it's for a couple of days Pat, but he's not just staying over, he's planning on moving back to fucking Sheffield, for good! I'm sorry, I should have said no but I didn't know how to. I was on the spot. I can't even call him back.' I was on the verge of tears now.

'Listen,' he said. 'It's for a couple of days. I'm fine with it. What time's he getting here?'

''bout four or five-ish.'

'Ok, no worries, I'll be finished up by then. Listen I'll see ya later. And stop panicking, it'll be reyt.'

I was glad that Pat didn't seem that bothered, but I was worried. Having a social drink with Dad in the pub was one thing. Living with him was something else entirely, and I should know...

# 2: Earliest Childhood Memories

I don't have many childhood memories of Dad. Perhaps that was because he wasn't around that much, and if he was around, he didn't really do the Dad thing. Mum tells me that he did have spells when he'd stay home and spend time with us as a family; apparently, he'd even cook. But it's not what I remember.

We lived on Alexandra Road in the Heeley area of Sheffield, next to a pub called The Myrtle. I remember this, because that's where Dad could usually be found.

At home, it was mostly just me, Mum and my younger sister Sarah, though we saw a lot of my Nan and Grandad, and Mum's sisters, Auntie Jackie and Auntie Glenda were nearby as well.

Sarah and I were brought up like twins: same hair, same clothes, mostly ones Mum made for us. Sometimes Mum went to the pub too, with Auntie Jackie and Uncle Richard and then we'd get to spend time with our cousins, which we loved. Our Paul, the eldest, was in charge of all five of us, and we'd wait excitedly for our parents to come home when we'd get a packet of crisps and a bottle of pop each, as a treat for being good.

Sometimes I helped Mum with the washing. At the time, we had one of those twin-tub washers and a mangle with two heavy rubber rollers which squeezed the clothes, draining all the excess water off, though I was never allowed near the rollers in case I trapped my fingers. We had an outside toilet and a tin bath, which was pulled into the kitchen at bath-times. Dad went first and we'd be ushered in after, to take our turns getting washed in his left-over water.

Mum was fair with us kids. We were the centre of her world, but she had strict rules. In her view 'kids should be seen and not heard' and we were frequently reminded that 'those that ask don't get'. I could never get my head around this one. If you didn't ask how would someone know what you wanted? I always sensed that these weren't actually Mum's rules, they were really Nan's, Mum just applied them to us like they were applied to her as a kid.

Dad kept ferrets in the cellar and used them for his shooting trips chasing rabbits. Mum would have the unenviable job of skinning any rabbits he caught. I remember the rifle – it was as big as me. These are the little things I remember.

One of my most vivid early memories of Dad was of a time when he had some mates round at ours. They were in the living room, playing cards, drinking and smoking. Dad called me over and placed me on his lap, parading me like a proud Dad. He made me puff on his cigarette. I remember coughing and choking, much to the amusement of Dad and his friends.

Another time, when I was still very young, Dad came home from work, all smiles; he'd probably been at the pub. It must have been teatime, because Mum was cooking in the kitchen. I was at the bottom of the stairs when he walked through the door. He whipped his hands behind his back when he saw me then beckoned me over.

'Come here, Trace. Ya Dad's got a present for ya.' I was thrilled and shot over to Dad, who passed me a small red box. It was lovely and I was excited to see what was in it.

I recall the catch being really stiff, but when I finally opened it, there, inside, was a lovely red watch. It wasn't even my birthday or anything! I gave him a hug and took it out of the box. It was far too big for me to wear, but I loved it.

I was playing with the watch when our Sarah walked into the room. Naturally, Sarah asked where hers was.

'You haven't got one.' Dad told her.

She cried because she couldn't understand why she hadn't been given a gift too. I remember Mum tried to comfort her, but Dad lost his temper and ordered her to bed. I still remember standing there, feeling ashamed and confused. Stomping towards the stairs, Sarah shouted that she was leaving home and she was packing her things.

'Well you can fucking leave, but you'll leave with what you came with – nothing,' shouted Dad.

This is the first time I genuinely felt what injustice felt like. I knew something was wrong and I didn't like the feeling. I wanted to feel special and loved but not at someone else's expense, especially my sister's.

It was the first act of kindness from Dad and should have been a happy memory, but it wasn't. It was tainted. This was my first taste of favouritism and, trust me, feeling special in our house was a double-edged sword that would have an adverse effect on my life for years to come.

# 3: D-Day: Dad Arrives

I broke the news that Grandad Ford was coming to stay when the kids got home from school. Fifteen-year-old Danielle immediately asked where he was going to sleep. When I explained that he would have to sleep on the sofa, Lauren wasn't having any of it.

'It's ok, Mum, he can sleep in my bedroom.'

Danielle was not impressed. 'And where are you going to sleep?'

'He can stay in my room, and I can share with you! It'll be fun, Dan!' Lauren was only ten and excited at the prospect of sharing a room she was rarely allowed in. However, Danielle valued her privacy. She looked at me and pleaded.

'Mum, NO! She can't share with me. Can't Grandad stay somewhere else? She'll do my head in!' and with that, she stormed out to see her mates.

She hadn't been gone twenty minutes before a car pulled up on the front of the house and Dad got out. He was looking good, dressed smartly as always. He waved as he made his way from the passenger seat to the boot of the car to get his suitcase out. I remember that moment well.

His suitcase was really old-fashioned, fake tan leather with bulky buckles. It looked like something out of Steptoe and Son. Dad was all smiles though. He looked like he was going on his holidays, but then I remembered he wasn't, he was coming to stay with me. Dad closed the boot and then made his way to the driver's side. He leaned down to talk to someone I couldn't see.

Dad stood tall. 'Hey shugs, you don't mind Steve coming in, do ya?'

I was just thinking *who the fuck is Steve?*

'Only he's been driving for the past couple of hours. He could do with a break before setting back to Stoke.'

*How could I refuse?* 'Sure, Dad, no problem?'

Steve took a bit more convincing, but soon he was parking the car whilst Dad made his way towards the house.

Lauren ran towards him as he walked up the drive. I could tell he was touched by her enthusiasm. Before he went to pick her up, he reached out to me. I expected a hug or a kiss, but he just handed me the suitcase.

'Here, love – take this, will ya? I'll wait here for Steve and then I'll be in.' This was the first time in over nine years that Dad had visited me at all at my home, and he'd only been here two minutes, and he was treating me like it was his place already! No 'Hi Tracey' No 'how ya doing?' Bleeding typical!

I could hear Dad brushing his feet on the doormat before entering the house and was glad I'd spent the day cleaning. Steve was still seeking assurance in a hushed voice.

'Stop being fucking stupid and come in, will ya.'

Dad joined me in the living room before ushering his mate Steve into the room. Dad looked around. I could tell he was impressed that I had a mortgage.

Steve was a lot younger than Dad. He was tall and skinny, with white bleached-blonde hair and he was sporting a long leather trench coat. He looked like a cross between Johnny Rotten and Sid Vicious, only with one eye. He wasn't like Dad's usual mates at all.

It felt weird to see Dad sitting there in my front living room drinking tea. I tried to ask Dad about his plans, but he was more interested in when Pat would be home so we could all go for a pint at our local pub. It would be on him of course, after all, it was the least he could do with us letting him stay and all that!

Being mid-week, we wouldn't normally have gone for a drink, but Dad had already finished his cuppa and was insisting Steve drive him down to our local. It was only a ten-minute walk from ours but then I remembered that Dad never walked anywhere.

Dad was standing at the bar next to Steve in the Best Room, when Pat and I arrived with Lauren an hour later. I was grateful that he wasn't in the Tap Room where all our mates would have usually been. I wasn't ready for that just yet! Dad offered to get the drinks in and quickly introduced Steve to Pat. They shook hands and Pat took Lauren into the kids' area whilst I waited with Dad at the bar to get the drinks. Dad wrapped his arms around me and thanked me again for letting him stay over. I tried to introduce him to Sharon, the bar manager, but Dad had beat me to it.

'We've already been introduced, Tracey,' she said. 'He's been telling me all about him being in the pub game and all that!'

'Ahh, I bet he has.' I didn't want him to get too settled in. 'Dad, come on. We need to take these into the kids' room,' I could tell he wasn't impressed at being prized away from the bar, but he reluctantly indulged me, and Steve followed like a compliant sheep.

We settled around the table. There was a lot of small talk, Dad asking after Pat and how work was going. Steve was still mainly mute.

'So, Steve, how do you know Dad?'

Before he could reply, Dad stepped in. 'Steve used to be one of me regulars in the pub down Stoke. That was until he was sectioned! I've been telling him he should have a chat with you, seeing as you've both been in't loony bin for't same thing, Steve wa' caning speed same as you Trace. He's not been out long.'

I was slightly taken aback, just because the mental health ward I'd been on wasn't a loony bin, and because I knew from my own recovery how fragile Steve must be. Driving Dad up the motorway seemed like the last thing Steve would have needed.

'It's early days,' Steve shared sheepishly, clearly embarrassed by Dad's open disclosure. 'But ya Dad's been good to me, so bringing him up here is the least I could do.'

Dad patted him on the shoulder. 'He's a good un, our Trace. Hey, perhaps you could give him some counselling and all that.'

It was a slightly awkward moment. I didn't mind offering a listening ear to anyone, but I hadn't signed up to counselling his mate in the kids' room in the pub whilst Lauren was there!

Steve quickly interjected. 'I'm doing loads better. I was only there for a couple of weeks. I'd been taking too much sniff, started seeing things, totally lost it, I did, but I'm doing ok.' He turned to Dad. 'Frank, I'm going after this one. I'd best be thinking about heading back soon.'

Only Dad wasn't having any of it.

'Don't be silly, tha can't get off yet! Ya can have a couple more wi us.'

Steve shouldn't have been driving already, let alone having a-bloody-nother but drink driving rules didn't apply in Dad's world. Totally oblivious, Dad took a cigar from his inside jacket. He was about to light it when I explained that in the kids' area, smoking wasn't allowed.

'Ah be reyt, there's only us in here,' and he continued to light his cigar.

Pat shook his head and with a dismayed look, offered to get the round in.

'So Dad, how comes you're back in Sheffield?' I asked.

Before he could reply, Sharon walked in to collect the empties. Dad had just taken his first drag.

'Hey Frank, ya do know you're not supposed to smoke in here, don't ya?'

'Ahh, our Trace just mentioned it, it's only a cigar and there's no one else in? No other kids? What's ya problem?'

Normally Sharon would have given him what for. She didn't take no shit from no one in the pub and folks respected her for it. But not Dad. It was one rule for him and another for every bugger else! Still, I was surprised when she just shrugged her shoulders and said 'don't let me catch you again' before turning and walking back to the bar.

And just like that, he'd got his own way. Again.

I steered Dad back to our conversation. 'So come on, Dad. How come you're back in Sheff?'

'Well, ya know I've been running The Pig Pen? Truth is, it's a bit too much on me own, so ya Uncle John and Dot are gonna take it over. I fancied a change. Time to come back to me roots.'

My mind was in a whirl. What was he planning on doing now? He'd done a bit of asbestos stripping in between managing pubs, but nothing seemed to last long these days. Dad could see what I was thinking.

'Hey, don't you worry about me, shugs, I'm sorted. I've got this insurance claim going through, so I just need to keep me head low. I'll get me sen a place and take it from there! Might get another pub!'

*For fuck's sake!* Pat returned with the drinks, but I was ready for off. I'd got to get back and sort our Lauren's room out and we hadn't even had tea yet.

Then Dad had an idea 'Tell ya what? You get yourselves off home. We'll have a couple more, then I'll get us a takeaway. What d'ya fancy? Chinese? Chippy? Pizza?'

We settled on the chippy and Me and Pat headed home. Before long, Dad arrived with a load of cans and Steve was in tow carrying the chippy tea.

'I reckon Steve should stay over. It's getting late. I told him you wouldn't mind.'

I could tell Steve did though.

'Nah Frank, honest. I'll have these and be off.'

'Nah, sod that! Anyway, ya over limit' He turned to me and Pat. 'You don't mind, do ya?'

*No, Dad. I don't mind Johnny Rotten sleeping on my sofa. I don't have work in the morning or nowt?*

That's what I was thinking, but not long afterwards, I found myself alone in the living room making up a bed for Steve. Even though I knew deep-down he could probably be trusted, I still felt uneasy having a stranger sleeping downstairs, so I stayed up a little longer continuing with the small talk.

It wasn't too long before Steve shared a little more about his past. He'd been introduced to speed during the dance scene, in the late eighties. Whilst all of his mates had moved on, settled down and got families, he'd continued to use. His life for the past few years had revolved around short bouts of recovery before relapsing and being sectioned.

I sat and listened, taking in his story. I never thought that I would have had anything in common with Johnny Rotten, but I did. I recognised the feelings of being the odd one out, never feeling like he fitted in. The only difference was that I had managed to break the cycle. I was in no place to judge him. Deep-down, he was a lovely guy. Shame he didn't know it himself. But I also knew that this was his journey.

I was just about to get up ready to go to bed, when he stopped me,

'I noticed you like your silver.' He was looking at the rings on my fingers and before I could answer, he was gifting me with a silver ring from his finger. 'Here, take this and thanks for listening.'

I tried to refuse. After all, the ring was bloody huge, far too big for me, but he insisted.

'You will never know just how much it has meant, you sitting here listening to me waffle on. Your dad was right – you do know your shit!'

I took the ring. I didn't want to offend him, but at the same time, all I could think to myself was that Dad didn't have a clue about me, not really.

When I woke the next morning and came downstairs, Steve had gone...

# 4: Grandad Was My Hero

Right back as far as I can remember, my Nan and Grandad on Mum's side were a significant factor in our lives. If Nan wasn't already round our house, we'd walk the two miles to Abbeydale to the terrace that backed onto the railway track.

On the way, we'd pass the black and white plastic cow at the old milk factory, and the steelworks where Grandad worked. His workstation was bang next to the footpath and his window would always be open, with the invisible smell of the steel works seeping out. He'd be there with his navy boiler suit covered in grime and always with a smile on his face, happy to see us.

I don't recall Nan smiling much at all. She was always wearing her signature pinny and cleaning or cooking. Nan had a selection of dolls, but they weren't toys, more like ornaments. We were never allowed to play with them. If we were lucky, she might let us play with this one toy monkey she had, but apart from that when we were round at hers, the 'Kids should be seen and not heard' rule always applied, well apart from when we were outside with Grandad – there were never any rules when Grandad was around.

Grandad was my hero. He was a very tall, handsome man with a look of Clarke Gable. He was amazing with his hands. You name it, he could make it. Grandad loved to spend time playing with us kids. He'd have us on his lap, grab our faces and rub his stubble against our cheeks whilst ticking us. I hated and loved it all at the same time. I would always walk away with a great big rash on my cheek, but also with a feeling of being loved. Grandad always called me 'Tatey' which made me feel even more special, more loved.

My mum was the youngest of three girls: Auntie Glenda, Aunt Jackie (my fave) and then Mum. When they were teenagers, Auntie Glenda's daughters, Christine and Stephanie, would be at Nan's too because they didn't get along with their mum's new bloke. Later, she married him, and they never returned. Little did I know then that they would soon be moving in with us.

# 5: Sid Vicious Was Gone

In the morning, it was just the usual routine, apart from the fact that we were tiptoeing around, trying not to wake Dad. Once the kids and Pat had gone off, I got ready for work, then took him a brew. I knocked on the bedroom door. No response. I tried again.

'Dad, are you awake?'

I could hear him stirring.

'Come in, Trace. I'm awake.'

Dad was lying under Lauren's pink quilt with one of her teddies lodged between his head and the wall. It was a sight to behold.

'Did you sleep well? I've got to be heading off to work soon. I brought you a cuppa.'

I could see it was taking him a couple of minutes to realise where he was himself.

'Tell ya what, Trace. Take the cuppa downstairs. I'll be down in two secs.'

I waited for Dad in the living room and handed him the tea as he settled into Pat's chair by the fire.

'Sorry I can't stay with you Dad, only I have got to be getting into work. Is there anything you need? I can do you some breakfast before I leave if you like?'

Dad was quite chirpy. 'No worries, Trace. I'm going to make a few calls today to the solicitors but if there's owt you want me to do around the house, let me know?'

The thought of Dad cleaning my house for me amused me, after all it had always been the other way around. But it also saddened me. I didn't know why, there was just something that I couldn't quite put my finger on. He seemed different somehow and I couldn't work out why. The mention of solicitors got my attention though.

'Dad, why have you got to call the solicitors?'

'I need to chase me claim.'

'What claim?'

'I was in the Hadfield train crash, wasn't I?'

I was shocked. I could vaguely remember something about the crash, but I didn't have a scooby do that Dad had been on it. And I couldn't work out why Dad had a claim. He seemed ok to me but then what would I know?

'I told you,' he said, looking bemused.

'Dad, no you bleeding didn't. This is the first I have heard of it!' I was pissed off, but it just highlighted just how much we had grown apart.

'I'd been doing some asbestos stripping. Ya know me, Trace, I'd been at the bar and was heading back to my seat when the lot went. I don't remember much. One minute I was about to sit down and the next, me drink wa gone, I was upside down, dazed as fuck with blood trickling down my face and all I could hear was screaming. It were a good job I'd left the buffet car where them people died but I was in't next coach.'

I was still staring at him as he carried on.

'So, I've got a claim in, for damages on account of the PTSD. It's no win no fee so it's not costing me nowt, but its fucking taking forever! Still dealing with it three years on but I've had some interim payments. Solicitors reckon I'm due a BIG pay-out! They've just paid one bloke half a million. He lost a leg though. Still, you see, Trace, once this is all sorted, I can get me sen a nice little place of me own, I can retire, go fishing to me little heart's content.'

It made sense now where Dad's money had been coming from. I wasn't as optimistic as Dad seemed to be though. Ok, he'd been shook-up but he seemed fine to me. Dad told me that his case was taking longer on account that PTSD was hard to establish, but that he was expecting £200,000. So, for the past few months, he'd been keeping a low profile and waiting for the appointments with the shrinks. Once they'd written their reports, they'd be going back to the railway to negotiate a settlement.

I was late for work. I started to make a move.

'I'll need to make a few calls. Is it ok to use the phone?'

‘Of course it is, Dad. Listen, you get settled in. I’ll call ya later.’

As I drove into work, I reflected on everything he’d said. I couldn’t help thinking how little I knew about Dad and what he’d been up to over the past few years. I could see how we’d grown apart. With Dad working away, our only contact had been the occasional telephone conversation here and there. I’d stopped relying on Dad like I used to, and we were both in very different places in our lives. Aside from the shock of the crash and the smoking episode in the pub, it hadn’t been so bad having him to stay. He wasn’t that overbearing, and he hadn’t taken over. Maybe it would be nice to have him around, after all.

# 6: Barbers Field

It was 1977, I was seven years old, and we were moving to a new house on a newish estate. I was full of nervous anticipation at the thought of starting at a new school and having to make new friends, but I was also filled with excitement.

Mum hadn't stopped talking about the new house which had its own back garden, meaning we would no longer have to play out on a concrete backyard in front of the outside toilets. The new house had an inside toilet too; no more peeing into a bucket at night or venturing out into the freezing cold for a pee. And it had its own bathroom, which meant the old tin bath was now redundant.

When we arrived at our new home on Fraser Crescent, I could see why Mum had been so excited. She let us explore the house before the furniture arrived. It was three-bedroomed, which meant me and Sarah would have our very own rooms. I loved it.

As usual, Dad was nowhere to be seen, but Nan was there, with the trusty old pinny and marigolds on, barking orders, giving instructions to poor old Grandad, who was left humping the furniture into the house. Mum sent us out of the way to play.

Our road was long. There were terraced houses as far as the eye could see. On our side of the road, there were steep grassed verges, with steps down from the houses to the road. It was the school holidays, and our arrival had caused quite a stir. There were kids playing out, itching to get a glimpse to see if there were any new potential friends or foes to be made.

We hadn't been outside long when Alison, who lived opposite, came over to introduce herself. She was a little older than us and pretty with a nice smile. Alison asked my mum if we were allowed to go down to Barbers field. I hadn't got a clue what or who Barbers Field was, but I was up for finding out.

We turned left and made our way down to the right onto Fraser Drive. There was another row of houses, but behind the houses was a huge green field. There were parents standing outside their doors chatting whilst the kids played on bikes. Others were playing cricket or rounders on the field.

As we got closer, the field seemed to get bigger. I couldn't believe we would have this much open space to play; it was certainly a stark contrast to our old street which didn't have any grass at all.

The field to the right was lined with trees, protecting a dense wood behind. As we walked, Alison introduced us to the local kids. I felt shy but underneath, I was excited. I couldn't wait to live here.

# 7: No Win No Fee

It had been over a week since Dad had arrived and, truth be told, it wasn't half as bad as I'd first feared. In fact, he was the perfect house guest; he would dust, wash the pots, put the washing out and tidy around the house whilst me and Pat were at work.

I'd been making enquiries to housing to sort out a tenancy. I was worried Dad would be picky, but he was easy-going. In his eyes, it was only temporary. Once the claim was sorted out, he'd be buying his own place.

When Dad wasn't cleaning, he was stalking the solicitors pursuing the claim and getting more frustrated each day. It didn't help that it was all over the news because one of the crash victim's widows was in high court seeking her own compensation. It didn't sit easy with me when Dad would complain about her getting her case sorted before his. I wanted to scream at him: 'for crying out loud Dad, she has lost her husband! What have you lost?' but the words never left my mouth.

Our Sarah, my sister, came around to see him. She'd been staying with Mum having split up from her long-term partner and had enough on her plate without worrying about Dad. Initially it was awkward; their relationship had been strained for years. She thought I was mad allowing Dad to stay. Apparently, unbeknownst to me, years earlier Dad had asked to stay at hers and she'd said 'no'.

'Well would he have done the same for me?' she asked, knowing from personal experience that the answer would have been a big fat no.

Sarah wasn't interested in Dad's big insurance claim. I could see her eyes glaze over when Dad talked about his big plans once he got his pay out. And to be fair, I couldn't blame her; it was starting to grate on me too.

Over the years, I'd come to admire my sister's attitude towards Dad. She was almost fearless in the way she approached him. She wasn't bothered if she upset him, in fact she could take or leave him. She'd given up trying to get his attention years ago.

Unlike me. I was like Dad's little shadow, always craving love and attention from him that never quite came.

# 8: Dog's Bollocks

I loved our new house and the newfound sense of freedom. There was always plenty to do and places to explore and play. These were some of the most innocent times of my childhood.

Where my sister could be found playing with dolls or making daisy chains on the field, I loved climbing the local trees. I had no fear and could go higher than any of the boys. Even though I was the only girl, I always felt accepted as one of the lads. But the best part about climbing the trees was when I got to the top, I could see for miles. It was quiet there and sometimes, I'd go and climb a certain tree alone, just for the feeling I got from sitting at the top, oblivious to any passersby.

Things were different when Dad was home though. He wasn't around much but when he was, everyone had to tiptoe around. It wasn't anything specific, just this invisible tension. I mean Dad had never raised his hand to us kids, but then again, he never had to. If he was angry, all he would have to do was raise his voice and it would be enough to make me want to literally pee myself.

If there was an unfamiliar flash car on the front, I could bet it was his. I didn't know what Dad did for a living, but when he was home, he always seemed to have cash on him, whilst Mum always seemed to be skint. She never seemed to stop; in addition to moving to a new house, she had taken a job in an accounts department. If she wasn't working, she'd be cleaning, or washing clothes outside in the back garden because the twin-tub washer leaked.

When Dad was home, he was either eating his tea, sleeping or getting ready to go out. Back then, the pubs opened at midday, closed at three-thirty pm then reopened at seven pm. Dad played darts, so was always getting ready for some competition at the pub. He must have been good at it, because our cabinet in the living room was full of trophies he'd won, the only evidence that he lived there.

As soon as Mum got back from work, she would make a start on Dad's tea and would take it into the living room on a tray for him to eat while watching TV. After eating, Dad would head upstairs to bed for a couple of hours. We always had to be quiet when Dad was in bed, so as not to wake him up. Just before waking Dad up, Mum would go upstairs and run a bath. Whilst Dad was in the bath, she would... wait for it... wash his hair and brush his false teeth! Then Mum would head back downstairs to iron his clothes and make him a large mug of tea, which would be placed next to the armchair ready for when he came back downstairs and sat in his chair. Nobody else could sit in Dad's chair if he was at home.

He would come downstairs and walk into the living room reminding me of a sumo wrestler, wearing nothing except a large bathrobe draped around his waist. Dad would sit in the chair whilst Mum blow-dried and styled his hair; she would then kneel in front of him to put his socks on for him. (Years later, Dad asked me to put his socks on for him. I told him to 'fuck off'. I swore I'd never do that for a bloke).

Once Dad had finished his mug of tea, he would head back upstairs, get ready, then come back down, looking the "dogs bollocks". Dad always smelt nice, and the smell of his aftershave would linger in the house long after he had left, the only evidence he'd ever been there at all.

I often wondered where he was going. I was never awake to hear him come back home and he never seemed to be around in the mornings neither.

Sundays were different though, I think on account of the pubs closing earlier. Even then, he didn't eat at the table with us, preferring to have his meal on a tray watching TV. Sundays are the only memories I have of spending actual time with Dad. I recall the times me and Sarah would be encouraged and goaded to fight each other for Dad's entertainment. I always felt that Dad loved us both in his own way, only his love was implied and assumed, Dad seldom displayed expressions of love. Any accomplishment was more likely to be met with a pat on the back rather than a hug and kiss.

On one particular Sunday afternoon, Dad asked me and Sarah: 'How would you feel if I got a new girlfriend?' Mum was actually sitting in the living room!

My reply was swift. 'I wouldn't have anything to do with her.'

Dad laughed. 'Yeh you would, if she gave you money you would!'

But I was adamant. 'I'd kick it outta her hands!'

It left me feeling unsettled. Mum was right there, and she never said a word. I couldn't quite make out if he was serious or not. I'd find out soon enough.

# 9: Fish and Chips

The date for Dad's appointment with the psychiatrist had finally come through. The only problem was that it was in London. Since the accident, there was no way he would even contemplate travelling by train, so muggins here offered to take him, even though the prospect of driving down to London filled me with fear. Driving with Dad as a passenger was almost more daunting; he was the world's worst backseat driver. And the timing couldn't have been worse.

Having worked at a day rehabilitation centre for addicts for the past five years, I'd just been given a new role as Carer Involvement Worker with Sheffield's Drug Action Team. With the National Treatment Agency only recently established and an increased emphasis on service user involvement, my new role was a big deal. I'd be continuing my work supporting and coordinating family support groups across the city, but now I would also be working alongside the commissioners responsible for funding our services and carrying the burden of making sure the views of families were heard.

I was still finding my feet in the new team, embracing the new ways of working and trying my best to make a good impression. The last thing I needed was to be taking annual leave to ferry Dad off to London, but I reasoned that the sooner he got the claim sorted, the better. So, off we went.

The three-hour journey felt more like thirty. Dad was anxious about what he should and shouldn't say and I had to listen to him all the way there. He was preparing like an actor who was up for the audition of a lifetime, his big break. Perhaps that's how he saw it. According to him, this BIG claim was going to change his life. He was bordering on obsessed. 'Once this is all sorted, I'll be able to properly retire, I'll be set for life,' he'd say.

Dad had been researching the effects of PTSD: nightmares, anxiety, guilt. I hadn't seen any evidence of any of it. I nearly choked on my fag when Dad started rehearsing about how his nerves were shot and how he'd turned into a virtual recluse since the accident. He was even going to use the fact that he'd had to move in with his daughter as evidence.

He said he suffered from guilt on account that others died but all I'd heard him say was: 'It's a bloody good job I'd left the drinks carriage or else it would have been me!'

I never challenged Dad about his claims or side-effects, but it didn't sit right. All I saw was a man who'd had a string of failed relationships and fallen on bad times, a fiercely independent, successful businessman, who'd lost it all through not paying the taxman. If he was suffering from anything, it was the shame of sleeping in his granddaughter's bed and relying on his daughter to help him out.

We finally arrived at the Maudsley. It was an impressive building, more like a university than a hospital. We sat in the waiting area, until Dad's name was called. I was planning to stay there but he wasn't having any of it, in fact he was so vocal that the whole waiting room could hear.

'Listen love,' he tried explaining to the secretary. 'I ain't going nowhere unless my daughter comes with me.'

Dad got his own way, and we were taken to meet the psychiatrist. The room was more like a library than a doctor's surgery, the walls lined with expensive-looking bound books.

The doctor rose from his chair and walked around his expansive wooden desk and introduced himself as one of the UK's leading specialists in treating trauma and PTSD. My stomach dropped.

Whilst I only had a measly diploma in counselling, I knew enough to know that Dad would require *all* his blagging skills to pull the wool over this guy's eyes. The session lasted just under an hour. It was painful and bordering on embarrassing, watching Dad talk about how the crash had affected him, especially in the head, in fact he'd tapped the side of his forehead on numerous occasions to labour his point. At one point, he'd even started to cry. This had been the first time I had *ever* seen Dad cry as he vividly recalled what happened on that fateful day. I was impressed. The psychiatrist never really probed or questioned Dad, in fact, if anything, it felt like he was almost prompting, leading him like a director would directing a film.

At the end, the psychiatrist stood and shook Dad's hand, reassuring him that he was satisfied that he had some form of PTSD and that he would be providing the solicitors a full report with his expert opinion, acknowledging the longer-term trauma Dad had experienced on account of the crash.

Dad's whole demeanour changed as soon as we were outside the hospital. It was like he'd won the bloody lottery. The relief that the appointment was over was clear to see. It was like I was driving a different guy home from the anxious passenger on the way there. Dad suggested that we call into the nearest service station and get something to eat on account of him being 'fucking Hank Marvin'. He also wanted to grab a couple of cans from the supermarket to help celebrate on the way home.

Dad treated us both to fish and chips. As we sat opposite each other, I realised that I'd spent more alone time with Dad over the past two weeks than I had ever done in my thirty plus years. Dad seemed to treat me differently too. He sought my opinion and valued my thoughts, and I somehow felt heard. He had every confidence that I would be able to pull some strings, use my influence with the local authority despite me explaining to him that I worked for the NHS and not housing.

Still, it was clear that the dynamics of our relationship had shifted. For the first time in my life, I felt that I was Dad's equal and after relying on him for most of my childhood, he now relied on me.

Our fish and chips arrived. Dad eagerly tore apart one of the small paper square sachets filled with salt and sprinkled it all over his food. The fish and chips were mint, fresh, almost like the ones you would get from the local chippy. I was tucking into mine when I realised that Dad had barely touched his, which surprised me. I asked him what was wrong. Dad looked at me coyly as he tried another chip, but he winced as he slowly chewed it.

'Christ Dad it's not a bleeding bush tucker trial, what's up?'

Dad pushed his plate away and picked up one of the opened sachets. Instead of salt, it was sugar! He looked pretty pissed off, but then out of nowhere, he just cracked. He laughed like I had never heard him before.

He laughed so much there were tears, but this time they weren't fake ones, they were tears of laughter. His laughing was infectious and before I knew it, I was laughing hysterically along with him. Christ knows what anyone else in the canteen must have thought, us two sat there laughing at his plate of fish and chips, but to be honest I didn't care. Even if the joke was on him, it was the first time I'd ever seen him laugh at himself. More importantly, it was the first time in my life that I had felt part of the joke.

# 10: Lose-Lose Situation

I'd been outside playing and had an altercation with a boy who lived across the street from us. He'd lamped me one and I'd run into the house crying. Mum was in the kitchen reassuring me and trying to calm me down when Dad came into the room to see what the commotion was about. I was hoping he'd go out and give Adam a piece of his mind. But instead he took me by the hand and led me outside onto the front garden. He made me point the boy out.

Dad called him over.

I'm thinking, 'Yeh, you're gonna get it nah.'

Adam was hesitant but Dad shouted, 'if tha don't come over here then I'm coming over there and I'll be having a word with thee Dad.'

Adam did as he was told and sheepishly came over the road to meet us in my front garden. The other kids stood back anticipating Dad's next move. But it wasn't Dad who was making a move, it was me. He was pushing me forward and commanding me to hit Adam. I was shitting myself and Adam looked as confused and nervous as me.

'Now fucking lamp him back!' Dad shouted. He then pushed me into Adam, who didn't retaliate. 'Either hit him or I'll hit you!'

I remember thinking that it was a lose-lose situation. Dad or Adam? And of course, Dad won. I did as I was told and hit Adrian in the face, then stepped back.

After I'd thrown my punch, Dad grabbed me by the arm before turning to Adam.

'You ever lay a fucking finger on my daughter again, you little bastard, I'll be straight over to yours and I'll beat the fucking shit outta you AND both ya parents, do you hear?' Dad then spun me round and took me into the house. I was sitting shaking on the sofa when Dad came and knelt in front of me, straight in front of me, looking directly into my eyes.

Listen In this world it's not about winning, it's about having the guts to have a go. Don't you ever let anyone push you around. I won't always be here, but if I hear you have ever backed down again, be sure as hell you'll have me to contend with, do you hear?'

Oh, I heard you Dad, loud and clear, thanks for that! Little did Dad know that those words would always stick, later on in my teenage years, not always to my advantage neither.

# 11: Showing His True Colours

Dad had already had a few drinks by the time Pat got home from work, but he wasn't pissed, pissed. We'd come home to a letter from housing that Dad would be eligible for a tenancy, so we had even more to celebrate. We regaled Pat with the fish, chips and sugar debacle knowing that the incident would be one that we'd laugh about for years to come and then the whole family had a celebratory takeaway together.

I reflected on the past few weeks. They hadn't been so bad really. I almost felt a sense of guilt for even dreading Dad's arrival, after all he'd been the perfect guest. Lauren loved having her grandad around and it filled my heart, seeing Dad laugh and joke at her cheeky antics. Even Danielle was warming to him, though he couldn't compete with the deep bond of her other grandad who had been around while she was growing up.

The kids went to bed, but the drinking continued. I could tell Dad was up for a proper drinking session. He even suggested that he and Pat should go off to the local pub, but it was too late for Pat. Instead, Pat invited Dad to meet him the following day for an afternoon pint which Dad was thrilled about. I was used to Dad practically living in the pub but he'd barely stepped foot in a pub since his arrival. He hadn't drunk much either, apart from the odd can here and there. I wondered if it was due to the claim or if he was trying to turn over a new leaf.

As the drinking continued, dread started to bubble in the pit of my stomach as I could see the old Dad gradually reappearing, morphing like Dr Jekyll and Mr Hyde. The previous week's conversations had all been amicable but now he just talked and talked about his great big plans, how he'd show everyone that Frank Ford was back. It seemed like he'd forgotten that he was in our front room and not in the pub, with some of the language that came out of his mouth.

When Dad was like this, on a roll, you couldn't tell him anything. He knew everything. He started reminiscing over his fighting days. There was a time when I would have listened in awe, but I'd lost interest years ago. I could tell Pat wasn't impressed either. He'd seen this side of Dad too many times before.

The very first night I'd taken Pat to introduce him to Dad, Dad had humiliated and embarrassed me. There he was, standing behind the bar of his pub in Attercliffe lording up his landlord status. The drinks flowed and all seemed to be going well but then Dad started talking about my ex. I could see he was sizing Pat up, almost taunting him, waiting for him to bite, but he didn't. Dad was trying to compare him but for me, there was no comparison at all.

Pat was a good bloke; he'd taken on my kids as his own, been there at my worst and in my eyes, I felt Dad's attitude was a total insult. I hated Dad that night and to add insult to injury, the cheeky sod ended the night asking if Pat would paint the pub for him! I apologised to Pat, but he'd got Dad's card marked already.

'It's ok,' he said. 'He's just a bully. He doesn't bother me.'

Tonight was no different and by the time we went to bed, I was gutted. The day in London and the early part of the evening had gone so well. I'd thought Dad had changed, but good old arrogant Frank Ford was still there, showing his ugly head and I hated it. Worst of all, I could tell that Pat was regretting his earlier invitation for Dad to join him for a pint after work the following day.

# 12: When Four Became Six

We'd only been living at Fraser Crescent for six months, before my cousins Christine and Stephanie came to live with us. They were about fifteen or sixteen at the time.

Social Services had got involved due to concerns around neglect since Auntie Glenda had remarried, and Mum had offered to let them stay with us, so they didn't have to go into foster care. Dad had insisted he should be the one to fetch them, just in case anything kicked off. So now there were five women and Dad living in a three-bedroomed house. Looking back, Mum had a lot on her plate at the time: as well as working full-time and having her own two kids, she was bringing up two teenage nieces, plus running around after Dad, and all at the tender age of twenty-two.

Nan and Grandad were practically daily visitors at Fraser but if Dad was still in the house, they would sit and wait in their car parked further up the street until he left. It was no secret that my nan hated my dad. She was always ranting about how he was no good and saying that Mum should just ask him to leave.

*Why don't you leave?* I'd think, but I never dared say it. I could never get my head around why she disliked Dad so much. I used to hate it when she badmouthed him behind his back, and he couldn't defend himself. There were a couple of occasions when I stood up for Dad in his absence. I can still recall the looks of disdain from Nan when she would shush me, telling me that I didn't know what I was talking about. I didn't know the history back then.

Dad came from a big family, so big that when my other nan gave birth to twins (Jane and Trevor), she couldn't cope with Dad as well as his older brothers, John and Mick, so she sent Dad and Uncle Mick to a foster home for a while. Later I wondered about the impact it had on him but at the time, he seemed invincible.

Dad's family weren't just big in number, they were big in reputation and by the time Dad met Mum, he was known for being the local "Jack the lad".

Nan wasn't impressed even then that Mum was dating one of the Fordy clan but for Mum, he was forbidden fruit, and she was flattered to go from little old Gilly Law to 'Frank Ford's bird.' Little did she know she wouldn't be the only one. 'Of all the girls, he could have chosen, he chose me,' she used to say. 'I felt like I was someone'. Nan must have been even less impressed when, at sixteen, Mum fell pregnant with me.

I don't suppose it was what either of them had planned, but I do think Dad loved Mum. The two of them got married to be respectable but there were no photos and no celebrations. Soon, Sarah came along to join the family to complete the family.

But now, we were a busy house of six. Chris and Steph would both head off to school in the morning, wearing the smartest school uniforms I had ever seen. I couldn't wait to be their age and to wear one myself. When they got home, all they seemed to talk about was boys, boys and more boys. I could tell Mum liked having them around; they were more like friends, doing each other's hair.

Steph and Chris would help Mum out around the house. They seemed to get on well with Dad too.

Occasionally Mum would go out with Dad, leaving Christine and Steph to babysit us. They'd let us transform the stairs into a makeshift toboggan run, using a pair of Mum's silk curtains out of the cupboard. Sometimes they'd let some of the other kids off the street indoors to play too.

Other times they would have boys around, which was great, because whilst they were being entertained by the boys, they didn't bother us, and we would be able to play out later than usual. We loved those evenings.

We'd often go and visit my Auntie Jackie, Mum's older sister. She was a lot younger than Uncle Richard, who never seemed to be at home because he was out driving lorries for a living. When he was home, his lorry would take up half the street, it was so big. They lived on a cul-de-sac, and it seemed like everyone knew everyone and I loved playing with my cousins: Paul, Debbie and Wayne, as we were all around the same age. Auntie Jackie's house was more laid-back than ours, with kids always coming and going.

I loved it at Auntie Jackie's. If the sun was out, she'd be in the back garden, covered in baby oil, sunbathing. I could relate to Auntie Jackie, because she wasn't a fan of Nan's either. She'd often rant on about Mum being Nan's favourite and that her kids didn't get a look in, not like me and my sister, though that's not how it seemed to me.

On very rare occasions, Dad would pop in whilst we were there too. Auntie Jackie and Uncle Richard were good friends of Dad's and would go out drinking with him regularly.

There was one particular day me and my cousin Paul were playing out on the front, when he said: 'I know where your dad's girlfriend lives.'

'What girlfriend?' I asked. 'Dad doesn't have a girlfriend. He's married to Mum.'

I ignored him, but he persisted, insisting it was true.

'Ok then, prove it,' I dared him.

Cock sure of himself he said: 'All right then, come on. She lives down by the side of the corner shop.'

Absolutely convinced that he was lying, I followed him down to the shop. Standing outside, Paul turned me and pointed to a house set in the middle of some terraced houses. That didn't mean anything. Anyone could live there.

But then he offered to take me to the house, on the pretence that he was calling to see if her son was in. I was convinced he was lying, but I started to feel uneasy as he seemed so sure and convinced. So I called his bluff.

'Come on then, let's go.' Part of me was hoping he wouldn't go through with it, but as soon as we started to walk towards the house, he stopped in his tracks. There was my dad, standing there bold as brass and dressed up to the nines, kissing a woman I'd never seen before. He seemed happy, carefree. She had short bleached blond hair, quite the opposite to Mum.

After he'd kissed her, he headed to his car, waved and drove off. I was left feeling stunned. Thankfully Dad drove off in the other direction, so he never saw me standing at the end of the street.

Paul was looking pretty chuffed with himself. He couldn't have timed it any better. I couldn't deny it. I had seen it with my own eyes. I played it down of course, like I didn't care, but deep-down I was hurt and confused. I wondered if this was the woman that Dad had talked about previously. I couldn't understand it. This wasn't normal, was it?'

We headed back to Auntie Jackie's house, but then I started to panic, wondering if I should tell Mum. If Paul knew, who else knew? When we got back, I decided not to say anything, especially not to Mum. What if I'd got it wrong?

Deep-down though, I knew what I had seen, but I was scared that if I talked, I would be the cause of so much trouble, so I kept me gob shut. After all, us kids were to be seen and not heard – right?

# 13: A Few Drinks

Just as he'd promised the night before, Pat came to collect Dad from ours straight after work before heading to the pub to meet the other blokes who'd finished for the week. It had become a Friday tradition that he'd have a few drinks and then I'd walk down to meet him and drive him home.

I didn't begrudge him that time. He worked hard and it gave him a welcome break from family life. Dad had been really looking forward to going out and when I got home from work, he was all ready to go. He'd pressed his clothes, had a shave, done his hair and the house was filled with the scent of his aftershave. I waved them off and got the girls their tea.

A couple of hours passed before I got a call from Pat to say that they would only be having a couple more, which was my cue to make my way down. When I arrived at the pub, I found Dad, Pat and Pat's brother, Rob, tucked up in the corner. The pub had quietened down, with only a few guys left drinking in their work clothes. Pat stood up and offered to get me a drink from the bar. I asked for a diet Coke.

'Put her a Bacardi in it!' Dad interjected It was more like an order than a suggestion.

'Dad, its ok, honestly a Coke is fine, I'm not bothered about a drink. Anyway I don't even drink Bacardi.'

'Well put her a Brandy in then!'

I could tell by the look on Pat's face that this hadn't been the first awkward moment.

'Look Dad, I really don't want to drink, I'm more than happy with a Coke.'

'Yeah well, I wanna treat ya.'

Dad was a hard man to refuse but I didn't need to. Pat did it for me.

'Look, Frank, she just wants a Coke.' And with that he headed to the bar.

I admired Pat for standing his ground. He didn't really do confrontation, in fact he was that laid back, he was horizontal, but I could tell Dad had pushed some of his buttons this afternoon.

Dad clearly wasn't happy either. Mumbling under his breath, he took a swig of his pint.

When Pat returned from the bar, there was an awkward silence which I tried to break.

'So, had a good time?'

'Ahh it's been sound, our Trace, turns out I already know the landlord! Me and Terry we go way back. I used to drink with him down the Wicker, I didn't know he'd got this place, he must be raking it in, it's a bleeding gold mine.'

Pat's eyes glazed over.

"Kin 'el, Trace! Turns out this is Max Andrews' local too!'

I was confused. Dad was good at that, expecting everyone to know who he was talking about. 'Dad, I don't know who you are on about?'

'Max Andrews, Tracey's uncle!'

Max Andrews was a regular, a well-liked bloke, everyone knew him including me. I just didn't know that Dad knew him too and I didn't know he was the uncle of my favourite of Dad's long-term girlfriends. Dad was in high spirits, I could tell he'd enjoyed himself, but clearly Pat hadn't.

Terry, the landlord, walked past our table, came up to me and placed his hands on my shoulders.

'Hey, Trace never knew ya Dad wa Frank! Me and thee Dad go way back!'

I knew straightaway that if Dad stayed any longer at ours, our local would soon become his local and I really didn't want that. If Dad started drinking here, he'd soon get his feet under the table, and it wouldn't be too long before he upset or offended someone.

Pat was clearly thinking the same, because when Dad left to go to the toilet, he turned to me.

'There is no way, Trace, he's going to start coming down here. This is my local and I'm not going to fall out with my mates or defend him if he upsets any of them.'

'What's he done?' I asked

‘Seriously, Trace I thought it was going to kick off!’ he said. ‘All I heard was someone shout ‘what the fuck you looking at?’ across the pub. It was Max and some other blokes. He was looking right at your dad who goes, ‘who the fuck you looking at, ya fat ugly bastard!”

Pat told me he genuinely thought there was going to be a fight when he saw Max and Dad staring each other out but then Max’s aggressive face had turned into a smile as he opened his arms to embrace Dad.

‘You’d better chase that flat up,’ said Pat.

I didn’t need telling twice. I had already resolved that when Monday came around, calling the housing was the first on my to do list.

# 14: A Man Possessed

Grandad could turn his hand to anything. If he was round at ours, he'd always be fixing something around the house or sorting the back garden out. A keen carpenter, he once made me and Sarah our own little chairs. Sarah's was faux leather in the shape of a dice. Instead of sitting on it, we would try rolling it like a dice, but we could only ever get it to turn once. Mine was a small chair with a white frame. The backrest and seat were filled with intricately woven reeds.

One day, I went into the airing cupboard on the landing to fetch a bath towel and there was my stool. It was all mangled and broken. I wondered what had happened to it, after all, I hadn't broken it. Mum was busy, as usual, in the kitchen. I asked her about the chair.

'Silly me,' she said. 'I tripped over and fell on it the other day.'

It didn't take me long to put two and two together to realise that was a lie. Only a few days earlier, Sarah and I had come downstairs for breakfast, to be greeted by Mum, who was wearing a pot on her arm. We were shocked; she'd been fine when we went to bed.

Mum had tried explaining to us how she'd slipped on the stairs the night before and had fallen awkwardly and fractured her wrist. My first instinct was to believe her. It wasn't the first time she'd banged into something or hurt herself; she would occasionally have the odd bruise, that was just the norm. I had never given them a second thought.

But instinctively, I knew there and then that, even though I'd never seen Dad be violent towards Mum, it was him that had done that to her.

I'd always suspected that Dad could be violent. I had seen first-hand just how intimidating and threatening he could be. Once, Mum had had a few cross words with the old guy who lived next door and when Dad came home, he had gone straight round to theirs with the hedge cutters and cut down their washing line, with all the clothes still on. He then turned his attention to the old man's prized privet. He was like a man possessed; the privet was ruined. I was sad because the old guy never spoke to us kids again. He went from being really nice to us kids to totally ignoring us. It always felt awkward after that.

Whilst I never saw the physical stuff, there were raised voices and an undercurrent of fear that clouded the house when Dad was around. I realised then that all my mum's accidents – the black eyes and bruised arms, weren't in fact accidents at all, they were done by Dad.

# 15: Drugs are For Mugs

Dad had been here for three weeks now and the atmosphere in the house was getting more strained by the day. The kids were still sharing a room and there was no alone time for me and Pat to off-load at the end of the day. Everyone was getting frustrated.

It had been nice to spend time with Dad though and to feel he was taking an interest in what I was doing workwise, even if he never really understood it.

Drugs are for mugs,' he'd say. He didn't have any sympathy for the addicts I worked with. He talked about them as 'scum' and 'thieves' who had nothing to offer to society, which was pretty ironic, considering I'd been one of those addicts myself.

I pointed this out to him, but in Dad's eyes that was different, as I wasn't 'like a real addict'. I don't think he understood just how low and unhappy I'd been or what had driven me to drugs. But this wasn't the time to start trying to explain. Instead, I was grateful to hear him say the words I'd be yearning to hear for years – that he was proud of me.

Sometimes I was proud of him too, but the pub visits were increasing, and I knew better than anyone that it wouldn't be long before he would piss someone off.

The pub was his stage, the place where he always needed to be the centre of attention, everyone's best mate. The trouble with Dad was that if he had an opinion about something, his would be the right opinion. There was never no room for manoeuvring, particularly if he was drunk. If he had an audience, he would never back down. So many times, I'd seen grown men silenced, out of fear of saying the wrong thing.

There was one time, I was standing at the bar with Dad and a few of his mates. One of the blokes started swearing. Out of the blue Dad was like: 'Nah then, watch ya fucking language! There are women here!'

The bloke looked at me and the other women standing with us and profusely apologised, before walking away like a scolded kid back to his seat. It was embarrassing and awkward. He didn't seem to understand his own hypocrisy.

'You do realise that you have just told him to stop swearing when you've been swearing. And since when were you bothered about swearing in front of me?' I asked.

Dad just laughed.

'I cannot stand the little twat.'

Dad wasn't bothered about the swearing; he was just fishing for a fight! An opportunity to assert his reputation as a man who couldn't be messed with. Even if he wasn't as young or agile as he used to be, he was still Frank Ford!

We needed to get him out of our pub as soon as possible. So, when the council called to say that they had a flat to view, I couldn't wait to take him to see it. I crossed my fingers, hoping and praying that he would accept it.

# 16: The Other Woman

One day, I came home from school to find the sofa had gone from the living room. It turned out Dad had left too. Aside from the fact that he'd taken Mum's bed, there wasn't any drama around him going. One minute he was there and the next he wasn't.

Mum seemed happier and the house felt easier somehow, more relaxed. With five women in the house, we all settled into a routine. Mum seemed to love her job and still had time to walk us to school, accompanied by Christine and Steph, who would go their separate ways once we got to the main road. En route, I'd listen to them talk about how many pounds they'd lost this week and would be very confused that they seemed happy about it.

We still saw Dad and, at first, we got to spend more quality time with him. One morning, when me and my sister came down for breakfast, Mum told us that Dad would be picking us up later that morning and would be taking us swimming. I was so excited and didn't need to ask twice to go and get my swimming stuff together. We sat and waited for an hour and eventually Dad pulled up on the front.

Heeley Baths was an old building. I'd walked past it many times on the way to Nan and Grandad's. I'd never been inside before though. The smell of chlorine was overwhelming as we entered the building. Inside, there was a large swimming pool, surrounded by little cubicles which had curtains instead of doors.

Dad ushered me and Sarah into one each and told us to get changed into our costumes. I waited for Dad outside my cubicle and laughed to myself when I saw Dad in his swimming trunks. I'd never seen him in trunks or pants before. We climbed into the shallow end of the pool and stood at the edge and watched in wonder as Dad submerged, pushed off the wall and swam underwater for the whole breadth of the pool. I didn't even know Dad could swim! He was like the man from Atlantis but Dad didn't buck his body like a mermaid, he swam straight like a bullet.

Outside the baths, there was a small canteen where families sat drinking hot chocolate from the vending machine. I was really looking forward to being able to sit like the other families, but Dad said we couldn't because he had somewhere else to go. I remember feeling disappointed that we had only spent an hour or so with Dad and not the whole day like we had been expecting, but I soon got over it.

Our next outing with Dad was very different. This time, instead of swimming, he was taking us to the fair. We were so looking forward to it and were happy when he arrived on time, but we were surprised to see Uncle John, Dad's older brother with him.

We were even more surprised to see him standing with another woman who we'd never seen before. I wasn't bothered that Uncle John was there, but I was bothered that he was holding hands with someone who wasn't Auntie June. Did all dads have other women too? I was consumed by dread again. Should I tell? Who Should I tell? And what would I say? It was all very confusing.

Then, I saw her, the other woman, the one from the house our Paul had taken me to. She was smiling at Dad as she made her way towards us. She greeted Uncle John and his lady friend; it was clear that they already knew each other. Dad reached out for her hand as she got closer and pulled her next to him before turning to me and Sarah.

'Kids, this is Elaine, she's a friend of mine,' he said.

She turned to us all smiles and said: 'Right, who's Tracey and who's Sarah?'

I was busy comparing her with Mum. Her short bleached blond hair seemed cheap in comparison to Mum's long, natural locks. She was pleasant and friendly enough, but I didn't like her. Obviously, I never let on. And on that Sunday afternoon with Dad, I didn't kick money out of her hand like I had threatened before.

Elaine spent most of the trip chatting and laughing with Dad, Uncle John and his new lady friend as opposed to getting to know us. I don't have memories of going on any rides or even doing hook a duck. Perhaps there was candyfloss. I just remember feeling like an inconvenience, a gooseberry, whilst Dad and Uncle John enjoyed the company of the two strange women.

I was worried about going back home. But it turned out, Mum must have suspected something about the other women, because when we got back, she asked us if there was anyone else there. I was reluctant to say anything, but I knew that she already knew. I told Mum that the other woman wasn't anything like her and that I didn't like her. Mum smiled. It was a relief that I didn't have to lie or keep secrets anymore.

# 17: Dad's New Flat

Dad's new flat was only a ten-minute drive from ours, on the Manor estate. I knew the estate had been notorious for anti-social behaviour but, as we drove up, I was relieved to find that the area around the flat seemed quiet and really nice. It was just as well. The Council would only offer Dad one place and if he refused, he'd be on his own.

Dad's flat was one of the two hundred and fifty Graves Trust Homes that had been built by J.G. Graves around the time of World War Two. They were grander than the other homes in the area, set back from the main road with a large grassy area outside and well-maintained flower beds around the edge. We entered through a communal door and found that Dad's flat was on the first floor.

Dad fell in love with it immediately. It was a simple one-bedroomed flat, with a decent-sized living room and kitchen area, a nice bathroom and plenty of storage space. And it was in decent nick. It was clean, and we agreed that it wouldn't take much to turn the place into a nice cosy bachelor pad for Dad.

Dad had just recently received another interim payment from the solicitors, and he was keen to get it decorated and kitted out with carpets, even though he saw the flat as a temporary arrangement. As far as he was concerned, as soon as his claim was settled, he would be buying a nice new place of his own. He'd be mortgage-free and spending his days fishing. I just hoped and prayed that the solicitors could deliver on their projected pay-out, because if they didn't, they were going to have one very pissed off customer.

For now though, I felt the heavy weight lift as we left the flat and headed back home knowing that, in less than a week, we would have our house back. Finally, Dad would have his own place, and life could go back to normal, back to the way it was before.

# 18: The Man with a Moustache

A while after Dad left, I noticed that Mum started to go out more on her own. It was weird seeing her get dressed up, as she'd hardly ever been out when Dad was around. I didn't mind though. When she went out, Christine and Stephanie would babysit us, which meant we could run amok for the night.

Usually we enjoyed it when Mum was out, but on one particular evening, as soon as Mum left, Chris and Steph informed me and Sarah that they were having a party, and we had to go to bed early. We weren't impressed, but they bribed us with party food and pop on the condition that we stayed in our bedrooms. The house was noisy; we could hear music and lots of laughing coming from downstairs. Unable to sleep, we decided to leave our room and check out what was happening.

The living room was rammed full of teenagers. We headed to the kitchen and hid beneath the large plastic sheet that was draped over the kitchen table filled with snacks and alcohol. There was still no sign of our cousins, but we could smell cigarette smoke coming from the direction of the front porch and we suspected that they would be there.

After a while, me and Sarah started to make dares, poking random feet or sneaking our arms from under the table trying to reach some of the snacks.

It wasn't long after that we were rumbled. Stephanie screamed at us to get back upstairs to our rooms.

'This is our house, not yours. I'll tell Dad what you have been doing!' I screamed back at her.

She just laughed at me, before dragging us from under the table and frog-marching us back to our room. Once in our bedrooms though, me and Sarah laughed at how long we had been able to stay under the table without being detected. It was a good night, and it certainly wouldn't have happened had Dad still been at home.

On another occasion when Mum went out, Christine and Steph had allowed us to stay up later and watch some more TV. After an hour or two, the phone rang. I rushed to answer it. I could hear music in the background.

It was Mum. 'Hi, love, it's just Mum checking you're ok?' She sounded happy.

'Yeah Mum. We're going to bed soon. Are you having a good time?'

'Yes, love. You go to bed when Chris and Steph tell you. I won't be late home.'

I could hear another person. It was a man. It sounded like he was standing right beside her.

'Mum, who's that?' I asked.

She laughed. 'Oh, it's just a friend. You will get to meet him soon enough.'

I was intrigued. I wanted to know more. 'What's his name? What does he look like? When will we get to see him?'

Mum laughed again. 'His name is Adrian. He has brown hair, and he has a moustache.'

A moustache? I'd never met anyone with a moustache before.

My sister had heard some of the conversation from the living room and now she was standing right beside me and joined me in pleading to speak to him. Mum soon conceded and we heard her pass the phone to this new man, called Adrian.

Adrian sounded so nice. We giggled as we asked him loads of questions. He told us how he liked Mum very much and was looking forward to finally meeting us in person. He didn't sound anything like Dad. His voice was a lot softer, not as harsh as Dad's. He seemed really keen and interested in us too. He was asking us both loads of questions about what we liked doing, unlike Dad, who rarely took any interest in us.

Satisfied, we said our good nights and handed the phone to Steph. Not long after the telephone call, we were sent to bed, but neither me nor Sarah could sleep. All we could talk about was this new man, someone who seemed to make Mum seem very happy.

# 19: Just Around the Corner

Pat had never decorated a flat so fast in his life! And, just to make sure that he got Dad moved as quickly as possible, he even roped in his brother in to help out.

In less than two months, Dad had gone from sleeping in his granddaughter's bed to having a place of his own and I was proud of what we'd been able to achieve in such a short amount of time. A couple of friends had helped out with some donations and soon he had everything he needed. Despite being extremely grateful for all the help, I knew that he didn't like feeling dependent on others, especially his daughter. In his eyes, it should have been the other way around.

I'd been getting it in the neck from some family members, who would remark 'he wouldn't have done the same for you,' and whilst I understood their cynicism, I felt good inside. My reward for helping Dad had been having the opportunity to build on what had become, for me, a fractured relationship even though Dad wouldn't have seen it that way. If someone had asked Dad about our relationship, he would have told you that we had a great bond. He was totally oblivious of the recognition, love and affection I'd craved all these years.

With Dad in the flat, life settled into a new routine. I would often pop by and see how he was doing or fetch some shopping from the supermarket at Manor Top. The first few weeks he didn't venture far; the furthest he would go would be to the corner shop for a newspaper, bread, milk and a four-pack of lagers. He even declined the invitation to come back to ours for his tea or Sunday lunch, claiming we'd done enough.

Dad knew his way around the kitchen, after all it wasn't the first time he'd lived alone. Sometimes, when I was round, he'd make his favourite dish which took me back to my teen years. He'd peel and cut chips, deep fry them old school in a chip pan, then place them in a Pyrex dish and smother them in Heinz Chicken Soup. Then he'd make a butty with slices of thick bread lathered in Lurpak.

In many ways life was back to how it had been before Dad came to stay. The only difference was he now lived round the corner...

# 20: Nothing Like Dad

It was the middle of the night, and I was woken by shouting I knew better than to open the door and I could pretty much hear what was going on. Dad was demanding to be let into the house. I'd never heard him so angry; he was swearing, calling Mum a slag and a flurry of other nasty words.

I was confused and scared. What had Mum done wrong? Why was Dad so angry? It wasn't long before the shouting woke Sarah up too. We were frightened. Should we go out? Or call the police? I opened the bedroom door slightly and saw Mum leaning out of the window at the top of the stairs trying to calm him down, telling him to call her tomorrow when he was sober. She was trying to placate him, but this only seemed to make him angrier.

Now his shouting was accompanied by loud banging sounds. It sounded like Dad was trying to kick the front door in. I feared for Mum. What would he do to her if he did get in? Mum turned around and she saw me and Sarah standing there. She told us to close the door and to stay in our bedroom. The shouting, banging and demanding continued, but Mum stood firm and still refused to let him in.

After what seemed a lifetime, the noise died down and Mum came into our room. I was relieved she was ok and proud of her too. She seemed so calm, and I was impressed by the fact that she hadn't backed down to Dad, like I had seen her do so many times before. This was a different Mum; she seemed stronger.

She explained how Dad had found out about her new boyfriend, and he wasn't happy. I wondered what Adrian had done to make Dad so angry. I mean we hadn't even been introduced to him yet. Did Dad know him? Did Dad want to come back home? It was all so confusing! Mum explained that Dad wasn't coming back, and we would soon get to meet this mysterious Adrian. And a few days later, we did.

Adrian, it turned out, liked to play cricket. When she took us to watch him, we were excited. The bus journey took forever, but it was an adventure. Mum let us sit at the front of the bus on the top deck as we took in new sights, passing roads, houses and shopping centres we had never seen before. It took two bus journeys before we finally arrived at our destination.

Mum held our hands as we walked down the long driveway toward the big building. I felt nervous, but Mum seemed to know her way around. She'd obviously been here before. We entered the building, walked past a bar and dance hall and down two lots of steps and eventually emerged outside, where a load of men in white stood watching the match.

I couldn't see anything but then Mum took us to an area where a group of mothers were chatting and picnicking with their kids. One of the ladies came over to give Mum a hug and introduced us to her kids. As soon as the introductions were done, I asked Mum which one was Adrian. She pointed to a man who was walking alone and rubbing a red ball against his thigh.

The next thing I knew, he'd turned swiftly and started running in the opposite direction before throwing his ball toward a man holding the bat. He whacked the ball then started to run. There was lots of shouting on and off the field before Adrian got the ball again. He looked in our direction. I could tell he'd seen Mum. He smiled and waved at us.

When there was a break, Adrian finally came over. He stood by Mum and kissed her gently on the cheek before turning his attention to me and Sarah. He leaned over and reached out his hand and introduced himself. We sat and chatted while he asked us lots of questions.

I remember his teeth were really white. He had a kind smile. He was nothing like Dad at all. He placed his arm around Mum's shoulder and told us that he thought she was very special and that he intended to take care of her. I had never seen Dad do that with Mum; in fact, I'd never seen them be affectionate towards each other at all.

Mum glowed as she smiled back at Adrian and any nerves I might have felt previously soon melted away. It wasn't long before lunchtime was over, and Adrian headed back to the pitch. Mum asked us what we thought? Both me and Sarah were in agreement that we liked him. Mum mentioned that she'd recently booked a caravan holiday for us, and we dived straight in asking if Adrian would be coming with us too.

After the match, Adrian came outside to where we were playing with the other kids. He'd changed and showered and was wearing jeans and a t-shirt. Even the way he dressed was nothing like Dad. He asked if we wanted a drink and some crisps and invited us to come with him to the bar with him. We helped him with the drinks and took them to Mum, who was sitting with the other women.

Mum was enjoying herself; she was laughing and seemed so relaxed around these people. I had never seen her so happy.

# 21: Dad's New Cronies

Dad had just received another interim payment from the solicitors, but it didn't appease him. He was getting more and more pissed off with how long the claim was taking. When I called round to see him at his flat, it was all he talked about; he was like a broken record.

He was so self-entitled and impatient that I found myself feeling sorry for the poor sods at the solicitors who'd been on the receiving end of his rants.

He'd recently started drinking in a nearby pub called The Ball Inn. I called in one evening after work to meet him and found Dad huddled in the corner of the pub with a few new mates. Dad ushered me to sit beside him, then introduced me to everyone before heading to the bar to get a round in.

Good old Dad! I could see why his new mates liked him so much. They were all half-cut by the time I got there. There was just one woman, who was thin as a rake, but she could still keep up with the blokes, drinking pint for pint. There was another guy parked up in a mobility scooter. He'd had far too much to drink to be driving anywhere, in my opinion. Then there was the toothless guy who looked like the local rag and bone man. I didn't reckon he'd seen a bar of soap for weeks. It seemed like none of them worked. They were all either retired or on benefits, passing their days chatting shit and getting pissed.

As Dad walked to the bar, I smiled at how smart he looked. He always dressed well with his pressed Farrar trousers, his polished shoes and ironed shirt. He looked out of place with his new drinking buddies. He seemed happy enough though. He had a captive audience and Dad loved an audience. They all knew about his impending pay out and they all knew about how he'd once been a successful businessman. When Dad returned from the bar with everyone's drinks, they listened in awe about his plans to get his own pub once his claim had been settled.

This amused me. Dad's plans changed frequently. One day, he was buying his own house, then another day he was going to buy himself one of those retirement lodges by a large fishing lake or he might have a look into a new business venture. Personally I couldn't give a toss what he did, but the sooner they paid him the better.

# 22: Gleadless Valley

Soon, Adrian moved in with us at Fraser Crescent. It was very different having him around. Some nights he'd cook for us, and we'd all sit around the table and eat our meal as a family, sharing stories from our day. Ada, as I'd started calling him, didn't go out on a night either, not like Dad. Instead he would help out around the house, and we would often sit in the living room together watching TV.

Sometimes Dad would phone. I could tell it was him straightaway. Mum's body language would tense. Sometimes she'd get upset after putting the phone down and Ada would wrap his arms around her and tell her everything would be ok. Dad rarely asked to speak to me or Sarah and, when he did, he'd just tell us to let him know if Ada laid a finger on us. I still couldn't work out why Dad seemed to dislike him so much, as he'd never done anything to hurt us.

It wasn't long before Mum was talking about a 'new start' and soon we were moving from the estate that had become my playground to a new home on Gleadless Valley. Mum reckoned we'd been lucky that someone had been willing to exchange with us, because it was a very popular estate, but I didn't want to move. The new house was very modern and new, bang in the middle of a small cul-de-sac with three houses on either side. At the top of the street, there were some flats reserved for old age pensioners and behind them was our new school.

Our old school at Woodseats had been built in the 1800s and the playground was all concrete, surrounded by walls and railings, but our new school, Hemsworth was modern-looking, sat in the middle of a big open field surrounded by privet.

So new house, new stepdad, new school, new life – it was all a little bit daunting. I felt out of my comfort zone as I walked around this new estate on moving day. Even with my sister by my side I felt alone. I was scared my days of innocence were behind me. I pined for my old friends and to go back to play on Barbers field or out in our local woods.

Our first day of school arrived. To make a good impression, Mum dressed us like twins in our smartest outfits. It was a handmade, velvet two-piece number: a skirt and matching waistcoat. I hated it.

I don't remember being introduced to our new teacher or class, I just remember the first breaktime standing alone, looking and feeling like a sore thumb in the playground. Our Sarah had no trouble fitting in; she'd already found a new friend and was off running around the school playground. Everyone clearly had their own long-standing friendship groups. I found a large concrete rock and sat alone, trying my best to look unfazed and cool, which was hard because of the stupid velvet outfit.

Eventually, a girl approached me. She was a lot smaller than me with long, dark hair and trendy clothes. She seemed very confident, sure of herself. She introduced herself as Tracy. Her name was the same as mine, so of course we had something in common straight away. I felt my spirits lift. She complimented me on my long blonde hair that draped all the way down my back.

I was grateful for the compliment, even though my hair was a source of irritation to me. I'd wanted to cut it shorter for years, but Dad had always been set against it. Tracy introduced me to her best friend, Jill, who was clearly Tracy's shadow. For a small kid, Tracy had a big presence about her.

She ushered me around the playground, showing me the ropes, pointing out who to talk to and who to stay away from.

By afternoon break, school was going ok, in fact it was going far better than I expected; I'd made a couple of new friends and lost the waistcoat and was feeling more confident and relaxed in my new environment.

I was standing in the playground chatting with Tracy and Jill, when a group of other girls approached us. I could tell that they weren't on friendly terms with Tracy. Tracy and this other girl started arguing and as the conversation started to get more heated, I felt compelled to stick up for my new best friend telling the girls to go away. That moved the ring-leader's attention onto me, and I started to wish I'd kept my gob shut as a fireball of anxiety swelled in my stomach, but I remembered what Dad had said to me about not letting anyone push me around.

I knew I couldn't back down now, so I stood my ground. Before I knew it, I'd agreed to a fight after school with the ringleader of the group, who unbeknownst to me at the time carried the reputation of being someone you didn't mess around with.

Sarah was buzzing on the way home. She'd had a great day and made some new best friends. I just wanted to go back to my old life, my old routine and back to my old friends. Mum was waiting for us in the kitchen, anxious to hear about how our first day had gone.

'Well apart from making plans later to fight the local cock the day went pretty well, Mum.' Of course I didn't tell my mother that part.

Me, Ada, Mum, Sarah, Christine and Steph all sat around the dining table eating our tea, talking about how our days had gone. I didn't have much to say and I couldn't eat my meal; I was too busy praying for a miracle that the fight might have been called off.

But at six o'clock, as planned, there was a knock at the door. Mum answered it and called me from the kitchen where I was washing the pots. It was Tracy and Jill and, behind them, further up the street, was a group of lads. I recognised a couple of them from school earlier. Mum introduced herself. I could tell she was chuffed that I'd made new friends so quickly. Little did she know that they were only here to see me have a fight.

Mum left us at the front door while Tracy explained that she'd heard that the other girl was bringing a crowd to the fight, so Tracy had been busy rallying some of the local lads for some moral support for me. Everyone except me was buzzing with anticipation, the lads especially.

We headed towards the pre-arranged meeting point, taking a path locally referred to as the black path, which ran through the whole estate. We approached a small bridge. The road above it was next to the field that was about to be the venue for my first fight. We were early and so we stood under the bridge for a while.

One of the lads who had gone up ahead came running towards us.

'There's about twenty up there!' he shouted. I thought I might pee my pants there and then. Like a scene out of Rocky, Tracy and some of the other lads were giving me my pre ring prep talk. I didn't hear them. I just wanted to run in the opposite direction, but my feet didn't move. All I could hear were Dad's words.

'It's not about winning, it's about having a go. Don't you take no shit from anyone!"

It was time, and we rounded the top of the steps and walked towards a small field – our meeting point. It was protected by a large shrubbery that obstructed the view from the main road, so nobody else could see what was about to happen.

The other girl was standing there with her gang of cronies behind her, some of whom looked a lot older than us. She stood in the centre looking confident and all self-assured, whilst deep-down, I was feeling quite the opposite, in fact I was shitting me sen. How the fuck had I ended up here?

I was soon standing face to face with her. I could now see she was bigger than me. The other kids formed a circle around us and then someone pushed into me. I fought back like my life depended on it. I have no idea how long we fought for; all I remember was the other kids screaming like animals. I felt someone else punch and push me. I continued to lash out, punching as hard as I could, just like Dad had taught me. At some point, the fight was broken up.

I stood, breathing heavily. My whole body was shaking, and my hair was all over the place and soaking wet. I didn't know where the water had come from. As we retreated from the fighting spot, boys were patting me on the shoulder telling me how I had whooped her ass. Others were complaining about how unfair the fight had been. I was still in shock. I couldn't take anything anyone was saying in, it was all just a blur.

We retreated back under the bridge. I was sweating and still panting. My face hurt. Jill was trying to comb my hair using her fingers as Tracy gave me a running commentary about what had just happened.

It turned out one of the older kids was this girl's auntie. It was her auntie who had thrown in a couple of punches when it seemed I was getting the upper hand; in fact, it was her that had thrown the water on me. My once long, straight golden hair looked like it had been backcombed within an inch of its life. I was covered in mud and still in shock but, according to my new-found mates, I was the champion, the overall winner.

I didn't feel like no champ. I was more concerned about how I was going to explain the hair and clothes to Mum and Ada when I got home. Luckily, they didn't see me come in and I was able to get washed and into my pjs without them being aware of my antics.

Walking to school the following morning, I was sick to the stomach. My body ached but there were no visible signs from the fight the night before. On the other hand, she was sporting a black eye, so based on the physical evidence, the verdict was that I was the new female cock of the school.

Now, Dad would have been proud. God, I wished he could have seen me, his daughter, taking no shit! I was now known as someone you didn't mess with. I wasn't a nobody anymore. I was Tracey Ford, the new bird, who could fight. And whilst the newfound attention felt good, I knew deep-down that it was also fake. This wasn't a title I had asked for or ever pursued. It didn't matter if I liked it or not though, I had it.

# 23: The Drinks Are on Me

It seemed like a lifetime since Dad had left ours, but our relationship had been transformed by his stay and, now he was in his own place, we'd often speak on the phone, and I'd visit him once or twice a week after work.

Work was busier than ever. I'd been working flat-out organising a conference, bringing together families and friends whose lives had been impacted by a loved one's addiction. It was a BIG deal, a first for Sheffield and we had David Blunkett, the Home Secretary, coming to speak.

Days were long and when I called to see Dad with some bits of shopping after work, I was often knackered. One day, I couldn't wait to get home to shower and get my Pjs on. The last thing I needed was to find Dad surrounded by unfamiliar faces and the smell of weed when I walked into the flat.

Dad was pleased to see me though.

'Ay up, lads, this is our Tracey, my eldest. She's the one I was telling you about!'

One of the guys stood up and offered me his seat. I had no intention of hanging around and I declined.

'Just dropping off ya shopping, I'll go and put it away.' I turned and went into the kitchen.

'There's some cans in the fridge, Trace,' Dad shouted. 'I've just sent Billy to fetch some more.'

'Looks like you've all had enough already,' I joked, but deep-down, I was seething. Dad was normally house-proud but today the kitchen looked like a bomb site. There were takeaway wrappings everywhere and on the draining board there was a pile of unwashed pots. 'Tramps!' I muttered under my breath.

I didn't mind tidying up for Dad, but I *wasn't* cleaning up for these two muppets. These weren't Dad's friends, they were parasites. I could see straight through them.

I came back into the living room. One of the blokes, who wasn't that much older than me, smiled and chatted to me like I was his long-lost mate as he rolled himself a spliff. I couldn't hide my disdain. He was oblivious, but Dad wasn't. I could tell he knew what I was thinking.

'They're good lads, Trace. They're going to sort me out a car, a little runner, been thinking I might pop over to Stoke for a couple of days.'

'Ah that's nice, Dad,' I said but what I really wanted to say was, 'I wouldn't buy anything off these two idiots.'

His new mate chimed in. 'Yeah, think we've got him sorted. I was telling ya Dad, I'll stay in the flat if he wants and look after it, whilst he's in Stoke.'

Dad laughed. 'Yeah, and there will be fuck all left when I get back!' Dad's quick retort reassured me that the guy wouldn't be house sitting whilst he was away, which was a relief.

The other bloke was half comatose on the chair. Christ knows how long they had been drinking. The coffee table was covered with stains from the cans, and the ashtray was overflowing with tab ends and there was a half-empty bottle of brandy. The brandy was Dad's. He had a bottle of Coke by his foot, but he looked like he'd had enough already though.

I had no intention of hanging around any longer. I promised to call Dad later, but I already suspected he wouldn't be answering; he was half cut already. I left him to his so-called mates and hoped he'd come to his senses soon.

# 24: Strutting At the School Disco

I preferred wearing jeans to skirts, trainers over pretty, girly shoes. Though my hair was long, it was always tied back and whilst my sister loved doing girly stuff, I loved hanging about with the boys in the woods, or exploring new areas of the estate, playing knock a door run, hedge hopping, doing more of the risky stuff. What I loved the most was that they just accepted me as 'one of the lads'.

I was rarely at home after school. I'd be itching to have my tea and go out with my mates. I hated the thought that I might be missing out on anything and sometimes resented the way things were now that Ada was around. I liked the fact that Ada was a fount of knowledge, but he was so passionate about educating us that he would test us on our knowledge on various topics whilst having the evening family meal which would feel like Chinese torture. I didn't give a toss about what the capital city of Greece was; all I was bothered about was getting tea finished, getting the pots done and getting outside to knock about with my mates.

And sometimes, in my haste to get out as fast as I could, the pots weren't up to Ada's standards, and he'd make us do them all over again.

Despite the rules though, Ada always had time and a lot of patience. So much so, I often found myself opening up to Ada as opposed to Mum. He was the one who I went to about advice around friends or my first period. He seemed more objective and didn't ever question or talk about Dad and his faults in public, like Mum and Nan.

Ada's only fault was that he could sometimes be a mardy arse, particularly if his football team lost. One time, there were raised voices between him and Mum and the next thing I recall was a defrosting loaf, flying through the air and straight through the kitchen window. One thing I always respected about Ada though was that, if he ever felt he'd been out of order he would come and apologise for his behaviour, unlike Dad, who would have never ever have apologised for anything.

Money seemed tighter than ever. Some of my friends would get a fiver a week as pocket money, but we got a quid at the most, and we had to do chores to earn it. When I asked Mum for more, she'd say: 'Ask ya Dad. It wouldn't hurt him to put his hands in his pockets every now and again.'

We would have to help out on the trips to do the food shopping at Sheaf and Castle markets. I always preferred the Sheaf Market, where Mum went for the fruit and veg. Sometimes, if Mum could afford it, she would treat us to a drink and snack in the cafe that appeared to float above the markets, overlooking all the stalls.

I could have sat there for hours, just people-watching and sometimes, I would throw parts of my napkin from above onto the heads of unsuspecting passersby.

Castle Market was on three floors and a lot bigger than Sheaf. As you walked through the main set of doors, there was the music stall to the left which would always be surrounded by teenagers sifting through the rows of vinyl.

In the far corner of the market, there was the Harrington's clothes store, famous for its jackets and jeans. I would always envy my friends who were able to buy the latest fashions from there, but all we ever did was walk past and look.

The only reason we were in that market was to buy meat and fish from the fish market in the centre. I hated having to go in there. It was always busy with men and women walking about with bloodied aprons. It was cold and smelt of death. We would have to walk all the way around until Mum found the best deals. Money permitting, we might have a small bowl of cockles soaked in vinegar.

Our other shopping trip was going to Asda, which had its own free bus service. Mum had a list, and we never deviated from it. Me or Sarah would go for the branded cereals with the free toys, but Mum would always say no. Mum never bought fizzy pop, treats or branded crisps, like my friends would have. Mum and Ada would bulk buy, to make large batches of food for the chest freezer.

It was nearly Christmas, and we'd been to Asda for the Christmas shop. As we were getting off the bus, I noticed a purse nestled into the seat as Mum got up to leave. I put it in my coat jacket.

I couldn't wait until I got home, back to my room to check out the contents for myself. I thought "finder's keepers" and all that, and couldn't wait to see how much was inside. I could buy as many fags as I wanted instead of constantly scrounging off my mates.

We'd just got off the bus when Mum started to panic, verging on crying. Then I realised the purse was hers. I handed it to Mum, trying to make out I'd been going to give it to her when we got home. She was so grateful and explained that, without the money in it, Christmas would have been ruined. I struggled, knowing that Mum and Ada would have given us more if they had it. But it didn't stop me feeling resentful, that we were somehow different to other families and that everyone else's families always seemed better off and happier than us.

There was a school Christmas disco coming up and money was extra tight, because Ada had just been made redundant. Everyone was talking about their new outfits and new shoes, and I felt left out again. We only had new clothes on birthdays, Easter and Christmas and even then, they were for best. And, whilst my mates went to Rebina, a popular shoe shop in town, if I needed shoes, we would have to get up at the crack of dawn and go to the Friday morning shoe market.

You had to get there early, before any of the good stuff had gone. I would see a pair of shoes and wiggle my way through to the front, trying not to get elbowed in the process, then I'd grab a pair of shoes, hoping and praying that they had my size.

One afternoon after school, me and my sister were beckoned into the living room. Mum seemed overly excited, and I wondered what the hell was going on, but then, as we entered the living room, everything became clear. There were two sets of brand-new clothes laid out on the sofa: one for me and one for Sarah. Ada had used some of his redundancy pay to treat us.

I was so touched by the gesture. I ran and gave them the biggest hug before checking out my new clothes. The trousers they'd bought were all the rage at the time, and we had two pairs each! There was a new jumper each, both the latest fashion, a couple of new tops, a dress for Sarah and a new pair of shoes each.

I was dumbfounded, amazed and ecstatic all at the same time. I couldn't take it in. I wasn't going to be the odd one out. I would be the same as everyone else, strutting into the school disco, looking the dog's bollocks. I don't remember the disco, just that act of kindness. It is something that will stay with me for my lifetime.

# 25: No-Win Situation

Work was going well and keeping me busy. The conference was getting closer, and we had over two hundred people who had confirmed their attendance. There were times when I thought I might have bitten off more than I could chew, but there was no turning back now. And, as well as work, I had family life to juggle. Not just the kids. I had Dad to think about too.

Dad's new "mates" had come through on their promise to sort Dad out with the car and he was planning on heading back to Stoke for a few days to stay with Uncle John, who'd recently taken over the Pig Pen. I thought it would do him good. Going over to Stoke for a couple days would give him a chance to catch up with family, and helping out with the pub would help take his mind off the claim.

He was obsessed with it and there wasn't a telephone call when it wasn't mentioned. It would give me a little breather too. I was sick of hearing about it and keen to spend time with Mum and Ada.

It was all change with Mum and Ada, who had finally taken the plunge and decided to sell up and move to the coast to run a B & B together. They'd talked about it for years while Ada was working nights and Mum days. They'd worked really hard over the years, profiting from the sale of several houses, and now they would finally be able to live their dream. I was excited for them and keen to spend as much time with them as I could before they finally moved down.

I knew it bothered Mum and Ada to see me helping Dad out. I was fully aware that Dad hadn't deserved my help but, even though I knew he was a grown, capable man, I was always mindful that he had no other family here in Sheffield. He only really had me.

It didn't stop me from feeling guilty and torn though. Sometimes I felt like a kid again, stuck in the middle of a no-win situation.

# 26: Excuse for Dad

We had no specific routine contact arrangements with Dad. If he was due to meet us, he was either always late or didn't turn up at all. One time, we stood for what seemed like hours on the street corner in the pouring rain and, even though Mum tried to persuade me to come inside, I kept waiting, just in case he was late. I was worried that he'd turn up and we wouldn't be there, that he'd think we didn't care, and then he might stop coming all together.

I told myself that the car might have broken down or that he was ill. I could always find an excuse for Dad; there always had to be a reason. Mum tried to comfort me, but I always felt that deep-down, she was pleased he hadn't turned up. I sensed that life would be so much easier for her if Dad wasn't in the picture anymore.

Dad was a constant reminder of a past she would prefer to forget, but I wasn't about to let her. I used to wonder if Mum had been weak or not up to scratch. I mean, why else would Dad have left? She never went out with him. Was that why he went with another woman?

The only way I would be guaranteed to see Dad was if he was in one of the local pubs. The John O'Gaunt was one of Gleadless Valley's busiest pub and Dad could often be found in there with his mates or playing darts. Us kids weren't allowed in the pub, but we could buy pop and sweets from a small hatch in the doorway. If I was knocking about at the shops, I would knock to see if Dad was in. All the bar staff knew Dad and would give him a shout, and he'd come outside.

He wasn't always chuffed to see us though. Sometimes, he would ask how we were, then chuck us some change and go back inside to his mates to finish his pint. Other times, he would seem irritated, saying: 'tha only ever wants me for money'. That would hurt. Little did he know that I would have preferred his time and attention over money any day.

Dad always seemed to be with his mates and seeing Dad spending his time with them instead of me only made me crave his attention more.

To me, Dad was like a legend. Everybody knew Frank and generally, apart from Mum and Nan, no-one had a bad word to say about him. He always seemed like a man who was going somewhere; he had a purpose about him. To me, he seemed elusive, unique, unlike the other Dads I knew or had seen growing up. He always drove a nice car, and he didn't follow the rules. He did what he wanted, when he wanted. He said what he wanted, even if it wasn't always nice or people didn't like what he had to say. When he talked, people seemed to listen.

Dad was still going out with Elaine, the "other woman" and she had recently moved onto the Valley. It wasn't far from where we lived. I could walk it in fifteen minutes if I took a shortcut through the woods. She lived with her two boys and Dad in a ground-floor maisonette. There were a couple of rare occasions when we would be invited around for tea, but I always felt like a spare part in her home, or an inconvenience.

Sometimes I'd drop in unannounced, which annoyed Elaine, but I didn't care, after all I wasn't there to see her, I was there to see Dad. When Dad was around, he always seemed to favour and fuss over her sons rather than us. He'd talk and have banter with the boys about football and girls, laughing at their latest antics.

Sometimes, watching them together hurt. It felt like my heart was physically aching for the same kind of attention that was always reserved for Elaine and her boys.

One day, me and Sarah had been hanging around Elaine's maisonette playing with her son Stephen and the other local kids who were around our age. Dad and Elaine were going out and Stephen asked if we could stay over. Elaine agreed on the condition that we behaved. It was late evening and, after playing outside all day, we went indoors to play darts on Dad's darts board. We were in the dining area with music on in the background, when Stephen dropped a bombshell. Dad was planning on taking him, his brother and his mother Pat away on holiday abroad later that year.

I was instantly consumed with jealousy. Not only had I never been abroad (the furthest I had ever been to was a caravan in Skegvegas), but I already envied all my friends who went abroad for their summer holidays. And Dad had *never* taken us away at all.

The feeling of rejection was overwhelming. I tried to hide my hurt and made out that I wasn't bothered, but as Stephen continued to brag about where they were going and what they would be doing, I could feel myself getting angrier and angrier. I tried to change the subject, but he wouldn't shut up. Like an elastic band being stretched to its full capacity, I snapped and in one split second, I had gone from having a friendly game of darts to stabbing him on the top of his arm with one of Dad's darts!

Our Sarah just stood there stunned, speechless, as he fled the room crying, heading straight to the phone at the bottom of the stairs to call his Mum at the pub to grass me up.

I didn't feel sorry for him at all. In fact, it felt good to finally shut him up; he got what he deserved. Stephen slammed the phone down.

'You've had it when me Mum and Frank come home!' he shouted, before running upstairs and slamming his bedroom door behind him.

Sarah and I considered leaving and going back home, but it was late. Ada and Mum would have been in bed, and I would have to tell Mum why we'd come home. I did briefly consider running away but decided I had best stay put and await my fate.

I lay in bed running through all the scenarios: would Dad disown me? I mean, he always seemed to favour the lads over us. Would he hit me? Shit! I'd seen what he'd done to Mum. Dad had never hit me before. He'd never had to, his angry voice alone sent shivers throughout my body and just the thought of those shovel-like hands giving me my first pasting made me nearly want to pee myself.

Dad and Elaine couldn't have come home straight away, because I had fallen asleep. I was woken by lots of shouting and screaming. Disorientated, at first, I thought I was back at home, but then I heard Stephen crying in the background and remembered where I was.

I had flashbacks to what I had done earlier, and I winced to myself, acknowledging that perhaps I might have gone too far this time. I could hear footsteps. I was shitting myself, lying in bed, waiting to get a pasting of a lifetime.

Dad came into the room. I could smell the alcohol and fags. I knew he was drunk.

'What's gone off?' he said.

Before I could reply, I burst into tears. I was trying not to, as Dad didn't do crying, but I was scared shitless that I was going to feel the full wrath of Dad. I told him what had happened and why I had stabbed Pat's precious son and tried justifying myself, saying 'it was only a pin pick, it's not like he needed stitches or owt!'

Rather than get angry, give me a slap, or shout, Dad calmly said to me: 'Listen, ignore what he said about the holiday.'

He then chuckled, telling me not to worry about it and to go back to sleep, he'd sort it. For a moment, it seemed like he was actually proud of me which was a first! He stroked my head, before turning to leave the bedroom, silently closing the door behind him.

I can still recall the relief that washed over me as I lay in bed, but what I remember more is the feeling that I had made Dad proud.

Dad went back downstairs, and I heard Stephen climbing back up then sobbing quietly before going into his bedroom and closing his door.

I could hear Elaine screaming. I heard my name being mentioned. She was like a banshee. I was convinced she would never speak to me ever again. I heard the front door slam and then there was nothing, just a deathly silence.

The next morning when I woke, I was not looking forward to going downstairs to face Elaine. I walked into the dining room; Elaine was sitting there at the table alone with her back to me. I knew I would have to get my apology in straight away to try and explain my actions.

I wondered whether she would ever let me in the house again, which would mean I would see less of Dad. She was sitting wrapped in her dressing gown, smoking a cigarette.

Upon hearing the door, she turned her head slightly and said good morning, nice as pie, as if nothing had ever happened the night before. She didn't seem angry at all; in fact she was quite the opposite, her tone was really friendly.

I took this as a good sign and went to take the seat next to her to try and explain what had happened. As I took my seat, Elaine turned towards me. One side of her face was a mixture of orange and black bruising. Her usually petite nose was now swollen beyond recognition. I was no doctor, but it looked broken, and remnants of blood were encrusted on the inside of her nostrils. She looked like she'd done ten rounds with Rocky, but I knew it had been Dad.

I was stunned, speechless, I didn't know what to say apart from: 'God. What happened? Was this because of what I did?'

But she was insistent.

'Listen, it had nothing to do with you. Me and ya Dad had too much to drink, ok?'

In fact, she tried telling me it looked worse than it was. Now where had I heard that line before?

It was like nothing had ever happened. It was weird. Her once pretty face would take weeks to heal. I couldn't look at her, it was such a mess, I did feel guilty, but part of me felt happy. Dad had defended me. Instead of taking the side of the boys, he'd sided with me. He did care after all.

# 27: "Fuck You, Look at Me Now"

Dad had been in Stoke for over a week. I'd spoken to him a few times and learned that he'd been helping out behind the bar. I could tell he'd been drinking too and there was no sign of him returning any time soon. The last time I'd spoken to him, he'd just said that he'd be coming back to Sheffield to fetch some more clothes. Most of my uncles, aunts and cousins had relocated to Stoke years ago and I was starting to wonder why Dad had even come back to Sheffield if he was just going to spend his time in Stoke.

I'd been working me tits off on the conference so, when Dad said he'd be back in the early afternoon, I took some time off to meet him at the flat and have a proper catch up.

I couldn't wait to share my news that, even though I didn't have the usual entry requirements, I had been accepted for university to do a Health and Social Care Degree, and the best part was that work was paying for me to go! I still couldn't quite believe that little old me, Tracey Ford, was heading off to university.

I wished I could go back in time and say to all those doubting teachers 'Fuck YOU, look at me now!'

I arrived before Dad. The flat was a mess, and it stunk of stale odour. The ashtray was still overflowing and there was a half empty bottle of Coke and empty bottle of brandy by the side of the settee where Dad would sit. The kitchen was no different either; the sideboard was littered with unwashed pots; some covered in mould. It looked like it hadn't been cleaned since I'd last been. I knew Dad wouldn't be doing it, as he'd made it clear that it was a flying visit, so I opened the windows, rolled my sleeves up and got started in the kitchen.

I was just about to make a start on the living room when Dad turned up.

He was unshaven and carrying a black sack. He looked like he'd aged a year, but he'd only been gone a week.

'Hiya, shugs,' he said, coming over to give me a hug, before setting the black sack beside him and sitting down on the settee. 'Shit. It stinks in here, doesn't it?'

'Wanna cuppa?' I asked. 'I've just washed the pots and cleaned the kitchen for ya.' Dad nodded as he rolled a cig.

I decided to make myself a cuppa too and took them into the living room. 'So, how's you? Ya look like shit, Dad.'

He laughed. 'Was there any post?'

I passed him some letters that I'd found on the doormat. He tossed them onto the sofa, clearly frustrated.

'Were you expecting something?'

'Yeah, the fucking solicitors rang me last week saying that now the train company want to see me medical records! What the fuck that has got to do with my claim. Apparently, they need my signature or summat. I've a good mind to sack these solicitors off. They're taking the piss!'

I tried reasoning.

'Dad, it's a big claim, perhaps it's what they do all the time.'

'Yeah, well they can fuck off! I'm claiming for PTSD. What's my physical health got to do with owt? I've got enough on me plate wi'out all this.'

I tried to change the subject.

'So what's in the black sack?'

'Washing. I'll do it when I get back.' He was sitting perched on the edge of the sofa with his hands in his head. He looked like he had the world on his shoulders.

'Tell ya what,' I said. 'I'll sort ya clothes out. Is there anything else you need me to do?'

'Yeah. Tha can sort this friggin claim out. It's doing my head in, Trace. It's taking far too long. They said it should be sorted this year, but that ain't going to happen now.'

'Well, Dad. Tha not going without. They keep giving ya interim payments. They wouldn't be doing that if they didn't think you had a claim, would they?'

When Dad was in one of these moods, there was no reasoning with him.

I offered to get Dad some clothes ready to take back to Stoke. His bedroom was in a better state, and the wardrobe was full of clean clothes, some still with tags on.

'You been shopping again?' I shouted from the bedroom.

'Ahh. I went to Matalan a couple of weeks ago.'

I folded his fresh clothes into a clean black sack for him and headed back into the living room.

There was a silence before Dad lifted his head.

'Thanks, shugs,' he said under his breath, and I knew he meant it. 'Listen, I'm going to get me sen a shower and shave. I need to be heading back, but thanks for cleaning the flat.' Taking the cue to get off, I decided that now wasn't a good time to tell him about work or uni. I would leave it for another time.

# 28: YPO Kid

It didn't seem two minutes since I'd started junior school, and now we were getting my uniform for secondary or "big school". Whilst my mates were shopping with their mothers at Tammy Girl, searching for the trendiest school trousers, I was at the YPO building, queuing with Mum for my free school uniform: a blazer, a horrific long A-line skirt and shirts with the biggest cardboard collars I had ever seen.

The first day was torture. I felt like a prize twat in my uniform; it had benefit kid written all over it.

I looked around for familiar friends, but there were lots of new groups of kids too, faces I had never seen before. And, unlike my first day at Hemsworth, my sister wasn't by my side.

We were all beckoned into the school hall, waiting anxiously to find out which class we'd been placed in. It was like being picked for the football team. Thankfully I was called early, and I dutifully made my way to my new form teacher, Mrs McDermott. When everyone was called, we followed her to our new classroom. I wished I had a best friend to sit with. Instead I sat by the window with some of the boys that I sometimes hung around with. Whilst I had many friends, I never really felt close to them. I was a social butterfly, flitting from one social group to another. Sometimes it felt like people only wanted to know me because I could fight their battles for them, battles that I always had to win because my pride, my status, was all I had.

You could always tell who was on benefits at school. We stood out like sore thumbs, with the cardboard clothes, standing in the queue for our free dinner tickets.

I'd watch my friends walking past with their lunch money and wonder what they were talking about when I wasn't there. Were they talking about me behind my back? Or planning things that didn't involve me?

Sometimes, I'd sell my free dinner ticket to someone else for half the price and spend the money at the tuck shop or go and buy myself some fags from the shop at ten pence a pop. I soon started to spend most of my breaks and lunchtimes hanging around the "fag corner", behind the gym or one of the mobile classrooms.

There would be a group of us, forever moving around, trying to avoid the teachers patrolling the yards at break times. The girls' toilets were another good place to source twos-up on a fag. The place always stunk of stale smoke. It was like a game. If they caught you red handed, you would be frog-marched to the headteacher's office to receive your verbal bashing or be given a detention slip.

School life for me was as much about dodging the rules and the teachers as it was about actually doing any work. I soon got a reputation with the teachers for being difficult, but really, I just didn't get what was being asked of me.

I wouldn't ask for help because I was afraid that I would look stupid or thick in front of my mates. I knew that the teachers thought I was just being obstructive and awkward, which made me just want to rebel more.

I would protest about having to shower with the other girls after gym class, convinced that my teacher was a lesbian. Some of the girls were more confident with their bodies, but I wasn't. I didn't want anyone seeing my private parts.

I questioned why I had to do a home economics class when I wanted to do woodwork or metalwork. Just because I was a girl. I once made the home economics teacher cry in class. She had a meltdown there and then in front of the whole class and sent me outside for the rest of the lesson. It turned out that after composing herself, she apologised to the rest of the class and explained that her sister had recently died. I felt a bit guilty but how was I supposed to know that?

I would never understand the purpose of RE. How would that help me in later life? And what was the point of French? Why was it acceptable that the PE teacher socialised with the older kids at Roxy's nightclub? And how come the teachers got to go out at lunchtime and have a swift one in the local pub, when we weren't allowed off the grounds?

I would often be found outside the headmaster's office or the staff room for one misdemeanour or another. Sometimes, I'd catch a glimpse of the teachers having their coffees, laughing and joking without a care in the world. I was sure they loved making me wait.

They would walk past and look down on me. They didn't care about me, so why should I give a fuck about them? I didn't. I had zero respect for anyone that school, apart from my mates.

There were times when I really tried hard. After a bad week at school, or after a telling off from Mum, I would resolve to behave better and take more of an interest in class. But it never lasted long before I was in trouble again.

'Just like ya Dad,' Nan would say when she was round ours.

It had been all over the news that our country was going to war with the Falklands. I was scared. Would all the Dads all have to go to war like they did back in the old days? Dad would most likely come back a hero, after all, he could fight and handle himself. But what about Ada? Would either of them make it back?

I fantasised about us kids being shipped off to the countryside, taken to a place of safety to live with temporary adoptive parents. I'd reinvent myself and make a fresh start. No more benefit clothes because my adoptive parents would be wealthy. I could drop all the fake shit and be the real me, the person I was underneath the attitude. I would excel in school, be the perfect kid. I could return home when the war was over, and Mum and Ada would love the new and improved Tracey, or even better, my adoptive parents would love me so much that they would insist I stay there in the countryside and start a whole new life.

But the war was short-lived and far away, and the opportunity to reinvent myself didn't come. And, though I had lots of friends, I still always felt the odd one out, the loner in the crap uniform, with no sense of belonging.

# 29: Hospital

The conference went ahead, and was a roaring success. It even made the headlines in the Sheffield Star, who did a two-page feature on the event. What with being so busy and distracted, I realised it had been a couple of days, since Dad had left for Stoke again.

I hadn't heard from him which was unusual and every time I tried his mobile, it was dead, so I decided to call the pub on the landline. Uncle John answered straight away.

'Hiya, Uncle John. I've been trying to get a hold of Dad. Has he lost his phone or something? I haven't heard from him for a few days.'

There was an awkward pause. 'Look, Trace, ya Dad's in hospital.'

'What d'ya mean, he's in hospital? How long's he been in? Why is he in? And why hasn't someone called to tell me?' I was incensed and Uncle John knew it.

'Look Trace, your dad insisted we didn't tell ya. He didn't want you to worry.'

'Well I am worried! I'm not a kid. What's the matter with him?'

'It's something to do with his liver. It's inflamed or something. He's been seeing the doc over here because he's been passing blood and they'd been running some tests, but the other night, he started with really bad stomach-ache, and they told him to get to the hospital.'

I was stunned that he was in hospital, but not shocked to hear that Dad didn't want me to know. Years earlier, when he had the taxi firm, he'd had a cancer scare and I'd only found out much later when he explained his rationale for switching to from fags to cigars was 'because of the cancer scare'!

Uncle John tried to reassure me. 'Look, Tracey. They're saying he'll be out in a couple of days. I'll tell ya Dad to call ya when I next go...'

I didn't listen to the last part. 'Don't bother! I'm coming over! Can you tell me which hospital and ward he's on please?'

I put the phone down and called Sarah to explain what had happened and she agreed to travel to Stoke with me, in my car. She hated my driving, but we were keen to get there as quickly as possible.

# 30: What Had God Ever Done for Me?

It was all change again. Christine and Stephanie both moved out and, though I was pleased to get my room back, I knew I'd miss them. Then, having asked for our permission first, Ada proposed to Mum. There was no denying that he loved Mum to bits. Apparently, he'd got down on one knee next to the fish tank in the hole in the road, soppy sod. I was really happy for Mum. She'd never had an engagement ring before and didn't even have any wedding pictures from being married to Dad.

It wasn't long after the wedding announcement that Mum and Ada took me and Sarah to one side to share their other news. In a few months we would be having a new brother. Back to sharing a room again! Ada was chuffed about having a son. I often wondered what the big deal was about boys. Dad always seemed to prefer boys too. But I was as hard as any boy I knew. I could climb trees better than them, win all the dares set by them and if there was a fight at school, I'd be the only girl amongst them or fighting with them.

As the wedding date was getting closer. Mum's dress had to be altered to fit her stomach, and I was going to be one of the bridesmaids. I'd just got my head around having to wear a dress and headband for the day when Mum and Ada announced that we had to start going to church. The vicar wouldn't marry them unless we went to church because they had both been married before, and me and Sarah hadn't been christened, so we would have to be baptised instead.

It was a blow; I couldn't stand religious education at school let alone having to go to church every Sunday just so Mum and Ada could get married. I hated trading my Sunday mornings playing out with my friends for sitting in a church. It was torture, sitting there listening to a bloke in a dress spouting the Lord's name. It felt like a cult, like they were trying to brainwash me, but I wasn't having any of it. I mean why did God have to be a bloke anyway? What had he ever done for me?

The day of the baptism came. I couldn't wait to get it all over and done with. I wondered how they would do it, seeing as I was too big for the vicar to hold me over the basin. The Baptism in itself, was painful. I was used to telling lies, in fact I had got it off to a fine art form, but standing there pretending that I was handing my life over to a bloke I'd never met before was next level shit!

The only saving grace was that none of my school friends got to see me being baptised. If they had, any street cred I might have had would have vanished in a nanosecond.

Baptism over, it was time for the wedding and there was a buzz about the house. The wedding day had arrived. Ada stayed with his best man the night before which I thought stupid, considering Ada had been living with us for nearly two years.

Granddad would be driving Mum and the bridesmaids to the church. There were five of us in total: me, my sister, my cousins Linda and Debbie, and Mum's mate Jenny who was going to be maid of honour. We had to have our hair done and I'm sure they used a whole tin of hairspray on my hair alone. Whilst all the girls seemed to love their dresses, I couldn't wait to get out of mine.

It was a sunny day, and people were all gathered outside the church waiting for us to arrive. Ada was standing there, looking so handsome in his suit and wearing the proudest smile. Dad and Elaine only lived around the corner from the church, and I wondered if he would turn up and disrupt the peace, but there was no drama, apart from when my cousin Linda was sick, having stuffed herself with sweets all day.

We arrived at the reception at the Polish Club, which was weird, considering that we weren't Polish. During the wedding meal, all the bridesmaids were presented gifts.

I couldn't wait to open the box to see what was inside. You can imagine my shock to find a book and not just any book, a bloody Bible. I was sure someone was taking the piss! The meal was over and more people, some I'd never seen before, started to arrive. The DJ took his place and invited Mum and Ada onto the floor for their first dance as husband and wife.

Mum was no longer Dad's wife. She was now officially Mrs Flude, content to be marrying the man of her dreams and carrying his child.

# 31: Visiting Dad

Visiting time was almost over by the time we reached the hospital, and it was easy to find a parking spot, even in the dark. Our next task was to find Dad. It wasn't hard to locate him on the ward; his was the only bed without visitors.

He was sat up on his bed, reading a newspaper and I immediately felt sorry for him. I was expecting him to be pissed off that we'd come, so it was a relief to see him smile at the sight of his kids standing at the foot of the bed.

'Ey up! What you two doing here?'

'I could ask you the same about you, Dad?' We got some chairs and nestled ourselves on either side of Dad's bed.

'You really didn't need to come all this way. They've said I'll be out tomorrow.'

I scanned his features, and to be fair he looked well. His skin was glowing, almost like he'd been abroad, but his yellow eyes told a different story. I made a mental note myself to ask the nurses about that before leaving.

I couldn't hide my frustration.

'Dad, you should have called!'

'I know, but I didn't want to worry you.'

'How would you feel if we had been in hospital and hadn't told ya?'

He put his paper down. 'Honestly, it's nothing to worry about. They reckon it's something to do with my liver, told me to have a break off the booze, which is stupid, I mean I haven't even been drinking that much of late.'

I knew that wasn't true, because I could tell he'd had a drink every time I called.

'Anyway, where's me grapes?' he said, smirking.

'They're still in the shop. So what about this bleeding from ya back passage. What have they said about that?'

'Who told ya that?'

'Look Dad, Uncle John told me, says you haven't been well for some time.'

His eyes rolled. Uncle John was going to get it in the neck, but I didn't care.

'Honestly, babs, there's nothing to worry about. I'll head back to Sheffield anyway. I need to get this claim sorted; it's fucking doing my head in.'

I wanted to scream at him: 'Fuck the fucking claim!' but I just said: 'That will sort itself out. What's important is you getting better.'

Dad gave me an exasperated look. 'It is important. The lawyers will try and use this against me. Fucking doctors don't know what they are talking about. They go on about everyone else's drinking and they're sat there wi' their cigars and brandy. They know fuck all!'

Sarah rolled her eyes. We both knew there was no point in trying to reason with him.

We made small talk and soon visiting time was over, but I wasn't going nowhere until I'd had a word with the nurses myself to try and find out what was actually wrong with him.

The nurse we spoke to was great. She explained that they'd run some tests and were concerned that Dad might have an early onset of cirrhosis of liver.

'Your dad came due to the jaundice, which is a classic symptom.'

The penny dropped. 'Which would account for the yellowing of his eyes, then?'

'Yes, ideally your dad really needs to cut down on his drinking.'

After the conversation we'd just had with Dad, I didn't think that was likely to happen.

Still none the wiser about this cirrhosis condition, my first priority was to get home and do some research. But I was also going to try and find out what else has been going on. I decided to call Uncle Mick, Dad's other brother, because something just wasn't quite right.

# 32: Ireland

On the 6th of October 1982, my baby brother, Mark, was born. With his wispy, blond hair and blue eyes, he was perfect. After bringing him home, the house was filled with visitors who all wanted a cuddle with the new arrival.

Nan was there too, of course. You'd think she'd been at the birth, and the way she went off, you'd think it was her who was battered and bruised by the epidural, not Mum. She was like an itch that wouldn't go away, always there, always having an opinion: *don't do this, don't do that!*

But despite her presence, I did love having Mark around. I loved the permanent smell of babies that would hit you as you walked in the house. Our Sarah loved looking after Mark, offering to help feed or bath him, or taking him for walks in his pushchair – to her, he was like her new doll. I preferred playing and cooing with him and couldn't wait until he started to develop his own little personality.

Just as Mum and Ada got married, Dad and Elaine split up. Dad moved out of hers and got himself a flat on the tenth floor of Kenwood Mount over at Norfolk Park. It wasn't that far away – a fifteen-minute ride on the bus.

Dad had done it out nicely. It was modern, with a corner sofa and a large modern cabinet that housed his prized darts trophies. He had a top of the range TV and video player; it was a proper bachelor pad with a view to die for.

I preferred my single Dad. At least I got more of a look-in that I did when he was with Elaine and the boys. It was pot-luck whether he'd be in, but I'd hang about the flats and got to know the Norfolk Park kids there.

Dad had his fair share of women who he'd bring back to his flat. I could tell when he would be planning to bring someone back as he'd make sure the flat was tidy before he went out.

One day, out of the blue, Dad announced he was taking us to Ireland to visit his sister, Jane. I was so excited that we would get to see our cousins again. I'd missed them since they'd moved away from Chapeltown where we used to visit them.

I was a little nervous as there were still the Troubles going on in Ireland, but I was reassured that there were no bombings or fighting in Cork, where we were going.

Early one morning, Dad came to collect us, but he wasn't alone: he was with a bloke called John who I recognised from the pubs. Dad told us that he and John were going to be doing some sea fishing while we were there.

John was a really nice bloke to be fair! He was the total opposite of Dad. Whilst Dad drove, John talked to us constantly and took an interest; it seemed he wanted to know everything he could about us.

We finally arrived at the ferry and crawled patiently with all the other traffic waiting for the overnight trip. Once we got onto the ferry, we headed straight to our cabins. Me and Sarah were sharing our own, with Dad and John next door. Then, once we'd dropped our stuff off, we all headed to the bar, and Sarah and I went off to explore. Later, it was John who took me and our Sarah to our cabins and made sure we were settled in for the night before heading back up to the bar to join Dad.

But Dad never made it back to the cabin. True to form, he copped off with someone he'd met at the bar and turned up in the morning, ready for the onward journey.

Ireland looked a lot like home: it was all green fields and housing estates, and there were no signs of war or any troubles. As we headed into County Cork, I vividly remember the bridge that grew bigger as we got closer and the blue water that sat below. It was just beautiful, and I was mesmerised.

It was a sunny day, and my cousins were out in the front garden, playing with some mates when we arrived. It had been a few years since I'd last seen my cousins, but the connection and familiarity were still there, though their fashion seemed out of date.

I couldn't believe how expensive it was out there: 50p for a Mars bar, where back home, they were only about 20p. We played with the local kids, whilst Dad and John went fishing during the day and went out to the pub at night.

Money was also tight for Auntie Jayne and her family. I showed our Marguerite how to use sugar and water instead of hair gel. We took the piss out of each other's accents and played outdoors till late. Despite all the Troubles, it felt safe here.

It was the kind of community I'd never seen before; neighbours didn't lock their doors and there was hardly any crime. It was a trusting community, where everyone seemed to know each other. It was like the place I used to dream of being evacuated to.

I could have quite happily stayed and reinvented myself, started afresh, put the past behind me, but sadly the trip had to come to an end, and in the blink of an eye it was time to go back to Gleadless Valley, back to all the bullshit. My heart sank as we left, envious of their life that seemed so uncomplicated.

# 33: The Pieces of the Jigsaw

I'd already looked up cirrhosis of the liver on the internet, but there was so much information to take in and I had to stop myself from getting carried away with worst-case scenarios. We still didn't know that it was what we were dealing with and no-one else seemed duly worried. In fact there was little or no sympathy forthcoming from anyone. As far as they were concerned, Dad was a grown man and could take care of himself.

I was relieved when Uncle Mick answered straight away. It was always good to talk to him. A lorry driver who liked a drink, like Dad, he was a straight talker who called a spade a spade. Unlike Dad, he was a family man first.

'Hiya Uncle Mick. It's Tracey. I wanted to have a chat with ya about Dad.'

"Hiya lovely. How's ya Mum and sister Sarah keeping?"

I loved that, even after all these years, he never forgot to ask after Mum. Mum and his missus had been close before she tragically died, leaving Uncle Mick to bring up my cousin on his own.

'They're grand, thanks. Look, can you tell me what's going on with Dad? I'm pretty pissed off that no one thought to tell us Dad was in hospital.'

'I'm sorry. I hadn't realised no one had let you know. I should have called ya. Now I feel guilty.'

'It's just that, ever since Dad moved back to Sheffield from Stoke, I've been worried about him. Something's not quite right and I can't put my finger on it. The nurses reckon Dad might have got something wrong with his liver, cirrhosis or summat, but Dad's playing it down.'

'Look Trace. His drinking had got bad. This isn't the first time he's been in hospital.'

'Ya what?' Now I was pissed off and I knew Uncle Mick knew it too.

'Look, love, I honestly thought you knew. I thought ya Dad might have told ya?'

'Well, he's told me fuck all, Uncle Mick. This is the first I have heard about any of this.'

Uncle Mick went on to explain how he and his new missus had agreed to take Dad in, to help him detox, and that's why Uncle John had taken over the Pig Pen.

'Why? How much has he been drinking?' I was confused. Dad had always been a drinker, but it had never been a problem.

'Look, love, it's not how much he was drinking, it's what he was drinking; he'd been hitting the top shelf hard, couldn't help himself.' I could hear Uncle Mick's voice deflate. 'The silly twat had been doing great at ours. Hadn't had a drink for weeks. He started having a couple of tinnies, but then our lass found out he'd been hitting the spirits again. She wasn't having any of it. She doesn't take no shit from no one, so ya Dad gave us no other option but to ask him to leave.'

I was stunned, speechless.

'I've tried telling him if he just sticks to the lager, he'll be fine. It's that fucking top shelf he needs to stay away from.'

I was just wondering if that had been the real reason Dad had moved back to Sheffield, when Uncle Mick read my mind. 'That's why he went back to Sheffield, for a fresh start. I warned him that coming over here to stay wi' our John was a bad idea, but tha knows ya Dad. Tha can't tell him nowt.'

After saying goodbye to Uncle Mick, I felt like I'd been punched in the stomach. It was like everyone had known what was going on except me and, despite wanting to know the truth, a part of me wished I'd never asked. I was glad I was alone at home. The pieces of the jigsaw were starting to fall into place. It just wasn't a picture that I wanted to contemplate.

# 34: Best Christmas Ever

Christmas was around the corner. Dad didn't usually do Christmas, so it was a big surprise when Dad asked if he could pick us up on Christmas morning to open some presents at his flat. I could tell that Mum wasn't impressed but she conceded on the condition that we opened our presents at home first.

I'd already had the best Christmas morning. After opening a mountain of presents downstairs, I'd walked into my bedroom to find a racer bike! There were shrieks from Sarah's room too and she came out of her room with a stereo.

'What's up?' Ada shouted from the bottom of the stairs.

Mum was grinning. Tears welled in my eyes. I'd been after a racer for ages, but Mum and Ada always said they couldn't afford one. It was second hand, but I didn't care, because it was mine. Overwhelmed, I ran downstairs to give them both a hug and told them how much I loved them, and I really meant it.

We were still finishing our special Christmas breakfast when Dad pulled up outside the house. Mum stood on the doorstep to wave us off.

'Merry Christmas, Gill!' Dad shouted as we got in the car, which I thought was nice of him.

Mum smiled. 'Same to you, Frank.'

Seeing them being civil to each other eased the usual awkwardness and I wondered if they might even be friends again.

On the drive over, Dad asked us how our Christmas morning had gone. We excitedly told him about all the presents and the bonus ones that had been waiting for us in our bedroom. He was smiling like a Cheshire cat. 'Well, let's see if I can top that then?'

When we arrived at the flat, Dad ushered me and Sarah into the living room and followed us. There were two mountains of neatly wrapped presents on each corner of the living room. The sight took my breath away.

Dad laughed.

'Go on, then.' He ushered us both into the living room. 'They won't open their sens, will they?'

Me and Sarah tore into the gifts. There was paper everywhere. We had the exact same as each other. We'd already each got a watch off Mum and Ada, but this one was more expensive.

There was an electronic Simon game, but it was a miniature one that wrapped around your wrist. I'd never seen one like it and Dad said they were new out. We had Walkmans, Pjs, toiletries, chocolates and a cuddly St Bernard's dog, which was the biggest teddy I'd ever seen.

I glanced over to Dad who was sitting with his cup of builder's tea watching us open our presents. I'd never seen him smile so much.

I rushed over to the sofa and gave him a massive hug. 'Thank you, Dad.'

He patted my back. 'You're welcome. Merry Christmas!' He stood up and looked around the room. "Reyt. I need to get you back. There's some black sacks under the sink. You'd better get ya presents in them and clear up the mess!'

So much seemed to have changed since Dad had been single. When he'd lived with Elaine, we only saw him on Boxing Day, and we knew the presents were all bought by her. Now, instead of snatching moments with him in the local pub, or having to compete with another woman's kids, he had an open-door policy with his kids, and the truth was that day, I'd never felt closer to him.

Dad dropped us off back home at the allocated time as promised. He was dressed up and stunk of aftershave. This was turning out to be the best Christmas ever.

Dad pulled up outside the house and peeped his horn. Mum came to the door. It was nice to see her smiling. Once Dad had gone, we were excited to show Mum and Ada what we had got. Mum was smiling but I could sense she was smiling through gritted teeth. Ada didn't hang around. He made his excuses about having to do something for the dinner.

Ten minutes after we had got back, Nan came. I thanked her for my presents and the obligatory brand-new copper coins which was a Christmas tradition of hers. I used to love them but now I just tossed them aside. I was eager to show her what we'd been given for Christmas, but she wasn't impressed.

She turned to Mum.

'Didn't you give him a list of what you were buying them?" Mum nodded.

Nan shook her head in disbelief. 'Then why has he gone and got some of the same stuff?'

'Just leave it, Mum, will ya?' said my mum.

But Nan didn't stop. 'He's got a nerve. He doesn't pay nowt towards the kids' upkeep and thinks he can show up once a year giving it the Big I Am. Who does he think he is?'

'Just leave it, Mum, will ya?' Mum's tone was firmer this time.

But throughout the day, every so often she'd mutter: 'he's not even a part-time Dad him' or 'he must have robbed a bank this time, where's he got all the money from?'

What should have been the best Christmas day ever had been tainted. There was a tension in the air, and it was all because of Dad.

# 35: Blackpool

Dad was being discharged and, most importantly, was on his way back to Sheffield. I was glad he was coming home but the timing couldn't have been worse because I was busy driving a removal van to Blackpool and helping Mum and Ada to move into their B & B.

The conversation I wanted to have with Dad about his drinking would have to wait. At least it would give me time to think about what to say.

It was all hands-on deck. Sarah, Mark and I were all driving over from Sheffield on the Saturday and staying over. After a few arguments about my driving, me and Sarah finally arrived and we were both surprised at how deprived Blackpool looked away from the seafront, especially in the daylight. The place was massive though and Mum had grand plans for redecorating each room and putting her personal touch on the place. It was nice to see her excited and putting herself first finally, but I still couldn't quite believe she wasn't going to be up the road.

Moving them was knackering and backbreaking work, but also fun. It had been a long time since I'd belly-laughed as much. Even when I dented the bleeding van trying to reverse it on Mum's back yard, we had a laugh. Thank fuck for insurance! That night, me, my sister, brother, Mum and Ada sat and drank and reminisced about the old days.

The next morning, I decided to have a walk on the seafront to get the girls some rock before heading home. There were some families on the beach building sandcastles and, even though the sea was a shitty brown colour, it was still a glorious view. I found a bench and sat down. I needed ten minutes to myself before heading back to Sheffield.

Even though Dad had moved out of our house a few months before, now it felt like he'd moved into my head instead. He was home now and had told me he had no plans to go out, but I was still worried about him.

I would normally have been able to talk through my problems with Mum and Ada, but I couldn't burden them with my concerns about Dad. As far as Mum was concerned, Dad was just a sperm donor. In her eyes, he'd never been there for us growing up and I knew that it bothered, even hurt her, when I would give Dad the time of day.

With Ada, it was even harder. I admired and respected how he'd stepped up all those years ago and, now that I was older, I realised that Dad's involvement had been sporadic and always on his terms. Dad didn't do hugs; he didn't do talking and emotions were for wimps as far as he was concerned. Whereas Ada was always there with open arms. He didn't walk away or give up on me, even after the times I'd rejected him. Poor sod, I never made it easy for him. I was the stepdaughter from hell.

I couldn't talk to our Sarah either. She'd cut the umbilical cord after the birth of her first child, Niall. Dad had insisted she should name her baby after him, but she'd told him where to get off and they hadn't really spoken since.

My train of thought was broken by some kids screaming on the beach. The fresh air had sorted the last of my hangover, and it was time to get my ass back to Sheffield.

# 36: Front Page of the Sheffield Star

My attitude at school wasn't improving; in fact, it was getting worse. The teachers no longer scared nor intimated me, and I would often be found standing outside the headmaster's office, waiting to be reprimanded for being insolent or disruptive. And then I got myself expelled.

One morning I'd been made to sit next to Mrs McDermott, my form teacher, at the front of the class. She kept on telling me to sit up straight, but I was automatically resting on my elbow to write. She nudged my arm, and I reacted, accidentally swiping her on the chin where she had a boil. It was a total accident but that was that. Violence against teachers would not be tolerated.

It's fair to say Mum wasn't impressed with the school's decision to expel me and decided if I was leaving the school, then so was my sister. She found us a place at the neighbouring school, Newfield Green. The only problem was that I'd previously been in fights with the kids from there and Sarah was furious with me.

I hated the new school and, to make matters worse, my maths teacher was Mr McDermott, Mrs McDermott's frigging husband! I could feel the hate reverberate off him as soon as I walked into the classroom. The only people I knew at the school were my cousins, Debbie and Wayne, but they were in different year groups.

I felt like a fish out of water, a loner. I would meet up with mates from Gleadless after school, but it wasn't the same. Just wearing a different uniform made me different. I was missing out on all the school gossip and plans and felt like a spare part all over again.

I'd only been there a couple of weeks before I was involved in a scrap in the school canteen. Mum could see how miserable I was at the new school and somehow, she persuaded the headteacher from Gleadless to let me and Sarah come back. I promised to behave myself, but it was easier said than done.

I'd been back at Gleadless for a couple of months, when I was told about a protest taking place in town. The protest was about the introduction of a new Youth Training Scheme (YTS), that paid school leavers twenty-seven quid a week to work. Mum had already said that when I left school. I'd have to start paying ten pounds a week in board, which would only leave me with seventeen quid to live on. It was a pittance!

There was a buzz about the school and a few of my mates agreed to meet at the bus stop at lunchtime. The headteacher got wind of our plan and was soon on the top deck of the bus, warning us that if we stayed on the bus then we'd be suspended. Some people got off, but I stayed. I didn't have that long left at school anyway, so what did it matter?

When we arrived outside the City Hall, we were greeted by what seemed like thousands of kids and adults. It was my first ever protest! There were flags; people were shouting into a microphone, whilst others chanted. The atmosphere was electric. I was in my element, surrounded by people like myself who were angry with the world.

I was approached by random people asking me my opinion; they seemed to understand how shit it was being a teenager. There was a stand promoting careers in the Army. No formal qualifications required and the promises of travelling the world and getting paid at the same time appealed to me.

I felt close to adulthood and the opportunity to reinvent myself, able to prove to everyone that I could be something other than a constant disappointment.

On a high, I climbed the City Halls steps and wrapped myself around one of the pillars to join in the chants. A couple of hours later, the protest started to disperse, but a few hundred kids had other ideas. We weren't ready to go home yet so we marched on through the town centre. We walked defiantly past the Town Hall and headed down to The Moor and gathered on the bandstand, chanting, continuing our protest.

A big group of kids stormed GT News, raiding the shop like locusts. There was nothing the staff could do. Eventually, the police were called and slowly, the crowd of kids started to disperse. My first real taste of freedom had come to an end.

Later that evening, I was sitting at the dinner table, bored by the same chit-chat. *How did school go? What lessons did you have?* My response was the usual grunt. I didn't dare tell them what I'd really been up to.

Suddenly, Ada pushed his chair away from the table and reached for the local newspaper. He threw it on the middle of the table.

'Explain this, then?' he said.

There I was on the front page of the Sheffield Star, smiling, hugging one of the pillars outside the City Hall. There was no point trying to worm my way out of it. I was busted!

I really didn't know all the ins and outs of the protest, but I stood my ground, justifying my actions. I repeated what the organisers had said. I had every right to be angry. Stuck in limbo between being a child and an adult, one minute I was being told to act my age, then grow up, I couldn't win. Eventually, Mum and Ada calmed down and soon we were laughing.

A couple of weeks later, I came home from school, and I knew immediately that was in trouble. I'd barely walked through the door before Mum started ranting about the National Front. I was friggin' clueless. I didn't have a Scooby-doo what she was going on about. I had never heard of the National Front. It transpired that whilst out on the march, I'd signed up for the National Front and they'd called round at ours earlier that day to talk about my membership.

Mum had flipped her lid and given them a few choice words before giving them their marching orders. I tried apologizing, explaining that it was a simple mistake, that I had no idea they were a racist group.

Mum couldn't look at me. She just shook her head in despair. 'The thing is, Tracey, you think you know everything, but you know nothing.'

# 37: Changing the Subject

I waited until after work on Monday to call to see Dad. It was already dark, but the flat was cosy and Dad seemed in a good mood. He was pleased to see me. I made myself a cuppa, before taking it into the front room and snuggled myself into Dad's spare armchair in the corner.

'So how ya feeling, then?'

'I'm good, shugs. Feeling loads better. I've decided to stay away from Stoke until this claim's been sorted. I'm sick of waiting. They're taking the fucking piss.'

A part of me wished I hadn't asked.

'Well, it shouldn't be that much longer, should it? I mean, you did the psychiatric assessment. Has the report been written and submitted yet?'

'Has it fuck! They are still insisting on wanting access to my medical history, which has got fuck all to do with the claim. It doesn't make sense. What's that got to do with the train crash!'

I tried to change the subject. 'What did the hospital say then, Dad? Do you have to go back or anything?'

'Nah, got the all-clear.'

'Yeah but I spoke to the nurse. She said they thought you might have onset of cirrhosis of the liver, Dad. I looked it up and it can get bad. Surely there should be a follow-up appointment?'

'Like I said, I'm ok now.'

I wasn't going to press him anymore, I knew it was a waste of breath.

'They can say what they want – this claim has got fuck all to do with drinking.'

'Well, I'm not being funny, Dad, but wouldn't that go in your favour?'

Dad looked at me like I'd grown two heads. 'How the fuck do you work that out?'

‘I know that this isn’t the first time you have been admitted. Uncle Mick told me. If your drinking’s got worse since the crash, then it actually supports your claim – depression, drinking more...’

Dad was pissed and it wasn’t the drink.

‘My drinking has got fuck all to do with the claim! I bet the bastards have got someone spying on me, trying to catch me out. Anyway, I’m going to stay low. It’s been two fucking years now. They are taking the fucking piss, Trace.’

He was clearly on one. There was absolutely no way I was about to push him further on his drinking.

‘I ain’t got a problem with the drink. I’m just sticking to me couple of cans of lager. I can stop anytime I want. Anyway, how did your mum’s move go?’

Good old Dad, he certainly knew how to change a subject.

I told him about Mum’s new place. He seemed genuinely pleased for Mum and Ada. I told him about me damaging the van and he laughed.

‘I bet Ada was pissed off wi ya. That won’t be cheap.’

‘To be fair, he was ok. There was a two hundred and fifty excess on it, but Ada reckoned I was worth it,’ I joked.

‘Actually, I’ve been thinking of taking a little weekend break me sen. Apparently Blackpool’s good this time of year...’

I just looked at Dad and shook my head, but I couldn’t help but laugh, and Dad was laughing to himself too.

‘Yeah, Dad, give ‘em a bell. You can be one of their first guests. I’m sure they’d give you a discount an’ all!’

# 38: Willy Do

I had a new obsession. Horses. A couple of our mates had recently started horse-riding lessons, but there was no way Mum, or Ada could afford it. Only there was a lady at Norton Oaks field who would let us ride her horse, Champ, if we mucked it out when she wasn't around.

Champ was old and could be grumpy and unpredictable, but it wasn't long before I had mastered the rising trot and felt confident going into a canter. Being around the horses kept me out of trouble, so Mum was happy I'd found a new hobby. It also meant I was spending less time around at Dad's, not that he would miss me. He was busy setting up his new taxi firm.

One of our mate's cousins had her own horse called Willy Do. She lived at a place called Ford, an hour's walk from the Valley. It was like another world. Concrete roads were replaced with fields and there were more trees than council houses. Willy Do lived in a field adjacent to her back garden. She was so lucky, but she was bored with Willy and was more than happy for us to help muck out and ride him when we wanted. Unlike Champ, Willy Do was much more placid; he was the perfect horse. And then Willy Do was put up for sale.

Mum and Ada couldn't afford that kind of money, but Dad could! I became obsessed, desperate to have this horse. Eventually, after a lot of pestering and persuasion, he finally agreed to buy him for us. I was elated. None of my friend's parents could afford to buy them a horse, but my dad could, and did.

Mum wasn't impressed though. 'It's ok him buying the horse, but is your dad gonna pay for the rent and food?'

Dad had promised he would provide the monthly fees. He even paid a month's stable rent in advance, and the farmer threw in some bales of hay for free.

As soon as me and my sister woke, the first thing on our minds was Willy. We would race each other to see who would get to the farm first. We were the envy of all our friends. He should have been called "Willy Won't", because he was a bugger to catch, but I'd spend hours at the farm.

The best times were those we spent alone, just me and him. I would talk to him, assuming he understood every word that I said. It felt like I finally had someone to share my fears and concerns with. I didn't even get into trouble off Mum if I was later home.

But the second month's rent never materialised and nor did the third. Dad was always out working, it was hard to pin him down and when we did, he would fob us off. It was just the rent neither; we ended up resorting to stealing bales of straw when the farmer had gone indoors. Mum would send up some peelings or carrots to feed him, even Nan would even bring him scraps.

Mum even got me and Sarah a Saturday morning job, working alongside her in a café. We would rotate weekends, and all the money went on Willie's upkeep, but even the extra cash didn't help.

I would see how well looked after the other horses in the field were and felt ashamed that we couldn't offer the same to Willy. I just hoped that the love we had for him made up for the lack of proper care.

I started to feel ashamed. The owners of the other horses would make snide comments and what hurt most was that they were right.

The tension at home grew and it was all Dad's fault. I absolutely adored Willy and the thought of not being able to keep him made my heart ache. But the worst part was that he'd proved Mum and Nan right. In their eyes, Dad was a loser who didn't care about us kids and shouldn't have made promises that he couldn't keep! I couldn't defend Dad, because I knew, deep-down, that what they were saying was true. Dad had let us down again and there was no way that we could keep Willy. He had to go.

It didn't take long for us to find him a new owner. Dad said we could split the money we made between us. It was one hundred and fifty pounds, the most money I'd ever had to myself ever, but I just wanted Willy. I took him out for our last ever ride and cried the whole way.

Dad had let us down and broken his promise. Worse than that, he'd broken my heart, I thought I might never forgive him.

# 39: A Steep Learning Curve

I'd spoken to Dad on the phone but hadn't seen him for a couple of weeks. My new role working with families of addicts was manic. When I'd first volunteered at a day rehabilitation centre, Dad had said I was mad working for free, but here I was, getting paid for a job I loved.

The new job was proving to be a steep learning curve. People thought the stigma was bad enough for addicts, but it was ten times worse for the families. Working with them was completely different; in fact it was harder.

Hearing some of their stories of what they had gone through forced me at times to reflect on some of the things I'd put Mum and Ada through. I remembered all the times Mum had questioned and blamed herself, wondering if there was anything she could have done differently or the shame she was forced to endure from the times she'd had to call the police on me.

One of David Blunkett's representatives from the Home Office, who had been at the conference a couple of weeks ago, had emailed. I'd mentioned in passing that I would love to be able to capture and share the stories of some of the families to encourage people to come forward for support sooner. Now the Home Office had offered to pay for it to be produced.

When I had spoken to Dad, it didn't sound like he'd been drinking, which was a relief. Apparently, he'd been keeping himself entertained with some pirate DVDs he'd bought off some shoplifters in Stoke. He was keeping true to his promise to lay low in case someone from the solicitors was trying to catch him out. He was even getting his groceries delivered. As far as I was concerned, he only had himself to blame if they were onto him; he'd laid it on pretty thick with the shrink a few months earlier. At least he'd finally given them access to his medical records and I was glad that there would be no more visits to Stoke for a while.

Christmas was just around the corner. It had been a mad year, what with Dad rocking up out of the blue, then Mum moving to Blackpool and even though work was going amazing, I was already glad to see the back of 2002.

# 40: An Attitude Problem

Deep-down, I knew it wasn't Mum's fault that Willy had to go, but that didn't stop her getting the brunt of my hurt and anger.

Me and Sarah got to keep our Saturday morning job at the café. The best part was being able to sneak fags off the shelves. It felt good to finally have some cash for myself, it meant I wasn't tapping off my mates.

I'd started hanging about with the lads again, having neglected them for Willy. We'd hang outside the local shops or venture out to other youth clubs outside the Valley boundary, meeting up with other gangs of kids.

In those days, we were territorial and would fight with other kids from neighbouring schools. There were some lads who sniffed glue; the older ones smoked weed. I tried glue a few times, but never liked the sensation it gave me. I didn't like alcohol neither. I was happy as a pig in shit just hanging out with my mates, having a laugh and just being accepted by the lads.

I was privy to all the lads' talk, about which girls were "easy", which made me resolute about not putting out and, though I had the odd boyfriend, it never lasted longer than a couple of weeks and we never went further than a kiss. Some of the lads would joke that I was frigid, but I would rather have been known as frigid than being a slag.

Sometimes I'd wonder what Dad would think of me if he saw me out with the lads. I thought he might like me more. But we rarely saw him; he was too busy building his empire to have time for kids.

Me and Mum had been butting heads for weeks. She claimed it was down to me having an attitude problem, but as far as I was concerned, it was her. One day we were having another spat. I don't know what started it, but it escalated quickly. I'd stormed out of the house, full of hatred and anger, but Mum was on my tail, screaming and shouting at me down the street, then suddenly from nowhere, I could feel myself being pulled back, something had a hold of me, dragging me back towards home. Mum was so fast and strong, I didn't even have the time to take my hands out of my pockets to retaliate.

The next thing I knew, I was being dragged up the stairs backwards towards Mum's bedroom where she threw me onto her double bed. Mum had never been physical with me before and I was in shock. Mum started showering me with punches from every direction. She was like a woman possessed, screaming in anger like a banshee.

I'd always thought I was stronger and harder than Mum but, in that moment, she was winning!

I could hear Ada shouting.

'Gill, that's enough!' He pulled her off me. When the blows stopped coming, I dared to look up and there was Mum, breathing heavily with tears running down her face. I had never seen her look like that. It was like she was a different person.

Standing firm, Mum demanded that I go straight to my room and stay there, until further notice, but I was pumped and there was absolutely no way I was staying at home now! In my eyes, this was abuse and I didn't have to stay there.

I didn't have a clue where I would go, but anywhere felt better than being stuck in this house under the same roof as Mum. I bided my time, then climbed out of my bedroom window before hopping onto the front porch. I was preparing my final descent when Sarah walked around the corner.

'What are you doing?'

I told her not to say a word to Mum, and with that I was off.

Determined that I was never returning home again, I walked the streets. I contemplated staying in the woods for the night, but in my haste, I'd forgotten a change of clothes. I hadn't thought this through, but I couldn't go back.

Walking the streets, I bumped into an old mate Richard, who was on his way to babysit for a lady who lived down the road from us. I told him what had just gone down at ours and he asked her if I could stay over too and thankfully, she agreed.

Relieved, I considered my options. I could go to social services, and they'd put me in a care home or foster care once I told them that Mum had beat me. I knew a couple of kids who were in a foster home and it looked ok to me. They even got a weekly allowance.

I sat with Richard; we talked about how shit it was being a kid, how we hated our parents, how we couldn't wait to leave school and escape from all the rules. It was bliss until we were woken by shouting. I could hear Dad's voice. I'd never heard him sound so angry.

I could hear a woman's voice too. It was the lady who Richard was babysitting for. She must have come home, left us on the sofa to sleep but then been woken by Dad at the door. Dad had her out of the balcony, threatening to throw her off!

Still in a daze, Dad dragged me out of the flat and drove me home. He didn't say a word. He didn't have too.

'We'll talk about this tomorrow,' he said to Mum as he dropped me home and then he was off.

Mum seemed relived but she also looked angry. I was too tired to fight, so I headed straight to my room. Sarah was up waiting for me. She filled me in on what had taken place after I'd left.

Apparently, Mum had tried all my friends once she'd realised I'd gone and then she'd called Dad who'd come round declaring that he had a sawn-off shotgun in the car and that Mum and Ada's kneecaps would be in the firing line if I wasn't found by morning. Like Mum, Dad had been to all my friends' houses, but Dad was a lot more threatening. I felt sure that I would never be able to face or be ever allowed at my friends' doors again.

Dad was back round at our house the following morning. I was still in my bedroom, but I could hear them talking in the living room. I could hear Dad raising his voice at Mum and despite still being angry at Mum, I felt sorry that she was on the other end of Dad's wrath.

Everything went silent and for a moment I thought Dad had left, but then Mum called to me. I walked sheepishly into the living room. As soon as I saw Mum crying, I wished right there and then that if I could turn back the clocks.

Mum broke the silence.

'Look Tracey, I don't know what's going on with you, but I know you're not happy...'

She didn't get to finish her sentence because Dad interjected. 'Right, lady, listen to me! I ain't got no time to be fucking running around in the middle of the night chasing after thee.'

I bowed my head terrified that I was going to get a pasting, but Mum was speaking again.

'Look it's up to you, but your dad has said that you can go stay with him for a while. Perhaps a break is just what we all need, eh, and you can always come back.'

I couldn't believe my ears. I felt like I'd just found a golden ticket from a Willy Wonka chocolate bar.

'Look, if tha comes to stay at mine, there'll be no fucking about, do you hear me, cos I won't stand for thee fuckin bullshit thas been giving thee mother! Are ya listening?'

I turned to Mum. 'What do you think?'

Mum just sighed and shrugged her shoulders. 'Look, love, it's completely up to you, but you're clearly not happy here.'

Mum looked awkward. I couldn't make out if she was trying to get rid of me or giving me the choice to stay. They both stared at me, waiting for me to respond, stuck in the middle. It felt like a trick question and I felt torn.

'Can I go stay with Dad?' As soon as the words left my mouth, I felt like a traitor. Mum looked gutted. I knew I'd hurt her. I tried to make it better. 'I mean, just for a while, give you a break from me if anything?'

I'd never seen Mum look so defeated and all because of me.

Dad stepped in. 'Right, that's sorted then, you go pack some clothes, but before you do, I think you owe your mum an apology, don't you?' It wasn't a request; it was an order.

Sarah was waiting at the top of the stairs, anxiously waiting, keen to hear the gossip. 'What's happening?'

'I'm going to live with Dad.'

'You're not!' She sounded indignant.

'Ah fuck off, Sarah!' I snapped. The last thing I needed was to feel even more shit than I already did. I started to gather my clothes when Mum appeared at the door.

'Here you go, love, you'll need these.' She handed me some carrier bags. 'You can always come back for anything you've forgotten.'

She was smiling but I couldn't face her. I just wanted to get out of the house as fast as possible.

Dad was already in the car with the engine running, waiting impatiently for me to get in. He turned to me.

'Got everything?'

I nodded.

'Right, let's get you to mine. I'm already late for work.'

And that was that.

# 41: Merry Christmas, Dad

Christmas brought the usual mix of tradition, nostalgia, and also sadness that this year, Mum and Ada would be in Blackpool and Dad would be on his own.

I wasn't used to seeing Dad at Christmas (he'd always been shacked up with a girlfriend's family), but this year he was in Sheffield. I couldn't invite him with us to Pat's mum's though; he was he complete opposite to Pat's family. And I could hardly invite him to our family Boxing Day celebration in Blackpool! So, he'd given me some money to buy presents for the kids, and we'd agreed they would open them at his. It was the least I could do, and I had some presents for him too.

It was like any other day entering his flat; there were no signs of Christmas apart from the kids' presents in the living room, which I'd already wrapped for them. I left the kids in the living room with Dad whilst I helped myself to a cuppa and made Dad a mug of his usual builder's tea.

I could hear the kids opening their presents and thanking him. I brought our drinks into the room. He wasn't dressed yet but looked cosy in his dressing gown and slippers. He was all smiles as Lauren excitedly told him about all the presents she'd got from Father Christmas.

Our Danielle was her usual reserved self. She'd plonked herself into the armchair and was scrolling through the channels to find something to watch.

'Merry Christmas, Dad,' I said, giving him a kiss and passing him his presents.

'I told ya, tha needn't have bothered, Trace, though it was nice watching kids open theirs.'

I smiled inside. I knew he would appreciate it; he'd missed out on so many Christmases over the years and on seeing the kids grow up, unlike Grandad Ada, who the kids had an amazing bond with. It made me sad, like history repeating itself.

'I hate leaving you on ya own Christmas day, Dad. Are you sure you don't wanna come round to ours later? I'll pick you up and you can have a couple of drinks with us.'

'Thanks love, but I've told ya, I'm sound. Anyway it's only another day. John Wayne's on later. I've got me sen a couple of tins, I've got plenty of food in, I'll be all reyt. Anyway, I need a shower. It's been lovely seeing ya, but you get ya sens over to Pat's Mum's and have a good day and that's an order, do ya hear me!'

I leant over and gave him a kiss. 'Loud and clear, Dad.' I turned to the kids, 'Come on! Give ya Grandad a kiss. You've got some more presents to open at Nan Wina's.'

They did as they were told, and off we went.

# 42: Chips and Chicken Soup

I felt like a hobo carrying all my belongings into the flat. The smell of stale aftershave and cigarette smoke hung heavy in the air.

Dad pointed to the spare room.

'Here, put ya stuff in the spare room. You're gonna have to sleep on the sofa until I get ya a new bed.'

I'd never ventured into the spare room before. Apart from a few black sacks in the corner of the room, it was empty. There wasn't even any carpet or curtains, and it felt cold.

My initial thought was to ask what about the rest of the bedroom furniture, but I decided to keep my gob shut; I was in enough shit already.

I just dumped my stuff on the bedroom floor and sheepishly followed Dad into the living room. He was busy getting all his stuff together to go to work.

'I'm sorry, Dad.' I wasn't sure if he'd heard me. I felt like an inconvenience already.

'Dad, I'm sorry.'

Dad turned to me and huffed. 'Look, what's done is done and like I said, there'll be no fucking about here, do you hear me?'

'I promise, Dad. I'll behave. You won't even know I'm here.' I meant it. The thought of living with Dad excited me and I really wanted to use this opportunity to start afresh and show him what he'd been missing out on all these years.

'Well, look. I've gotta go to work. I'll be back about four. There isn't much food in so you'll need to go to the shop.' He pointed to a shopping list on the sofa. 'There's a list and money on the side there.'

I turned to see a crisp twenty-pound note on the side.

'And I want the change,' he added in a stern tone.

And with that, he was gone.

I started cleaning the living room, dusting and polishing all the surfaces and Dad's prized trophies. I cleaned the ashtrays, saving the tab ends to smoke later. Soon the smell of Mr Sheen had replaced the smell of stale smoke. I cracked on with the kitchen and then headed into Dad's bedroom. I wasn't sure if I should even be in there, so I decided to just make the bed and open the windows to let some fresh air in. Then I took some damp clothes from the bathroom to dry on the veranda and admired the view, which was breathtaking.

I fetched myself a cuppa and enjoyed the silence. Never in a million years would I have dreamed that I would be living with Dad and here I was. This was the start of a new adventure. I wasn't about to fuck it up.

I took a slow walk to the shopping precinct instead of the fifty pence shop on the main road, (we called it that because it was shaped like a fifty pence piece).

I'd only ventured down to the main shops a couple of times since Dad had moved in the area. It reminded me of our shops on the John O'Gaunt – perfect for the oldies to do their shopping and gossip, and the perfect hangout and meeting point for us kids. I passed a couple of small groups of kids my age and recognised a couple of faces, but I kept my head down and carried on walking; kids were territorial even though I wasn't an outsider anymore. I was now officially a Norfolk Park resident.

I must have been knacked from cleaning and lugging the shopping back to the flat because the next think I knew, I was woken by Dad slamming his money bag and taxi radio on the side.

'Someone's been busy!'

I was still half asleep but couldn't help noticing the impressed expression on his face as he took in the living room. I sat up, feeling pretty proud of myself.

'You like it? I did the kitchen and bathroom too. I would have put some washing in, but I don't know how to work the washer.'

Dad chuckled. 'Well, I suppose that's one way to make ya keep! Have you eaten? I'm having some chips and chicken soup, do ya want some?'

I didn't need asking twice. 'Yeah please.'

I sat smugly snuggled up on the sofa, whilst Dad busied himself in the kitchen. This was the first meal that Dad had ever prepared for me. Chips with chicken soup sounded weird, but I didn't care. I'd never even sat down for a meal with Dad before.

After five minutes, I popped my head around the kitchen door. 'Want any help?'

Dad smiled and nodded to the bread on the side. 'You could butter some bread if tha wants. Do me two slices, will ya, and don't be shy with the butter.'

'I've never had chips with chicken soup before.'

Dad chuckled, 'well tha dun't know what tha's been missing out on! It's the best! But it's gotta be Heinz soup and ya can't have ya bread without butter, none of that margarine shite – and it's got to be Lurpak.'

Dad shared the chips before pouring the chicken soup over the top, then picked up his bowl and bread and headed into the living room. There were no trays, so we used newspapers on our laps. Mum would have never allowed that at home.

Chips and chicken soup was the best thing I think I'd ever eaten.

Dad picked up on my delight as he made himself a butty 'Good, innit. I could eat this for the rest of my life.'

'Watch out for the butter dribbling if you make a butty. It gets fucking everywhere!'

This butter was next level. We only ever had Vitalite at home. I got up to get myself another slice of bread and butter.

'Addictive, innit! Here take us that in when you go in kitchen.' Dad passed me his dish. 'And make us a brew, will ya?'

I came back in with his tea and my extra slice of bread and Lurpak and finished my tea in silence whilst Dad smoked and flicked through the TV channels. Ten minutes later, Dad was standing up, stretching.

'Reyt, I'm off to bed. Can tha give me a nudge at five thirty?' A grin appeared on his face. 'Oh and a mug a tea would be nice.'

'No worries, Dad, see ya in a bit.'

I found something to watch on tv and supped my tea. I knew Dad could be a bastard at times. I thought I might never forgive him for not letting us keep Willy Do, but at that moment I'd forgiven him everything.

I no longer cared about what happened in the past, because all that mattered was the future. It was me and Dad against the world now.

# 43: Still My Dad

I wasn't sure if I could stomach another Christmas dinner, but I was really looking forward to spending some quality time with our Mark, Mum, Ada and our Sarah.

Mum and Ada had closed to paying customers over Christmas, so we had the place to ourselves for our Boxing Day buffet.

Ada looked the part behind the bar. The kids were all nestled in a small group in the snug, laughing and joking. I had some amazing memories growing up with my own cousins and it was nice to see them making their own.

In fact, it was a rarity to get us all together in the same place at the same time. Our Mark was working now and had his own place, and our Sarah worked full-time at the newsagents on Norfolk Park. It seemed a lifetime ago since we were kids and I loved it when we got the chance to reminisce about the old days.

The drinks were flowing, and the piss-taking started. We reminded Mark how as a toddler, he'd take himself behind the sofa to play with his todger, and laughed about the day Ada had shoved a trifle in our Sarah's face when she demanded the best one, and about the time he made us eat the fags he'd discovered on top of my wardrobe.

Ada ended up force-feeding Sarah until there was tobacco everywhere, in her teeth and her hair, whereas I just snapped them in half and smugly swallowed them like tablets.

Ada laughed and shook his head.

'Tha was always a clever little git, Trace.'

Sarah laughed, still protesting the injustice of it all. I loved that we could look back and laugh at the times I had made Mum and Ada's life a misery.

By early evening, my thoughts had turned to Dad so I went outside for a fag and tried calling him but there was no answer. I turned around and our Sarah was standing behind me.

'What are you doing?'

'Just tried calling Dad, but he's not answering. I hope he's ok.'

Sarah huffed. 'I'm not being funny, Trace, but I don't know why ya bother. Do you think he worried about us all them Christmases? Did he fuck!'

I couldn't argue, I knew she was right. I also knew she'd been to see him on Christmas evening. 'If you didn't care, you wouldn't have called round Christmas Day.'

'I'm not a heartless cow, Trace. I couldn't see him alone Christmas Day, but I'm not going out of my way for him. He's a grown-ass man. He can take care of himself.'

My phone started buzzing. I could hardly hear Dad on the other end.

He was clearly in a pub.

'Ey up, love, how's Blackpool?

'It's sound, Dad. Where are you?'

'Oh, I'm in the Ball. I couldn't stay in, not on Boxing Day, I've only come out for a couple.' But I could tell by his voice, he'd had more than a couple already.

'Well make sure you don't have too much. We don't want ya back in hospital again, do we?'

'Listen, them docs don't know what they are fucking on about. I'm fine. Get ya sen off and enjoy Blackpool. Anyway, send my love to ya Mum, will ya? Tell her I'll be down in the New Year!'

He couldn't help himself. I said my goodbyes and turned to our Sarah.

'See?' she said. 'We rushed to see him in Stoke. He knows he shouldn't be drinking and what's he doing now? He's in the pub getting pissed. I told ya, Trace, leave him to it!' And with that, she went back indoors. Deep-down, I knew she was right, but he was still my dad.

# 44: Silver Blades

Dad and I soon slipped into a routine. He would leave me some change for bus fares and to get some lunch every day. I would always clean up, make sure the flat looked tidy, something I'd never done at home.

I felt more like an adult living with Dad, and it felt nice making him happy. It was Dad who showed me how to iron, and I'd take great caution ironing his shirts and Farah trousers. I'd make him a mug of builder's tea whilst he bathed and prettied himself up getting ready for his night out I wondered if this was how it was for Mum when she used to get him ready for a night out when I was younger.

I finally got my own bed, but the room was still cold and empty, and I was finding it hard to sleep in the flat alone. I was always on high alert, convinced that someone was trying to break in. It was even worse when it was windy or raining; being so high up on the tenth floor, it felt like being in the middle of a hurricane and I swear I'd felt the flat sway on more than one occasion.

Sometimes I would stay awake until Dad got home. I could sleep better knowing he was in the flat. I liked drunk Dad best. He was more affectionate then, like the alcohol helped him let his guard down. He'd ask me about my day or tease me about having parties in the flat whilst he was out. One night, he even surprised me by coming home early with a Chinese which was another first for me. It was that same night Dad offered me a fag.

'Ere, does tha want one?'

At first I wasn't sure if this was trick question, so I declined.

'I know tha fuckin' smokes, Trace! 'Ere, have one.'

He sounded irritated, and I knew that if I refused again, he would have got annoyed. My hand shook as I took a cigarette from the packet. Dad tossed me the lighter and sat silently, waiting for me to light up.

I could feel his eyes boring into me as I took a drag on the cigarette. I was honestly expecting him to snatch it out of my hand at any minute, but he didn't.

'Well at least tha can smoke it reyt and takes it back, not like them who pretend to smoke!'

I turned to watch the telly whilst I finished my fag, paranoid he was watching me. It felt weird smoking in front of him. He never offered me a fag again.

Another night, he told me about this bird he was seeing. It turned out she was a bit younger than him. My heart lit up when he said that he'd told her all about us kids and how she couldn't wait to meet us.

I wondered why he'd never brought her back to the flat, but he explained that they had to keep it secret on account that she was the daughter of one of his best mates who was the landlord of his local – the White Lion on the Wicker. She was called Tracey like me, and she had two horses. I liked the sound of her already!

Then I put two and two together. It must have been Tracey who'd bought the previous Christmas presents on Dad's behalf. I wondered if she'd been the reason that Dad had bought Willy Do. I could tell Dad was smitten, because he was even talking about asking her Dad's permission to get engaged.

I imagined my new life with them both. I would be able to ride Tracey's horse to my heart's content, and I'd be the perfect kid. I just couldn't wait to meet her.

It didn't matter how late Dad went to bed, he was always an early riser, but he wasn't always a morning person. I'd quickly learned how to gauge his moods. One morning, I could hear noises in the kitchen, but when I walked in, there was a woman there. She looked nothing like the description Dad had given me of Tracey.

'Ooops, Don't mind me,' I joked as I manoeuvred around her to get a glass of water. 'So did you come back with Dad then?'

She seemed relieved when I confessed to being Dad's daughter. Christ knows who she must have thought I was!

Dad was having a tea in the living room. 'Good night then?' I teased him.

'Aye, but you didn't see her, reyt.'

I knew that what he meant was not to tell Tracey, if I ever met her.

'And don't worry, tha won't be seeing her again. She wa' just a one-night stand.'

It wasn't long before I started to make new friends on the estate. I'd been waiting for the bus on East Bank Road, heading to call for some mates on the Valley when I met the Cherry Twins. I don't even know which one of them broke the ice, because they were identical, but we hit it off straight away. Nicola and Keely were both tomboys at heart, just like me. They had the most mesmerising eyes and long flowing blonde hair, and it didn't matter how many times they told me who was who, I'd still get confused. It was them who suggested I go to Silver Blades, the ice rink, with them.

The cold hit me as soon as I walked in, but the atmosphere was on fire. The twins seemed to know everyone, and it wasn't long before I started to get to know the other kids from the estates. I've never had problems making friends, but being friends with the twins gave me instant kudos.

I could already roller-skate, so it didn't take me long to master ice-skating. The only shitty part was that I had to skate in "spaz" boots, (that's what everyone called them). They were navy blue or black and were the ugliest and smelliest things I'd ever seen.

There was a small shop next to the canteen with a display of fancy boots, but even the second-hand boots were out of my range. The older kids would hang about outside the front of the DJ booth, watching their mates show off their new ice-skating skills. Every so often, the music would ramp up, indicating it was speed skating time. That was the time to get out of the way to allow the older, more confident skaters to speed around the ice ring, showing off their skills and tricks.

There would always be someone snogging behind the DJ booth. I copped off with a couple of lads, but, in truth, I wasn't that interested in boys.

I'd never really experienced a life outside of the boundaries of the valley, but Silver Blades attracted kids from all over the city. I was like a social butterfly because I would either know someone or have a mutual mate and as my self-confidence grew, I would happily make my way down to the ring on my own. At Silver Blades, I no longer felt like a kid. I was transitioning into a young adult and I liked it.

# 45: Self-Pity Mode

I blinked and Christmas and New Year had been and gone, and Dad seemed to have spent most of it in The Ball. I'd invite him over to ours for Sunday dinner, an opportunity to spend some quality time with the kids, but he always declined, saying that he liked his own company, which was funny because he was becoming the Ball's best customer. I was disappointed. I'd honestly thought that this time it would be different.

Even though we'd had the odd tense moments, when Dad had stayed over at ours, it had been lovely having him around. I'd loved our little chats and loved seeing him getting to know the kids. I honestly thought when he left and got his own place that he'd come back and visit more often, but he hadn't, in fact, he'd been in Sheffield for six months now and he hadn't been back since he moved out and most of our contact was by phone.

The interim payments from his lawsuit kept coming, which would pacify him for a month or so, but then the rants would start up again. Sometimes it felt like I was dealing with a petulant teenager, not a fifty-two-year-old man! After the pleasantries were out of the way, he always wanted something or other: some shopping or something he'd forgotten to order, which was normally something he could have got his fucking self as there was a local shop only a hundred yards away. Sometimes I might pop into the Ball on my way home from work as it was the best way to see him. It was like being a kid again.

I was starting to get pissed off with him. One week when he'd called and I was out he'd phoned in full self-pity mode. I knew his money must have been running out because he was staying in.

'It's ok for you, Trace,' he said. 'Don't you worry about me. You go enjoy ya sen wi ya mates.'

For a split second, I did feel guilty, him being at home alone and me being out wi me mates but then I was fucking speechless, the cheeky bastard! He didn't need or think about me when he had cash in his wallet. Nah, when he did, he'd be spending it on buying the local pissheads in the Ball drinks or having mates around for a takeaway or drinks, the same knobheads who got him the car, which didn't last long.

They'd clearly ripped him off, but Dad couldn't see it. And I had my own shit to deal with, like running my own house, working and sorting two hormonal teenagers out. The only time I had a break was at weekends once I'd got the house done, when me and Pat would walk down to our local, The Birley, for a few drinks. I deserved that time with my mates!

I knew Dad was never going to win Father of the year award, but when he first came back to Sheffield, part of me had thought Dad had changed. Now I was thinking that Sarah and everyone else was right. Dad didn't care about anyone else except his mates and himself.

# 46: Moving Back

I'd been living with Dad for about four weeks, and the school holidays were nearing the end. I'd already floated the idea of leaving school early with Dad, half hoping that he might give me a new job when he started his new taxi firm. But he wasn't having any of it.

I still hadn't spoken to Mum. Some nights when I was alone in the flat, I wondered if she was back home thinking about me like I was her. My feelings towards Mum were all over the place: one minute, I resented her, blamed her for everything and the next I craved her presence and wanted her back in my life. There were times I was tempted to telephone or pop in unannounced whilst visiting the Valley, but I hadn't. I took her not reaching out as a sign that she was happy with the arrangements. And the longer we didn't speak, the harder I found it to make the first move.

It was a Saturday. Dad had left me some money to go to town with my mates and to get some new jeans. I was desperate to wear them for the skates that night, but they needed taking in. And the only person I knew with a sewing machine was Mum. I kept all my fingers crossed that a) she'd be in and b) she'd have time to do them before Silver Blades opened.

I rang first. Part of me was scared that she might tell me to piss off, but she seemed more than happy to oblige. So, me and a couple of mates off Norfolk Park headed to Mum's house.

Sarah opened the door with a smug look on her face and for a split second I wanted to wipe it off her.

'What's that fucking look for?'

She just shrugged her shoulders and ignored me. 'Mum! our Tracey's here!'

Mum came to the door. She had a big smile on her face and was carrying my little brother on her hip. 'Look who it is, Mark, it's your big sister, Tracey.'

I put my arms out to hold him, and my heart skipped a beat when he leaned towards me to accept a cuddle. I realised just how much I'd missed him and when I looked at Mum, I realised just how much I'd missed her too. I wanted to wrap my arms around her, but my pride wouldn't let me, plus I didn't have the time.

'Come on then. Where's these jeans?' She gestured for me to follow her into the house, like nothing had ever happened. I followed Mum into the kitchen and changed into my jeans whilst she set up the sewing machine.

Mum got on her knees and spoke with a mouthful of pins. 'So, you, ok?'

'Yeah, I'm good, thanks.'

'Our Sarah tells me that you're at Silver Blades all day long lately.'

'Yeah, I love it!'

'Ah that's nice, and how ya getting on at ya Dad's?'

'It's ok actually,' I said, but that was partly a lie. Dad was barely around. There had been talk of him moving in with Tracey, but there had been no mention of me in his new plans. Truth be told, I was starting to feel like his flatmate instead of his daughter.

Our conversation felt weird, and I couldn't make out if this was Mum's attempt at small talk or if she was really interested in what I was up to. Part of me had hoped that she'd wrap her arms around me and tell me she loved me and that she'd forgiven me for being a little shit, but the words nor the hug never came.

'Right, take them off, it won't take me long.'

I changed back into my other trousers, but wasn't sure I should stay in the house, or wait outside. 'I'll wait outside, if that's ok, my mates are waiting for me.'

'No worries, pet.'

Ten minutes later, Mum called me back into the house to try them on. They were perfect.

'Thanks, Mum. I really appreciate it.'

Mum smiled. 'They look nice,' she said, admiring her handy work. 'You're welcome, pet, and you do know you are welcome to come back home anytime you like, don't you?'

She took me a little off-guard. I knew this was Mum offering me an olive branch and I could tell she wanted to talk, but my mates were outside waiting impatiently for me to finish.

'I'm sorry, Mum, but I've got to get off.'

Mum, seemed to understand.

'Go on, then and don't leave it too long until next time, will ya?'

And with that, I was gone, it wasn't until I got on the bus that I realised I hadn't even given her a kiss to say thank you. I felt such a bitch. So, I made a pact with myself to go and see her the following day. But before I could do that, Sarah turned up at Dad's flat. She barged into the living room screaming.

'You are a fucking selfish cow, do ya know that?'

I went straight into defence mode; I hadn't got a clue what she was on about.

'Who the fuck do you think you are, barging in here gobbing off!'

'It's Mum!'

'Why, what's up wi' her?'

"No, she's fucking not fine! And it's all because of you!'

I was just going to explained how I'd planned to go see her later that day, but she didn't give me the opportunity

'As soon as you left yesterday, she broke down. Honestly, Trace, I've never seen her so upset.'

She was venomous and on a roll. According to her I didn't care about anyone else apart from myself, which wasn't true. I couldn't tell her that I found the nights lonely and that I lay awake, scared and alone in my new bedroom, wondering whether Dad would be coming home.

I couldn't tell her that I missed the home comforts, the family nights in watching TV. Or that I was sick and tired of sandwiches and chips and longed for a home-cooked meal or that I missed my little brother. I missed Ada too. At least he was able to show emotion which was more than could be said for Dad. I didn't even get the chance to tell her that I even missed sharing a bedroom with her, because as soon as she'd finished laying into me, she was out of the door, leaving me once again.

I was surrounded by lots of new friends, and yet I'd never felt so alone. I couldn't shake the feeling that Dad had only agreed to take me in out of self-pride and to prove to Mum that he could be a dad. He'd never once sat me down and asked why I was playing up at home. He never asked how I was feeling, or how my day had gone.

I was secretly hoping that he might one day crack and wrap his arms around me and tell me: 'Hey, I do really love ya, ya know,' but it never came.

My friends envied me being able to come and go as I pleased but I envied their curfews, knowing that they were at home with their family. I knew, deep-down that I wanted to go back home, but I'd never been sure how to engineer it. Still, I knew I had to call her, at the very least to say sorry.

I could tell she didn't sound right as soon as she picked up the phone.

'Mum, I'm sorry.'

'Look, love, this has gone on far too long, I think we need to talk, don't you?' I knew she was right. 'Why don't you come round, and we can have a proper chat, eh?'

A feeling of relief washed over me. 'No worries, Mum. give me an hour and I'll be over.'

I still hadn't spoken to Ada and wondered if he would be as happy as Mum about me coming home, but I needn't have worried because when he answered the door, he even looked pleased to see me.

'Why are you knocking? This is your house!' he joked, before taking me into his arms for a big hug. He kissed me on the head. 'Go on, ya Mum's waiting for ya in the living room.'

The long lecture I was expecting never came. For the next hour, we both shared our regrets. Mum agreed that it had all got out of hand and that she'd overreacted and that she regretted laying into me. I apologised too, because I knew I'd pushed her too far. She explained how she understood what it was like being my age, stuck in-between being a kid and adult.

We talked for what felt like hours; we even laughed about me jumping out of the bedroom window and Mum joked that she'd have to put locks on. The saddest part was that for all this time, both of us thought that the other hated each other, but were both too afraid to pick up the phone out of fear of being rejected. Mum was right, our stand-off had gone on for too long. It was time to come home.

I knew, deep-down, Dad would be ok about me going back home, but I was still scared to tell him. I was afraid that he would see me wanting to go home as some form of rejection, that might leave him feeling like he wasn't a good enough Dad or that he'd failed, but I needn't have worried, because when I told him later that afternoon, he seemed relieved. In fact, he helped me pack my bags and offered to drop me back home.

As I left his care, he told me I was welcome back any time, but really, we both knew that I would never be coming back to stay with him.

# 47: A Good Little Pub

I was at work when Dad called. He sounded in a good mood, and I was about to find out why.

'The Cuthbert Bank is up for grabs!' he said.

I thought he was joking at first, but he was deadly serious. I knew the pub well because it used to be owned by one of Dad's mates. I'd even done a couple of shifts there myself. It had once been a busy pub, but I wasn't sure it would be now.

'Dad, how you gonna run a pub on your own? And what about keeping a low profile?'

Dad snapped. 'I haven't said I'm going to fucking take it, have I?' Then his tone changed. 'I only want to go have a look. Used to be a good little pub. Anyway, I was thinking I'll stump up the cash, then I'll get someone else to work the bar. I'd be like be a silent partner.'

This was a bad idea, but I could tell in Dad's voice that there was no point in even trying to reason with him. 'So, when are you going to take a look?'

'That's why I've called. I could do with you running me over.'

I wanted to say: 'Well, get one of ya mates to take ya! You know, the same ones who sold ya the shit car!' But I didn't, and instead I found myself saying that I'd take him.

'You're a fucking diamond, ar Trace, pick us up. See ya Thursday, 'bout twelvish?'

Lyn, our admin assistant, shook her head. She'd listened enough to me talk about Dad and I could tell she thought this was a bad idea, but what I could do? I couldn't just let him go on his own and buy a fucking pub!

I didn't agree with Dad that buying a pub was the answer to his loneliness and boredom, but I could see that staying indoors wasn't good for his mental health.

He was a social creature by nature and needed something to do, and some proper friends instead of the blokes who'd sold him the car, who were just using him. I'd tried to say as much, but Dad wouldn't have any of it. All he talked about was that fucking pay-out, which in his eyes was going to solve all his problems and set him up for life.

His plans changed daily. One day he was going to buy a static caravan and go fishing, the next he was going to buy a couple of houses to rent out. And now there was the pub idea. He'd talked about getting a nice little village pub that didn't take much running, which I knew didn't exist. Pubs were hard work and being around alcohol all day was never going to be a good idea. But the stubborn git still refused to accept there was anything wrong with his health or that drink was a problem.

I couldn't argue really, because in all fairness since being in hospital, he'd stayed away from the top shelf and seemed ok just on the cans in the flat. Even though I was far from happy about his new idea, I'd rather be there and know the ins and outs than let him get carried away and make a big mistake.

# 48: Leaving School

Soon after I moved out of Dad's flat, he bought his first taxi firm. He also moved in with Tracey. She was just as special as I'd expected and when she met us for the first time, she greeted us like long lost friends. She looked like she'd just come back from the farm and apologized for being in her scruffs, but she needn't have worried. I liked her already. Tracey certainly wasn't Dad's usual type; there wasn't a trace of make-up, and her long, jet-black hair was messily tied up, but she had the warmest of smiles.

Her love of horses was evident; there were pictures of them and rosettes all over the house and mucky riding boots in the hallway. She also had two huge dogs, Sultan and Kelly, who scared the shit out of me initially, but they were both friendly.

Tracey prepared us some tea and Dad joined us at the table to eat. I could tell he was smitten. I listened to their banter and laughed when she gave him as good as she got. I could tell that despite all the smiles she wasn't a push over. Dad left the table to go for his daily snooze, leaving me and Sarah with Tracey, which gave us a chance to get to know her and to find out more about their plans.

I wondered if she might have kids with Dad, but she seemed happy being home with her animals and didn't mind Dad going out. And when she wasn't tending to the horses, she was working for Dad at the taxi firm.

She told us that Dad had also bought the fruit shop next door to her house and had got her sister Karen running it. Tracey even mentioned that Dad was looking to convert the shop below the taxi firm into a carpet shop. He seemed to have big plans and instead of being his bit on the side, Tracey was very much part of them. She was so easy-going, and it felt nice not to have to compete against other women's kids.

I could tell she was good for Dad; she had a calmness about her which brought out a side to Dad I'd never seen before.

Dad joined us in the living room a couple of hours later, all spruced up to go out for the night, but not before dropping me and Sarah back home. We said our goodbyes and Tracey gave us both a big hug before telling us that we were both welcome there anytime and I knew she really meant it, although it would be a while before I saw her again.

It was the final year at school, and I couldn't wait to leave. Some friends were talking about going to college and others had jobs already lined up, but me? I still didn't have a clue. There were rumours that Silver Blades was shutting down and I was devastated until Angela Baxendale's dad opened Sheffield's first under 18's nightclub.

Once a week, Rebels nightclub would transform from being a sweaty rock club into a magnet for under-eighteens from all over the city, and the place was buzzing. Sometimes, I couldn't afford the entrance fee, but that didn't stop me; we'd arrange to be let in through the back door fire escape or distract the cashier while one of us sneaked in. But my lifestyle was set to get easier because Mum had got me a part-time job in the canteen of the student hall of residence where she worked.

I knew Mum had put her neck out getting this job for me, and I was eager not to fuck it up. I towed the line and did what I was asked to do. One of my jobs was washing the pots, shoving crates of dirty places through a machine and monitoring the other end waiting for them to come out sparkling clean. It was a constant conveyor belt, but I enjoyed it. I was on my own and the time flew by. Fat Peggy would pick faults with my work, but I'd bite my tongue. I wasn't going to let no Fat Peggy get in the way of that weekly wage.

Sometimes I would be asked to serve on the canteen. I didn't like that as much though. The students weren't that much older than me, but I felt like we had nothing in common. I imagined they all had servants at home; they were so privileged. And, how sad did they have to be to want to carry on studying?

Working gave me a purpose and, even though it wasn't the best job in the world, it did mean that I had a little independence. I still had the exams to go though.

The first exam arrived. The school hall resembled a mortuary; it was so quiet. We had to sit on individual tables and not speak to anyone. We couldn't even speak to the teachers unless we needed our pencils sharpened, or if we were desperate for the toilet. None of the teachers smiled; it was like being in mass detention for two hours.

The timer was set, and everyone's heads went down, focusing on the exam paper. I opened my exam booklet. It was full of multiple-choice questions and at first, I thought it was piss easy, but after a couple of pages, my confidence started to wane. I didn't understand half of the questions, let alone know the answers. I could see the teachers looking at me with their condescending faces. I didn't give a fuck!

Halfway through the exam, I really didn't see the point of sitting there any longer, so I got up and left and I didn't go back to do anymore.

On the last day of school, there were tears, hugs and laughter all round. Kids were writing all over each other's shirts and some kids had bought presents for teachers and were crying about not being able to see them again. Weirdos! Apart from not seeing my mates every day, I couldn't wait to see the back of the place.

It wasn't just schools that had broken up for the summer, the universities had too and now, instead of catering for students, I was catering for old age pensioners. And instead of serving people through the canteen, we would be waiting on them and serving them at their tables. I had to wear a black dress with a white pinny (which I hated).

Mum showed me how to serve holding three meals at once. I was a natural, apart from the one time I accidently spilled cold gravy down an old dear's neck. It was longer hours, but the pay was great. I'd come out with a hundred and fifty a week. I had to pay Mum twenty for board then the rest was mine.

‘Put it towards driving lessons,’ Mum would say, but as soon as my shift finished on the Saturday, I’d order a taxi from Dad’s taxi firm. Usually Tracey or Uncle John would give me a freebie, so my money was all mine.

I could now shop in Harrington’s if I wanted jeans, and I could buy shoes from Rebina. I started to get to know some of the older lads who hung out on Fargate. They were all into football, so I’d meet them at the Blue Bell pub on the High Street after matches.

I still preferred the company of boys, but I wasn’t interested in having a boyfriend, unlike my girl-friends, who would spend hours getting ready for a night out clubbing at The Roxy. I went once but hated every minute of it; I looked like a clown in make-up and couldn’t walk in the heels my friend loaned me. I’d have never felt more out of place in my life in this huge place. Even in the loos there, older women lined up against the mirrors, applying makeup and giggling.

I’d heard Dad mentioned this place before and the prospect of bumping into him scared me shitless. I could see why Dad liked this place. There were women strutting around like peacocks and I figured this must have been where he’d found the random birds he’d brought back to the flat.

I was sitting alone having a drink when a pissed old man about dad’s age started trying to pull me. He wasn’t getting any of me, dirty old bastard. I told him as much before letting my mate know I was off. I decided there and then that nightclubbing wasn’t for me.

# 49: It Could Do with a Lick of Paint

Dad was outside waiting for me. He looked like he was off to an important business meeting, which, in his eyes, he was, but I still couldn't help but think he was deluding himself. As we drove, all he talked about was how busy the pub used to be. But he hadn't drunk in Walkley for over ten years, and a lot had changed.

'As soon as everyone hears I've taken it on, they'll be back. Trust me.'

I had to admire his confidence. I just wished I had as much as he did.

I couldn't park on the main road because of the new tram tracks. I'd have to pull up on the estate opposite.

Dad must have read my mind, 'Drop me off here! That could be the bloke from the brewery. Don't want to keep him waiting.' The lazy git would always avoid walking if he could help it!

I dropped him off and got parked as fast as I could, so as not to miss out on what they'd be talking about. Knowing Dad, he'd have signed for the lease before I got there!

I'd only glanced at the pub as we passed, but after parking the car and walking towards it, I realised it was far from being the bustling place it used to be. The pitch full of parked cars had gone and was now a jumble of weeds and rubbish. The pub didn't look much better. The external walls could do with a lick of paint for starters.

Dad was standing outside the pub, talking with a slim-built bloke with an unironed suit and slimy smile. There was no way he was going to blag me. The place was a fucking shithole.

The agent went in for the handshake. 'Good afternoon and you are...?'

I was tempted to say: 'I'm here to make sure you don't fucking rip him off.'

Instead, I said: 'Hi I'm Tracey, Frank's daughter. Used to frequent this place years ago. Looks like it could do with a lick of paint.'

'Nowt our Pat couldn't sort out, Trace.' Dad said, already assuming Pat would decorate the place.

We eventually got inside. The place stank of stale beer and other unpleasant odours.

'So how long's it been empty then?' I asked.

'Trace, stop wi' the interrogation, will ya? Let the bloke show us around.'

I was pissing Dad off I could tell. I shrugged.

The place needed more than a lick of paint; it needed fucking knocking down. But Dad was already starting with the negotiations. The agent was saying he'd need a three grand deposit and be tied in for three years.

I laughed, a little too loudly.

'Just you go outside and leave this to me, will ya?'

'No worries, Dad, I'll leave you to it.' I needed a fag anyway. 'I'll be outside.'

Whatever they were discussing, it didn't take long, because soon they were outside with me and Dad was sparking up a fag while the agent locked up.

'You have a think and get back to me ASAP As I said, someone else is interested, so you don't wanna be leaving it too long.'

*Bullshit!* I thought as Dad went in for the handshake.

'Yep, no worries, mate, but like I said, tha gonna have to come down a little.'

As we headed back to the car, I could tell Dad was a little deflated. I was sure he'd changed his mind.

'So what ya think?' he said.

I turned and just stared at Dad blankly. 'You're joking, right? The place is a shit hole, Dad – there's nowt and no one around here anymore, the Kelvin Flats have gone, that car place must have been shut for a good couple of years...'

Dad interrupted me. 'Look, Trace, I've turned worse pubs than that around.'

'Yes but, you're not supposed to be running it, right? I thought the plan was to get someone else in. And where you going to get three grand from?'

'Who said owt about not working? I said I wouldn't be working the bar, but I never said owt about not being in the bar – someone's got to make sure it's being run reyt.'

'So who you got in mind then?'

'Les Lawson and his missus.'

'What, them two from the Ball?' I'd met them a couple of times when I'd popped into to see Dad. They hadn't seen a toothbrush in fucking years, or a bar of soap for that matter.

'You are joking, right? The only experience they've got is drinking pints, not pulling 'em.'

'Actually, they used to run a pub, years back, and they've got plenty of experience.'

We drove the rest of the journey in silence.

As we pulled up outside Dad's, he turned to me.

'Look, I haven't even said I'm taking it yet, so it isn't a done deal. I'll call ya later.'

I wasn't looking forward to that. If he was going to take on that shithole, he was going to be on his own. I wanted no part of it.

# 50: Chips and Scraps from the Friary Chippy

We were moving again. Ada had got a new job as a caretaker at Charnock Primary School which came with a house. I was sad to be leaving the Valley, but these days my life revolved around going to work and hanging about in town with my new mates anyway, plus I was chuffed to finally get my own room.

The summer holidays were drawing to an end, and Mum was keen for me to take on an apprenticeship as a chef at the halls. The only problem was that I didn't have any interest in cooking, and I would have to go down the YTS route, the same scheme I'd protested about. I'd be getting £27 for a full week's work! In my eyes, it was slave labour.

The thought of going from a hundred plus quid a week to seventeen made me feel physically sick. I even called to see Dad to ask if he had any jobs going, but he was no use. He was distracted by a blonde bird with huge tits who was giggling and hanging off his every word. Apparently, she was the local Boob a Gram. Anyway, he said I was too young, and he didn't have anything.

I didn't want to be a chef, but I felt backed into a corner and, without any other options, I conceded and agreed to try the YTS scheme out.

The scheme was based on Furnival Gate in town. I took an instant dislike to the place and the staff. They claimed that this wouldn't be like being at school, but the room looked like a school, lined with desks and a member of staff preaching from the front. They explained that they had to do a morning register (something about it being a government requirement), and if we weren't there, or were late, we would be penalised out of our already shit wage.

We'd be expected to spend the first three months attending classes five days a week, before we would be offered a placement, and then we still had to be back in the classroom one day a week. I'd already worked out that after paying, board, bus fairs and getting lunch, there would be nothing left out of my wage to even buy a packet of ten fags. I only lasted two days before I jacked it in.

Mum was absolutely furious when I got home. I got a full-on lecture about it being time for me to grow up and start acting like an adult, and that if I wanted to continue living under her roof, I would have to either get a job or go back to the scheme.

There was no way I was going back there. The following day, after walking around the steelworks, I got a job as a cutlery polisher. It's fair to say Mum was stunned and though she didn't think it was a "proper career".

She couldn't really argue because I had done what she had asked and got myself a job, which I was due to start the next day.

The shifts were long and monotonous, there was no time for idle chit chatter, and we were all expected to work at a consistent pace to make the daily quota. The shift supervisor would do regular surveillance walks on the shop floor, as a reminder that we were all there to work. The break times were short, and I could see why the factories had a high turnover of staff. Every week, I would get the Thursday night Sheffield Star and look through the pages of jobs, but they wanted qualifications and experience which I didn't have.

After work, I'd treat myself to a cone of chips and scraps from the Friary chippy, then walk along the arcade before heading over the bridge to the escalators which took you down to Pond Street bus station. There was always someone I knew down there. I'd be in my work scruffs and covered in soot from the factory, but I didn't mind because at least I was working, which was more than some of the other groups. There were the Mods, in their khaki Parkas, and the skinheads, wearing tight jeans and high-laced Doc Martens. The Skins and Mods didn't mix.

Then there were the trendies or rockers. I wasn't into music or interested in dressing a certain way to look cool. I could mix with pretty much anyone.

A couple of weeks into starting the job, I was at the bus station after work with some mates, when a group of lads approached us. I'd not seen them before. One who stood out from the rest. He was much taller, with tanned skin and short jet-black hair. He was very good-looking. We soon learned that he was called Paul and that he and his mates hung out on the Manor.

I must have looked right sight, dressed in my scruffy jeans and covered in soot from the factory, but that didn't stop him making a bee line for me every time we all got together.

All my friends fancied Paul, and they were envious about the attention he gave me. I had to admit, I was flattered. So, when he asked to meet me alone, I accepted.

# 51: It's Ok for You

It had been over a week since I'd seen Dad. I'd been keeping my distance. At least it sounded like the enthusiasm he'd had about getting the pub was waning, though he was still adamant that he could turn it into a goldmine.

I knew that it wasn't about the money though. It was like he'd fallen in love with the idea of being a landlord again, the status that would come with it and the social network. There was a time that his bleeding phone never stopped ringing; he was forever wheeling and dealing. Nowadays, the only phone calls he got were from the solicitors.

Lately, it felt easier dealing with my own hormonal teenager than dealing with him. His moods swung like a fucking pendulum; I never knew which version of him I'd get. He was either wallowing in self-pity or angry about the status of the claim.

I had thought that after getting his own place and being more independent, he would have felt better, but it seemed like he was getting worse. His life over the past few months revolved around sitting alone in the flat or drinking with a load of piss heads in the Ball and bragging about plans that were never realistically going to come to fruition.

I didn't care so much about him having a pub; he could do whatever he liked, just like he always had done. What worried me more was I felt like I was being sucked back into his world again, the one where I couldn't say no.

Somehow, Dad had started to assume that I could fix everything. He seemed to have my number on speed dial. At first, it had been nice to feel like an equal and that he wanted to be speak to me, but increasingly, he was dependent on me and some of his calls were unnecessary.

He'd get a letter off the council about fixing a door and want my advice on what to do. Other times, he'd call out of boredom: 'Hiya, shugs, what you up to?' and my reply would always be the same: 'Same old, same old, Dad, work, kids, house, sleep and same again next day.'

But the worst calls were when he was pissed. He'd be either slathering down the phone, ranting about someone who had pissed him off, usually the solicitors, or was complaining about being bored shitless. What was worse was when he repeated himself; he was like a broken record.

Sometimes I wondered if he was actually depressed, but I was sure it was nothing to do with no train crash. He'd been complaining about having stomach-ache again too, but he wouldn't see the GP, so there wasn't much that I could do.

All he could focus on was being on his arse – no job or relationship, and no real friends. I tried to sympathise. I knew first-hand how it felt to feel totally fucking alone, empty, worthless; there was a time where I could count the only friends I trusted on one hand. Not that Dad understood this.

'You haven't got a clue,' he'd say. Or: 'It's ok for you.'

This would piss me off no end. He wasn't around when I was effectively in the same boat, was he? Recalling his absence always left a bittersweet taste in my mouth.

I had loads going on though. The guys from the Home Office had sourced a film company to help make the family support film.

Our Lauren was due to move from primary to secondary school too, and our Danielle didn't have long left at school either and she had no clue what she wanted to do. All I knew was that I was adamant about her breaking the cycle.

I didn't want her to become another young mum like I had been, and my mum before me, with me. Thankfully, she was turning out to be the complete opposite of me.

I was proud of myself. I'd done alright, got myself a decent job, and a decent bloke who was amazing with the kids. We'd worked and saved hard for this house. I still had to pinch myself sometimes, to remind me that I was a homeowner. We didn't have much money, but we were getting by. Life was good, really. All I needed now was for Dad to sort his shit out too.

# 52: Our First Date

Paul met me on Gleadless Town End for our first date. He didn't have money for a proper date, but I didn't mind. We walked and talked for what seemed like miles. Turned out that we had a lot of things in common.

His parents were divorced and both in new relationships. His mum had cheated on his dad, so he was now sofa-surfing at a mate's flat, waiting to get his own place off the council. He told me about how he hated cheats. Like me, he didn't have many qualifications, and he wasn't sure what he wanted to do for a job, but he had grand ideas about being rich and was adamant that he didn't want to rely on benefits. He wasn't interested in going out drinking and took immense pride in his appearance.

I even wondered if he might be too good for me. He seemed so much more worldly and mature, and the two years' age difference unnerved me. I'd only just left school and was still a tomboy at heart. I didn't even wear makeup! But none of that seemed to faze him, in fact, the fact that I didn't look like all the other girls seemed to make him like me more.

For years, I'd felt like the odd one out, but he made me feel wanted. A kiss at the end of our first date sealed the deal I was smitten.

As the days turned into weeks, we became inseparable. Behind his good looks and charm, he was insecure and there was a vulnerability that I was drawn to. He was fiercely protective and would sometimes get jealous and moody if we'd bumped into any lads I knew from school or from Silver Blades. He could even be jealous when it came to his own mates, paranoid that I might be interested in them, which was ludicrous, especially after I'd opened up about how I'd seen first-hand how Dad's infidelity had impacted on my own Mum.

I eventually took him home to meet Mum and Ada. I could tell straight away that they weren't impressed with him not having a job, but he managed to win them over, talking openly about how he adored me. I was keen to meet his family too, however Paul seemed in no rush to introduce me, and when I met his mum, I could tell why. My first impression of his mum wasn't brilliant. She was more interested in the food he'd brought than in me or him.

I could tell that Paul hadn't inherited his good looks from her, but she was loud and didn't have anything nice to say about Paul, in fact she mocked him for not having a job, which I thought was ironic, considering both her and her new bloke were unemployed. I could immediately tell why Paul had moved out. It felt like Piccadilly Circus, what with people coming and going, including the Shopacheck man, who'd come to collect repayments on loans.

When we left, Paul sheepishly explained that he'd had to take out a loan whilst his benefits had been sorted, but he was quick to reassure me that the debt had nearly been paid.

Paul was the first boy I'd ever taken to see Dad. I'd half-expected Dad to give Paul the third degree, but he was preoccupied with getting ready to go out that night and didn't say much apart from: 'If you can't be good, be careful.'

I wasn't sure what he meant until Paul suggested on the way home that he might have been referring to us having sex. I remember getting all embarrassed at the time.

I felt insulted that Dad could even think I might have already had sex, especially considering I was still only sixteen, but then again, he was used to women putting out. The closest I'd ever got to having sex was letting a lad feel my tit, and even then, it didn't feel right.

And anyway, even if we had wanted to have sex, there was nowhere to have it. Mum and Ada were always home, and I wasn't putting out behind a shop on Manor Top.

Paul had reassured me and said that he was willing to wait, but part of me wasn't sure if he would. I already knew that he'd had sex in all his other relationships and part of me still worried that once I'd put out, he'd be off like a shot. But, after a couple of weeks, Paul told me that he loved me, and I found myself saying it back. I mean, it felt rude not to.

One month into the relationship, Paul announced one evening that his mate was going to be out for the night. This was a rare chance to be alone and even though sex hadn't been mentioned, I knew that sex was on his mind.

The bus journey over to his flat was torture. I was nervous as hell and still wasn't sure if I was ready. Part of me wished I'd taken more of an interest when the girls at school had talked about sex, because I didn't have a clue how to pleasure a man. I was paranoid about him seeing me naked and he laughed when I made him wait outside the bedroom whilst I got undressed before climbing into the bed.

Paul seemed to know what he was doing and promised to take it slow and insisted that we could stop at any time, so I decided to trust him and let him take the lead. After the act, Paul seemed pleased with himself and loved the fact that he'd been the one to take my virginity. In fact, he said that because of that, he loved me even more.

However, it wasn't quite the same for me. The fireworks that I had been expecting never arrived and I just felt like a cheap slag, sore below and exposed. On the bus journey home, I was disappointed in myself. I felt like I had offered myself up too easily. Even though I thought I might love him, part of me was scared that everything seemed to be going so fast.

# 53: It's Only for Medicinal Purposes

I'd arranged to call in to see Dad after work and was looking forward to some quality time with him. I called him before setting off. He sounded in a good mood, which was a relief.

'Hiya, Dad, do ya need owt from the shop? Milk, bread?'

'Nah, I'm all sorted, shugs.'

'Ok. See ya soon.'

'Oh, Trace, I tell ya what, if you don't mind, you couldn't get me a small bottle of brandy, could ya?'

Brandy? Uncle Mick's warning about the top shelf preyed on my mind but I could hardly say no. I'd just asked him if he wanted anything. 'What kind do you want?'

'Napoleon or Three Barrels. Owt'll do. Only a small one though.'

When I arrived, Dad was in his usual spot, on the edge of the sofa by the window, sat rolling himself a fag.

'Ey up, shugs.'

'Hiya, Dad, here ya go.' I passed him the bottle of brandy and gave him a kiss. 'Don't be drinking that all at once, will ya?'

I went to make a coffee and was pleased to see that the kitchen looked relatively tidy and that there was food in the fridge as well as cans.

I sat down. 'What you been up to then?'

'Nowt. Not been out for a couple of weeks. I can't be arsed with the Ball. One of the lads, Dawson, has done me some shopping.'

I wasn't sure if the shopping comment was a dig or not, so I tried to let it go over my head. 'So how you feeling? How's the stomach-ache?'

'Ah that's sound, but I have been to docs about this. Have you seen the state of my fucking arms and hands?'

I moved to take a closer look. His hands were covered in small red blotches.

‘What is it?’

‘Doc reckons it’s either psoriasis or eczema. Had it for weeks now. It’s driving me mad *and* its spreading. Started on my hands at first, now it’s going up me arm.’

‘Has he given you owt for it?’

‘He’s given me some cream, but it doesn’t seem to be working. Says he’s going to make a referral to Hallamshire for some more tests if it doesn’t start clearing up.’

I could tell he’d been drinking, but at least he wasn’t pissed. Dad lit the fag he’d made earlier. ‘So, how’s you? The kids? Work?’

Settling into the sofa, I curled my legs up and brought Dad up to speed about what I’d been up to. Dad laughed at the prospect of Lauren starting big school and told me that Sarah’s son, Niall, had been popping in and going to the shops for Dad.

‘I reckon he only comes for the quid tip.’

‘Chip off the old block I reckon, Dad.’

Dad didn’t mention the pub, and I certainly wasn’t going to bring it up; the less said about that the better. I didn’t want to ask about the claim, but I knew I would have too.

‘So how’s the claim coming along? You heard owt?’

Dad perked up. ‘Solicitors reckon it should be ready to make an offer soon.’

I don’t know who was more relieved, me or Dad. I couldn’t wait for that bleeding claim to finally get sorted. ‘So, have you decided what you are going to do then?’

‘Dunno yet. Depends what they offer. Solicitors reckon over a hundred grand. I’m not accepting the first offer neither.’

I looked at Dad and shook my head. ‘But Dad, won’t that just drag it out even longer?’

‘Trust me, Trace, ya never take the first offer.’

I tried to change the subject. ‘You heard owt from Uncle John or Mick?’

‘Aye. Your Nan’s not been well. They think it might be cancer, so I’m planning to pop over to Stoke as soon as I can to see her.' Dad turned to me. 'You should go too. When was the last time you went to see her?' His tone was accusing.

'Can't remember, Dad. It's been a while.'

But I remembered exactly the last time I'd seen her; it had been years ago, when Dad invited us all over for Christmas at Grenoside.

Nan had sat regally on the sofa, all fags and red lippy and pretended that she hadn't known we were coming, to excuse herself from buying Danielle a present. It was a downright lie. She'd never been interested in me or my daughter.

It was like Dad was reading my thoughts. 'She does love ya, you know.'

Before I could disagree, Dad's phone rang, and he was arranging for a mate to come round.

'Well, I'll get off then?'

'Nah, don't be silly, you don't have to.'

'I know I don't Dad, but ya know what, it's getting late. I'll try and bring the kids over at the weekend, shall I?'

'Yeah, that would be nice, not seen 'em in ages. Oh, and thanks for fetching me the brandy.'

I couldn't help myself. 'Ah well, don't be drinking it all at once, don't want ya back in hospital, do we?'

Dad lifted the bottle off the coffee table.

'What, on that? It's only for medicinal purposes. Got a bit of a chesty cough coming on.'

I put my coat on and gave him a kiss.

'Listen, let me know what the doc says about your arms. I'll call ya about bringin' the kids.'

I was pleased I'd made the time to go see Dad. I wished he could be in a good mood more often. As I left, the main thing on my mind was how he would cope if there was something wrong with Nan.

# 54: Official

Any fears that I'd had about Paul bolting now we'd had sex disappeared. I was now officially "his bird", which would have been nice, only now his mate had been kicked out of the flat and Paul had nowhere to stay. The Council was of no use, and he didn't have the deposit for private accommodation.

'I've called everyone,' he said. 'I even called Mum, but she said there isn't room.'

'Surely she wouldn't leave you out on the streets!'

He shook his head, 'you really don't know my mum, do you?'

I felt so sorry for him; he looked like a rejected homeless puppy. 'Tell ya what, let me have a word with Mum and Ada, I'm sure they wouldn't mind you staying for a bit, plus Mum works for the housing, perhaps she could pull a few strings?'

Mum was in were we arrived home and thankfully Ada was still at work. Paul looked on sheepishly while I tried to persuade Mum to let him stay for a couple of days.

'But where is he going to sleep?'

I laughed. 'With me, of course.'

I could read Mum's mind. I knew she was worried about us having sex.

'He can sleep in the dining room if it bothers you.'

I thought I was winning her round when Ada walked in carrying Paul's suitcase.

'What the fuck's this? I've just nearly broke my neck on it.'

'It's Paul's. I was just asking Mum if it's ok for him to stay at ours for a couple of days.'

Ada looked at Mum.

'She's kidding, right? Where's he going to sleep?'

Paul stepped in. 'Look, its ok, I'll find somewhere.'

I turned to Mum and begged her. 'Mum, please, just for a couple of days.'

She turned to Ada. He looked at her gone out. 'I'm not having owt to do with it.'

Mum sighed in resignation. 'Ok, but it's only for a couple of days.'

My heart skipped a beat. I rushed over and gave her a hug. I felt sorry for the predicament that I'd placed Mum under, but was so relieved that, for now at least, Paul had somewhere to stay.

# 55: Action!

Dad's worst fears had come true. Nan had cancer and I could see that he was devastated. It was clearly affecting him badly because every time I spoke to him, he sounded pissed. I was worried about him but, when he said he was going over to Stoke, I was almost relieved that other people would be keeping an eye on him, because it was time to shoot the family support video.

The filming was taking place at Kenwood Hall Hotel. The film crew planned to do one-to-one interviews in different locations around the impressive grounds but the first day of filming was focused on recreating a support group. Someone had dropped out and I roped Mum in at the last minute to make up the numbers. I'd promised her she wouldn't have to say much, as the rest of the group had plenty of experiences to share.

My role was to facilitate the group. The film crew had set up what looked like a mini train rack around the room to help them film from different angles. We were in a really posh room, and everyone was a little nervous but also excited at the prospect that sharing their stories might help someone else. The film crew were all in place. We settled into our positions then the director called: 'Action!'

One by one, I went around the room, asking each participant when they'd first realised that their loved ones had a problem with drugs.

Vera started us off. She was one of the founders of RODA (relatives of drug abusers) and her son Richard had been through numerous rehabs. Then we heard from Eddie, whose two sons were hooked on heroin. Jeanne told us about her brother who had died of a heroin overdose and then Pauline, the founder of FADs (Families affected by drugs) talked about caring for the families of her two daughters who were also addicted to heroin. Next, Charlotte who ran a support group called SPACE 2 for families bereaved from addiction talked about having lost her own son to an overdose. A new woman called Steph shared the story of her daughter's amphetamine addiction, and then there was Mum.

'So Gillian, when did you start to realise that there was a problem?'

Mum took a deep breath. I could tell she was nervous. 'Well she'd lost a lot of weight, and her behaviour was so erratic: one minute she seemed fine but then the next minute she would be freaking out, lashing out. It was like she'd been possessed. She really scared us at one point. We even had to call the police. It was like living in a nightmare. You just want heaven and hell to open up together, swallow you all up. You just want someone to just lift you all away. You want someone to take that person from you, do something, whatever it is and bring them back like they were before.' She was starting to cry now.

I had thought asking Mum to step in at the last minute wouldn't have been that much of a big deal. After all, I'd been clean from drugs for a few years. But listening to her speak hit home about just how much pain and suffering I'd put her through. I knew I'd put her through some shit with my own brush with addiction, but she had always put on a brave face. I'd never really realised how bad it had been for her.

I felt awful, watching her so upset. During the break, I even suggested she leave early as we did have enough people in the end, but Mum insisted on staying.

'Honestly, Mum, you've done your bit, you don't have to stay and what about work?' Mum had taken two days of last-minute annual leave on my account already.

'Ah, sod work, love, this is far more important. I know I am crying, but they are happy tears too. I couldn't be prouder of you, and look at you now! If it means that more families will be willing to come forward for support, then the tears will have been well worth it. There was sod all like this when I was going through it. Just knowing that you are helping others, people like me, makes it all worthwhile. Anyway, the coffee's great here and I am actually enjoying myself.'

It had been eons since I'd spent any quality time with Mum. And even though it was a sad and draining experience, when we'd finished, it felt like a really positive and productive day.

# 56: It's Positive

A couple of days turned into a couple of weeks. I contributed to Paul's board and Paul tried his best to be helpful around the house whilst everyone was at work. He cut the grass, washed the pots, and even offered to babysit my brother a couple of times, if Mum was running late at work.

But he still wasn't having any luck with a job. Although he never said anything, I knew that Ada wasn't his biggest fan; every so often he would drop little digs about Paul not working or ask if he'd found somewhere else to stay.

I was glad Paul wasn't on the streets, but it was starting to feel suffocating, having him around all the time. His jealousy was starting to get on my nerves. He'd question why I was late from work or quiz me about my day and who I'd been talking to. Sometimes I'd snap.

I found his interrogations insulting, as if he thought I was cheating. He would always apologise, claiming that it was because he'd been cheated on in the past. He sulked for days when I mentioned that I was planning on going to see a school mate off the Valley who'd recently had a baby. He even suggested that he could tag along, but I insisted that I was going alone.

As soon as I got off the bus at the John O'Gaunt terminus, I immediately felt at home. I missed the carefree days, just hanging about on the shops with no responsibilities.

The place hadn't changed one bit, but I knew I had. I was still only sixteen, but now I was a grown up and had responsibilities. I didn't particularly like work: the hours were long and monotonous, but the weekly wage was a necessity. I was in a serious relationship and now somehow felt responsible for us both, and even though I couldn't wait to leave school, I found myself missing it.

It felt weird seeing Michelle open the door to her new home with a kid on her hip. The last time I'd seen her, we'd been at the Silver Blades, sharing a smoke and speedskating against each other. I brought her up to speed with my life, and work; I talked to her about Paul, sharing my concerns about him being slightly possessive and the tensions back at home due to him not having a job.

She reckoned I should get rid, but I said it was hard because I knew deep-down that he did love me and part of me felt sorry for him. She wasn't convinced; she shared her own relationship woes and how the father of her son had been the exact same, claimed he loved her but as soon as he'd heard she was pregnant, he was out of the picture. The bastard was even questioning paternity, but none of this seemed to faze her; in fact she reckoned they were both better off without him.

Apparently, she'd received a decorating grant off the social and with the support of family, she'd managed to turn what was once an ugly maisonette into a lovely family home.

Her parents occasionally helped by babysitting, but instead of going out, she much preferred staying in. She joked about how the last time she'd been out, she'd had to make a mad dash home after her tits had leaked milk through her top.

I moaned to her about how I'd been having problems with my own tits, they felt like they'd grown two cup sizes and had been really tender.

Instead of laughing, she gasped. 'You're not pregnant, are you?'

Her comment took me back. 'Me? Fucking pregnant? You are joking, aren't you? I've only had sex a couple of times!'

Karen picked up her baby from the crib and smirked. 'Yeah, that's exactly what I said.'

'Not a fucking prayer, mate.'

I was adamant and quickly changed the subject. I didn't want to say it out loud, but whilst I envied her independence, there was no way I'd be stupid enough to get myself pregnant. Hours passed and part of me knew that Paul would be back at home getting his knickers in a twist, so I made my excuse to leave.

I couldn't stop thinking about what she'd said. She'd got me worried. The thought of being pregnant brought me out in cold sweats. There was no way I could talk to Mum. I racked my brains, then remembered my mate's mum. I knew I could trust her and decided to call her the following day at lunch time from a phone box around the corner from work.

Armed with some paper and pen and a pocket full of ten pence pieces, I called her house, and she answered straight away. But instead of dismissing the ideas, she confirmed that there could be a slight chance, because sore breasts was a symptom.

She gave me the number of a church which did pregnancy tests for free. I called the number and got an appointment for the next day.

The manager on shift had reluctantly agreed to let me leave early on the condition I made up the lost two hours the following day. But I wasn't bothered; I was prepared to do anything. I needed to know one way or another.

I felt like a walking pressure cooker about to explode. I berated myself on the walk over. For years, I'd slagged off girls of my age for having sex and now after only having sex a couple of times, I might be fucking pregnant.

When I arrived at the church, I recognised it as a place Mum used to do an exercise class. She'd bring me with her as a young child and here I was getting a pregnancy test.

I pressed the buzzer and was buzzed in and told to go to the second floor, where a woman who looked like Nan was waiting for me. She smiled but I could feel her eyes judging me. Jesus was looking down at me from the wall too and I felt ashamed to be there.

The woman sat me down and talked about who they were and what they did, but it went straight over my head. All I wanted was a test and to get out of there as fast as I could. She handed me a test tube and told me to pee in it.

After covering myself in piss, I sealed the tube and washed my hands and handed it back to the old lady. She left me alone in the room, with only Jesus staring down on me for company. I didn't believe in God, but I found myself praying.

It seemed like a lifetime before she returned to the room, and she sat opposite me and handed me a small sheet of white paper. The word POSITIVE stood out, in black and white.

'Are you ok?' she asked me in a quiet voice.

I wanted to scream at her: 'Do I fucking look ok?' but the words wouldn't come out. My mind was in a spin, and I had Jesus staring at me. I looked at her.

'Are you sure this is right?'

She gave me that fake smile again. 'Yes, so by your reaction, I assume that this wasn't planned?'

'Planned! Are you kidding me? I only had sex a couple of times; I can't be!' I handed her the sheet of white paper. 'Can you do another just to make sure?'

She placed her hands on my knee. 'Listen, lovely. That is the second one. We always do two just in case.'

I couldn't take it in. My hands started to shake, and I could feel the tears coming, I tried to hold them back, but I couldn't stop them and before I knew it, I was sobbing like a pathetic baby.

I could see Nan's face now, that disappointed one, the one which was always reserved for me, the black sheep of the family. Then I thought about Mum. How could I tell her? Mum had always said she'd wanted more for us kids; wanted us to get a career and all that before settling down and having kids and now I'd let her down too. How could I have been so stupid?

The lady in the clinic was talking. I could see her lips moving, her face gesturing reassuringly but all I could hear was white noise; none of it was sinking in. I heard her mention adoption, that it was available and made a point of telling me that abortion could cause infertility as she handed me some leaflets. She kept on going on about how I had a living human growing inside of me, that bringing a child into the world was a beautiful thing: 'a child of God'. But all I could think was: *if this was an act of God, he could shove his faith up his arse. Fuck! Fuck! Fuck!*

# 57: There's More Coke Than Brandy

It was the last day of filming and a beautiful day. Everyone was hanging about in the courtyard, chatting away like old friends as they waited to be called for their one-on-one interviews. Even Mum had decided to stay. I'd already made a mental note not to sit in on her interview! The whole atmosphere had been brilliant, and it had been great to catch up with everyone.

Chris Scott, an ex-heroin/crack user turned keyworker had joined us today for the interviews with support workers. He'd done amazing, returning again and again to support programmes, having relapsed and then worked his way into a paid role. He joined me for a fag while the producers set the room up.

Chris was his usual bubbly self. 'So how's the filming been going, Trace?'

I sighed. 'Ya know what? It's been a bit heavy going. It hit home a bit when Mum shared her bit. We'd never really spoken about it before. There were no support groups like there are now.'

'I know what you mean,' he said, taking a long drag on his fag. 'I dunno what Mum would have done without RODA, especially after all the shit I've put her through.'

'Yeah, but look at you now? You're doing great!' I was so proud of Chris. He'd had so many challenges: prison sentences, addiction and homelessness, but one of the hardest challenges had been rebuilding the trust between him and his family, especially his Mum. 'Who would have thought you'd be working as a drugs worker?' I said.

Chris blushed. 'I know. That's why I agreed to do this, Trace. I reckon Mum might have given up on me years ago had it not been for RODA.'

Chris went in for his filming and I was left alone for a moment. Dad was niggling in the back of my mind. He was back from Stoke earlier than I expected and I'd said I'd call to see him later on that day. I didn't know which version of him I was going to get. I'd been listening to families sharing stories of loved ones for the last few days and, even though it was all familiar stuff – lies, deceit, theft, manipulation, shame and humiliation – the common theme was families not being able to recognise their loved ones anymore, which really struck a chord.

Even though they were mostly talking about heroin and crack and not alcohol, I was wondering if there was a parallel with Dad's drinking. I was thinking about the bottle of Brandy. Dad had told me not to worry, but I was worried, so later in the day, I had a chat with Joy from RODA.

We found a quiet spot out in the hotel gardens, and I shared my concerns with her. I told her about what Uncle Mick had said about Dad and how his drinking had been spiralling out of control in Stoke, before coming to Sheffield and that Dad had just brushed it all off, accusing them of overreacting, and I wasn't sure if I was or not? I mean, though he was drinking more, it wasn't like he was demanding money for drink or stealing! Yes, he could be obnoxious or lairy after a drink, but Dad was like that without alcohol.

Joy sat and listened; she was good at that. She didn't seem overly concerned about Dad but did advise me to just keep an eye on him, especially after him asking for the bottle of brandy. As she was called away by the producers, she suggested I call Jean, who chaired the Al-anon support groups.

I took her hand. 'Joy, thanks for listening, mate.'

Joy smiled. 'Anytime, Trace, tha knows that – now come on let's get back to that filming, I'm fucking dreading my bit, I hate being interviewed.' She took me by the hand, and we headed back indoors.

Finally, it was a wrap, in fact we'd managed to finish earlier than expected, which was a bonus. My intention was just to pop in to see Dad for ten minutes, show my face and shoot off. I was ready to have a couple of drinks with Pat at home to celebrate.

I rang Dad before setting off and found myself regretting my decision as soon as he answered. By the sounds of it, Dad was already pissed, and it wasn't even four o clock. He was like Worzel fucking Gummidge, you never knew which version you would get. There was the sober drunk, where he'd been drinking but he was pretty much compos mentis, and you could have a reasonable two-way conversation with him. Then there was the happy drunk, with a splash of optimism; it was like he didn't have a care in the world.

The flip side was the angry drunk. You couldn't reason with him when he was angry. He was good at blaming everyone else, but I could see he was frustrated with himself. But what was even worse was when he'd got his maudlin head on. Dad played the victim role off to a T. In fact, if he'd been an actor, he'd have an Oscar by now.

The front door was unlocked so I let myself in, calling from the hallway.

'Dad?' But there was no answer. As I headed to the living room, I couldn't help noticing the state of the kitchen directly in front of me. I turned to the living room and found Dad. He was bang-out on the sofa, completely out of it. Thankfully, he was alone.

'Dad!'

He looked up at me.

'How are you feeling?' I knew it was a stupid question. He looked deflated. I'd never really seen him look this vulnerable before.

'Look at me, Trace, I'm fucked.' He reached down by his foot and produced a larger bottle of brandy. He topped up his glass. 'Don't worry. There's more Coke than brandy.'

I knew getting off his face wasn't going to make him feel better, but now wasn't the time to go there. 'Listen, it will have meant a lot, you going over to stay with Granddad. I bet it was nice to spend some quality time with him and I'm sure

Nan will have appreciated it as well, knowing he wasn't alone.'

'That's not going to help her get better, is it? She looks fucking shocking, Trace,' he said, moving to the edge of the sofa, and pressing his fingers into his eyes, like he was attempting to stop the tears, but it didn't work. He started to sob.

I placed one hand on his knee and the other arm around him to comfort him. 'Come on, Dad. She'll get better.'

Dad leaned into me, giving me permission to comfort him. I just didn't know what to say. What could I say? The uncomfortable silence was broken when Dad composed himself, took a deep breath and reached for another drink.

I took my cue and sat back. 'You going to be ok, Dad? I'm not used to seeing you this upset.' I wasn't lying. I don't think I had ever seen Dad cry before. There was a sombre mood in the air, and he hadn't even mentioned the claim! I didn't want to leave him, but it was getting late. I gave him a kiss and promised I'd call around the day after to check on him. Dad smiled but didn't get up.

'Lock us the door and push the keys through the letterbox, will ya? I'll see ya tomorrow, eh? Oh, and thanks for tonight, it means a lot.' I knew he meant it.

My elation at the film's success had been replaced by sadness. Dad was hurting, and it hurt me to see him so upset. But, as I drove home, I also knew deep-down that apart from being there for him when he needed a shoulder to cry on, there wasn't much else I could do to help.

# 58: Dropping The Bombshell

I couldn't get away from that building quick enough. I lit a fag and, two drags in, I remembered that I shouldn't even be smoking. I was like a walking zombie. I passed girls my own age who were laughing and joking without a care in the world and envied their innocence.

As I walked through the bus station, I prayed that I didn't bump into anyone I knew. I still had no plans of telling anyone, not even Paul. I suspected that, despite all his declarations of love, he'd probably just do one. I couldn't even comprehend being a single Mum. On the bus journey home, I stroked my belly. There was no swelling, and I didn't even feel pregnant, but according to that sheet of paper, I was. I berated myself mentally – how could I have been so fucking stupid?

Thankfully, the house was empty. Paul was out visiting his mum which gave me time to go to my bedroom and read the leaflets that the lady had given me. I chucked the one about church and how much God loved me straight in the bin. Then there was the piece of paper with PREGNANT stamped on the front; that went back into my pocket.

The one I needed to read was the one about my options. According to the leaflet, I needed to know was how far gone I was. If I was early enough, I could take some pills, but if I was too far gone, I would have to go down the surgical route and have the baby sucked out. The guilt of killing another human weighed heavy as the words from the old lady replayed around in my head.

The leaflet went on to explain that one out of four pregnancies end in miscarriage. Then an idea popped into my head: What if I miscarried? If I did, then the decision would be out of my hands. I'd heard somewhere that falling down the stairs could cause miscarriage. So I jumped up, checked the house to make sure nobody was in and headed to the top of the staircase.

My first attempt was pathetic, I didn't even make it to the bottom of the stairs, so I headed back determined to make this time count and do some proper damage. This time, I launched myself forward headfirst. Just as I closed my eyes, I heard the back door. Sarah found me in a heap at the bottom of the stairs, sobbing.

'Tracey, are you ok? I heard a bang!'

I was still crying, I couldn't look at her in the face, let alone tell her what the matter was.

'For fucks sake, are you ok? Come on, tell me.'

'I'm fucking pregnant!' Even saying the words made me feel physically sick.

'Nooooo way!' I could tell by her face she was stunned, but then her expression turned into concern. 'You are going to have it, aren't you?'

'Are you fucking kidding me?'

I should have expected this response from Sarah. She loved kids whereas I didn't have a maternal bone in me.

'Come on Tracey, you'll be fine, I'll help out. Have you told Paul yet?'

'No, I haven't told anyone, and you can't neither!' I snapped.

'Told me what?' My heart sank as Paul came into sight.

As soon as he saw me on the floor, he panicked and rushed to my side. 'Trace, what's happened, are you ok?'

There was no way of hiding it any longer. My secret had been exposed. I'd been expecting Paul to run in the opposite direction, but in fact he was ecstatic.

'Wow, this is brilliant!' He was buzzing. Then he was confused. 'What are you doing on the floor?'

Irritated, I snapped: 'Look, I don't even know if I'm keeping it yet!'

The hurt on his face was visible, and I immediately felt guilty.

'Look, it's gonna be ok,' he said. 'I know it's a shock and it wasn't planned but Trace, this is brilliant!'

I shook my head in disbelief. 'Is it though! You're saying that now, but you can walk away anytime you want. Michelle's bloke did.'

He looked hurt again. 'Yeah, but I'm not him. I love ya, and I've told ya I'd never leave ya.'

Part of me believed him, but the reality was we couldn't bring a child into the world on love alone.

'Look, Trace. We'll make a better job of it than our Mums and Dads.'

'This isn't a fucking competition, you idiot! We don't have anywhere to live, and you don't even have a job!'

'Trace, you being pregnant means we'd get priority on housing, and I can always get a job. Look, you said it yourself. Ya mate's doing ok, so why can't we?'

We were going around in circles until Sarah stepped in. 'Let her have some space to think this through. It's her decision, after all.'

Paul was indignant. 'But it isn't just hers, is it?' He pointed to my stomach. 'It's my kid too. I have rights.'

I just wanted it all to go away. It was like a bad dream. I've never felt so trapped in my life. I felt like I was the one taking all the risk.

Whilst Paul hadn't said it out loud, his tone had implied that our relationship might not survive should I abort "his" baby, and there were no guarantees that he'd stick around if I chose to keep it. I was in a no-win situation.

I'd been planning on keeping my news a secret from Mum, but now I knew I needed her.

I stayed in my bedroom until I heard Mum's voice. My stomach started to do summersaults. I had no idea what I would say or when the best time would be to tell her.

Paul offered to be there when I broke the news, but I told him I thought it best that he stayed out of the way, especially if Ada was home. I found Mum in the kitchen; I stood by the door frame watching as her and Ada worked in harmony preparing tea, oblivious about the bombshell I was about to drop on them both. A feeling of shame engulfed me, and for a second, thought about backing out. I just didn't have the heart to ruin both their days, but I knew that it had to be done.

'Mum, Ada. I need a word.'

'What's tha done nah?' Ada joked, but I knew he wouldn't be laughing when I broke the news.

'I just need a word, can you come in the room.'

I went to sit on the sofa. Mum sat beside me, clutching a tea towel, with concern etched all over her face.

Mum patted my knee. 'Hey, what's up, pet?'

'I'm pregnant.'

I kept my head bowed and my eyes were welling with tears. I could feel the words hanging heavy in the air and then I heard clapping. It was Ada.

'Ahhh, great! Well done, Tracey. It's like history repeating itself all over again.'

Mum glared at him. 'Not now, eh?'

'Whatever! I need some fresh air.' And with that, he stormed out of the house, leaving me and Mum on our own in the living room. She took a deep breath and turned to me. I shook my head in shame. I still couldn't look her in the eye.

'Look, Tracey. These things happen. It's not ideal, but it's not the end of the world neither.'

I couldn't believe how calm she was.

'When did you find out? Do you know how far gone you are?'

Mum listened intently as I ran through the timeline of events.

'What's Paul said? I'm assuming he knows?'

'He's over the moon and wants me to keep it!'

'Okay, but what do YOU want?'

'Thing is, Mum, I don't know what to do. I didn't even feel pregnant, but now, it's hard, cos I know I've got something growing inside of me. I don't know if I have the heart to kill something.'

'Listen, you don't know this, but I had an abortion once.'

I looked at her shocked. This was news to me.

'It was after you and Sarah had been born. I wasn't in a good place, in fact I was recovering from a nervous breakdown at the time.' She sounded so matter of fact, but I could still hear the regret in her voice. 'I was in no state to look after myself let alone another child, and your dad was barely around.'

I was still trying to absorb Mum's confession. I couldn't help thinking that had things been different, that I might have had another brother or sister.

'Look, it wasn't easy, but at the time it was the right thing to do. I'm not suggesting that you do the same – this decision has to come from you – but please know that whatever you decide, I will stand by you.'

Mum's reaction took me by surprise. 'But what about Ada? He hates me, doesn't he?' I started to sob again.

'Come here.' Mum embraced me. 'Look I know it feels like it, but it isn't the end of the world. I should know. First things first, we need to get you booked in at the doctors and we can take it from there, ok?'

Mum left me in the living room alone, whilst she made an appointment for the doctors. The feelings of guilt and shame enveloped me, like a long-lost friend and I knew whatever I decided I couldn't please everyone. My pragmatic head was screaming 'don't do it!' But my heart was saying different.

I knew the baby was only the size of a pea and yet I found myself already getting attached to it. I couldn't help wondering if I was carrying a boy or a girl, or whether it would take after Paul with his good looks. I didn't believe in God, but I did wonder if it was a sign or if this was all part of His plan for me?

Afterall my career prospects were grim: I had no qualifications; I knew that I didn't want to work in a factory for the rest of my life. I'd never aspired to be a Mum at such a young age, but Paul seemed so confident that we could make it work. I was scared that my murdered unborn child might haunt me in my dreams. Then there was Paul, I knew deep-down that he would never forgive me and that our relationship would never survive.

Mum came back into the living room. ‘I’ve made you an appointment for tomorrow, ok, love? And I’ll come with you if ya want?’

‘Thanks, Mum.’ I meant it. After years of pushing Mum away, I realised in that moment she was the only person I wanted by my side. But what I didn’t tell her was that I had already made my mind up. I was keeping my baby.

# 59: Officially A Swot

I'd spoken to Dad on the phone a couple of times since my last visit. It didn't sound like he'd cut back on the brandy; in fact I suspected he'd been drinking more. I didn't know what state I'd find him in when I visited later, but for now I needed to get on with my university module on research methods.

I'd been struggling with it, blagging my way through all the lessons. Statistics, graphs and data would just go straight over my head. So I'd stayed late to work in the library. Even though I struggled with that system too and could never find the books, at least I could get my head down in the library. At home, there were too many distractions.

The students around me were all younger than me. They reminded me of the students I used to serve in the canteen when I was sixteen: sad, privileged losers and swots who'd chosen to keep studying. I silently laughed at the irony that I, Tracey Ford, was now officially a swot. But I wasn't young and carefree these days. Now, I had two kids at home, a mortgage, a full-time job and, more recently, Dad to contend with.

I got my head down and had managed to get quite a bit done on the assignment, I was feeling pretty chuffed with myself and even though I was knackered, I went to see Dad as planned.

I found him into the living room. The room was like a bloody furnace. What was worse was the smell of stale cigarettes.

'Christ, Dad, it's boiling here. Can I open a window?'

'Ahh, please thee sen.'

I went to open the window. I spied a bottle of Brandy by the side of his foot.

'Ya going to have to get a set of keys cut, Trace. Our Sarah's got the other set. You could get a copy cut off them. She was round earlier.'

I was surprised. She hadn't said anything about going round.

'She ok then, Dad? I've not spoken to her for a couple of days, what wi filming and uni an all that.'

'Ah, she's sound, although she did have a little dig about this.' He lifted the half-empty bottle of brandy and started to pour himself another shot.

I tried not to sound too patronising. 'Well, it's not going to help is it, Dad.'

Dad snapped back. 'Fuck me, Trace, don't you fucking start an all. What do ya fucking expect? I've got thee nan dying over in Stoke and I'm fucking stuck here! And I've had the solicitors on the phone. Them twats are dragging their feet. If they'd sorted this claim, I could be living in Stoke nah!'

He started coughing and topped his glass up with some Coke and took a sip.

'Anyway, it's not like I'm drinking it fucking neat.' He waved the glass in the air as if to prove a point. 'I'm a grown man, tha knows. I don't need you having a pop an all.'

'Look, Dad, no-one's having a go. We know you're going through some shit at the moment. We're just worried about you ending up in hospital again.'

'I'm sorry,' he said, and I could tell he was. 'Don't you worry about me, ok? I've told ya before, them doctors talk shit! There's nowt wrong wi me. Trust me, I ain't going nowhere.'

I was tempted to try and have a chat about his drinking, raise my concerns, but I was exhausted. I didn't have the energy to fight with him, not tonight. So I let myself out and posted the keys through the letterbox.

When I finally arrived home, I told Pat about my day. He was receptive until I started sharing my concerns about Dad. His eyes rolled at the mere mention of Dad these days. He wasn't interested at all, and he told me so regularly.

'I know he's your dad and all that but, he's taking the piss. I just know why you bother. He's done fuck all for you! It's all you talk about lately and if I'm honest, I'm sick of hearing about him.'

His words stung; I needed his support, not a telling-off from him.

'Look, Pat, I hear what you're saying. It's just, what if he ends up back in hospital?' Pat looked confused, 'What if he does, Trace? You can't see it can you? Ya Dad is going to do whatever he likes, just like he has always done. You worrying about it or him all the time isn't going to change that!'

I'd worked in the addiction field long enough to know that until a person even acknowledged that they had a problem, they had to feel the consequences of their actions. But it felt like Dad was giving up on himself and I couldn't just sit back and watch.

Even though I'd disapproved of Dad spending too much time in the pub, at least then he'd still been taking pride in his appearance and getting out and socialising. Lately, he'd become like a hermit, confined to that dam flat, justifying his drinking as he wallowed in self-pity. His hygiene standards seemed to be slipping too. And he was like Jekyll and Hyde, he was so unpredictable. There would be times I could have a rational and reasonable conversation with him, then other times he just didn't make any sense, which was all down to the drink. It worried me.

And now, on top of worrying about Dad, I was worried about my relationship. Usually Pat had the patience of a saint. He was a rock, my stability and my biggest supporter, but it was clear he couldn't support me with this. It was time to give Jean from Al-anon a call.

# 60: What Kind of Man is He?

Who knew that someone could still have periods when you were pregnant? The nurse reckoned I was three months gone, which meant we had seven months to get our shit together.

The news of my pregnancy went down like a fart in a church with Nan. She couldn't even look at me. The best she could muster was the occasional tut whilst in my presence. But I wasn't bothered about her opinion, because we still had to break the news to Dad.

I wasn't just terrified about what he would say. I was worried about what he would do to Paul. His parting words had been: 'if tha can't be good, be careful.' He'd said it jokingly, but the threat wasn't lost on me. I was talking to Mum in the living room with Paul, asking her advice on the best way to break the news to Dad, without him breaking Paul's legs in the process.

'I'll do it.'

'What?' I couldn't believe my ears.

'Would ya, Gill?' Paul looked relieved, but I was worried. I knew that going to see Dad was a big deal for Mum. Over the years, she'd always made a point of keeping contact to the absolute minimum, but now she was going to see him to protect me, and she was adamant.

'I'll do it. It will come better from me, trust me.'

Tracey's mum and dad had swapped the busy pub in the Wicker for a local village pub called the Angel in Grenoside. Tracey's family had welcomed Dad with open arms and soon Dad and Tracey had followed them. Their large, detached cottage was nestled on one of the most beautiful hills just up the lane from the pub, and Tracey was able to keep her horses on the land behind. Dad was now a regular in The Angel and this was where Mum had arranged to meet him.

I could tell she was nervous before she left. I tried telling her she didn't have to go, but she insisted and reassured me she'd be ok. But it wasn't just her I was worried about. Dad could be so unpredictable, I was scared that he might take his anger out on Ada.

We waited anxiously for hours and finally, I heard the car pull up on the drive. Mum stumbled into the house. She was drunk and I mean, really drunk. Ada rushed to her aid to help her into the house.

'Mum, are you ok? What's happened? What did Dad say?' but Mum was incoherent. Ada interjected.

'Look, love, leave it will ya? It's been a long night. I just want to get ya Mum in bed.' Ada didn't say anything else, leaving me and Paul still none the wiser.

The following morning, Mum emerged in the kitchen.

'Morning, you two.'

She looked dreadful and headed straight for the cupboard to get herself a couple of paracetamols.

'Hiya, Mum. You look shocking. Are you ok? How did it go? What did he say?'

'Well, obviously he's not impressed, but to be honest, he talked more about himself! Sounds like he's doing ok for himself now, flashing his money about, giving it the Big I Am.' Mum was gesticulating now with her arms. 'Oh, and did you know he's just bought a house now with that Tracey? Apparently, it comes with an acre of land too!'

'So come on, Mum, what did he say about me being pregnant?'

'Look, obviously he wasn't chuffed,' she said, 'And of course, I got the blame.' She turned to Paul. 'And I reckon you'd better stay out of his way for a while, cos he's not impressed with you, laddo.'

Paul bristled. 'Well, it doesn't matter what he says, does it? He's never been there for ya and anyway you've got me now. We don't need him!'

But it did matter. It mattered a lot. I knew all too well that Dad could be a bastard at times, but he was still my dad.

Mum was still talking.

'Oh, by the way he's already made a claim on the baby's name. If it's a boy, you've got to name him after Dad.'

'Really?' My heart skipped a beat, hoping that my unborn child might bring us closer together.

Mum picked up on my enthusiasm.

'Don't you be getting all ya hopes up. Tha knows what ya Dad says and what he does are two different things.'

Mum sounded bitter and I couldn't blame her. I gave her a hug. 'Thank you, Mum. I really mean it. I know it feels like history is repeating itself, but I promise this will be different.'

Mum hugged me back. 'Look, love, it's what us Mums do. You'll learn that soon enough.'

I'd left it a week before calling Dad, and tracking him down wasn't easy. Eventually I got hold of him at The Station pub in the Wicker. The barman called Dad to the phone. The place sounded busy and wasn't the ideal place to have a heart to heart.

'Hello?'

'Hi Dad, it's me Tracey.'

Dad laughed. 'I was wondering when you would call. Oh, and nice work getting ya Mum to come and break the news!'

I tried to explain, but he wasn't listening.

'And what about that bloke of yours eh! Didn't have the balls to come and tell me his sen? What kind of man is he?'

'I know, Dad. I'm sorry. It was a mistake.'

'Well, it's a mistake that tha's got to live with, Trace and what about him, has he got a fucking job yet?'

'No Dad, but he's looking.' Which was a lie. Paul had made no real effort to look for a job.

'Tha better tell him that we're due a man-to-man talk when I next see him. That cunt better not hurt ya. If he does, he's got me to contend with. Do ya hear me?'

'I hear ya, Dad.'

Then his voice softened. 'Listen tha's still my babby and if ya need owt, give me a bell.'

It was all the reassurance I needed, to know that he still loved me, but the reassurance was short-lived.

'Listen, I was in the middle of a meeting when tha called, so this really isn't a good time.'

'Dad, look, I just wanted to say I am sorry and is there any chance of us meeting up proper, face to face?' But I realised he couldn't have heard me because the phone was dead.

'Are you ok? What did your dad say?' I couldn't answer Paul. I was choking on tears. I never knew where I stood with Dad, and it hurt. One minute he was claiming to love me and the next he couldn't wait to get rid of me.

'Look, we don't need ya Dad's approval and we certainly don't need his money!'

I wasn't in the mood for an argument, so I just shrugged him off. Everything was happening so fast, and Paul was starting to irritate me. It was easy for him. He wasn't bothered about his family, but I was and despite all his words of reassurance, I still couldn't shake the fact he could still walk at any time.

'Just leave me alone a bit, will ya?'

# 61: Hi, my name is Tracey

My chat with Jean had been helpful. She listened as I brought her up to speed about Dad and told me that there was a meeting later that evening. I didn't need any encouragement, just talking to her had eased the invisible weight that had only got heavier over the past few weeks.

As promised, Jean was there waiting for me, and I felt comfort in seeing a familiar face. One by one, the other members started to arrive; I couldn't help myself mentally sizing them up.

I knew I had nothing to be afraid of, but I still wasn't sure if I was at the right place. Dad was an annoying pain in the fucking arse when pissed, but was he an actual alcoholic?

Everyone greeted and hugged each other like long-lost friends in between making themselves coffees. One bloke approached me, asking if I needed a hug too and for a moment, I wondered if he was there under false pretences, just there to get his hands on a woman.

I mentally berated myself for being such a judgemental git and had to remind myself that I didn't know anything about him yet to be making sweeping assumptions.

When everyone was seated, Jean opened the meeting. It felt like everyone's eyes were on me as the newcomer.

'We welcome you to the Al-Anon Family Group and hope you will find in this fellowship the help and friendship we have been privileged to enjoy.' Everyone nodded in agreement.

'We who live, or have lived, with the problem of alcoholism, understand as perhaps few others can. We, too, were lonely and frustrated, but in Al-Anon, we discover that no situation is really hopeless and that it is possible for us to find contentment and even happiness, whether the alcoholic is still drinking or not.'

Ok, so far so good, I thought. Yes, I felt lonely, and I was definitely frustrated, but I wasn't sure how the fuck I was going to find any contentment while Dad was drinking I smiled as Jean continued, I had to keep an open mind.

'We urge you to try our programme. It has helped many of us find solutions that lead to serenity. In this support group, we share our experiences strength and hope, to help us accept that alcoholism is a family problem.'

*Okayyyy.* I wasn't sure Dad's drinking was a family problem. He just needed to have a fucking word wi his sen. I let Jean continue.

'Our family situation is bound to improve as we apply the Al-Anon ideas. Without such spiritual help, living with an alcoholic is too much for most of us. Our thinking becomes distorted by trying to force solutions, and it's then that we become irritable and unreasonable without knowing it.'

I kept on having to remind myself to be open-minded, but it was hard. I just wanted to Jean to stop talking so I could spew everything off my chest and see if anyone had any ideas on how the fuck I should deal with Dad. It felt weird being part of a group instead of facilitating it.

Jean opened her book again, to a bookmarked page. The chapter she was about to read was apparently called Live and Let Live. She started to read out loud again, before passing the book to the person sitting next to her. The lady picked up from where Jean had left off and read for a while before passing it to the next person. I was hoping that someone would finish the topic before the book got to me, just so I didn't have to read out loud. I mean, fuck me! I came here for support, not to take part in an English lesson.

Thankfully, by the time it got to me, there were only a couple of lines left. I couldn't wait to hand the book back to Jean.

Finally, Jean opened the meeting.

'Right, let's talk about how we learn to live and let live?'

There was silence before a lady introduced herself. She was the daughter of an alcoholic.

'I still really struggle with this one,' she said. 'I mean, I know Dad's been gone now for over two years, and yet I still find it hard to forgive him.'

Everyone was nodding, knowingly, but I was confused. If he was dead, then why was she here? I was dying to ask, but I had to wait my turn. I was used to running support groups where people were invited to offer advice and share experiences but here, no-one gave feedback. The woman just carried on talking about how she struggled to accept herself. She barely even mentioned her dad. I didn't get it.

When it came to my turn, I didn't even know what to say.

'Hi, my name is Tracey. I'm not even sure my dad is an alcoholic? I mean he's drank for as long as I can remember, but he's never had a problem with it. As much as he does my head in, I do feel sorry for him. His head's up his arse and he's waiting on this claim, that according to him is going to solve all his problems and now he's just found out his Mum's got cancer. He's always had a bird on his arm. I reckon this is the longest he's been single. He's just not the same Dad I knew a few years ago.'

I waited for a response, but nothing came. All I got was knowing looks and nods, so I continued. 'You see, it's the brandy that's worrying me. He's not long been out of hospital. They were concerned about his liver. Then I find out that my Uncle Mick and his missus had helped Dad detox. I was totally unaware of all this when Dad came back to Sheffield.' Again, silence. I shrugged. 'So basically, I don't know what to do?'

Thankfully, Jean broke the silence.

'Just keep coming back. As affected family members, we have to learn to understand and accept the things we can't change. I know it seems hard, but your dad is on his own journey. What's important is you and how you respond to his behaviour.'

'I know everyone keeps telling me that, but it's hard, especially when it's me who he turns to. He hasn't got anyone who'd got his back! Everyone keeps telling me to leave him to it, but I can't, I just can't.' I could feel the tears bubbling I couldn't stop them. 'All I want is for my life to go back to normal. Honestly, I wished Dad had never come back! I mean, how bad does that sound?'

Jean patted my hand. 'You're entitled to feel a mixture of emotions and that's where Al-anon can help.' She handed me a couple of leaflets to read at home.

Walking towards my car, I mumbled to myself. 'Well that's an hour of my life I ain't gonna get back!' I knew they meant well, but I still wasn't sure how attending these meetings was going to help. Right now, I just wished I'd never answered that fucking phone eighteen months ago.

# 62: Kamikaze Dash

I'd been trying to keep news of my pregnancy low-key, but word had spread around like wildfire. Some mates claimed to be chuffed for me, whilst others thought I was mad.

I could already feel myself excluded from conversations about their future plans, because my freedom and my short-lived independence had been snatched away. All because of my own stupid naivety.

The only saving grace was that Paul was true to his word. He hadn't done a bunk, and if anything, he'd been more attentive and protective than ever. We were like Siamese twins and did everything together.

Paul wanted to be involved at every stage of the pregnancy, and I was more than happy for him to take the lead and to lean into him for support. Soon I was handing my notice in at work and, even though Ada made constant snipes about Paul getting a job, his words were like water off a duck's back. Paul reckoned we'd be better off making a joint benefit claim and getting a start-up grant for essentials when the baby arrived. He reckoned that Mum and Ada should stop interfering, but I knew they had my best interests at heart, and I'd remind Paul that if it hadn't been for them, he'd have been out of the streets. He apologised but it would only be a few days before he started up again.

I still hadn't seen Dad since breaking the news, but I had more important things to be worrying about, like finding a place to live. It turned out Paul had been right, and I was eligible for priority housing status.

The only sticking point was that I would have to present at the housing department in person to explain that Mum was kicking me out. I laid it on thick and cried when I explained about Mum being furious about me becoming pregnant. I could tell she thought that I was just another promiscuous young girl who'd got herself pregnant in an attempt to jump the housing queue. She telephoned Mum whilst I was sitting there to confirm my story. Mum was an even better liar than me. I could hear her raised voice on the other end of the phone as she assertively explained that I had to be out of the family home before the baby arrived.

When I was offered a place, it was at a place called Walkley behind Kelvin Flats, which had a reputation for being rough. It was also just down the road from Dad's taxi firm.

When we arrived, my heart immediately sank. The house on Exley Avenue wasn't at all what I'd been expecting. It was old and reminded me of Nan's house. Like hers, you had to access the back door via a shared gennel. At the end of it, we were greeted by a set of four old toilet blocks, which instantly took me back to being a toddler doing the Kamikaze dash to the bog in the cold when we lived on Alexandra Road when we were toddlers. But Mum joked that we wouldn't have to use it, because the council had recently installed a new bathroom, which was a relief.

Ours was the end terrace. The garden was overgrown, and it appeared the council workmen had forgotten to take their crap with them. The smell of old people hit me as we opened the back door, which led into the kitchen. The wallpaper confirmed that the previous tenants had been really old, and I feared they might have even died in the house. There were large chunks of bare brick in the kitchen where cupboards had once been and an open pantry that sat underneath the staircase with a trap door that led to a cellar that resembled a dungeon.

The living room was bare. It had a new gas fire, but that was it. Upstairs, there was a bedroom and bathroom and a flight of creepy stairs to the attic, which Mum suggested could be the baby's room.

The whole lot would need stripping, papering, painting and new carpets throughout. I couldn't see beyond the smell or the walls, but for once, Paul and Mum agreed, they both thought it had potential.

Mum also said that the council had offered us a grant to help decorate and that if we stuck to using some cheap blown vinyl, we might be able to have enough to get some cheap cord carpet laid. But I wasn't convinced. It was nothing like Michelle's large, airy place, and Paul could tell I wasn't impressed. He wrapped his arms around my waist and stroked my stomach.

'Come on, Trace. This is cosy. It'll be plenty big enough for the three of us.'

I looked down at my belly. I had finally started to show. I felt like I should be excited, but the reality that I was going to be a Mum in only a few months scared the shit out of me. Everything was happening so fast, and I wasn't sure if I was ready to be a Mum and all the responsibilities that came with it. But the reality was, I didn't have a choice.

I didn't have a choice about my new home either. This was the only offer the council had been prepared to make, so the following day, we signed up.

# 65: Wide Berth

I'd tried giving Dad a wide berth, but it was hard. He was still calling at least three times a day. I attempted to keep conversations brief and tried to not take his moods personally, because I knew it was the drink talking.

One minute, he seemed reasonable but then if something didn't go his way, he turned into a petulant teenager I couldn't count the number of times he'd put the phone down on me accusing me of not listening and I was sick to the back teeth of hearing him using Nan's ill health as an excuse to drink.

The worst was when he'd call for no other apparent reason, just to talk. It was these calls that tugged at my heart strings. I could hear the loneliness down the phone. Where I'd once felt grateful that, after all these years, Dad was confiding in me and telling me that he trusted me, lately it was becoming a burden. What was worse was I felt like a fraud. I felt like I should know what to do and say. For fuck's sakes, I'd been supporting families in similar situations for the past couple of years and yet I found it hard to practice what I preached.

I would encourage the family members to educate themselves about addiction. I'd be going through the cycle of change with them, explaining the different stages, but I didn't need educating. I knew full well that Dad was stuck in the denial stage. According to him, he didn't have a problem and that he could handle his drinking. I knew at this rate; it would take something serious to happen before he'd even consider his drinking a problem.

The small bottle of brandy I had agreed to buy for him weeks before was still playing heavily on my mind. Had it been my fault that he was on the hard stuff? Uncle Mick had warned me about the top shelf, but just that time, I hadn't listened. But he could have been drinking it before that, and it wasn't like he didn't have the cash. He could have asked one of his so-called mates to get it for him. They were still hanging around, taking what they could from him, and he didn't see it. It felt like I was the only one who could see what was happening and the only person who knew that, behind all the bravado, Dad was hurting and in a bad place. Everyone else was sick of listening. I knew, deep-down, that Dad didn't deserve any sympathy. I mean, no-one was forcing him to drink. Still, a little compassion wouldn't have gone amiss.

It was hard staying away, but I knew that I had no control over his drinking, and this was something that Dad would have to figure out for himself. All I could do was be there when he was ready, but in the meantime, I just needed to back off and leave him to wallow a little more until he came to his senses.

# 66: All Hands on Deck

I'd called Dad to let him know we'd been offered a place just down the road from his taxi firm, and he'd promised to pop in to see the place. Meanwhile, it was all hands on deck. Well, my family's hands; Paul's mum just called round to have a nosey but didn't offer to get stuck into help or offer any support.

Mum had already been out to the hardware store and bought some scrapers, for the stripping; she'd bought buckets and sponges and loads of much-needed bleach. She'd also bought us a kettle as a housewarming gift and put a box together, filled with cups, teaspoons and coffee and milk. Unlike Paul, I was happy to take direction from Mum about where we should start, after all, she had far more experience than us.

After expertly showing us how to score the walls and dampen the wallpaper with a wet sponge, we all set about stripping the rooms. It was exhausting work. There were layers upon layers of paper to cut through but by the end of the weekend, we had all managed to do the whole ground floor.

The next week, me and Paul spent full days stripping the rest of the house. As soon as the walls had been stripped, Paul cracked on with painting the skirting boards and doors and by the following weekend, all that was left to do was to blast the whole house with some cheap blown vinyl.

One of Mum's friends was getting new carpets fitted and was throwing her old one out, so we used that for the living room and carpeted the rest of the house in cheap cord. Mum's friends gave us bits and bobs, and Nan even agreed to buy us a cooker. I had insisted that we had a phone installed I needed a lifeline to Mum. Dad still hadn't called in but I gave him the number anyway.

It wasn't perfect, or how I'd envisioned my first home, but it gradually started to take shape and after a couple of weeks and hard graft, we finally moved in. It wasn't that long ago that I'd been skating around the Silver Blades ice rink without a care in the world and now here I was, sitting on a sofa, sharing my first night in my new home with a guy I'd only known for a few months, whilst carrying his unborn child.

Paul was engrossed watching a TV programme, but I wasn't listening or watching, because I was trying to digest the past two months. I was still only sixteen, but to the outside world, I was officially a grown-up; me and Paul were like an old married couple. I looked over at Paul, who was laughing at something on the TV, oblivious to the thoughts going around in my head.

He could be loving and attentive, but he could also get paranoid, jealous and moody. Sometimes I wondered if we'd even still be together if I'd not got pregnant. Nothing in my life seemed to go right.

'Hey, what's up? Aren't you watching this?' Paul snapped me out of my daydream. 'Come here.' Paul gestured for me to snuggle up beside him. I moved over, and he wrapped his arms around me.

'Isn't this perfect, eh, just you and me?'

'Yeah.'

I berated myself for having any doubts, because I knew that he had my back. Now it was me and him and our unborn child against the world. All the ifs, buts and maybes didn't matter anymore, because this was happening whether I liked it or not. Nan was right, the fact was, I'd made my bed now and it was time to lie in it.

# 67: Northern General

I was just about to go into a family support meeting when I got the call. The meeting was a big deal; I had all the support group leaders around to discuss the next steps for the Family Support Forum.

'Hi. Is this Tracey Ford?'

I felt like someone had just punched me in the stomach. 'Yes, who's this?'

The woman must have sensed my anxiety. 'Hi, love. It's nothing to worry about. It's ya dad. He's had a fall and hurt his hip. He was brought into hospital last night. He was rather intoxicated when he was brought in, so the doctors wanted to keep him overnight just for observations. There's no fracture, but he's going to be sore for a while. Your dad has given me your number, to see if you could come and collect him.'

I was tempted to jump into the car and drop everything, but then I remembered what someone had said in the support groups about rescuing. I quickly assessed the situation. This wasn't an emergency. Dad could wait.

'Look, I can come and collect him, but it won't be for another couple of hours.'

'No, no that's fine, there's no rush. He's on Huntsman 2.'

Joy had just finished going through the minutes from the previous meeting when I made it into the meeting. I reassured her that I was okay to continue, and we carried on. Perhaps a couple of hours' wait would give him time to think about his drinking.

The afternoon's meeting went really well, though I found it pretty ironic that I was in a meeting surrounded by family support advocates and yet couldn't share my concerns. Dad was always there at the back of my mind. I looked around the room. Everyone there had a unique bond.

I'd always had the utmost respect and admiration for the families I'd been working with. I'd often questioned whether I would have had the same resilience to go through some of the shit they'd been through. In my eyes, they were the real, unseen victims of addiction – they weren't injecting drugs, and yet they felt every single consequence.

I was thinking about the conversations we'd had as I drove to the Northern General. It had taken me over half an hour to finally find a parking spot before making my way to the ward to locate Dad, but first, I wanted to speak to one of the nurses. Dad wasn't going to blag himself out of this one. I managed to get a hold of the nurse who'd called me earlier.

'Hiya, love. You come to fetch Frank?'

'Yeah, I'm Tracey. Could I have a word with you before, please?'

'Yes, of course. I wanted to catch you anyway. Let's talk over here.' She winked. 'Out of the eyeshot of your dad. Ok, so apparently your dad was in quite a tangle last night.'

'You mean pissed?'

She smiled apologetically, but she needed have. 'The doctors are more than happy with his hip, but they were concerned about your dad's stomach. They've run some tests and put in a referral to the Hallamshire.'

'He's been waiting for an appointment for his arms. Is this the same thing?'

'His liver function was abnormal.'

I told her about the last time he'd been in hospital and that he'd been drinking a lot more of late, especially the brandy.

'Look, I know it's not my place, but it might be worth having another chat about his drinking.'

'I've tried, but according to him he hasn't got a problem. He's in total denial. I know how it works. I work in the addiction field – Christ, the team I work in commission the alcohol services.' It sounded ridiculous when I said it out loud.

'It might be an idea to give them a call,' she said.

I thanked the nurse and made my way to Dad.

‘Thank fuck you’re here! What took you so long? Been sat here waiting for hours.’

‘Er, it’s called work, Dad.’

‘Sorry to have put you out.’

‘Forget about it. How’s the hip?’

Dad pulled down his trousers. ‘It’s fucking sore. Look, it’s black.’

‘So how did it happen? Who called the ambulance?

‘One of the lads. I told ‘em not to bother, silly twats. I fell in’t taking a piss. To be fair, I couldn’t get up. It’s just bruised, that’s all.’

At least his so-called mates had done something right!

‘Were you pissed?’

‘Nah, honest Trace, I’d just had the usual. Look just get me out of here, will ya. I fucking hate these places.’

It was dark when we finally arrived at Dad’s. Sarah had agreed to meet us there and I parked behind her car.

‘What’s our Sarah doing here?’ Dad seemed confused.

‘I didn’t know If I might need some help.’

‘I’m not a fucking cripple, tha knows.’

‘I didn’t say you were, did I? Look, let’s just get you inside, eh?’

I didn’t have much patience left. I’d had no thank you! So, I left Dad to manoeuvre himself out of the car, the stubborn old git. He headed straight for the living room to sit in his usual spot. I was just about to go and find Sarah when she came from behind me.

‘Looking for this?’ she asked, waving a half empty bottle of brandy.

‘Fuck me! I’ve only just sat down. Give it a rest, will ya?’

‘Give it a rest! I haven’t stopped since I got here, this place was a bleeding tip. I’ve got enough on me plate cleaning me own house without cleaning up after you an all, and this isn’t going to help, is it?’ I could sense a row brewing.

‘Look, look I know you’re pissed off at me.’ Dad snapped back. ‘Can you leave the lecture for another time, eh?’

Sarah dropped the bottle. 'I'm just making a brew. anyone want one?'

'Yeah, go on then, leave the tea bag in too, that hospital tea is like piss.'

I sat on the sofa with Dad and tried to talk to him about how worried we were about his drinking, and about what the nurse had said, but he didn't want to know.

Sarah came in with the drinks. She handed Dad his mug of tea before sitting in the other armchair. Dad took a drink of his tea, then looked up to Sarah. 'And don't look at me like that neither.'

Sarah shrugged. 'I'm not looking nowt at thee, Dad.'

He placed his mug on the coffee table and started to roll a fag. 'Look I know I have been hammering it, but I have had good reason, what with ya Nan and all that, but I promise ya both I'm knocking the Brandy on the head for a while.'

'So does that mean I can pour what's left down the sink then?'

Dad looked nonchalant. 'Tha can do what ya want. Told ya both before I can stop whenever I want.'

I thought about what the nurse had said. 'Look, Dad I can make a referral for ya into the alcohol service if you like.'

Dad smiled. 'There's no way you'll get me into one of them groups sat wi a load of saddos saying hi my names Frank and I'm an alcoholic, nah fuck that!'

I laughed. 'Dad, you don't have to do that. I could arrange for you to see an alcohol worker. They could even help with prescribing you something, to help with the cravings.'

'Thanks, shugs. I know ya mean well, but honestly, I'm good. I just need a good kip. I promise ya. This time next week, I'll be reet as rain.'

'Famous last words,' I thought, as I kissed him goodnight and left him with his denial. I knew it wasn't my fault he was drinking but that didn't stop me feeling responsible.

# 68: Dress Ring from Argos

Me and Paul soon settled into a routine. We did everything together, including the household chores. Money was tight. Mum and Ada had offered to drive us for a big shop at Morrisons, but Paul wasn't having any of it, continuing to interpret Mum's suggestions as interference. Meanwhile, his own mother did fuck all to help us out and Dad was nowhere to be seen.

Unlike Mum and Dad, there was no pressure for us to get married, but sometimes I wanted to get engaged, not for romantic reasons but because I couldn't shrug off the judgemental stares from strangers when they looked at my growing bump. I knew what they were thinking, that I was another silly young girl who'd got herself pregnant to jump the housing queue.

Finally, we saved up seventeen pounds to get me a dress ring from Argos. It wasn't how I imagined getting engaged, but it did the job. When we weren't on the bus visiting family, we spent our time window shopping in town, fantasising about things we could never afford. On a couple of occasions, Paul shoplifted something we'd been looking at. He thought it was a thoughtful gesture, but I was furious. The last thing we both needed was for him to have a criminal record. If we ran out of money, I'd have to sheepishly go and ask Mum or Nan for a small loan, which I hated.

Two months after moving in, we'd had settled in for the night watching TV in our PJs when there was a heavy knock at the back door.

'Come on! Open up! It's freezing out here!' a voice bellowed from outside.

Paul scurried around the living room trying to tidy up, whilst I went to answer the door to Dad, who looked like one of the Kray twins in a long Crombie coat.

'Aren't tha gonna invite me in then?'

I smiled. 'Yeah, sure, sorry Dad.' I stepped back to let him in.

'Where's the man of the moment then?'

On cue, Paul appeared from the living room, looking nervous. This was the first time we had both seen him face to face since Mum broke the news.

'Alright, Frank.'

'Aye. I'm better nah I've seen tha hasn't done one.'

Paul came up behind me, protectively placing his arms around my shoulder. 'I'm not going anywhere, Frank, I love her.'

Dad looked down towards my belly. 'I still can't fucking believe my babby is havin' a babby. I'd have loved to have been a fly on the wall when ya nan found out. How's the old hag doing?'

I offered Dad a cuppa.

'Nah, I'm not stopping – just thought I'd see how ya settling in.' He was eying the decorating. 'Ya know what would look good is some suspended ceilings. I'm having 'em fitted in the video shop. Can get them to do yours after, shouldn't take 'em too long?'

'What video shop?'

'Oh, have you not heard?' He sounded surprised, which was ironic because I'd barely spoken to him. 'It's on Langsett road. Video USA next to Morrisons – ya can't miss it.'

Paul jumped in, all impressed. 'Is that yours? We've walked past it loads.'

'Gonna be a reyt little gold mine,' said Dad, rubbing his hands together.

Dad clocked the Betamax video player that one of Mum's mates had donated to us. 'They're gonna be extinct soon. I can sort ya a VHS one out if tha wants?'

'Ah Dad, that would be ace.' I was so happy that he was being so supportive.

'Give me a couple of days. I'll get one of the taxi drivers to drop it off. And you can rent as many films out as you want for nowt. Not the new releases, mind!'

I went over to give Dad a hug. 'Thanks, Dad and thanks for calling round. It means a lot.'

'You can thank me by naming me first-born grandson after me.' He said like he was making a joke, but it made me wonder again if he'd have preferred me to be a boy.

'We'll be sure to consider it,' Paul smiled.

'Reyt, I'd better be off. Borrow those films when you like.'

I went to give Dad another hug. 'Thanks, Dad.'

'No need to thank me, it's what us Dads do, innit?' He winked at Paul and reached to shake his hand, only he didn't let go. 'Just you make sure you look after her alreyt, or you'll have me to answer to.'

Paul smiled. 'I promise, Frank, I'll take care of her.' Paul saw him out and closed the door behind him. I was relieved that it had gone so well, but my relief was short-lived.

'Well, he's got a nerve 'an't he! Coming round here, demanding we call the baby after him. If owt, it'll be called after me. Cheeky git!'

'It's just his way. And he did offer to get us the ceiling done and get a new video player.'

'What if I don't want a new ceiling?'

I could feel my hackles rising. 'Well, you should have said something then! Don't start kicking off now he's gone!'

Paul was getting good at this. He'd never say anything to anyone's face, but as soon as their back was turned, he'd start sniping. He had more fucking faces than Worzel Gummidge.

We didn't speak for the rest of the night. I hated feeling stuck in the middle, constantly having to apologise for my family, especially after all they had done for us.

I'd even considered ending the relationship, but I couldn't, because I had nowhere to go and a mardy, ungrateful bastard didn't seem like a valid reason to leave; it wasn't like he'd hit me or cheated on me. The reality was, I was stuck and somehow, I needed to swallow my pride and hope that things would work out.

In the end, Paul managed to win me around and the argument was laid to rest. True to his word, two days after

Dad's impromptu visit, a taxi driver knocked on the back door with a VHS player.

A week later, despite Paul's initial complaints, he welcomed the workmen who'd arrived to install our suspended ceilings in the kitchen. All we had to do know was wait for the baby to come.

# 69: New Territory

Dad was starting to look ill. He was gaunt, and he'd stopped taking pride in his appearance. When I phoned, it seemed like he was always hammered, and I could hear his mates in the background.

To say I was pissed off was an understatement. I knew Dad was lonely and I could see that he was struggling but I couldn't help feeling let down. I'd tried my best, but clearly it wasn't enough. I'd always had his back, when everyone around me had written him off. I'd rallied around him, tried to support him, not just practically, but emotionally too. He knew how worried we had been about him and yet he still continued to drink.

I called Uncle Mick, hoping he could make Dad see sense, but apparently Dad had told him to fuck off and to mind his own business.

'It's like he's pressed the self-destruct button, Trace. I'd leave him to it; he'll see sense soon enough.' I was hoping he was right, but I also couldn't help thinking that it was easy for Mick to say, when he was miles away. There was absolutely nothing I could do and despite being surrounded by people who loved me, I'd never felt so alone.

I reached out, in confidence, to Giz Sangher, one of the consultants at one of the treatment providers we commissioned and was on the phone to her for over an hour. I went through everything.

She explained that Dad really needed to make the planned appointment at the Hallamshire and that I was right to be concerned. According to her, frequent hospital admissions were common with people with drink problems.

Having a medical professional on my side helped reassure me that I wasn't overreacting and she'd confirmed what I already knew already – that there wasn't much I could do unless Dad was willing to accept support. She did say that, when he was ready, she'd be more than happy to do an assessment with Dad herself, which was a relief. I'd already told her about how difficult and stubborn Dad could be, but she reassured me that she'd worked with worse.

In some ways, talking to Giz helped lift a heavy weight, but she also got me questioning myself. I fully understood that Dad was in denial about his drinking, but it was now clear that I'd been in denial myself. Despite what Uncle Mick had told me about how bad Dad had been before coming back to Sheffield and despite what I already knew about addiction, somehow, I hadn't been able to accept that my dad was an alcoholic.

I knew, deep-down, that there was absolutely nothing I could do to stop Dad drinking, not until he came to the decision himself. I would just have to step back and leave him to it. But I was still terrified. His inability to see how his drinking was changing him scared me. This was new territory for me, and I wasn't sure I was up for it.

# 70: You Are NOT Allowed in This Room

My due date came and went. I'd tried everything: eating hot curries and helping Ada out at the school buffing the floors, but nothing happened. Two weeks later, my induction day arrived. I'd decided to go to the hospital alone as the staff reckoned it would be a few hours before I started in labour, let alone give birth.

Everyone else was planning on calling up during visiting hours later. I had a small suitcase with a couple of new nighties Mum had bought me, some toiletries and a selection of white baby grows as I still didn't know the sex of the baby. Deep-down, I was hoping for a boy. Boys had it far better than girls and I knew Dad would have loved a grandson.

There were two other women on the ward. I was the youngest. I smiled, hoping to make a connection, but they weren't interested in me. They were first time mothers too, but I could tell from the way they talked about all the preparations they'd made that both of theirs had been planned pregnancies.

A nurse called Louise came round and drew the curtains around the bed. It was time to insert the suppository which apparently would help start the contractions. She left me with my thoughts as I waited for the suppository to kick in. Nine months ago, I could never have predicted that I'd be here, waiting to be a mother. I was living with a guy I was still getting to know and responsible for running a house. How the fuck had that happened? But the reality was it had happened, and I was going to be a mother whether I liked it or not.

An hour had passed before I started to get stomach cramps. They weren't too bad at first, but as the hours passed, the pain intensified. I asked Louisa for some pain relief, and she returned with two paracetamols. I looked at her gone out.

'Are you kidding me?' I said. 'Can't I have some of that gas and air?'

She smiled sympathetically and explained that I could have some of that later. I wasn't impressed.

As soon as Mum popped her head around the curtain at visiting hours, I started to cry. Paul rushed to the other side of the bed, whilst Ada stood at the bottom. My little brother Mark jumped on the bed, wanting to play with the food trolly, asking how long it would be before he became an uncle.

Mum shushed him. 'How are you doing, love?'

'They have started, Mum. It's agony and they won't give me nothing stronger than paracetamol! It hasn't done a thing!'

'Told ya,' said Ada, rubbing his back. 'I reckon I'm coming out in sympathy pains.'

Mum laughed. 'He's been complaining all morning.' She turned back to me. 'How far gone are you? Have they said?'

'Only two centimetres!'

Ada smiled sympathetically. 'Ahh well, you had better hurry up, love, cos I don't reckon I can take this much longer.'

'Have they said how long then, Trace?' I could tell Paul was excited.

Mum interjected before I could answer. 'This baby will come when it's good and ready.'

The next thing I knew, I could feel something warm around my bum.

Mum saw my face change. 'What's up, love?'

'I think I've just peed myself,' I said, embarrassed. My little brother laughed.

'Trace, you haven't peed yourself, love. Your waters will have broken.' She pressed the buzzer to call for a nurse. 'Well, there's no going back now, love. Don't worry, it won't be long now'.

It was another eight hours before the staff moved me to my own room. I must have walked miles, pacing the hospital corridor, trying to take my mind off the pain.

I needed my own space where I could cry without looking like a wimp. Then it was time for the nursing staff to change shifts. I was gutted; I'd been hoping that Louisa would have been there to help me give birth, but I'd only dilated another two centimetres, and her shift was finishing. She introduced me to Maggie, the new nurse, and wished me luck, promising to call back to see me the following day.

'Right, poppet,' said Maggie. 'Let's see if this baby has moved.' And she didn't mess about. I wriggled in agony as Maggie prodded about. I wanted Louisa back.

But when Maggie had finished and announced that I was now eight centimetres dilated, I was ecstatic. I was even more ecstatic when she offered me some pethidine to help with the contractions. I decided I liked Maggie after all.

I wanted to start pushing, but Maggie insisted I wasn't ready, explaining I would have to wait until I was ten centimetres dilated. My sister had called the hospital to check on my progress and to also let me know she'd managed to get a hold of Dad to tell him I was in labour.

It was about eleven o'clock when Maggie decided that it was time to try pushing. Mum and Paul were stood opposite each other, encouraging me to push. I was convinced I was pooing myself, but after two hours of pushing, nothing was happening.

I was exhausted. All I wanted to do was sleep. Soon, a doctor was there, explaining that they would be moving me to the theatre, just as a precaution. The only problem was that they would only allow one person at a time in the theatre. Panic set in. I was worried that something was wrong and for a moment I feared that I might lose my baby, and I wasn't alone. Paul was freaking out, pacing the room and crying.

The only person who seemed to be keeping it together was Mum. I was writhing in agony; the contractions were only seconds apart. I even wondered if I might die, but Mum reassured me that I wasn't going anywhere.

Soon, I was being wheeled down to theatre. Paul walked alongside the trolly stroking my hand, but all I wanted was Mum.

'Oh, by the way,' said Maggie. 'Your sister just called. Sounded like she was in a nightclub?'

Sarah wasn't even old enough to go to clubs yet, but I just shrugged it off because my priority was to get this baby out.

I'd sworn I wasn't going to have an epidural but at this point I'd have done anything.

Maggie sat by my side, solid as steel and stroked my back, whilst the doctor inserted the needle into my spine. I had to stay deathly still. 'It's going to be fine, poppet, you've got this, you're doing great,' said Maggie. I loved it when she called me poppet.

Having the epidural wasn't as bad as I'd expected, in fact I wished I'd had it sooner. After ten minutes, the contractions finally began to ease and I could breathe, but more importantly, sleep. I was knackered and at this point, I could hardly keep my eyes open.

At first, I thought I was dreaming. I could hear Dad's voice as clear as day. It was getting louder, and I could tell he was angry. I felt dazed and for a second forgot where I was and found myself wracking my brains trying to recall what I might have done wrong.

'Try fucking stopping me! That's my daughter in there!'

Then I heard Maggie. 'You are NOT allowed in this room. I'm sorry, Mr Ford, if you don't leave, I am going to have to call the police.'

'Fucking call 'em!' he raged.

I could hear Mum. 'Look Frank, calm down. Tracey's doing ok.'

I soon realised that it wasn't a dream and that Dad was there; this was really happening. He looked like a giant as he stood over me, stroking my hair with one hand and stroking my hand with the other. I could smell stale smoke and aftershave.

'Dad, is that really you? What time is it?'

'Don't you worry about the time. How ya doing?'

Mum was at the other side of the bed. It seemed weird seeing them both there together.

'And where's he?' He was referring to Paul.

'You've just missed him, he's just gone out for some fresh air,' said Mum.

'Good fucking job!' He took a deep breath, 'Cos when I get me hands on the dirty bastard!' Look what he did to ar Trace!'

I squeezed Dad's hand. 'Dad, look. I'm ok.'

'I'm sorry, Mr Ford. I've called the police.' It was Maggie.

'AND!' Dad didn't flinch. 'This is my first grandkid. You just try getting me to fucking leave.'

Mum tried to reason with him, but he wasn't having any of it. Whilst it felt nice that Dad cared so much, I wasn't sure about him being there whilst I gave birth.

It wasn't long before a police officer arrived in the theatre. Dad agreed to go outside to talk with them and Mum followed him. I could hear raised voices outside and then Paul and Maggie came back into the room.

'What's happening? Have they arrested Dad?'

'No, poppet, ya Dad's outside with ya Mum. He's calmed down now. We've agreed that he can wait outside on the condition your mum stays with him.' She smiled. 'They can come back in when you have finished delivering this well overdue baby.'

I was embarrassed and ashamed about the way Dad had spoken to Maggie; he'd been horrid. I felt I didn't deserve her smile, not after all the compassion and support she'd given me for the past few hours.

It was four am on the 8th of September 1987 that my daughter made an appearance, weighing in at a healthy 8lbs, 2 oz. Mum had been right. As soon as I held my baby, I forgot all about the pain. She was perfect and looked just like Paul, with the most perfect black hair and blue eyes.

As soon as the doctors had finished stitching me up, they allowed Mum and Dad in the theatre. Dad stormed in front, heading straight over to the bed.

'You've just missed the sarnis!' he said, 'I had one of the taxi drivers fetch me and thee Mum some snap! It's been a big night. I were out clubbing!'

Then it made sense. It wasn't our Sarah who'd called, but one of Dad's birds!

Dad went straight over to the crib, where my baby was sleeping. 'She's a looker, ar Trace.' Dad smiled, drinking her all in.

Mum gave me a hug. 'It's been a long night, eh love. I bet you're bloody shattered.' She turned her attention to the crib. 'Do you mind?' She gestured, wanting to pick up her first grandchild.

'Of course not, Mum.'

'8lbs 2oz, that's a good weight that, Trace.'

Mum was right. She was perfect. 'Are you ok, Mum?'

'Well, that will certainly be a night I won't forget in a hurry!' Mum joked and then she looked down at the baby. 'I am now' she cooed.

'So, have you decided on a name then?' asked Dad.

Me and Paul had already both decided on Danielle, and we'd agreed to give her the middle name, Francis, after Dad.

His face lit up. 'Ahhh really, that's sweet.' I could tell he was disappointed that I hadn't had a precious boy. 'Better luck next time, eh.'

'You are joking me, aren't ya Dad? I'm never doing this again, EVER,' and I meant it.

The family left, and soon it was just me, Danielle and Maggie who came in, armed with some toast and a cup of tea.

Dad had said that he'd apologised to her, but I was still embarrassed about how he'd spoken to her. I apologised again to Maggie, but she wasn't having any of it.

'Listen, poppet, don't you be worrying about me. It will take more than the likes of ya Dad to intimidate me.' I believed her.

I couldn't stop staring at my baby. She was perfect, and despite wanting a boy throughout the pregnancy, part of me was relieved she was a girl. I mean let's face it, one Frank Ford was enough.

# 71: I Didn't Mean What I Said

It was a Saturday afternoon, and I'd just finished ironing all the holiday clothes ready for a trip to Newquay when my mum and sister called in unannounced. They were off on an impromptu shopping trip and had called to see if I wanted to join them. I couldn't think of anything worse. Pat and the kids would be out for the rest of the day, and I just wanted to be alone.

I'd decided I could no longer collude with Dad's refusal to stop drinking so I hadn't seen him for a while, but he was on my mind all the time. Though I was trying to carry on as normal, inside I was hurting. This wasn't a man drowning his sorrows at his own pity party; this was serious. The only problem was that I was the only one taking it seriously. I was like a ticking time bomb of dread, fear, anger, shame and hopelessness about to erupt. And Sarah lit the fuse.

'Come on, Sis! It'll be a laugh. We haven't done anything together for ages.'

I knew she meant well but I really didn't share her enthusiasm. 'Honestly, Sarah. I'm really not up for it. I've had a manic week at work and what with Dad...'

'Are you still flapping about him? I've told ya leave him to it, he's not worth it! Come on, come with us you know you want too.'

And then it happened. The emotional volcano erupted. I started pacing the living room.

'It's fucking ok for you, isn't it! You have every right to hate him. I know he's treated you like shit and that you've always thought I'm the favourite, the chosen one, but I wish I fucking wasn't! It's not you who he's calling every two minutes, is it?'

Mum came rushing into the living room with the drinks she'd been making.

'Hey. What's going off?'

But I was on a roll.

'And there's no point coming to you, is there?' I directed my anger at Mum. 'You've always wanted Dad out of our lives! It's not my fault you married a bastard and had a kid with him! You got to walk away, but we didn't.'

I could tell she was hurt, but my pain was overwhelming. 'No... It's me, fucking muggins, the one who's always dropped everything for him, his fucking puppet. I wish I could just walk away, but I fucking can't. It's like he's got this hold over me and I feel like I'm choking. No-one else gives a fuck! I'm sick of being there for everyone, pretending to be strong, when I'm not! I'm not! I'm not fucking coping!'

The anger had finally been released, making way for the hurt and pain I'd been bottling up for what seemed like a lifetime. I sat and sobbed. I hadn't had an outburst like this since Middlewood, years earlier, and it scared me.

Sarah edged herself round to where I was sitting and placed her arms around my shoulder.

'Ah Trace, I'm really sorry. I didn't realise it was that bad.'

'It's worse than bad, Sarah. He's a fucking alcoholic. This isn't going to go away, ya know. I know how it works. I've sat in enough support groups and I've seen the impact. The worst part is, he doesn't get it, he just doesn't fucking get how bad he is.'

I could feel the tears brewing again and broke down.

'I'm losing it! I don't think I can do this.'

I could sense the silence in the room. Trying to compose myself, I looked at Mum.

'I'm sorry. I didn't mean what I said.'

She put the drinks down and spoke.

'Yes, you did and it's ok. I get it! I know first-hand just how difficult your dad can be. You can always come and talk to me.'

I knew she meant well, but I would never burden her with Dad. Dad was in her past for a reason, and I knew there were some wounds, memories that were still raw; memories I knew she still hadn't healed from.

Sarah interjected. 'Listen, I'm here for you and you *are not* on your own, do you hear me? And don't you worry about Dad whilst you are away. You need a break, so I'm taking over.'

I heard her, loud and clear and for the first time in months, I didn't feel alone.

'Right, when's his next appointment?'

# 72: 200 Fags and Four Cans of Lager

The baby was perfect with her little button nose, dark skin and dark hair which brought her blue eyes alive. My heart skipped a beat when she wrapped her tiny fingers around my finger whilst suckling on my breasts, which felt like two cannonballs.

Even though I felt awkward feeding her on the ward now I'd been moved, Danielle took to feeding easily. The nurse showed me how to burp her before switching sides and seemed satisfied with my ability to feed my baby.

After feeding, the nurse watched over me whilst I changed her nappy for the first time. I was all fingers and thumbs and part of me wished I'd changed more of my brother's nappies when he was younger.

It was a couple of hours before visiting hours, the nurse suggested that I take the opportunity to have a bath in plain warm water, to help soothe the twenty plus stitches that I'd acquired during my labour. I was just about off the bed when Dad popped his head around the curtain again.

'Ey up, chick.'

I couldn't believe it. Were there no rules that applied to Dad?

'Hi, Dad. You do know it's not visiting hours yet, don't you?' I was surprised the staff had even let him in after his antics the previous night!

'Ah, they're reyt! Told 'em I've got a business to run and an important meeting, so they let me pop in for five minutes. Here, I brought you these.'

Dad passed me a carrier bag containing a packet of two hundred fags and four cans of larger.

'Cheers, Dad,' I laughed, packing the carrier into a cupboard so the staff didn't see.

Dad headed straight over to Danielle's crib. 'She is a belter, Trace.'

My heart swelled seeing Dad gushing over my child and I wondered if he'd been the same with me as a baby.

'Look, I didn't get nowt for this little one, but I've got Tracey on the case. Oh, she sends her love, by the way.'

I wondered if she also knew about Dad being out with other birds the night before, but thought better of it.

'Like I said I can't stay long. Just I wanted to pop in. I'll be out later, wetting baby's head, but I thought I'd treat you, seeing as it's you what's done the hard work.'

I laughed.

'Dad, I can't even drink anyway. I'm breastfeeding.' Not to mention being only sixteen.

'Ahh, well, save 'em for when you get home. Anyway, I'd best be off.' He came over to give me a peck on the forehead. 'Give us a call when you get out, ok.' And with that he was gone.

I couldn't remember the last time Dad had kissed me. All I knew was it felt nice. And even though his presents weren't exactly appropriate, it had been the most thoughtful thing Dad had ever done for me. I wondered if this baby might just be the glue that brought us together.

Paul was one of the first visitors to arrive after I'd finally had my bath. After giving me a kiss, he walked over to the crib and stroked the baby's head gently.

'How's she been?'

I told him about my first attempts at breastfeeding and my unexpected visitor.

'Is he taking the piss?'

I looked around the room to check that none of the mothers or staff had heard him.

'Look, he didn't stay long...'

Paul cut me off before I could finish. 'I'm serious, Trace. Fancy fetching you some fags? You're not going to start smoking again and you don't even drink!'

I didn't like his tone.

'Who said anything about smoking? I can't help it that Dad bought them. I didn't ask for 'em,' I hissed. 'But if I do decide to have a fag, I will!'

'Well not in front of my baby, you won't!'

Now he was really starting to piss me off.

'I can't believe you would even think I would!'

'I'm still mad about your dad turning up last night.'

'Look, can we forget about Dad? I'm too tired to fight.' And I was, emotionally and physically. 'I just want to get out of here. Just a couple of days at Mum's so I can get into a routine, and then we'll be home.'

'I've been thinking about that. I don't see the point now. You said yourself that you're doing ok. I reckon we should take Danielle straight home with us.'

I shook my head in disbelief. Going to Mum's for a couple of days had been planned for months. I was too exhausted to fight, but I wasn't shifting on this.

'No Paul, you can do what you want, but I'm staying at Mum's. I'm shattered. We're gonna need all the help we can get! Her crib and everything is there already.'

He huffed heavily. I could tell he wasn't happy, then he noticed her hospital wrist band.

'How come she's called Ford on here?'

I was confused and at first, I wasn't sure what he was talking about.

'What do you mean?'

'This.' He pointed at her wrist. 'I thought we'd agreed that she'd take my surname.'

'It doesn't matter. She'll soon have your surname when we register her.'

I could tell he wasn't happy, but I wasn't about to get the staff to change it, after all it was only a tag.

Thankfully, his mood soon changed as soon as he held her in his arms. He was grinning like a Cheshire cat.

'She's beautiful, int she, Trace? I reckon she just looks like me.'

I couldn't deny it, she did. My heart melted watching him hold our new-born child and I knew right there and then that he wasn't going anywhere.

# 73: Cancer

The holiday was just what the doctor ordered, and Sarah had been true to her word, popping in to check on Dad, giving me some much-needed time to recharge my depleted batteries.

Sarah had made sure he'd attended his appointment at the Hallamshire but, as he'd insisted on going in alone, we were still very much in the dark about what was actually wrong with him.

When I'd tried to call the hospital, patient confidentiality had prohibited them from talking to me, so, as soon as I was home, I called round to see Dad.

Although I'd been away from Dad, it hadn't stopped me thinking about him. I'd accepted that he was an alcoholic, but I still felt powerless. I'd already made a pledge with myself that I wouldn't buy him drink, but he didn't need me for that anyway; the interim payments from the solicitors meant he had a steady supply of money coming in.

Meanwhile, he was still bugging me about chasing the claim. Sometimes it felt like he'd put his life on hold waiting for the big payout. At this rate, he'd be fucking dead before they paid up.

I was glad Dad's divvy mates were nowhere to be seen when I arrived.

Dad looked pleased to see me. 'Ey up, shugs. How did the holiday go then?'

As I went in to give him a kiss, I couldn't help noticing the residue of cola in the dried cracks of his lips.

'So how ya feeling?'

'I'll feel a lot better once this fucking claim's sorted. Have you spoke to them today? What have they said?'

I took a deep breath. 'Look, Dad I have spoken to them. They've got your medical records now...'

Dad cut me off before I could finish. 'I still don't understand what my medical records have got to do with this claim – a fucking waste of time, if ya ask me!'

Dad started to pour himself another drink.

I could feel myself getting more and more angry, until I snapped.

'I'm not being funny, Dad, but that ain't helping, is it?'

'Look don't you start, I'm sick of you and your sister coming around here, fucking preaching.' He took a long slug of his brandy and Coke. 'Look, I've got fucking cancer, ok.'

His words stunned me, and I wondered if I'd heard him right. 'What do you mean you've got cancer? When did you hear about this?'

'Ya know, that hospital appointment! You know the one *you* insisted I go to? It was fuck all to do with my drinking – they were testing for cancer. You happy now?'

'Dad, I don't know what to say. Have they said how long? How bad is it?'

'Look I don't wanna talk about it, ok, just leave me be.'

I took that as my cue, I knew not to push any further.

'Look I'm sorry for snapping, shugs. You get yourself off home and I'll speak to ya tomorrow, eh.'

I closed the door on Dad's flat. I didn't want to leave. I wanted to be there for him. I couldn't help feeling guilty that Dad had been coping with this diagnosis alone.

I saved my tears for the car, but I was inconsolable and suddenly, the drinking all made sense.

# 74: On Each Other's Nerves

Danielle was an amazing baby. She slept well and hardly cried. Sometimes she was so quiet that I'd have to go and check she was still breathing. Even so, it was nice to be at Mum's, surrounded by family, where I could make use of the washing machine and dryer.

Mum never interfered, but she was there to help when I needed her, even offering to hold Danielle while they did the Guthrie test. My heart ached when I heard my baby cry out in pain after having a pin pricked into her foot.

Despite only being five years old, my little brother Mark loved the idea of being an uncle and even Nan melted a little when she got to meet her great grandchild.

Dad had called round on the second day, carrying a bag full of baby clothes that had obviously been purchased by Tracey. I don't know who was most uncomfortable, him or Mum. Thankfully, he didn't stay long. But he did promise to call round once I was back at home. Even Paul admitted in the end that staying at Mum's had been a good idea after all.

Me and Paul went into town to register Danielle's birth. It was the first time we'd been out in public with our baby. Walking was still hard. I'd had twenty stitches and there was one stitch that pulled down below. It was a good job Paul was there because Mum had been right, the pram we'd spent a small fortune on wasn't very practical.

I'd been a little anxious and self-conscious of going out in public, paranoid that people might judge me, so I made sure that my engagement ring was on show for everyone to see. Shame enveloped me when the registrar took our details though. She didn't say anything as she took our dates of birth and realised we were both unemployed, but her face said it all.

Paul seemed oblivious. He was more than happy now his name was officially on the birth certificate. On the way back to Mum's, all he talked about was going back to our own home so we could be a little family. I could have stayed at Mum's forever, but I knew he was right. It was time to go it alone.

Back at home, Danielle was a perfect baby. I let her dictate her feeding times. In fact, from four weeks in, she was practically sleeping through the night, and she certainly wasn't going hungry.

Every few weeks, me and Paul would take her to check-ups with the midwife, who assured us that she was meeting all her healthy milestones. Any of my previous reservations about being a good mother had evaporated. I was a natural.

Paul was the perfect father too. He didn't shy away from any of the chores, including changing her nappies. I would have much preferred to use the disposable ones, but we couldn't afford them, which meant the twin tub washer was out most days, and we became expert with the nappy pins.

I'd turned into a right little housewife, getting my kicks out of seeing a line of perfectly pegged nappies on the line. Fifteen months earlier, I had no aspirations to be in a relationship, let alone be a mother and now I couldn't imagine life without her, nor Paul in it.

Sadly, any hopes I'd had about Dad had soon evaporated. The only time I would see him would be at the video shop and that would always be brief because he was always on a mission off somewhere. I was hurt but had to remind myself that I wasn't a kid anymore, I was almost an adult.

My eighteenth birthday arrived, and Dad called out of the blue, offering to take me out to buy my first official drink.

I was surprised that he'd even remembered my birthday. Mum offered to babysit, and Dad arranged for a taxi to pick me and Paul up.

It wasn't until we were in the taxi that it dawned on me that this would be the very first time that me and Paul had been out socialising together.

It felt weird that I was finally able to spend time with Dad inside the pub after all those years of hanging outside them, hoping he would give me the time of day. As soon as we arrived, Dad handed me a large birthday card and a small red velvet box which reminded me of the one he'd given me as a kid.

Inside was a gold pendant in the shape of a cross. It was the first ever piece of real gold jewellery I'd been given I decided that I would treasure it forever. Dad had even written in the card. It wasn't much, just 'Happy 18th Birthday Love Dad', but it meant the world.

Dad was popular; he seemed to know everyone in the bar and showered his mates with rounds of drinks, like money was no object. Throughout the night, I hung on Dad's every word and I got a fuzzy warm feeling in my stomach every time he introduced me as his daughter.

He was talking of expanding his business empire and offered Paul a job in the video shop. It wasn't a lot of hours, but it would be cash in hand, and God knows we needed it. We were ecstatic.

The joy was short-lived though. After Dad bought me a Babycham and brandy, I threw up in the taxi home and woke up with a raging hangover and a row with Paul.

I couldn't remember much about the night apart from the necklace and Dad's offer of work.

Paul fobbed me off.

'Ya Dad was pissed, Trace. He'll have forgotten what he said. Anyway, who said I wanted his job?'

I was confused. I thought he'd seemed chuffed when Dad had asked him. 'Are you kidding me?'

'Look Trace, leave it, will ya?'

I could tell Paul was in one of his moods again. I was infuriated, but too hungover to start a fight. I put his mood down to being hungover, but I was determined not to let it go, because we needed the extra cash, so I dragged him to the shop.

Dad was there as promised. 'Morning, birthday girl – has tha recovered?'

'I have, just.'

Paul stared at me smugly with an 'I told ya so' look written all over his face.

I was undeterred. 'Dad, were you serious about offering Paul a couple of shifts?'

'Oh, shit, yeah, I'd forgotten about that!'

Karen chirped up from behind the counter.

'Well, I bloody hadn't. I was thinking of setting up a bed in the back of the shop and moving in,' she said, laughing.

'Alright. You can take Karen off at five/sixish, Paul, then close up. In fact, you two could pop into Hillsborough now and get another set of keys cut.'

I was buzzing. I went in to give Dad a hug. 'Thanks, Dad.'

'Don't be thanking me. Just don't fuck up, do ya hear, Paul?' Dad joked, and Paul laughed, but I could tell by his face that he wasn't laughing inside.

I was on cloud nine as we left the shop.

'Told you he meant it!'

Paul kept his head down. 'I don't want it!'

'What do you mean you don't want it? We ain't in a position to be turning down work and its cash in hand!' My excitement was turning into anger.

'I don't need ya Dad to find me work.'

I was incensed. 'I haven't seen you looking for fucking jobs.'

We walked in silence. 'I can't do it. Ya know I'm not good with people. He looked up, 'But you are! You get on with anyone, why don't you do it? I'll look after Danielle. It's only for a few hours at night.'

I was speechless but by the time I got back to the shop, I'd come round to the idea. I wasn't going to let the chance to bring some extra cash in the hand pass us by. We needed the money.

I was getting sick and tired of being the one who had to ask for a quick loan from my family to tide us over until payday. The monthly repayments on the large fridge we bought on tick were getting harder to meet, and then there was the phone bill. My only vice was the occasional fag, but Paul hated parting with any money, which meant I would have to make a packet of ten last me a week.

Dad had already left the shop, but Karen got him on the phone.

'Hi Dad. I've got the set of keys cut. Listen, about the job, Paul's just waiting to hear about another job, so I was wondering if you'd mind me stepping in instead?'

'He didn't say owt about another job!'

I wanted to tell Dad the truth, tell him that there wasn't another job and that Paul was just an ungrateful bastard, but decided against it.

'Look I don't mind who does it. I'll leave you and Karen to sort shifts out.' And with that, he was gone.

'Well, it looks like we'll be working together,' I said to Karen, still not quite believing it myself.

Karen smiled. 'Tell ya what, why don't you come back about five-ish and you can shadow me. I'll show you the ropes and how to cash and lock up, then you can start tomorrow.'

I didn't bother trying to catch Paul up. I was too mad. The more that I thought about it, the idea of spending a couple of hours away from Paul appealed to me.

It wasn't surprising that we were starting to get on each other's nerves considering that we hadn't left each other's side in the past eighteen months. Perhaps this was just what we needed.

# 75: Blurring the Lines

I was in the kitchen at work making a drink and bringing Lynne up to speed about Dad's cancer diagnosis. It had been a few days since Dad had broken the news, and I was still in a daze, struggling to process the information.

I assumed Dad was struggling too because, when I'd tried to revisit the subject, he'd looked at me like I'd grown two heads. In some ways, it was making me understand his drinking, but I was worried about what would happen next.

Lynne was a good listener but, like everyone else, she had little sympathy when it came to Dad. I was used to that but what she said next shocked me.

'Look Tracey, I hate seeing you like this. I know your dad has got his problems, but surely if it was cancer, he would have been to Western Park and not the Hallamshire? Personally, I think he's either very confused or he's lying to you.'

Her words stung. Who would dispute a cancer diagnosis? If I hadn't had the respect I did for her, I would have probably lashed out, but something inside me recognised that she might have a point. I told her about what had happened the other weekend and how Sarah was stepping up and helping out a little more, taking on some of the burden.

'Good! It's about time and maybe, just maybe, we might start to see a little of the old Tracey back then, eh?'

I felt like I was being told off, but I knew she cared. She offered me a smile.

'I know you love him, but this has got to stop, mate! I can tell straight away when it's your dad on the phone. I can see you tense up! He's got ya running around after him like a headless chicken – you haven't been yourself for ages.'

I knew she was right. I'd tried my best not to let what was happening interfere with my work life, but it was fucking hard at times. I prided myself on not dropping the ball, but

I'd dropped it a few times over the past few weeks, missing deadlines and forgetting about meetings.

Lynne's words replayed over and over in my head. What did she mean when she said 'we?' Were other people talking about me behind my back? It was hard. I had access to all the support resources at work, and yet my professional boundaries stopped me from accessing them; my job was to support the support groups, and I didn't want to blur the lines.

As for Dad, I didn't want to even consider that he might have lied to me. But, looking back, he'd been pissed off when I'd challenged him about his drinking. Was it his way of getting me to back off? I knew Dad could be manipulative, but this was next level. I mean, who tells their kid that they have got cancer when they haven't?

I gave Giz, the alcohol consultant a call and filled her in on the situation. I asked her bluntly.

'Giz, do you think he's got cancer?'

Her hesitance didn't go unnoticed.

'Look Tracey, you can only go on what your dad's told you. Without seeing his notes, I can't offer much. He might be confused. Only time will tell. What I will say though is that if he has got cancer, the hospital will be looking at treatment options and what with ya Dad's history of drinking, they'll be advising that he cut down on his drinking.'

I was still none the wiser. I'd just have to wait. But I did make a mental note to start checking any letters that he got from the hospital in future.

# 76: Broken Trust

Landing the job at the video shop was just what the doctor ordered. It was only a few hours in an evening, and it would give Paul and I a break from each other.

I couldn't help thinking that being a stay-at-home dad wasn't good for his self-esteem, and it was getting hard to have sympathy for him. He seemed so different from the cocksure young man I'd fallen for. He never went to the footie with his mates anymore and he refused to take driving lessons so that he could work for Dad taxiing. Paul said that me and Danielle were all he needed, but I needed more.

The only downside of the job was that I couldn't put Danielle to bed at night, but it felt like a small price to pay, if it meant we could bring some extra money in.

I was tired of asking for handouts from family and had even had to pawn the necklace that Dad had bought me. Paul had promised that we would go get it back, but I knew that I would never see my necklace again.

Working in the shop was a breeze. I was a natural with the customers and the conversation and banter became a welcome distraction from the monotony of daily life back home. My favourite film was *Rita, Sue and Bob Too*. It reminded me of my teenage years on the Valley, and I'd watch it over and over, having to pause it every time a customer came in because of the swearing.

As soon as I got home, I would hand over my cash for Paul for him to pay the bills. I was only getting fifteen quid a shift, but at least it slowed the red letters coming. Sometimes I missed logging a rental payment at the shop and used the money to buy my own cigarettes, instead of begging Paul for some money or scrounging the left-over tabs in the ashtray.

My cousin had just joined the video shop. He was working down the road as a hod-carrier on the demolition site of the old infirmary and he'd call in on his way home to get a film for his missus. Part of me envied her because my cousin was a grafter. I loved my little part-time job at the shop, but I would have much preferred to be a stay-at-home mum.

I mentioned this to my cousin and was excited when he called at ours with news about a part-time job going. He said Paul could have it and all he'd have to do was sweep the cabins out, keep the site clean and do the occasional sarni run for the lads. There'd be the chance of getting a full-time hod-carrier job in future, or even learn how to do bricklaying.

I decided the best approach would be if my cousin mentioned it instead of me and when he had, Paul seemed up for it but as soon as my cousin left, he started kicking off.

'I've told ya, I don't need nobody to get me a job.' he yelled.

I couldn't believe how ungrateful he was. 'Well, why didn't you say something then?

This was becoming a habit of Paul's. He'd be all smiles to someone's face but as soon as their back was turned, he'd change.

'He put me on the spot, didn't he? It's ok for you. You can talk to anyone. Just phone him and tell him I've changed my mind.'

'Like fuck I am! Ya can tell him ya sen. I'm sick of doing ya dirty work.'

'I didn't ask for the job.'

'Neither did I, working at the video shop!' I screamed. 'It's hardly a career but at least I'm doing something to support this family.' I tried a different tack. 'Come on, Paul, it will do you good, get you out of the house AND imagine how much better we will be off.'

'We're managing ok on your money.'

I felt like screaming but tried to keep my cool. 'It's not just about the money! This isn't how it's supposed to be. You should be the breadwinner. You won't know what it's like until you try it, and you never know, you might actually enjoy it. Just try it, will ya, please.' I was practically begging now.

'Ok, ok ok, for fuck's sake.'

I knew he felt backed into a corner, but even if he couldn't see it, I reckoned it was just what he needed; it was what we both needed.

Monday morning came and I got up early with Paul to wave him off. I was looking forward to spending some quality mum and daughter time with Danielle. I'd just put her in the bath with some bubbles when I heard the downstairs door slam. I wrapped Danielle in a towel and went downstairs.

There was Paul standing with his back to me in the kitchen. It was only ten am.

'What are you doing home? Are you on a break? How's it going?'

Paul turned round. 'I'm not doing it.'

I was stunned. I could quite believe my ears. 'What do you mean, you're not doing it? You haven't even given it two hours?'

'Like I said, I ain't doing it! It's just a fucking glorified cleaning job.'

'Yeah, but think of the bigger picture. In a few months, you could be learning a new trade.'

'I don't wanna be a fucking brickie.'

'Look, just go back. No-one will have missed you. You've only been away ten minutes.'

'Trace, I ain't fucking going back, ok!' He dumped the pack-up I'd prepared for him just hours earlier onto the floor.

'So what am I going to tell my family?'

'I don't care what you tell 'em. I'm not fucking doing it!'

My shock turned to anger. He was behaving like work was beneath him. I was incensed. Danielle started to shiver, and I realised she was still wet from the bath. I stormed upstairs and placed Danielle back into the bath. I tried to keep a smile on my face for her sake. Bless her, she didn't have a clue that her Dad was a lazy selfish bastard.

I even considered packing in my job at the video shop to make a point, but we needed the money, and since I'd started working for Dad, I finally felt part of his inner circle of trust, and I couldn't break that. My trust with Paul was broken though. I knew that I couldn't look at him in the same way ever again because any respect I might have had for him had died as soon as he'd walked back through that door.

# 77: Is It Contagious?

Dad was in hospital again. Apparently, the poor old man who lived on the ground floor had found Dad, on the main stairs in just his boxers and a t-shirt. Dad had been confused, saying he needed help, but the old guy couldn't work out what with. He'd tried to get Dad back in his flat, but Dad had started getting abusive, so he'd ended up calling for the ambulance.

Instead of feeling anxious about Dad being in hospital, I felt a sense of relief. This was a perfect opportunity to find out more about what was going on with Dad's health and this damned cancer diagnosis.

Having waited for an hour in A & E with Sarah, I was shocked when I finally saw Dad lying there in the bed. He was asleep, content almost, but he looked like shit. I noticed he had that yellow glow about him, the same one he had when he'd been admitted in Stoke a few months earlier and his stomach was swollen like he was pregnant.

One of the nurses came to take his obs, which stirred Dad from his sleep.

'Ey up, Frank, are you in a better mood?' I picked up the tone of sarcasm in her voice and my heart sank. I knew better than anyone that he could be a cantankerous git at the best of times. I dreaded to think what kind of grief he'd been giving the staff.

Dad either didn't hear her or ignored her.

I smiled apologetically. 'I'm sorry about Dad. He can be a real pain in the arse at times.'

She laughed. 'Don't you worry, Mrs. We've had worse than him to contend with.'

But I did worry. 'Have they said what's the matter with him?'

'The doctors think that your dad has developed ascites, which would account for his swollen stomach and him being confused. I'm still not sure he knows where he is. They also want to run some more tests because of his hepatitis.'

I was confused. 'What hepatitis? Look I'm sorry, but the last time Dad was admitted, a nurse mentioned concerns about cirrhosis of the liver. In fact, he had an appointment at the Hallamshire a couple of weeks ago, but we still don't know what that was about. According to Dad a doctor had told him he's got cancer? Would that be right?'

She did well to avoid my questions. 'Look, love, they're moving him in a minute. You'd be better speaking to the doctors when he's on the ward.'

Dad was still out of it, oblivious to the conversation we were having over him. Exasperated, I stood up. I needed to get some fresh air. It was freezing outside.

I fought the urge to just walk away and leave Dad there and not return, but I couldn't.

Sarah joined me. She lit a cigarette and offered it to me. 'You, ok?'

'Honestly, Sarah, I don't know what to think.'

Sarah took a long drag on her fag 'So is it contagious? What is it?'

'I've heard of Hepatis C before. All I know is that it's transmitted by sharing needles, which I am sure Dad hasn't done…' I huffed, 'but then nothing would surprise me to be honest, what with the idiots he has around the flat.'

Sarah laughed, shaking her head.

'No chance, Trace. He's many things but he's not a drug addict.'

I knew she was right. Dad despised drug users. Well, that was unless he was getting something out of them. He never thought twice about buying off shoplifters, knowing full well what they would be spending their money on. I lit myself another cigarette. I wasn't ready to go back in, not just yet.

# 78: Everyone Could Fuck Off

We'd planned to call and visit Mum and Ada, on the Sunday afternoon. I suspected that Mum would have heard through the family jungle gossip drums about Paul and the job. I was going to suggest that I go visit on my own, but I didn't need to because Paul had already made up his mind that he wasn't going. I felt suffocated and couldn't wait to escape.

When I arrived at Mum's, my suspicions were confirmed when Ada greeted me with: 'Where's that work-shy git?'

I wasn't about to try and defend him.

'He's at home. Leave it will ya, Ada. I don't wanna talk about it.'

My brother took Danielle out to play, and Mum made me a cuppa. 'Are you ok love?'

I wanted to offload and tell them that I'd made a mistake and wanted to come home, but I couldn't because I didn't want to admit that I'd fucked up again.

'I'm ok, Mum. Where's our Sarah?'

Mum chuckled. 'She's probably dying upstairs. She didn't get in until late.'

As if on cue, Sarah popped her head around the corner. I couldn't help but laugh. She was a wreck, but she still looked beautiful.

I couldn't believe just how much the tables had changed. I'd gained weight and lost track of the latest fashions and the confidence that I'd once had now seemed to elude me. I'd always envisioned her being the first to have kids and settle down. Instead, Sarah was working full-time and when she wasn't working, she spent her weekends out socialising with her mates downtown.

'Hiya, sis, where's Danny?'

'She's out back with our Mark. Late night, eh?'

'Oh my god! I wasn't even supposed to be going out! She groaned. 'Argggghhh. Mum, make me a coffee, will ya? So

Trace, are you coming out for my eighteenth? Steph and Christine and Mum are coming out.'

'Nah, ya alright. Anyway I can't really afford it.'

Mum chirped up. 'It's ok, pet. I'll pay. It will do you good to get out.'

I still wasn't convinced, then I found the perfect excuse. 'Anyway, I can't, I'm working evenings, aren't I?'

'Ah fuck Dad. He can get Karen to cover for ya.'

'Have you heard anything from him?' Part of me was hoping that he'd been in touch to celebrate her eighteenth, like he had with me.

She scoffed. 'Ya joking, aren't ya? I only hear from him when he's giving me a bollocking for using his taxis!' She laughed. 'The other day, one of 'em told me I couldn't have any more credit, and I said 'what ya gonna do? Leave me in town all alone? What if something happens to me? What'ya gonna tell Dad then?''

I couldn't believe her ballsy attitude towards Dad. I would never have dreamed of taking the piss like that.

'Anyway, stop changing the subject. Are you coming or not?' She pulled a silly baby face and pleaded. 'Pleeeese, come on, sis. It won't be the same without you.'

I knew Paul wouldn't be happy, but at that point, I really didn't give a shit what he thought, so I agreed on the condition that I'd join them after I'd closed the video shop, and then realised that I was going to have to spend the following week scouring the C&A extra-large sales section for something vaguely stylish to wear.

The big night came around. A couple of our Sarah's mates joined us. I couldn't help comparing myself with everyone. I felt completely out of place. I was smiling, trying to make the best of it, but inside I just wanted to go back home. But, after a few drinks, my anxiety waned. In fact, the more I drank, the less I gave a fuck.

We headed to a small club on Carver Street. Being a Thursday night, it was empty when we arrived, but that meant we had the dancefloor to ourselves.

It was all going well until I saw Sarah having a heated argument with a group of girls I'd never seen before. I was just about to go over and see what was going off when Mum said she'd go and sort it.

I could see Mum from the other side of the dancefloor. She had placed herself firmly in between the two groups of girls. One arm was on Sarah, trying to hold her back, whilst the other arm was in front trying to calm the other bird down. I could feel my body almost explode. I was itching to get involved and defend my sister. And then I saw it!

One of the girls had pushed Mum's hand away. I was by her side in a nanosecond, ready to attack. Mum, however, was still calm, trying her best to reason with the girls, insisting they leave whatever beef they had with each other for another night.

One of the girls swore at Mum. 'Who the fuck are you?'

But before Mum could reply, I was showering punches on the girl. I completely lost it. For a moment, I forgot who I was and where I was. All I knew was I felt alive.

The next thing I remember is being dragged up the stairs of the club and being thrown onto the street by the bouncer. I was pumped. I was having a full-on adrenaline rush, the exact same rush I used to get after a scrap at school. I was pacing the street, thinking of ways of getting back inside when my cousin Steph came walking out of the club. I thought she'd come to check if I was ok, but she strode across the street clapping slowly.

'Nice one, Trace,' she said, sarcastically.

I was incensed. Did she think I was about to stand there and watch someone start on my sister, let alone my fucking mother? 'You are kidding me, aren't you? Did you see what happened?'

'All I saw is that you ruined the night. You really can't help yourself, can you?'

I was incredulous. Who was she to look down her nose at me? She'd always thought she was better than everyone and nowadays she lorded it about, thinking she was the bee's knees just cos she was at university. Well, she could fuck right off. I was about to kick off, when Mum and everyone else in our group started to come out of the club.

I rushed over. 'Are you ok?'

'I'm fine, love. Listen, I think it's time to go home.'

Sarah chipped in. 'Well, you can go home, Mum, but I'm waiting for them to come out of the club. I'm not letting 'em get away with that.'

I was still pumped. 'I'm staying with Sarah.'

'Don't you think you've done enough for one night?' Steph snarled again.

She was starting to get right on my tits.

'Ah fuck off, Steph. If that silly slag hadn't touched my fucking mother, then I wouldn't have done anything.'

And then she said it. 'It's you who's the slag. You who got her sen pregnant at 16! You're a fucking loser! You'll never change!'

It was a low blow, and it hurt, but I didn't have time because Mum was hitting Steph over the head with her handbag and insisting that she take back what she had just said.

Now Steph and Mum were rowing, and it was getting nasty. The next thing, I was on the concrete floor, fighting with Steph. There were tits, arms and hair flying all over.

Mum managed to separate us. She was like a woman possessed. When we emerged, her hair was all over the place and judging by her eye, she'd copped for a punch whilst trying to split us up.

A feeling of shame enveloped me. I tried to apologise to Mum, but she wasn't having any of it. I could tell she was on the verge of crying.

A taxi came around the corner and Mum hailed it before frogmarching me and pushing me in it. Sat alone in the cab, my face was starting to sting but the comments from Steph hurt more. Mum said I should ignore what she'd said, but I couldn't help wondering if that's what all the family really thought about me. I didn't want to go home. I wanted to go back into town to get some retribution. I'd completely forgotten about being a mum, I felt like I was fifteen again, back in the day when I didn't take no shit from no one. Part of me felt guilty for ruining Sarah's night but another part was unrepentant. I had been sticking up for Mum, after all.

Paul was sat waiting up for me. He looked relieved to see me home early.

'Good night?'

I was still pumped as I regaled him about the night events. I was hoping he'd understand, but instead all I got was a look of disappointment.

'You can't even go out for a drink wi' out getting into a fight, can ya?'

I was venomous. 'Fuck off, Paul!'

I should have known better than to think he might be on my side or understand where I was coming from. As far as I was concerned, everyone could fuck off. I hated everyone, including myself.

# 79: Getting Nowhere

It was getting late when we headed back indoors to locate Dad on the ward. When we found him, he was still bang out, oblivious to all the chaos going on around him. I saw no point in going to sit beside him. Sarah sat with him whilst I tried to track down a doctor to find out more about what the hell was going on.

The nurse's station was empty. The only staff on the ward I could see were cleaners, and auxiliary staff handing out evening meals to patients. Smelling the food made my stomach growl and I remembered I'd missed lunch. Now I wasn't just pissed off and tired, I was hungry. I waited for what seemed like ages before a nurse started to approach the station.

'Erm excuse me, I'm sorry to bother you.' I paused and made a mental note to myself to stop fucking apologising all the time. 'I'm Frank Ford's daughter. He's just been brought in. The nurse in A&E mentioned that they think he has hepatitis and something else...'

I could tell by her body language that she had far more important things to be getting on with than dealing with an hysteric relative. 'He's only just come in, so I don't know much...'

I interrupted her. 'Well, is there a doctor who I can talk to then?'

She smiled apologetically. 'I'm sorry, the doctors won't be doing their rounds until tomorrow.'

I rolled my eyes. I was getting nowhere.

'Look', she turned towards the bay gesturing me to follow. 'Let me have a look at his notes and see if there's anything on them.'

The nurse took the board from the bottom of the bed where Dad was still sleeping and carefully inspected his notes. She looked up. 'It looks like we're treating your dad with antibiotics, which will be for the Hepatitis.'

I couldn't help interrupting. 'Well, does it say anything about cancer in his notes?'

She looked confused. 'I'm sorry, it doesn't say. Look, your dad's sleeping for now. Why don't you come back tomorrow and speak to the doctor? Or you could phone at lunchtime.'

It wasn't the response I was after, but I knew she was right. It was getting late, and people were leaving. Visiting hours must have almost been up. 'I'll call tomorrow then. Can you do me a favour?'

'Yes of course,' she smiled.

'Can you tell him that we have been here and that I'll be bringing him some clothes. I can tell you now, he won't be impressed with that nightie you've given him!'

# 80: It's Only for One Night!

A few weeks had passed since Sarah's eighteenth and things had calmed down a little. Steph and I had both apologised to Mum but the family rift between us remained. Every time I thought back to that night, my chest tightened. Steph's words had cut deep, and I vowed to never speak to her again. I also vowed never to go out partying in town again. I wasn't young, free and single anymore. I was a mother, with a family. I had responsibilities which included working more hours at the shop.

Out of the blue, Karen had decided to go work for a bloke she'd been dating who had his own company and it wasn't long before I was working full-time to help Dad out. I would snatch some quality time with Dan before work, then Paul would push her in the pram to walk with me and spend a couple of hours with me before heading back home for lunch.

One morning on the way to work, a little old lady stopped us.

'Can I just say, it's lovely to see a dad spend so much time with his daughter.'

Paul lapped up the praise whereas I felt like she was judging me for being a crap mum. All I wanted to do was scream at her and tell her that it should have been me pushing the pram every day, not him, but instead I swallowed my words and pushed the hurt to one side. I worried about Dan. Whilst she seemed to love being able to run around the shop, she was toddling now and needed to be playing with other kids, not empty video boxes. Some days, she didn't want me to leave, and my heart ached hearing her crying for her Mum as Paul pushed her out of the door.

I'd tried talking to Paul, but he'd fob me off. He didn't want a job, but Paul was obsessed with money, and despite the extra shifts, we never seemed to have any spare cash. He liked the nicer things in life and was great at being able to justify ordering stuff from the catalogue that we didn't need.

I felt stuck. Deep-down, I knew the relationship wasn't working but I had no other option but to make it work.

Then there was Dad. I wouldn't get home until nine some nights. I felt like his gofer instead of his daughter and I knew that the new staff that he'd promised would never materialise. Part of me felt like he was taking the piss, but at the same time, it felt nice that Dad trusted and depended on me. I felt like he no longer treated me like a kid, and I loved it when he asked my advice about what films he thought he should buy for the shop.

One day I'd tried talking to him about Paul and how unhappy I was, but all he did was look at me gone out.

'What's up wi' thee? Tha's got a good un there, Trace. He doesn't drink or go out, he doesn't hit ya and there's not many blokes willing to be a stay-at-home Dad.'

I wanted to scream that some days I wished he would fucking hit me, to give me a valid reason to leave. It was clear that Dad wasn't interested in me, nor my relationship, I should have known better than to go to him for relationship advice – he was two-timing Tracey with some rich woman he'd met whilst in Cornwall.

Paul shook his head in disbelief when he asked if he could bring her to ours for a night, but thought it was funny. 'You are unbelievable, Frank!'

'And what about Tracey?' I said, shocked.

'What about her?' Dad said innocently. 'Look, this is a transactional relationship. I'm trying to get her to invest in the video shop and what Tracey doesn't know won't hurt her will it. It's just one night. I'll pay ya. It's cheaper than a hotel.'

I couldn't believe my ears. 'Dad, you are kidding, right?'

'Well, I can hardly take her back to mine, can I?' he laughed.

'And where is she supposed to sleep?' I was incredulous.

'We can have your bed. Look, it's only for one night! He tossed me forty quid. 'Here – you and Paul go pop into town and treat yourself to some new clothes, get our Danny something with whatever's left over. Go on, I'll cover the shop, whilst you are gone.'

The following evening, I closed the shop early as agreed. I hoped he wouldn't follow through, but then Dad arrived at ours carrying an overnight bag.

'Have you brought the takings from today?' he asked.

I passed Dad a bag of cash and coins. 'Here. What time is she supposed to be arriving, then?'

'Anytime now. Come on, I need to drop this in the bedroom before she gets here.'

We headed up to our bedroom. Paul had already changed the bed with fresh sheets. Dad threw his bag onto the bed and a pair of red lacy pants fell out.

'Dad, are these supposed to be for this bird?'

Dad was at the window looking out for her arrival. 'I dunno what's in the bag. Tracey packed it for me.'

'Dad, look!' I said, dangling the lacy pants in the air. 'I'm telling ya Dad, she knows.'

'And I'm telling you, she doesn't suspect a thing.'

'So, what if someone sees you and what am I supposed to say to her?'

'*All* you have to talk about is the video shop and how well it's doing.' Dad looked exasperated. 'Look, Trace. It's no big deal, ok? Just be yourself and keep her company whilst I'm playing darts, that's it. She's here now.'

I peered over his shoulder and saw a black BMW pulling up in front of the house. I was expecting a floozy blonde getting out of the car, but she was pretty plain, defo not Dad's type, but then again, I reckon he would shag owt with a pulse.

Susan seemed nice enough, but I could tell she wasn't interested in me as we arrived at the Far Lees pub.

It was heaving as we walked through to the bar, where people greeted Dad like a long-lost friend. We got to the bar and there was a group of guys standing in their work gear, who looked like they were already pissed. Dad was tapping his fingers on the bar. I could tell something was irritating him and then he snapped.

'Nah then!'

One of the guys who had his back to Dad, turned around.

'Aright Frank, I didn't see ya there...'

But Dad didn't let him finish his sentence. 'Does tha mind, wi ya fucking language! There are women in here, including me daughter.'

The guy looked terrified. He addressed me and Susan. 'Ahhh, sorry. I do apologise, ladies. I didn't see ya there.'

'Listen,' Dad said. 'Why don't you and ya mates take ya drinks over there?'

Without another word, the bloke and his mates walked away like scorned teenagers, taking their drinks with them

'Fucking wanker, can't stand him!' Dad muttered under his breath.

'Dad, you do realise that you swore at him, whilst telling him off for swearing in front of us?'

'Did I?' Dad said smirking, 'Ah well he's gone nah. What ya drinking?'

I couldn't help thinking that this was bullying at its finest, but Dad was oblivious and so was his new bird. I felt like a gooseberry all night and it was clear that she was enamoured by him, clinging onto his every word.

To her, Dad was a bit of rough. To him, she was just a cash cow. I couldn't wait for the night to end and for her to piss off back to Cornwall where she belonged.

# 81: A Step Too Far

I had called at Dad's flat before work to get him something more suitable to wear to come out of hospital. The flat was a mess and there was a half-bottle of Coke and an empty bottle of brandy on the coffee table. I didn't have the time or the will to try tidying up.

'He can clean his own shit up,' I thought, grabbing a t-shirt, bottoms, some pants, and his slippers before heading off to work.

When I phoned, the nurses still couldn't tell me anything, so I left my number and asked if the doctor could call me as soon as he'd finished his rounds.

I was in the middle of chairing a meeting when a call came through on a withheld number. I made my excuses to take the call.

'Good afternoon. Is this Tracey Ford?'

'Yes, it is.'

'I understand you have some questions about your dad?'

I had so many questions, I didn't know where to start. So, I went straight in from the beginning, giving the doctor the full lowdown on Dad's recent medical history. The doctor listened patiently.

'Well, his blood results have come back, and we are treating him with antibiotics for the alcoholic hepatitis. We are also treating him for his ascites. However, if it doesn't react to medication, we may have to drain the excess fluid, but we don't like doing that unless we really have too, due to increased risk of infection, you see?' He paused. 'The thing is that these types of issues are going to reoccur and get worse if your dad doesn't cut down on his drinking.'

'It's not for want of trying,' I snapped. I apologised before going on to explain that I worked in the addiction field and that alcohol consultants were more than willing to assess him if only I could get Dad to accept he had a problem.

'I get it, I really do. I can make a call to the alcohol liaison nurse and have him to pop in and have a word with your dad, whilst he's here? Would that help?'

I felt a faint sense of relief. 'Yes, yes please, that would be great! Thank you so much.'

'No problem. Is there anything else you wanted to ask?'

'Actually, there is. You see at Dad's last hospital appointment at the Hallamshire, apparently, they told him that he'd got cancer, is that right?'

I could hear the keyboard clicking away in the background. 'Your dad must have been confused. There's nothing on his records indicating a cancer diagnosis. The appointment at the Hallamshire was to discuss his liver function results.'

I couldn't work of if I was angry or relieved.

The doctor continued. 'Don't get me wrong, cirrhosis can progress to liver cancer. Perhaps that's where the confusion has come from.'

I thanked the doctor, before ending the call. My first instinct was to head straight to the hospital and lay into Dad. I had so much I wanted to say but I couldn't, not yet.

I headed to the toilets; I needed some space to collect myself. I caught my reflection in the mirror and there was a split second when I didn't recognise myself. I washed my face with cold water. I needed to put my game face back on and get back into the meeting. But no amount of washing could rid me of the hurt Dad had caused. This was a step too far and I wasn't sure how much more of his manipulation and lies I could take.

# 82: Dad! What's tha done?

Sarah had moved to a flat in Upperthorpe and Mum and Ada were busy helping her out with the decorating. It was only a ten-minute walk away and I was desperate to see it, but I was always working, and Sarah was out partying most of the time. I offered her some free films, but she wasn't interested in anything that had to do with Dad. I envied her independence; unlike me, she answered to no one.

Dad hadn't been his usual self for a few weeks. I wondered if Tracey had found out about the one-night stand, who thankfully had disappeared without a trace, or if he was having money problems.

A new Blockbusters video store had opened in Hillsborough and takings were suffering. Dad had stopped calling in, instead ordering a taxi for me to drop the takings to him at the pub, where I'd watch him spend the takings on rounds of drinks for so-called mates.

Sometimes I'd stay and have a drink and have a catchup with Dot, the same woman that I'd met at the fair years ago with Uncle John. I hadn't liked her at first but now I realised that adult relationships were complicated, and I'd admired Dot's spirit. She sported what looked like a borstal spot on her cheek (a small blue tattooed circle) and didn't wear any makeup.

She didn't have airs or graces, nor did she take any shit from anyone, especially men. When she wasn't working in the taxi firm for Dad, she could be found sinking pints at the bar with Dad and Uncle John.

She was one of the few people I could talk to about Paul.

'I know, I shouldn't complain, he's a great dad and all that, but he won't work, and he moans about everything, especially if he doesn't get his own way.' I sighed

'Yah know, Trace, no man is perfect and I should know.' She nodded in the direction of Uncle John.

It felt nice to have someone to confide in; in fact, there were some nights I didn't want to leave. Paul didn't like it when I was late, especially if I had been to the pub. He'd try to complain about him being stuck at home all day, but as soon as I mentioned that I'd be more than happy to swap places, he'd shut up. Sometimes, he'd admit to feeling jealous, or scared that I might meet someone else, which was ridiculous considering I didn't have time to date myself, let alone anyone else.

I knew I'd been right to be concerned about Dad when only weeks after Susan's visit, he announced that he and Tracey were splitting up. According to him, it was an amicable split, in fact he claimed to still love her; that's why he'd agreed to leave her the farmhouse. He'd got himself a flat on South Road, above a fruit shop, a stone's throw away from the taxi company. I could always find him in the pub, and it didn't take him long to move on.

One night, I was dropping the takings for Dad at the Blake and found him standing at the bar with a bird's arm slung around his neck, snuggling her face into his neck.

I looked over to find Dot sat in her usual spot and she rolled her eyes and started laughing, it was like she was reading my mind.

I tapped Dad on the shoulder.

'Or reyt, Dad.'

They both swung around.

'Ah Trace.' Dad retrieved the bag of takings from my hand. 'This is Judy? Wanna drink?'

'Aye, why not.'

Dad's new woman and I exchanged pleasantries as I tried to ignore the huge shiner on her eye. She saw me looking and seemed embarrassed. Dad broke the awkwardness when he turned to hand me a drink.

'So, what do you think of ya new stepmum then?'

'Frank, stop it!' Judy giggled like a love-struck teenager. It was pathetic.

I made my excuses and went to sit with Dot.

A week or so later I knew the shit was really unravelling when the bailiffs started to become frequent visitors to the shop. Then two months after Blockbusters opened, Dad announced that he was closing the shop.

As a consolation, he offered me some hours on a Friday and Saturday night answering phones at the taxi firm. The pay wasn't great but at least it was still something coming in, and even better it meant I'd be working alongside Dot. It also meant I could spend more time with Danielle and finally go and visit our Sarah's new pad.

Readjusting to being at home was awkward at first. Paul and Danielle seemed to have their own little routine. Some days, I felt like I was imposing, and I felt jealous of their special bond. Which just made me even more determined to spend as much time as I could with her.

I had almost forgotten what it was like to spend most of my days around Paul. Some days it was like we had the perfect relationship; he could be charming and say all the right things, then the next, he'd find fault in everything.

I never knew where I stood with him. The one thing that hadn't changed was Paul's insatiable sex drive. It was like he was obsessed but I found myself going along with his demands just for a quiet life.

Despite not wanting to work at all, I found myself looking forward to the weekends. Being stuck in a smoke-filled room taking bookings and calming irate customers was preferable to sitting at home with Paul.

When Dad offered me the chance to make some extra cash cleaning his flat for him, I jumped at the chance. Despite the extra cash, Paul even sulked at that, but I didn't care – it was just an excuse to have some breathing space from him.

Dad's new flat was only a fifteen-minute walk from ours. I banged on the door and Dad answered. He looked dog rough.

'Rough night, eh?' I joked as I stepped inside and followed him into the flat.

'Aye, tha could say that.'

I glanced around Dad's new pad and was impressed It reminded me of his old flat on Norfolk Park, only it was more spacious.

'Ahh, this is nice, Dad. I might have to move back in with ya!'

Dad grunted and turned to sit in his chair. It was then I noticed his back; it was covered in scratches.

'Dad! What's tha done?'

Dad looked confused.

'Ya back! what have you done to it, looks like you've taken a reyt whipping. Don't tell me you are into the S&M stuff.' I joked.

Dad felt his back, then groaned. 'It's her, that Judy,' he exclaimed.

'What her from the other week, are you still seeing her?'

'I'm not seeing her or anyone.' Dad snarled. 'She's just been back to the flat a couple of times. Fuck me, she's sex-mad!'

I laughed.

'It's not funny!'

'It is, Dad. Have you seen your back? It's a reyt mess. She's proper marked her territory on you.' I was on a roll. 'I reckon you've got a proper bunny boiler on ya hands.'

'Ah, fuck off will ya and go and put kettle on?'

I made us both a drink, Dad's usual strong builders' tea with two sugars, I couldn't help admiring the flat. I would have loved live somewhere like this, instead of the old terrace house we lived in.

'So, this is nice, in it? Like the old days, just me and you.' I smiled whilst reaching for one of his fags.

'Oi, ya cheeky bastard!' Dad went to pat my hand away from his cigarette packet, but he wasn't quick enough.

'What?' I smirked, lighting the fag. Dad shook his head, smiling.

'Tha still a pain in my arse nah, forever tapping.'

'Well, I don't know if you heard. I've just lost my job and moneys a bit tight.'

He stood up to go get dressed. 'You are a cheeky git.'

'Mmm, I wonder who I take after?'

I made a start on the flat, whilst Dad got himself ready for work. It wasn't long before Dad reappeared.

'Here!' He tossed me thirty quid. 'Go get another set of keys done and keep the change and come back in a couple of days – oh and can ya do me that bit of ironing too?'

I shook my head. 'Now who's the cheeky bastard Dad?'

I finished cleaning. I could have stayed longer but I knew Paul would be getting mad.

There was twenty-five quid left after I'd cut the keys. I decided to tell Paul that Dad had only given me fifteen quid so I could spend the rest on some fags, which was the only indulgence I had nowadays. As soon as I got home, I made sure to hide my stash away.

I felt like a kid all over again, sneaking into the house tucking fags down my pants to avoid being caught by Mum or Aca. Part of me wished I could turn back time and start all over again, but the reality was that I couldn't. All I could do was try my best to make it work.

# 83: Seeing Sense

Dad's face lit up when he saw me on the ward.

'Ey up, shugs!'

Jekyll was back, or was it Hyde? I never knew which version of Dad I was going to get but I took it as a good sign that he was smiling and figured he might be more receptive to what I had to say, even though I still had no idea what that was. I noticed the swelling on his stomach had gone down. That was a good sign too.

I passed him his bag of clothes. 'Ey up, Dad. Here I brought you some clothes. Tha's not gonna pull anyone wearing that hospital gown, are ya?'

'Ahh, thanks Trace. I'm hoping that they will let me out soon.'

Dad rummaged in the bag. 'No grapes again.'

'Nah Dad. Can you imagine if I had? You could have set up a winery wi' all times tha's been admitted.' I hoped a bit of humour might ease the conversation along.

'Oooo touché.' He pressed his hand to his heart. 'That hurt.'

'Look Dad, this is serious.' I took a deep breath. 'I spoke to the doctor. You know as well as I do that the drinking has got to stop, Dad.'

Dad raised his hand. 'Let me stop you right there. I know I've been hitting hard of late. It's just a phase that's all, once this...'

I knew what was coming and I wasn't prepared to be fobbed off, not this time. 'Dad, you've got cirrhosis of the liver, that means your liver won't repair itself. It's only going to get worse if you carry on drinking. I mean look at you, for crying out loud. When they brought you in yesterday, you were completely out of it, you looked fucking nice months pregnant! That's all down to the drinking and now you have got hepatitis.' I was on a roll. 'Oh and while I'm at it, turns out you haven't got cancer neither!'

I immediately regretted mentioning the cancer, but it was out there now, the elephant in the room had been exposed.

Dad was indignant. 'I never said that I had cancer. I said I 'might' have cancer!'

I shook my head. 'Dad, you told me point blank the other week that you had been told that you had cancer. You just don't say shit like that!' I could feel myself getting emotional. 'My head's been all over the place since you told me. I don't think I can cope much more and if you carry on as you are doing, ya can forget that claim! Tha'll be dead before it's settled!'

'I'm sorry you've been worried,' said Dad. 'But you must have heard me wrong.' But I knew I hadn't. I also knew by the tone of his voice that he was never going to admit to it.

'Ok, so you haven't got cancer, Dad, but you have got cirrhosis of the liver. That damage can't be reversed, you know?'

'Stop fretting, will ya, I know all this. In fact I spoke to a bloke today about the drinking. We had a good chat actually. He said there are drugs to help with the cravings, and he said I should cut down slowly. Apparently, it's dangerous just to quit.'

I wanted to wipe the smug look of his face. 'Yeah but, Dad, you've already done the hardest part of the detox. They'll have been giving you drugs to help with the withdrawal, so there's no need to go back to drinking when you get out, is there?'

'What and stick to tea all day...'

I cut him off. 'Well, you did it before, Uncle Mick told me'

'Well, ya Uncle Mick needs to mind his own fucking businesses, dunt he? Dad snapped. 'He knows fuck all and has no business talking to you about it.'

I had to defend Uncle Mick. It wasn't his fault. I'd called him. 'I'm glad he did tell me. You can't keep hiding or pretending that this ain't happening, Dad!'

'Look, I promise you I won't be going back to the top shelf. Hey, I hear that Somerfield's got that alcohol-free lager, I could try that! I can't drink on these antibiotics anyway, so stop worrying.'

'Well, you're my dad, and I do worry.'

'I know, I know. Look, can we change the subject now please?'

There was no mention of the claim, and we passed the rest of the time with small talk.

I left the hospital with mixed emotions. Part of me was relieved that we had actually had a serious and honest conversation about his drinking, but I wasn't sure he was going to follow through. At least the alcohol liaison officer was going back to see him. Maybe they could make him see sense.

# 84: A New Friend

There was a hive of activity in our neighbourhood as a removal van reversed into the street. Peeping from the upstairs bedroom, I watched a young woman barking instructions to the removal men, whilst juggling a toddler on her hip and trying to entertain a girl who looked about the same age as Danielle.

For over a week, we exchanged smiles and nods to each other from a distance, then one morning when she was sat on the doorstep having a fag and a cuppa, she invited me in.

'Hi, love. I'm Donna. Do ya fancy a cuppa?'

I was chuffed to bits. 'Hiya, I'm Tracey. Let me get this shopping in and I'll be over.'

Paul was washing the pots. He looked bemused as I rushed in and put the stuff away in the cupboards. 'What ya rushing about for?' he laughed, bemused.

'I'm just popping over the road to have a coffee with that lady who's moved in over the road.' I beamed.

'Who? That fat bird?'

I shook my head. 'You can be such a judgmental bastard sometimes, Paul. *And* she's not fat!'

'I hope you're taking Dan with ya?'

'Of course, I am. She's got a little girl about the same age. It'll be good for her to have her own little friend.'

Paul shrugged his shoulders. 'You're not going to be long, are ya?'

I couldn't believe him. 'Why? Are we supposed to be going somewhere?'

'No, I'm just asking.'

'Fuck me, Paul, I'm only across the road *and* it's only a coffee. Jesus!'

I'd expected to leave after one coffee, but the time flew by, and we ended up spending the whole day together, filling each other in about our lives while the kids played without a care in the world. Danielle had a good time too.

I learned a lot about Donna in those few hours. She was married, but her bloke worked away. Donna didn't need to work. I envied the fact that not only did her fella work, but he also handed her a weekly allowance towards bills and shopping – no questions asked. She even had some money left over to indulge herself. She had a busy social life, and she lived for the weekends.

Apparently, every Friday night, they went out separately with their own friends and then would meet up at the end of the night for last orders. It sounded perfect. She suggested that I should go out with her one weekend and 'let my hair down.'

I didn't dare tell her about the last time I'd been out on the town, or that Paul would never agree to me going out alone.

Donna was easy to get along with. She had an air of confidence about her that I admired. It was infectious. I immediately felt at ease in her presence.

I felt that I could have told her anything, but I didn't want to be a Debbie Downer and put her off me, so I didn't mention the issues with Paul. I just told her about how we got together. She admitted that she'd noticed him and remarked about how handsome he was. Little did she know that looks could be deceiving.

We soon moved onto talking about Dad. She seemed impressed when I told her about Dad and his businesses, and I found myself telling her about some of Dad's antics.

'Your dad sounds quite a character!'

I laughed. 'Yeah, you could say that!'

I didn't want to leave, neither did Danielle. But it was close to teatime, and I knew that Paul had been spying on me on account of the curtains twitching across the road. We said our goodbyes and promised to meet up again.

I floated back home, on cloud nine. It had been the first time for as long as I could remember that I felt comfortable in my own skin. She was the least judgmental person I had ever met. I felt like I could relax and be the real me around her – whoever the fuck that was.

Paul was waiting for me in the kitchen. 'You've been gone ages.'

'*And*?' I wasn't in the mood for any of his jealousy. 'Well, we have had a lovely time, and our Danielle has made a new friend too, haven't ya, Dan?'

'Is it time to go back yet?' she asked.

I laughed. 'We'll go to the park with them soon.'

'Sounds great,' said Paul sarcastically. It was like he was mocking me, but I didn't care. I wasn't about to let him spoil my day. I'd had the best afternoon in a long time, and I'd made a new friend, and God knows I desperately needed a friend.

# 85: Maybe It Was Just a Blip

Dad was out of hospital, and I'd gone to visit. The smell of furniture polish and air freshener hit me as soon as I opened the flat door. Sarah had worked her magic. There was no alcohol in sight in the living room, and I was hopeful that he'd do as he'd agreed with the alcohol liaison worker and stay off the drink. Dad was sitting with a steaming mug of tea, and the news was playing in the background as he read his paper. He still looked weak, but he looked better already.

'Ey up, Dad, tha looking loads better.' I went in for a kiss. 'Fuck me, tha smells better too!'

Dad saw the funny side. 'I know. Eh, even had a shave. Kettle's just boiled if ya wanna cuppa.'

I headed for the pristine kitchen and opened the fridge, which was full of food. I smiled at the thought of Sarah softening toward Dad. Had it not been for my mini meltdown weeks earlier, he wouldn't have even got a glass of milk out of her.

I made myself comfy on the chair. 'So Dad how ya feeling?'

Dad reached for a bag on the windowsill. 'A few more of these and I'll be reyt as rein,' he said as he unloaded the bag of tablets that the hospital had given him. 'Trace, I need to apologise. I know I've been a bit of a dickhead.'

This time I wasn't going to brush his behaviour off. 'Well, you certainly haven't been the Dad I'm used to.'

Dad looked sheepish. 'I know, I know. It's the top shelf, innit? I'm alright if I stick to lager, but I'm gonna have a break from that an' all.'

I didn't want to push him too hard, but this was my perfect opportunity to have a proper chat about his drinking. 'Dad, can I ask a question?'

He laughed. 'Tha gonna anyway.'

'Is that the reason you came back to Sheffield?'

He looked confused. 'What do ya mean? Don't you want me here?'

'Don't be silly, of course I want you here. It was great having you at ours. What I mean is, did you come back to Sheffield because of the drink? I mean, this isn't the first time this has happened, is it?' I shrugged. 'I'm just going on what Uncle Mick said. It isn't the first time ya got yourself in a pickle.'

Dad started to look uncomfortable.

'Come on, Dad. You're talking to me now. It just makes perfect sense. It can't have been easy in Stoke when Uncle John's got the pub and everyone's drinking? I was thinking it might help if you got a little more support?'

Dad scoffed. 'I've told thee. You ain't gonna get me in no support group. I know what I need to do.'

'And what's that then, Dad, cos sitting in this flat alone ain't gonna help, is it? Look, I'll go along with ya. There are grown ass men just like you. You're not the only person to have a problem with alcohol, ya know?'

Dad laughed, 'Look, I've told ya, I ain't got a problem, ok! Anyway, I'm feeling a lot better nah, it was just a blip, that's all.'

It was time to try another tactic. 'Ok, then, how about I make you an appointment at the alcohol services eh? I know this consultant...'

'Honestly, Trace, I know you mean well, but I'll be fine, I promise. Once this claim's sorted, I'm gonna buy me sen one of them holiday homes, one of them wi' a fishing lake. Did ya know you can pick' em up for about 30k?' He reached to under the coffee table. 'Here.' He tossed me some brochures.

I sat a flicked through them and they looked really nice. 'So you're going to become a professional fisherman then, eh?'

Dad scoffed. 'What d'ya mean become? I'm already the best!'

I couldn't help but smile. It was nice to see that Dad's dry sense of humour was coming back. The flat was clean and Dad was clean. Maybe it was just a blip after all. I crossed all my fingers that Dad would finally get himself back on track and stay true to his word.

# 86: Behind Closed Doors

Me and Dad were like passing ships in the night, I'd barely seen him since he'd sold the shop, and he was usually up and out before I got to his flat to clean it. According to Dot, he was still seeing Judy and had apparently met her two teenage kids. It felt like history repeating itself all over again, being pushed to one side while he played Daddy to other women's kids. I wasn't naive, I always knew that Dad wouldn't make Dad of the year, but deep-down it still hurt.

The only consolation was Donna. We were joined at the hip, and Danielle loved going round to play with her daughter. We'd embarked on a healthy eating regime and were following a calisthenics exercise programme together. It wasn't as easy as it looked and sometimes it felt like a game of twister.

There had been many a time that one of us had got stuck, which was hilarious. As well as our weight loss pact, me and Donna started taking the kids to the local mother and toddler playgroup and it wasn't long before I started to make friends with them too.

Their conversations revolved around how dull their lives had become since having kids and complaining about how it was left to them to do the shopping and cleaning.

They reckoned I was lucky that I had a bloke at home, but I would have traded places with them in a nanosecond. He might have looked like the perfect dad, but behind closed doors, he could be spiteful and nasty.

Now instead of complaining about the hours I worked, his attention had now turned to my female friends. I tried to introduce him to Donna's bloke, in the hope he too might find a new buddy, but he wasn't interested, on the account that he was a Blade and supported Sheffield United, which I thought childish. All he wanted and needed was his little family unit, but unlike him, I needed more.

Some of the mothers from the playgroup had invited me to go out for drinks with them one weekend, but I used work as an excuse; there was no way Paul would let me go or give me the money.

Donna could never understand why I had to justify asking for money, especially when it was me who earned it. Deep-down, I knew it wasn't right but if I ever complained or challenged him, he always had a way of justifying what the money was being spent on, and it wasn't worth the hassle.

Paul put a dampener on everything, even ruining our trip to Primrose Valley with Mum and Ada with his constant complaining and moaning behind my family's back. My whole week was spent having to overcompensate for his mardy behaviour. In fact it was so bad that I ended up calling Grandad to collect us early.

The more I confided in Donna, the more I realised just how miserable I was. Paul was quite content in his little bubble, just me and Danielle. Whereas I felt like I was suffocating. I'd tried sitting him down on numerous occasions to explain how unhappy I was, but it was like talking to a brick wall.

Things were changing. I was developing a new-found confidence and even though I was tied into a relationship and didn't have control of my own money, I felt stronger. I could just about cope with Paul and his controlling ways if I had Donna by my side. All was going great, and then I found out I was pregnant again.

# 87: Just the Tonic

The change in Dad had been amazing. Though the stubborn git was still point-blank refusing to access any other source of support, he had been true to his word, with no alcohol passing his lips since he'd been released from hospital.

Thankfully, apart from one mate, Lawson, the rest of his divvy mates had stopped calling round. Lawson had a dishevelled appearance and a few missing teeth, but he wasn't a bad influence, and it was good to have someone else keeping an eye on dad and keeping him company.

Dad had treated himself to a new DVD player and was gaining a pretty impressive collection of DVD films. He loved John Wayne and the old cowboy films and could watch them over and over again.

The claim seemed to be progressing well too, which was also a massive relief. Apparently, the solicitors were finally preparing their case in readiness to argue over a settlement fee. It genuinely felt like we were turning a corner, and I could see some light at the end of what had been a very dark tunnel.

One night, I called round and could hear him on the phone. I could tell it was a woman by the flirty banter, so I left him to it and went to make a brew. When I returned, I was surprised to see him holding out the phone to me. 'Wanna say hello?' he asked.

I was bemused but Dad looked like the cat who'd got all the cream. Dad handed me the phone.

'Hello?'

There was a giggle from the other end. 'Hello, Tracey.'

I recognised the voice, but I couldn't quite place it.

Dad laughed at my confused face. 'It's Tracey, ya silly sod!'

'Tracey, Tracey.' I could hear her laughing at the other end.

'Oh my god, Tracey!' I exclaimed. 'How are you doing?'

It didn't feel like years we'd last spoken. It was great to chat, and we exchanged numbers before I handed the phone back to Dad. I left them to carry on chatting. It was nice to see Dad happy. He sounded like a lovestruck teenager, just like when they'd first started dating.

Eventually he returned to me.

'Soooooo...' I laughed. 'How long you been talking to Tracey? Tha kept that quiet, ya sly old dog.'

Dad laughed. 'Aye, tha knows.'

Apparently, he'd got Tracey's number off her uncle in a pub and had left it a while before calling. I found myself thinking that it was a good job he had, because she wouldn't have got a straight word out of him a few weeks back.

Dad brought me up to speed. It turned out Tracey was living in Lincolnshire with a young son called Malcolm. For a spilt-second I wondered if he might be Dad's son, but it would have been impossible as they hadn't seen each other for years.

The best news though was that she was single, and Malcom's dad wasn't on the scene. My mind went into overdrive and Dad picked up on my smirk.

'Don't you be getting any ideas. It's early days and a lot of time has passed since we split. It's just nice we're talking again.'

I held my hands up. 'I totally get it. I'm just chuffed that you are back in touch again. You know I've always liked Tracey.'

Dad smiled. 'I know, she's always been a good egg, hasn't she?'

She was. Tracey was just the tonic Dad needed right now.

# 88: The Bombshell

I couldn't believe it. Six months earlier, I had changed my contraception and now my breasts were sore and a second test at Donna's confirmed it.

I thought I'd been careful. I hadn't even had that much sex, but the result was positive – I was pregnant and I knew right there and then that, as much as didn't want an abortion, I couldn't have this baby. I'd missed out during my first attempt of motherhood, and I wasn't about to make the same mistake again.

The guilt weighed heavy on my heart, and I wondered if I would ever forgive myself, but I knew deep-down I couldn't keep it. I just hoped Paul would see it the same way.

I made sure Danielle was asleep before I broke the news to him. I'd been psyching myself up all day. I had no idea what he was going to say. The best-case scenario was that he'd agree with me and be supportive. After all, even he must be able to see that our family set up was far from perfect.

Paul was playing a video game in the living room, oblivious of the bombshell I was about to drop on him.

'Paul, we need to talk.'

As usual he hadn't heard me, so I raised my voice. 'Paul.'

'Give me a minute. I'm close to the next level.'

I waited for him to finish and then I told him. He still had his back to me.

'I'm pregnant.'

He spun round and his face lit up. I had to get in quick and break the second part of the news fast. 'But I'm not keeping it.'

The silence was crippling, but I didn't say a word. I reasoned that I'd been afforded the time to get used to the idea and that he still needed to process it. It wasn't long before he broke the silence. He stood up and began pacing the room, then stopped and snarled.

'But you don't get to fucking decide! That's my kid too!'

He was furious. It couldn't have gone any worse. I tried to reason with him, reminding him we barely had two pennies to rub together, that we could barely afford the kid we had already, but he wasn't having any of it.

Then Paul changed tactics. Instead of being angry, he softened. 'Look Trace, I can't see how you would think that this is bad news. We've always talked about having a brother or sister for Dan. Ok, I know it's sooner than we'd planned but we'll cope. We have done ok so far, haven't we?'

I couldn't bear to tell him the truth; I couldn't tell him that the relationship was already suffocating me. That the burden for being responsible for bringing the money in was weighing too heavily on me. I couldn't tell him that, given half the chance, I would have been off like a shot ages ago and that the only thing that was keeping me there was the fact that I had nowhere else to go.

'Look, Trace, we can cope.'

I laughed before snapping. 'I don't want to just cope! And I don't want to bring another kid into this world and not get to look after it! This is all fucked up!' I was pacing the room now and on a roll. 'I don't know any other man who doesn't want to go out to work and provide for his family. It's not fucking normal! You never go out, you won't socialize. This isn't a fucking life, it's an existence.'

'Are you fucking kidding me? This is all your fault! It's you who fucking trapped me!'

I just shook my head; I was wondering when I'd start getting the blame for everything.

*Of course it was, Paul, of course it was*, I almost said. But I was determined not to bite.

'Look, we are going around in circles here.'

'So, who else knows?' he asked. 'I bet she knows, that fat bitch across the road. You haven't been the same since tha made friends with her.'

I was furious. 'This has got nothing to do with Donna. I have got my own mind, you know.'

'Do you actually think I'm going to sit here and let you murder my child and say nothing about it?' He shook his head and started smirking. 'Let's see what everyone else has to say about it.'

'You can tell whoever the fuck you want Paul. My mind's made up.'

I tried to put on a brave face, but deep-down it felt like a small part of my soul had left my body. I wanted to storm out of the house but didn't have anywhere to go. I could have gone running over to Donna's, but that would have just given him more ammunition. Instead, I headed upstairs to the bedroom, hoping he wouldn't follow.

I lay on the bed, wondering what I could do and then I had a thought. Dad was barely at the flat anymore ever since he'd been dating Judy. I wondered if push came to shove that he might let me and Dan go stay at his, just until I sorted somewhere else to live.

The next day, I dropped Danielle off at school then headed to see Dot at the taxi firm. I filled her in on what was happening, and as predicted, she was fully supportive.

She even suggested that I could stay with her but there was no way I was living in her small, scruffy place.

'What about your mum?'

'I've already put her through enough shit already. Anyway, that would mean Dan moving schools and Paul wouldn't let me take her.'

'So, get him to move out, then!'

'There is absolutely no way that Paul will leave that house...'

'Oo, oo,' she said excitedly. 'I heard one of the drivers has a bedsit going in cheap in Upperthorpe. I think he only lets it for thirty quid a week, and that's including the bills. I reckon he'll waiver the deposit for Frank's daughter!' Then she looked all deflated. 'Then again, I don't think he takes kids.' She shook her head again. 'Anyway, it won't come to that. Ya Dad wouldn't see you out on the streets, Tracey. Trust me, he's in the Blake now. Go down and catch him whilst it's early.'

I knew the pub wasn't ideal, but right now, Dad was my only hope. I found him at the bar in his usual spot, drinking with his mates.

'Dad, can I have a quiet word?'

Dad laughed. 'What? Tha wants some money?'

I didn't laugh; this wasn't funny. 'Nah Dad, it's not that. You got two minutes?'

Dad rolled his eyes, gesturing to the beer garden. 'Come on then, we can go out back.'

Thankfully, the beer garden was empty. I sat opposite him on the pub bench and took a deep breath.

'What's up? Spill.'

'Dad I'm pregnant.'

'Oookay. And that's good, isn't it?'

'Not really, Dad. I'm not keeping it, I can't.'

'What's Paul said?'

'He reckons it's great news. He's completely opposed to me getting rid, but I can't keep it, Dad.'

'Well, he does have a say in the matter.'

I couldn't believe he was siding with Paul. 'I get that, Dad. Under normal circumstances, I'd be over the moon. Do you honestly think I want to do this?'

'Has he hit you?'

His question threw me. 'No, he hasn't. Why would that make a difference?'

Dad took a drag on his fag. 'Well yeah, if he ever lays a hand on you, I'd wanna know about it, do you hear me?'

I tried to explain that I wasn't happy, that I was sick of working, how I didn't want to have another kid only to go out and work, how I didn't feel like a proper mum already and that Paul was never going to get off his arse to work.

'So, what do you want me to do?'

'I'm not really sure, Dad. Only I'm not happy, and Paul's already threatened that we will split up if I don't have the baby. I don't know what to do. I was hoping that if the shit hits the fan, you might let me and Dan stay at yours, just until I find somewhere else.'

'Thing is, I would, but I've been thinking of giving the flat up. Me and Judy have been looking into taking the Palm Hotel over.'

'Bit soon, isn't it? Tha's only been seeing her a couple of months.' As soon as the words left my mouth, I knew I'd pissed him off.

Dad shook his head before stubbing out his fag in the ashtray. 'That's rich coming from you, innit. Listen Trace, go back to Paul. I'm sure you will both figure it out.'

He started to stand up, a signal that the conversation was over. My heart sank. I could feel the tears coming. I looked at Dad, hoping he could read my eyes, hear me, see me and tell me everything would be ok. But there was nothing. And I knew right there and then I was on my own.

Dad walked back into the pub, leaving me sitting alone. I was gutted. I'd never ever asked him for anything. I'd lied for him, covered up his cheating. I was the one who'd had to deal with the bailiffs and all the shit in the shop. I'd done anything he'd asked of me and thought we'd had a special bond and now, when I needed something from him, he didn't give a fuck!

I walked back through the bar on my way out.

'Are ya staying for a drink?' Dad shouted. 'Oh, I'm sorry, I forgot. You can't. You're preggers!' And with that, he turned his back to me.

I couldn't believe how insensitive he'd been. Now everyone would know that when I didn't start to show, that I'd got rid of it. I didn't say a word. I couldn't get out of the place fast enough, plus I had a doctor's appointment to keep.

# 89: A New Ally

Tracey had invited Dad to stay over at hers for the weekend. I don't know who was more excited, me or Dad. They'd been speaking regularly, which was respite for me because he was calling me less. Tracey was clearly having a positive influence on him, but I couldn't help wondering how much she knew about Dad's recent drinking activity. With Dad's impending visit, I owed it to her to bring her up to speed. So I finally took the plunge and made the call.

'Hiya,' I said. 'It's me, Tracey.'

'Hello lovely. It's so nice to hear from you.' I could tell by the tone of her voice that she meant it.

'A little bird tells me that you've invited Dad down to yours for the weekend.'

She laughed and we chatted for over half an hour, whilst I brought her up to speed. I'd had another child since I'd last seen her and I was in a relationship with a new guy. A *lot* had changed.

When it was her turn, she explained that Malcom's dad wasn't on the scene and that she hasn't dated anyone since then. I really didn't want to throw a spanner in the works, but I had to...

'Look Tracey, I'm not sure how much you know about what's been going off, but I need to have a chat about Dad.'

I filled her in about the hospital episodes and the doctor's concerns. She listened so intently, without interrupting me, that I was worried that when I'd finished, she might have a change of heart.

I was so relieved to hear that he had been transparent with her. In fact, it sounded like he'd opened up a lot more to her than he had with me and had even disclosed to her that he had scared himself.

'I know your dad hasn't had it easy over the past couple of years but I'm not naive either. I know he's not the easiest of people, but ya know what? He'll always have a special place in my heart.'

She paused. 'That being said, I have got Malcom to consider, and he'll always come first. Anyway,' she laughed. 'Let's not get carried away, it's only a weekend. I thought it might do him good to get away for a bit and I've also said, there'll be no drinking.'

Dad was a lucky sod to have someone like Tracey on his side. It didn't seem to matter that he didn't have much to his name these days. She could have easily have backed away, but instead here she was, embracing him with open arms! And it wasn't just Dad she'd embraced; it was me too. Just confiding in her confirmed that I had a new ally. All I could hope for now was that Dad didn't fuck this up.

# 90: Backed Into a Corner

The doctor confirmed the pregnancy and made another appointment with the nurse to go through the arrangements. I only had to take some tablets, but they needed to confirm how far gone I was first. I couldn't believe how easy it was.

Before going home, I walked around the estate, going through my options again. My only practical option was the bedsit. I could afford to cover the rent with my wages from the taxi firm, and it was only five minutes away.

I reasoned I could still be there to take Danielle to school etc. The only difference would be I wouldn't be sleeping overnight, *and* it wouldn't be for long. I could then go to the council and, even though Paul had never been violent, I was prepared to lay it on. I could even take Danielle into a mother and baby home, if that's what it took to get re-housed.

But hopefully it wouldn't come to that. I prayed Paul might have had a change of heart by the time I got back home.

He was waiting for me in the kitchen. 'Where have you been?'

'I went for a walk. I needed to think.'

'And...?' He smiled. I could tell he was thinking I might have changed my mind.

'Paul, my mind's made up. I'm not keeping this baby.'

Paul erupted. I'd never seen him so angry. 'I'm telling you now, Tracey, if you get rid of my kid then we are done, that's it! There's no coming back. I don't think I could ever forgive you!'

Once again, I tried reasoning, but he wasn't having any of it. Then he pointed to my stomach.

'That's my kid.'

'No Paul, it's ours and I have a say too.'

'So, that's it then? I've told you if you get rid of that baby, we are done!'

'That's your choice Paul, not mine. The last thing I want is to split the family up.'

'No, it's not!' he screamed.

In the years I'd been with Paul, I'd never dreamed he would get violent but, in that moment, I wasn't so sure. Then he changed tactics.

'Anyway, where do you think you're gonna go, cos if you think I'm leaving here you've got another thing coming.'

I was prepared. 'Well, there's a bedsit going in Upperthorpe.'

'Ahhhhhh, I get it now!' He started laughing cynically. 'Who else lives there, eh? Who is he? I bet it's not even my kid, is it?'

I couldn't believe my ears.

'Is that why you wanna get rid of it, eh, just in case it comes out and don't look like me?'

'Are you taking the piss!' I screamed. Just the implication that I would sleep around wound me up further. 'Fuck me, when do you think I would have had the time for an affair? You know I am no slag. I'm just not ready. We're not ready!'

'To be honest, Tracey, I don't think I know you at all. I'm telling ya, you've changed since you have started hanging around with her.'

'My decision has got nothing to do with anyone else. How many times do I have to tell you? It's not the right time. Look, Paul, I'm not saying I want to leave, that's the last thing I want, but you are giving me no other option.'

'You can't do this Trace, you can't!' I could see his eyes welling up and it hurt to know that I was the cause of his pain. I tried to comfort him, but he pushed me away and wiped his eyes.

'So, what're you gonna tell Danielle then? Mummy's going to kill your baby brother or little sister, then leave?'

His tone was venomous and spiteful. It was a good job that there wasn't a knife close by, because I could have used it in that moment. 'Don't you dare mention anything to her or I will never forgive you. This isn't her fault!'

'No, it's yours.' He turned his back to me. 'I can't even look at you.'

I came behind him and placed my hand on his shoulder, hoping he wouldn't push me away. 'I've already told you I don't want to end the relationship. It's you who's saying it's done. We can get past this.'

He shook me off. 'Nah, trust me, Tracey, if you go through with this, you're going to regret it.'

I didn't like his tone. 'Is that a threat?'

'It's a promise,' he snarled.

My heart sank. I had thought that I might be able to win him around, but I'd failed. He'd backed me into a corner, leaving me with no other choice but to leave.

# 91: Staying Positive

Dad had ended up staying for the whole week and clearly things were going well. Despite Tracey having told Dad that she'd put on loads of weight, when I spoke to him on the phone, he said she hadn't changed one bit.

He seemed to be enjoying the slower pace of life and being part of the family. He'd been taking little Malcom to the park and swimming, and Malcolm had given him the nickname "Dolphin" because of his ability to stay underwater. While he carried on talking, my thoughts returned to the one time when Dad had taken me and Sarah to the pool, and part of me felt sad because it seemed like Malcolm might be the son Dad had always wanted.

I'd never felt that kind of affection from Dad when I was a kid. I quickly stopped myself from being maudlin though, and reminded myself that that was in the past and that I was a grown-ass woman now.

When Dad mentioned that Tracey had asked if he would like to stay for Christmas, I was absolutely elated. I had previously offered for Dad to come to ours, but like the year before, he'd declined.

I couldn't help but laugh when Dad told me about how Tracey had roped him into a pre-arranged photo shoot. The photographer had come round to Tracey's house and Dad had taken an instant dislike to him, claiming that he was over-familiar with Tracey. I could just imagine Dad getting all jealous and protective.

I could hear Tracey in the background, laughing. It warmed my heart that they were getting on so well. The news about him staying longer was the best Christmas present ever. I'd been worried about him being alone and drinking again.

It had been a rollercoaster since he'd returned to Sheffield and, though I was trying to stay positive, there were still some doubts which would niggle away at me. I knew Dad well.

He was an extrovert at heart and whilst he seemed to adapt well to playing the man at home, I was scared that he would soon get bored. Dad thrived around people, he loved being the centre of attention, propping up the bar, being around his mates. He needed a purpose, and status was important to him.

But for now, I had to try and push this to the back of my mind and try and get on with life and make most of the much-needed respite that had been gifted by Tracey. My only hope was that Dad would have some sort of epiphany whilst staying with Tracey, but until then, the threat of him relapsing would always be there.

# 92: Just the Beginning

I'd called the landlord the following morning and was relieved when he'd agreed to meet me straight after my appointment with the nurse. Dot had been right; he'd also agreed to waive the usual deposit on the basis that my dad was Frank Ford, even though the likelihood of Dad bailing me out was less than nil. He was more interested in his next business venture with Judy, managing the bar instead of propping it up.

After dropping Danielle at school, I headed straight to the doctors to see the nurse for the abortion pills. She told me to take one tablet with water, then four more twenty-four hours later. She warned me to expect cramps and reassured me that I would hardly notice a thing, apart from a little show of blood.

As soon as I got my tablets, I headed to the bedsit, where the landlord was waiting for me as agreed. He explained as we walked in the house, that there were no kids or pets allowed, and as soon as I saw the inside of the house, I knew that this wasn't a place for a kid. The whole house smelt fusty; the kitchen and bathroom looked like they hadn't been cleaned properly for years, and the worst part was that I would have to share it with three complete strangers.

We'd bumped into one of the other residents in the hallway, who could have done with a wash himself. He greeted me excitedly and told me I would fit in, but I wasn't interested in making new friends. This place was just a temporary measure, a place to sleep, which was just as well, because it was just a room. There was a single bed covered by an old-fashioned candlewick blanket, a bedside cabinet, with an empty glass, and a set of drawers and a single wardrobe.

I explained to the landlord that it might be a couple of days before I could move in, but he handed me the keys anyway.

'Listen, you're Frank's daughter. There's no pressure. I know you're good.'

As soon as I accepted the keys, I knew that there was no turning back. The bedsit was less than half a mile away, but that morning, walking back to the house, it felt miles further. Instead of going home, I called in at Donna's.

'Come on, then. What's it like, Trace?' Donna seemed excited for me.

'It's a reyt shit hole. There's no way I'll be able to let Danny stay over.'

'Trust me. You're doing the right thing.'

I couldn't share her enthusiasm. 'I don't have anything to my name. I don't even own an alarm clock. How the fuck am I going to be able to get up in the morning to take Dan to school? I stood up and started to pace the kitchen. 'What if I'm making the wrong decision? Even if I get a place with the council for me and Danielle, he's not going to give her up without a fight.'

Donna huffed. 'Look, it might just be the kick up the arse he needs to go out and get a job then!'

'And what about the rent? I'm going to have fuck all to live on after paying that out!' My stomach started doing butterflies. 'Fuck, Donna, I haven't thought this through properly.'

'Trace, calm down, everything will be ok.' She stood up and started rummaging in her cupboards before producing a small alarm clock. 'Here, and I've got a kettle you can have.'

'But what about Dan? Everyone is going to hate me. I mean what kind of mother leaves her daughter?'

'Trace, it's not like you're not leaving her with a mass murderer for fuck's sake. She's with her Dad, and like you said, it won't be for long, and who knows, you might even be able to come back from this.'

I shook my head. 'I don't ever think I would be able to forgive him.'

'Have you been to see the nurse yet?'

I went to take the tablets out of the bag and placed them on the table. 'I'm ready. All I need to do is get my clothes and leave.'

Donna leaned in to give me a hug. 'C'mon, Trace. You've got this. You know I'll always be here for you.'

I knew she was right and conceded that there was no time like the present. I took the first of my tablets and picked up the alarm clock before heading over the road to pack some clothes. As usual, Paul was playing on his games console.

I had no time to lose, so I went straight to the cupboard under the sink to get a couple of carrier bags before heading upstairs to pack my clothes. I was just grabbing some underwear when Paul turned up.

'What are you doing?' He looked confused.

'I've told ya. I'm leaving.'

'I can't believe that you are actually going through with this,' he sniggered.

I ignored him and continued packing.

'You are making a *big* mistake, Trace.'

I continued to ignore him, which only seemed to make him angrier. 'I'm telling ya now. If you leave, you are never coming back!'

I didn't bite back. I didn't have the energy. I continued to pack.

His voice softened. 'Look, we can work through this, there is no need to go.' He crossed the room and towered over me as I packed my carrier bag. 'I cannot believe that you are actually going to get rid of our kid and leave Danielle. What fucking kind of mother are you?'

I snapped. 'Trust me. If I could take her with me, I fucking would, but don't worry, it won't be for long.' I pushed him out of the way.

He laughed. 'You're nothing without me.'

It was weird, like I was having an out of body experience. I could hear his venomous words but somehow, they'd stopped penetrating. I felt numb. It took me less than ten minutes to pack the rest of my essentials, whilst Paul looked on.

I had to push past him to get out of the bedroom. I half-expected him to try and physically stop me but thankfully, he didn't. He just followed me to the back door.

'I'm telling you, Trace, you are going to regret this.'

'The only regret is being stupid enough to get pregnant again.' And with that, I walked out of the door.

As I walked to school to fetch Danielle, I replayed over and over what I would say and how she might react. I knew she was only young and that it might just go over her head, but I remembered what it felt like at that age myself.

I couldn't articulate it, but I wasn't stupid, and I could always sense the tension between my parents. Maybe this was for the best. The less me and her dad were around each other, the less tension there would be in the house.

Donna was right, it wasn't like I was leaving my child with a mass murderer, and Paul was her dad; she was used to him being the main carer with me working all the time. The only change would be that I wouldn't be around in the morning when she woke up. My main priority was to reassure her that I wasn't going anywhere.

In the end, I needn't have worried. She was more interested in playing on the swings in the park than she was about the news that Mummy was going to be sleeping somewhere else for a while.

I dropped her back to Paul with a hug and a smile and a promise to pick her up in the morning and, aside from a few snipes from Paul, that was that.

Striding purposefully to my new home, the tears that I'd anticipated never came. Instead, I felt elated, liberated, and proud that I'd been able to stand my ground.

I still couldn't believe that I was going through with it, But I also knew that this wasn't time to get complacent. This was just the beginning, and I still had another round of tablets to take. I just hoped that my unborn baby might be able to forgive me for what I was about to do.

# 93: It's Tradition, Innit?

Christmas had been going so well, but on Boxing Day afternoon, I got a call from Tracey. I knew something was wrong, just by the tone of her voice.

'Ey up, Trace.' There was a resigned sigh. 'I'm sorry to call ya, but ya Dad's been drinking.'

I could hear Dad in the background, shouting. 'If that's our Tracey, ask her...she'll tell ya!'

I was confused. 'Tell me what?'

Tracey took a sharp breath. 'Well, according to ya dad, he can drink if he sticks to lager.'

I felt like having a temper tantrum. I knew it had been too good to be true!

'Where's he been?'

'He was only supposed to be going to the shop but didn't come back until three hours later. He's defo had more than a couple.'

Dad was still chuntering in the background.

'Here! Gimmee that phone!'

Tracey passed the phone to Dad.

'Ey up, shugs!' He was slurring his words. 'Will you tell Tracey she's getting all wound up all about nowt. I have literally had a couple of pints and a small G&T. I mean it *is* Boxing Day. It's tradition, innit?'

I was so pissed off. 'Dad, I'm not being funny, but you aren't even supposed to be drinking and now it's gone from a couple of lagers to a small G&T!'

'Oh, for god's sake, not you an' all. I've had all this from her!'

I knew there was no reasoning with him. 'Look, Dad, put Tracey on, will ya?'

'Aye, that's all I need, you two ganging up on me.'

Tracey was back on the phone. 'I'm so sorry, Trace.'

I cut her off. 'Hey, you've got nowt to be sorry for. It's him who's fucked up!'

She went on. 'Hopefully he'll sleep it off, but I'm going to have to ask him to go back to Sheffield in the morning. If I didn't have Malcom, it might be different, but I've got him to think about. He doesn't need to be seeing this.'

She had every right to kick his sorry ass outta the door. I still couldn't believe he could have been so stupid. Part of me hoped that Tracey might have changed her mind in the morning, but deep-down I suspected she wouldn't and when the morning came round, nothing had changed. Dad was on his way back to Sheffield.

# 94: Whispers From My Heart

I'd only been asleep for a couple of hours when the cramps started, a reminder that I was terminating my child growing inside me.

Despite knowing that my decision was for the best, it was hard to ignore the whispers from my heart that told me I was making a mistake, and I found myself wondering if it would have been a boy or a girl. I didn't have time to wallow in the guilt and the shame though, because I had more important issues to contend with, like getting Danielle to school and getting my sorry ass down to the housing.

Paul barely acknowledged me when I entered the house. Danielle was in the living room eating her breakfast, engrossed in a kid's programme. She hadn't said anything about the fact I hadn't slept at home the night before either. It was all bizarre. It was like nothing had changed, but, of course, everything had.

My next challenge was getting into the housing department without bumping into Mum or her workmates.

I managed to slip into the waiting area unnoticed, then took a ticket from the machine before waiting my turn to see one of the housing officers. I still hadn't properly thought through what I might say or what reason I could give.

Sitting there, I hoped and prayed that I didn't cop for the same housing officer from a few years earlier. I couldn't cope with the look of distaste again. Then again, she'd have every right to judge me. I mean, look at me. Here I was, sitting in the same spot I'd been in only a couple of years earlier, begging for a roof over my head.

Only this time, I was just another single parent, and any dreams of having a fairy tale ending had vanished. This was far from a fucking fairy tale. It was a fucking nightmare, and there was certainly no Prince Charming waiting around the corner to come and rescue me from my sad, pathetic little life.

Then again, the last thing I was interested in was another man, fuck that! They were all useless. Even Dad didn't give a fuck about me, not now he had hooked up with Judy and was signing the lease on a new pub.

I thought back to Mum and wondered if I could be a single mum like her. She'd coped somehow. She'd managed to hold down a full-time job and take care of us kids, and Dad was ten times worse than Paul. I just hoped and prayed that whoever called my number would have the same faith in me.

I'd planned on being composed when my name was called, but I broke down as soon as I stepped into the booth. The poor guy behind the counter couldn't introduce himself because I was practically begging before I knew it.

'It's not working out. I've made a mistake. I have nowhere to go. I couldn't bring another child into the world, that would have been cruel. I can't afford to pay the rent on the bedsit. I can't go back. I promise I'll never ask for help again!'

My hysteria was broken when, out of nowhere, the guy, who would have only been a couple of years older than me, passed me a tissue. I immediately apologised.

Realising I'd made a right fool of myself, I was convinced I'd fucked up my chances, but instead of sending me away with my tail between my legs, the housing officer explained that I would need to take my name off our joint tenancy before they could offer me anything. He then explained somewhat apologetically that the only area they could offer me would be a flat in the Kelvin flats, which would be perfect for me. Dan wouldn't have to move schools, and I'd still be near work and Donna.

I left the housing office on cloud nine and was relieved that I hadn't bumped into Mum or any of her mates. I'd already decided that I was going to wait to move into my place that the council offered me before breaking the news to Mum or Ada about me leaving Paul. They had enough on, helping Sarah into her new flat on Norfolk Park. I hadn't even met her new bloke yet. I hoped he was better than Paul.

I still could believe how fucking stupid I'd been. I'd always said that I would never allow a man to treat me like shit, and here I was. Looking back, the manipulation and controlling ways had always been there, but I'd stupidly translated it into love. As far as I was concerned, the world could shove love up its fucking arse.

# 95: Breaking the Spell

I'd left it a day before calling Sarah to tell her about the call with Tracey and she was as pissed off as me. 'Ahhh, for fuck's sake! Well, I've got plans, so I won't be calling in on him when he gets back. What're you doing?'

'I'm working. That family support video that we had filmed in the summer's ready to be signed off. I'm well behind on making the training booklet...'

My phone started buzzing. I checked the number. 'Look, that's him now, let me call ya back.'

'Ey up, shugs. I suppose you've heard, then?'

I was bemused. 'Of course I have. We spoke on the phone last night, remember?' The phone went quiet. 'Dad?'

'I'm here, I'm here.' I could tell he was on the defensive. 'Actually, I do remember speaking to you last night. Look, I only called into the local for a couple.'

I interjected. 'Sounded like you'd had more than a couple, Dad.'

'Oreyt, maybe I had more than a couple. But fuck me, that's the first drink I have had in months. I still think Tracey overreacted, but hey, that's her prerogative. Anyway, we're still mates. A little break from each other will do us some good.'

I wanted to give him what for, but I didn't have the energy to try and reason with him.

'What you up to anyway? Are ya calling round?'

'I'm at work, Dad and I'm not sure when I'll be able to call, to be honest. I'll call ya.'

'No problem. I was just letting ya know I've got back ok. See ya when I see ya.' And with that, he ended the call.

There's a saying that you can love someone but not like them and it's fair to say that, in that moment, I didn't like Dad.

One minute, he didn't seem to have a care in the world and then the next, he acted like the world was against him and making excuses. If it wasn't his mum, it was the claim or the fact he'd been holed up in what he'd started to refer to as his 'shitty flat,' which pissed me off no end. He had no idea how hard it was to get that flat, let alone furnish and decorate it for him.

I decided to give Jean a bell. She'd been having her own challenges with loved ones over Christmas, and we shared our woes. It was whilst talking to Jean, I had a sort of epiphany.

For months, I'd been banging on about Dad being in denial, when I suddenly realised that I had been too. I'd been running around like a headless chicken, trying to fix Dad. I'd naively thought that Sarah stepping up and Tracey coming back on the scene was going to help, but it wasn't enough.

I was starting to get more and more exhausted and angry and, even though I knew I wasn't to blame for his drinking, I still couldn't help feeling guilty, like I had somehow let him down.

I felt constantly torn. But then again when it came to Dad, I always had been. As a kid, Dad was like my drug. He was my kryptonite, my Achilles heel. I'd always craved his attention, addicted to the high I'd feel after receiving recognition or praise from him. If he'd said 'Jump!' I would have said 'How high?' I literally would have done anything for him and, even though my efforts weren't reciprocated, I was still doing it.

I'd thought I'd built my own life that had nothing to do with Dad and that I wasn't dependent on him anymore. I'd worked on forgiving him too. I knew deep-down that he loved me, despite his fucked-up way of showing it, but I also knew that his ego would always come first. I'd thought I'd broken the spell Dad had over me, but I clearly hadn't.

# 96: Saving Grace

Just when I thought things couldn't get any worse, they did. The rumours about Dad selling the taxi firm turned out to be true. The staff were kept on, but things were changing. The new boss was okay, but he wasn't Dad, and I was no longer the owner's daughter, just another telephonist.

The new owner had grand plans, including relocating the office to the other side of town, making it impossible for me to sustain my current arrangements. Then, to make matters worse, Uncle John and Auntie Dot took the lease on a pub at the other side of town too.

It especially hurt when I heard that Dad had put up the money for the lease. He could have helped me, but he never had. It was like being a kid again, always coming second best to his mates or bird.

The only saving grace was that the new taxi office was just up the road from their new pub. The Rose and Crown was an imposing building and sat on the corner of Darnall. Barely being able to afford the rent on the bedsit, Auntie Dot suggested I could stay with them rent-free. The downside meant I would be further away from Danielle. But I had no other option but to return the keys to the bedsit.

I'd thought that not paying any rent might have made my life easier, but I was stuck between a rock and a hard place. I could have done more hours at the taxi firm, but that would mean spending less time with Dan. And I couldn't claim my own benefits because a) I didn't have a permanent address, and b) Paul had kicked off monumentally about how if I applied for benefits, it would be the equivalent of me taking food out of Danielle's mouth; he justified it as being akin to child maintenance.

Our relationship blew hot and cold. Some days, he seemed okay with the arrangements; he'd even invite me to stay for tea, and it was just like in the old days. Other nights, he would encourage me to stay over, saying 'no strings attached', but there were always strings attached. I soon figured out that my staying over was another opportunity for him to try to win me around.

Even though I'd left him, he was still in control. He was Danielle's dad, something he never let me forget. We were fused together by the DNA that had created our child. He'd tell me that although it had been hard, he still loved me. Or that he'd forgiven me for having an abortion.

But when he didn't get his own way, or his words didn't work, he'd flip. He'd be obstructive, arranging to go out when he knew I was planning on calling around, and doing everything he could to make life difficult. But if I complained, he would throw the fact that I was the one who had left the family home back in my face.

Some days, when it got tough, I would wobble and consider going back, but I had to stick to my guns.

I was surprised when, one day, Paul announced that he'd been invited out and asked if I'd babysit. He'd reconnected with some of his old mates, and I was relieved. He hadn't been out for over four years and had become a shadow of the guy I'd met years ago.

I knew it would be good for his self-esteem to have his mates back in his life, and I was grateful that it would take the attention off me. It also gave me and Dan quality time together and soon it was a regular thing on Saturdays and then Fridays too. I was tempted to ask him how he was paying for it but was too afraid to rock the boat.

Suddenly, Paul seemed to be living his best life, out socialising every weekend while I was living like a hobo, sofa surfing and constantly on the scrounge. I was starting to wonder if I'd made the right decision after all. Then I got the news that the council had found me a flat on Kelvin.

Paul even offered to come and view it with me, which I translated into him coming to terms with our separation. Dan was excited, too and couldn't wait to choose her bedroom.

I couldn't help thinking that after all the heartache over the past few weeks, my luck was finally starting to change. That was until I walked into the flat, and my heart sank.

There was no way I could move into it. The place was a mess; all the walls would need decorating, and then reality hit me: I didn't have the financial means to pay for paint. Even if I claimed benefits, that would only cover the rent, food and bills; there would be nothing left over to decorate or furnish it. I was on the verge of crying when Paul turned to me.

'Look, Trace, you've made your point. Why don't you come home, eh?'

I was stunned and snapped. 'This wasn't about trying to make a point. You gave me no choice but to leave.'

'Yeah, I know, and I was wrong. I admit it. I did take you for granted but so much has changed.'

I couldn't answer, because I knew he was right; so much had changed. I'd changed and he'd changed. I was so confused. I didn't know who I was anymore.

Paul pressed on. 'You know I've always loved you. Remember? Me and you against the world? I promise I'll try harder. You can have your own friends, your freedom.'

I wasn't sure.

'You were right. I'd got into a rut, but it's done me good getting out of the house with the lads. Plus, I can earn a bit on the side selling a couple of Es. One of the lads is raking it in!'

I couldn't help but laugh. 'So, you're gonna be a drug dealer now, are ya?'

'Don't be daft! I'm just saying there's easy money to be made. You won't have to work as many hours either.'

It did sound tempting.

'Look, you don't like living at the pub, so just come home? Keep the keys to the flat. I'll even help you decorate it. We could even let it out, make some cash.'

'Sounds like you've got it all sussed out.'

Paul shrugged his shoulders. 'Look, all I'm saying is let's just try, eh? This has gone too far. But there's no pressure.'

His declaration of love and reassurances felt convincing, and the thought of not having to return to the taxi firm or sleeping on a mattress on the floor like a hobo at the pub was tempting. Still, I wasn't ready to throw the towel in fully. I held my hands up in the air.

'Ok, but this isn't us getting back together, ok? I'm not giving up the flat and I still need to find a new job.'

Paul started grinning like a Cheshire cat, then turned to Danielle excitedly. 'Guess who's coming home, Danny?'

The smile on Dan's face was enough to tell me I was doing the right thing. I just hoped for all our sakes that I was.

# 97: Fuck Life, I'm Done

It was New Year's Eve. Me and Pat were getting ready to go out when Dad called. Pat suggested I ignore it, as we were already running late as, but I couldn't.

I still hadn't seen Dad since he'd got back from Tracey's, and I knew from our phone calls that he'd spent most of the week at The Ball. I didn't know what to do with him. I'd just known that I'd needed space. Pat rolled his eyes and left the room. I could tell Dad was well pissed already.

'Ey up, shugs.'

'Hi, Dad, you ok?'

'Aye, I just got back from Ball. I wa' just calling to see when babbi was callin' in to see me?'

This was the last thing I needed. I tried my best to sound chirpy. 'Well, it won't be tonight, Dad, sorry. Me and Pat are just getting ready to go out. Is everything ok?'

'Well, no, actually it's not! I ain't seen or heard from you since I got back. What's up? You avoiding me too?'

'I spoke to ya yesterday. Who else is avoiding you?'

Dad huffed down the phone. 'Tracey is.'

I'd only spoken to Tracey the day before and she'd said she couldn't get a straight word out of him when he'd rang her. So I guessed Tracey might have been dodging his calls too, not that I could blame her.

'Nah, Dad, not avoiding ya. I've just been busy. Ya know I've been working.'

'Whatever tha says.' There was a sarcastic undertone in his voice, and I didn't like it. I was tempted to tell him to fuck off, this was the last thing I needed right now, but I didn't.

'Ah, come on, Dad, don't be like that. You know I've been busy with work.'

'Well, ya not working now, are ya?'

'Look, Dad, I'll call up to see you tomorrow, eh?'

'Aye, whatever. You get thee sen out and enjoy ya sen. Don't you worry about little old me. I might as well not be here, I mean what's point, what's the actual fucking point?

Dad's tone unnerved me. I'd never heard him talk this way before. I tried my best to pacify him. 'Dad, listen, I have really got to go, but I promise I'll call up tomorrow.'

'Well, I might not be here tomorrow.'

I was confused. 'What d'ya mean? Where ya going?'

'I know you think I'm a burden. I may as well not be here. Ya know what? Fuck it! Fuck the claim, Fuck life, I'm done.' And with that, the line went dead.

I tried calling him back a couple of times, but he didn't answer. I called Sarah and relayed the conversation and my concerns, but she was of the same opinion as Pat, that he was pissed and would sleep it off.

I knew they were both right and that it was probably the drink talking, but it didn't stop me worrying. My mind was going a hundred miles an hour. Was he having a breakdown? What if he did something stupid? I even tried recalling what tablets were round at his and whether they would do some damage. It's fair to say that I didn't have a good night.

# 98: True To His Word

Paul was true to his word. He accepted my friendship with Donna now he'd got his own mates back, in fact, he encouraged it, which was a relief because the tables had turned.

Donna was having problems in her marriage and now she was pregnant with a third child which, unlike me, she'd decided to keep. Her decision almost felt like a betrayal as she'd supported the choices that I'd made, but there was no way I would have turned my back on her as she was the only true friend I had.

Paul and I had slipped back into a routine, and we were sleeping together again, only this time, it was different. We talked more and Paul openly admitted that he'd become paranoid and possessive, and he promised to never throw my decision to have an abortion back in my face, which was a relief, because I still doubted whether I had made the right decision, which was becoming the story of my life.

There were still occasions when I would see snippets of the old Paul resurface. 'I always knew you'd come back,' he'd say, which got under my skin because I knew that if Dad had helped me out, I still might not have returned. But Dad had turned his back on me and here I was.

The change in Paul was physical, too. He'd lost weight and started buying new clothes with his ill-earned gains from the weekend. Though there was never enough left over for me, which made me even more determined to find another job.

I even swallowed my pride and asked Dad if any hours were going at his pub, but then he dropped the bombshell that he and Judy had been offered a tenancy for a pub in Leeds. I didn't care what Dad did with his life; he'd made it clear with his actions that he didn't give a fuck about me.

After scouring the Sheffield Star Thursday job page, I saw an advert for a telesales job with no experience necessary, so I called them and was ecstatic when they asked me to come in for an interview.

The company specialised in house alarms. They had some fancy offices located by the hole in the road in the city centre. I joined the bunch of smartly dressed candidates for an interview and by the end of the day, I'd got a job.

All we had to do was call members of the public out of the phone book and tell them that we had security advisers working in their area due to a spike in burglaries. Once we'd booked the appointment, the sales advisor would do the rest, and according to the management, the alarm kit sold itself, so it was easy money, with a basic salary and plenty of opportunity for earning commission. The hours were good, too; we only had to work from five to eight-thirty, which meant I could still take and collect Dan from school.

Though it was hard, I was good at my job. I had the gift of the gab and never had a problem getting appointments. In fact, I was often top of the leaderboard. The only problem was relying on the sales reps to turn the appointments into sales, and I quickly realised that the management had exaggerated how much we could make, but I didn't care.

I loved the job and the banter with the other telesales staff and sales team; they became my second family; even Donna got a job working there. But it did mean I had to hand the keys back to the flat, which was only accumulating debt whilst it was empty.

There was a girl called Shauna who worked in the reception. I was drawn to her instantly; there was something about her. I loved her innocence, sense of adventure, and optimism; she reckoned that working at ATI was just a stopgap. She was planning to go to university but wanted to live a little first and had grand plans to travel the world.

I envied her freedom, but more importantly, her confidence. Every Thursday night, the sales team would arrange for the staff to go out for drinks, with the first round being on them, or more if we'd had a good week in sales, and it wasn't long before me and Donna started joining them. I would laugh my tits off at Shauna and her flatmate Claire flirting shamelessly with the sales guys, who lapped up all the attention.

As soon as the guys at work heard that Paul could get hold of some speed, they asked if I could bring them some in. I didn't mind, and Paul was more than happy for me to help shift some more gear for him.

It wasn't long before Donna and I would stay out longer on a Thursday night with them. We'd head off to the Thursday "grab a granny" night at Roxy's, a chance for me to really let my hair down. I would come home in a right tangle which would piss Paul off no end, but he could hardly complain, considering I was selling his drugs. Besides, he got a green card to go out and do what he wanted over the weekend, and plus, I wasn't getting off with anyone. Cheating just wasn't in my DNA, and the break had actually brought us closer together in the end.

Perhaps he was right that we were meant to be together. Maybe the grass wasn't always greener. And as for Dad, he could go and fuck himself as far as I was concerned.

# 99: A Whole New Territory

When I woke up on New Year's Day, I felt like absolute dog shite and wondered how Dad did it daily. I could have quite easily stayed in bed for the rest of the day to nurse my banging headache, but I couldn't rest until I saw him, and he still wasn't answering his phone, which was unusual for him.

The flat door was unlocked, and the old familiar smell of stale drink and cigarette smoke hit me as soon as I entered.

I found Dad in the living room. He wouldn't have looked out of place sat on a park bench drinking out of a brown paper bag; by the looks of him, he must have slept on the sofa all night. Thank God, the sofa was leather, because there were burnt out fag ends littered on it.

At this rate he would be more likely to die from a house fire instead of the drink. There was an empty brandy bottle and another which was a quarter full by his leg. There was a kitchen knife on the coffee table, and I immediately started looking for signs that he might have already tried harming himself. Thankfully I couldn't see anything, but the intent was there, which unnerved me.

I started to nudge him gently. 'Dad, Dad, it's me, Tracey.'

He slowly opened eyes that were red and sore. It looked like he'd been crying all night.

'Ey up, shugs.' Dad looked pleased to see me, which was a good sign.

'Happy New Year and all that bollocks, Dad. How ya feeling?'

'It's not good, Trace, I'm fooked.' Dad's lips looked parched.

'Do you want me to get you some water?'

I was just about to move when Dad grabbed my hand.

'Trace, I need help. I can't go on like this.' Before I had time to reply, Dad was breaking down right before my eyes. He was sobbing so much, he couldn't talk. My hand was still entwined with his, his grip getting tighter the more he sobbed. I stroked his hand, trying to comfort him. It broke my heart seeing him like this. I sat, patiently waiting for the tears to abate, whilst wondering if this might be just the wakeup call Dad needed.

Dad finally stopped crying and pleaded. 'Trace, I need help. You said you knew someone. Can you call 'em, get me in to see 'em, today?'

'Dad, I can, but it's the bank holidays and the services will be closed.'

He threw his arms in the air. 'Well, I don't think I can wait. I'm not gonna last a couple more days! I feel like I'm going fucking mad, me head won't switch off.' He started punching his head with his fist, before breaking down again. The desperation in his eyes scared me. I knew I had to act fast.

Even though it was New Year's Day, I called Giz for advice, and she told me to call the mental health services out-of-hours team. It didn't take long to Google the number and for someone to answer. I felt nervous. This was a whole new territory for me.

I explained to the person on the end of the phone about my concerns about Dad, threats to harm himself, the knife on the coffee table. Desperate, I laid it on, telling them about the train crash and that he was suffering from PTSD. I didn't want them thinking he was just another attention-seeking drunk.

Having spoken to Dad briefly on the phone, the guy asked if I would be able to bring him down to a place in Nether Edge called Burbage, so that they could properly assess him. He also suggested that I bring a change of clothes just in case they decided to keep him in overnight as a voluntary in-patient. I took note of the address, before thanking him and ending the call. I relayed to Dad what had been suggested and all I got in return was a defeated: 'I'll do owt, Trace.'

I probably shouldn't have even been driving, but soon, we reached the right building. It had been years since I'd stepped into a mental health ward, only that time, it was me being admitted. I still couldn't comprehend how the tables had turned.

As we sat in the waiting room, Dad moved his hand to pat my knee. I instinctively knew that I had done the right thing, that he was in the right place and that, more importantly, he knew it too. Having asked Dad and I some questions about his mental state and his drinking, the mental health worker agreed.

'Look, Frank,' he said. 'Tracey did the right thing by calling us. Here's what we can do. We can admit you for a couple of days to allow us to do some more assessments.'

Dad looked up.

'I need to be clear that this is only a voluntary arrangement and that you are free to go whenever you like but seeing as you have been struggling at home alone, I think for now, this would be the best place for you. We can also help with the drinking. How does that sound?'

Dad nodded. 'Where do I sign up?'

# 100: Comedowns

I finally felt like my luck was changing. I'd lost weight and had my own job and new friends. Me and Paul were getting on better than ever, especially now he'd got his mates back in his life and his own little income coming, which took the pressure off me financially. He'd even started returning to football matches which he used to love.

I barely saw Paul over the weekends; if he wasn't out on Friday or Saturday night, he would be lying in bed recovering, after rolling in at an ungodly hour. Occasionally, he would bring some of the lads back, and they would spend the early hours doing bongs in the living room to help with the comedowns from the night's highs. None of it bothered me, just as long as the lads didn't make a noise or leave a mess. Having his mates back in his life was just what Paul needed; it was what we both needed.

However, I soon learned Sarah wasn't as accepting of our new arrangements. She'd recently given birth to a baby boy called Niall, and I'd gone around to her new flat to visit them both. I tried to hide my envy of how nice she'd got the place. Apparently, Dad had been well pissed off when he'd heard she was pregnant and she hadn't introduced her new bloke to him, and was even more pissed off that she hadn't named his first grandson after him. But, as usual, she didn't care what he thought.

'Trace, we need to talk.'

I didn't like her tone. 'Why, what's up?'

'It's Paul. He's cheating on you.'

I shook my head and raised my hand because I knew what was coming. Paul had already told me that one of her mates had accused him of cheating.

'I already know about your mate having a pop at him in the club last weekend. He's told me.'

'He's a sneaky bastard,' she muttered, putting Niall in his crib.

'So, come on then, have you seen him cheating?'

'No, but there is this one bird, she's always with him.'

I shook my head; I didn't believe a word of it.

'Paul would never jeopardise our relationship, not after everything we have been through. He might be many things, but he's never been a cheater.'

Sarah smirked. 'Okay then. Did you know about the drugs?'

'Yeah, I know about the drugs. It's only a few Es and a few bags of Speed, *and* everyone's at it!'

Sarah shook her head in disbelief. 'Sooo, you're not bothered then?'

Her words hit a nerve, making me lash out angrily. I'd never asked her for anything, and I didn't even feel like I could turn to her when I needed her the most. And here she was, trying to plant seeds of doubt, threatening my relationship.

Well, I wasn't having any of it.

'What do you care anyway? I barely see you anymore. I haven't even met your new bloke and when was the last time you called round, eh? You haven't got a fucking clue, Sarah.'

I could tell she was hurt but I didn't care.

'So, in answer to your question, no, I'm not going to do anything. I don't want to hear any more, end of story.'

I didn't stay for much longer; there was nothing more to say, but I knew Paul would have plenty to say when I returned home and relayed our conversation.

And, though I had to ask him, I knew deep-down that he wasn't a cheater. Despite his faults, Paul loved me, he always had. His reaction said it all, and if anything, the allegations just made me even more determined to make us work and prove everyone wrong.

# 101: Cherry Twin

Before me and Sarah went to see Dad, we called in at the flat to tidy up and get him some fresh clothes. Though she was shocked about what had happened, she agreed that he was in the right place.

'Well, it worked for you, didn't it?' she said proudly.

It was nice to see the pride in her face. We'd had our ups and downs over the years but here we were, working together. Walking through the doors of Middlewood hospital years earlier had certainly been life-changing for me. I just hoped and prayed that Dad took advantage of the opportunity and accepted professional help.

We arrived at the ward, and the staff directed us to his room. I couldn't help but compare this place to the one I'd been in years before. It looked like a hospital, but the pictures on the walls and soft furnishings made it feel less clinical. Dad wasn't in his room so one of the staff nurses suggested we look for him in the TV room.

When we found him, he wasn't alone. He had his back to us and was courting a few of the residents with some story, which must have been funny as they were all in hysterics. You'd have thought he was in the pub and not a mental health ward.

'Ey up, Dad!'

All eyes were on me and Sarah.

'Ey up, shugs. These are me girls.'

I had to do a double take when the woman next to Dad got up out of her seat.

'Oh my God, I don't believe it!' It was one of the Cherry twins, only, what with them being identical, I wasn't sure which one she was. I hadn't seen either of them since Dad left Norfolk Park when we were in our teens.

She picked up on my face.

‘It’s Nic!’ She turned around to Dad and playfully slapped him, before heading to embrace us both. ‘I already knew these two!’

It was good to see her, though a shock to realise that she was an in-patient and not a visitor.

Nic laughed. ‘I can’t believe that these two are your kids, Frank.’

He smiled proudly. ‘Yep. They’ve been little fuckers I’ll tell thee, but they ain’t half stepped up when their Dad needed em! In fact, I don’t know what I’d do wi’ out em, to be fair.’

Dad was a proud man and rarely dished out compliments, especially to us kids. His behaviour and attitude over the past few months had been intolerable at times, but for him to acknowledge that we’d been there for him meant a lot.

‘Come on, Dad, ya sloppy sod, let’s go outside for a fag and you can fill us in on what the docs have said.’

I turned to Nic. ‘Catch up in a bit, eh?’

She laughed. ‘Well, I ain’t going anywhere, am I?’

We made our way to the garden and found a bench. ‘C’mon then, Dad. How are you feeling and what have they said?’

‘Well, when you’d gone, they did some more assessments and gave me some sort of sedative. I slept like a baby, I’ve had a session with one of the councillors this morning, well I think she was, anyway.’

‘And did it help?’

Dad seemed distracted and tried to roll his fag. He shrugged his shoulders. ‘Well, all we did was talk, but I do feel better than I did, so that’s good, innit?’ Dad lit his fag and took a deep drag. ‘She reckons that the claim’s not helping me mental health.

I was tempted to mention that the copious amounts of Brandy weren’t helping neither but I didn’t.

‘In fact, Trace. I need you to do me a favour. Can you get in touch with the solicitors and let ‘em know I’m in here?’ Dad took another drag on his fag. ‘In fact, I reckon this might be a blessing in disguise, tha knows.’

‘How do ya work that out then?’

He was looking rather pleased with himself. 'Well, me being in here might help support me claim for PTSD!'

'Dad, I wish you could park the claim for one minute and see the bigger picture here.'

'And I wish you would stop focusing on the drink, Trace. It's only been since this fucking claim stated that I have been drinking more. Once this claim is sorted, I'll be reyt, don't you worry.'

I was starting to lose my patience. 'Ahh well, Dad, I do worry. The fact still remains that you shouldn't even be drinking, ya livers knackered already and at this rate tha won't be alive to spend the money from the fucking claim!'

Dad shook his head.

I tried reasoning with him again. 'Look Dad, I don't wanna fall out with ya, but I am seriously worried about ya, don't ya get that? Two days ago, ya wa threatening to kill yourself for crying out loud!'

Dad stubbed his fag out. 'Listen, I know ya worried and I'm sorry about that. I know I've let you down.'

Sarah stopped him in his tracks. 'This isn't about us, Dad. This is about you. There's nowt we want more than for you to get this claim sorted, and our Tracey's right, you have got to get on top of this drinking. And before ya say owt, no one's saying you have got to completely stop, but tha has got to stay away from that top shelf.'

The brewing argument was broken up by Nic. 'I'm making a cuppa, ya want one?'

'Ah cheers, mate.' Dad chirped in. 'Don't forget I like builder's tea, two sugars.'

Nic laughed back. 'Piss off, tha'll get what tha given,' and with that she headed off to make a brew for us.

'She's a good egg, int she? Such a shame, young lass like that being in a place like this.' I couldn't help wondering if Dad thought the same about me when I'd been admitted, but now wasn't the time to be bringing up the past.

I was feeling a little more optimistic when I got home. Overall, it had been a good visit and at least I could sleep a little better, knowing he wasn't sat alone in the flat drinking. My optimism was short-lived though. Uncle Mick called to say that Nan was in a bad way.

He explained that he'd not mentioned it to Dad because he knew he'd been hitting the top shelf again. Sooner or later Dad was going to find out and when he did, I wasn't sure how he'd handle it. All I could hope was that he engaged with the support services and could make it through the next few weeks without relapsing.

# 102: Going To Be Different

Just weeks after the news of Donna's pregnancy, I found out I was pregnant again, and this time I was hopeful. Paul and I were in a different place and with mine and Donna's due dates being only a week apart, we could share and support each other through the various stages of pregnancy.

Then there was Paul, who was ecstatic. 'I'm telling you, Trace. This was meant to be!'

And he was right. He was the only person who had always been there for me. Sarah had been the only person to encourage me to give it a go with Paul when I'd got pregnant, but she'd been nowhere to be seen in recent years and now there were the cheating allegations.

Then there was Dad. I'd naively assumed that moving to the other end of the city and working for him might have brought us closer together, but that hadn't worked out. All Dad was bothered about was himself. Dad had never cared about me or Sarah, he never had. He'd always put other women's kids before us; in fact, he was doing the exact same now, playing happy families and playing the Big I Am.

Then there was Mum. After all the shit Dad had put her through, she'd finally found a guy who adored her and, more importantly, a guy who would never dream of abandoning his kids for another woman. Mum had been promoted at work, and they had finally managed to buy their first home. They'd even swapped caravan holidays to go abroad and were planning a trip of a lifetime to Disneyland Florida with my little brother, Mark. He didn't know what it was to go without.

I'd also come to realise that no relationship is perfect and no one else was perfect, including myself. Despite not agreeing with me aborting his child and forcing me to leave him, Paul had still always been there for me, waiting. If that wasn't a declaration of love, I don't know what was.

Getting rid of this baby just wasn't an option. The last time I'd fallen pregnant had been a mistake, a naivety on my part, but this was just downright careless of me. There was just no way I could abort another child due to my inability to take proper precautions. No, this time, it was going to be different.

# 103: Drinks Are on Frank

Dad was nowhere to be seen when I arrived back at the hospital. This time there was just Nic sitting alone in the TV room so, I headed over to see her.

“Ey up, mucka, how ya doing? Have you seen Dad?’

‘He’s in with one of the doctors.’ She shuffled to the side of the sofa. ‘Here, sit down – I missed you before you left. I said to our Keely last night, you’ll never guess who’s in here. She couldn’t believe it!’

I couldn’t help thinking it was shame Keely wasn’t here too. Still, Nic and I had a lot of catching up to do. Like me, she had two kids. It should have been three, but she’d lost one just after childbirth, triggering depression, and then they’d diagnosed her as being bipolar too.

She confessed that she’d turned to drugs occasionally to help, and I couldn’t help thinking I’d got off lightly. She was shocked, when I told her about being in a mental health unit myself, but at the same time, I think it brought her some comfort, especially when I explained how I’d managed to turn it around. She nearly pissed herself laughing when I told her about Dad rocking up back in Sheffield unannounced with his one-eyed mate Sid Vicious, who had also just got out of a mental health unit himself.

‘He does love thee, tha knows. He didn’t stop talking about ya after ya left. Telling me how ya put him up and sorted him with the flat and all that.’

‘He’s got a funny way of showing it sometimes.’

I couldn’t help noticing the dark bags underneath sad eyes which had once been mesmerising. It was a reminder that we were all fragile. I was supposed to be offering Nic some support but found myself confiding in her instead.

‘Honestly, Nic, I didn’t realise he’d got a problem with the drink until he’d been back for a few months. It’s so frustrating, cos I know he can do it. When he’s not drinking, he's sound, but he can flip in a nanosecond. He's like fuckin' Jekyll and Hyde.'

'Well, all I can say is that I'm glad he's in here. Me 'n' him are the only sane fuckers in here!'

'Are my ears burning?'

We both turned round to see Dad.

Nic piped up. 'I wa' just tellin' Trace, me and thee are only sane uns in here.'

Dad laughed. 'Looks like they are letting me go home in a couple of days.'

'Tha fuckin not! Tha not leaving me in here with all these nutters!'

Dad went all serious. 'Don't thee worry Nic, I've told ya my door's always open for thee if tha needs a break.' I knew he meant it. When it came to his mates, he'd do anything for them.

It was time to break my news to Dad.

'Guess what?'

Dad rolled his eyes. 'What?'

'I've been on the blower to the solicitors. They're starting negotiations for a settlement!'

'Fuckin' get in!' Anyone would have thought Dad was at a footy match the way he was going off. I was just relieved and pleased for him that it was some good news for a change.

'Drinks are on Frank, then!' Nic laughed, before turning to me. 'Only joking!'

# 104: Three-Way Exchange

After months of rumours, news broke that the council had approved demolishing Kelvin's flats. Everyone was to be rehoused, and they'd been given a clearance key, meaning they got priority status and could relocate anywhere in the city. Part of me was kicking myself for handing back the keys to my flat too soon, but Paul had an idea.

'Trace, this is a perfect opportunity for us to have a proper fresh start! Loads want to stay in the area. I've heard some people are even offering money to anyone locally who might be prepared to do a three-way exchange. It means this time we get to choose wherever we want to move to.'

Paul was right. This was our perfect opportunity for a fresh start. Apart from Donna, there was nothing keeping us in Walkley, especially now Dad was moving to Leeds with his new family. And when Donna announced that she and her husband were planning on doing the same, it was a no-brainer.

Literally hours after placing an advert in the local post office window, someone had got in touch offering us two hundred pounds if we exchanged with them. All we had to do now was choose where to move to. We debated for hours about where to move and kept on coming back to Base Green, which was bang in the centre of where Paul's mates lived.

It had a reputation for being a nice, quiet estate and was in the catchment area for Charnock Primary School, the same one my little brother went to. The only problem was that the houses were like rocking horse shit to acquire, but we could wait. We had more important things to consider, like our second baby.

I'd already decided that if needed, I would have an epidural as soon as it was offered. There was no way I was putting myself through any unnecessary pain again. And now that Dad was living in Leeds, there was zero chance that he would be rushing over to my beside whilst in labour. I wouldn't be going through the pregnancy alone either, not now I had Donna.

When I wasn't working in the evening, I spent all my time with Danielle, trying to make up for lost time before she started school in September. I finally felt like the Mum I should have been and was determined to make sure that she wouldn't be pushed out by the new baby.

Danielle was especially thrilled about moving to live closer to her uncle Mark. Ever since Paul had started going out on the weekends, we'd both started spending more time visiting Mum and Ada and we all loved it. As well as missing out on a relationship with Danielle, I'd neglected my relationship with Mum, too. Mum was especially hurt when I finally confided in her about the abortion and my failed attempt to leave Paul.

'Trace, you should have come to me – we could have helped out. You could have moved back home.'

I knew she meant well, but we both knew I couldn't have moved back home. I hadn't lived at home for nearly five years, and so much had changed since then.

'Mum, I couldn't have. Did you go running back to Nan to live with her every time something went wrong with Dad?'

Mum was clearly taken aback with my bluntness. 'Well, no, but that's not the point.'

'It's exactly the point. You and Ada have got your own life now and like Nan always says, I made my bed so I have to lay in it.' I grinned. 'Anyway, me and Paul are fine now. Everything is going to be different this time.'

# 105: Nan's Funeral

One minute Dad was calling me to tell me he was being discharged, and the next he was off to Stoke. Nan had died. Now we just had to wait to see what the impact on Dad was.

Sarah and I went over to the funeral, but we felt like detectives trying to figure who was who. In fact, there were some people I'd never met. I felt out of place and awkward. Despite being surrounded by family, I felt like a stranger.

Some of my cousins were crying over the loss of their precious Nan, but I felt nothing because I never knew her. Dad was nowhere to be seen, so we went inside to find him in the kitchen. He was standing with Grandad and Auntie Jane. They were all drinking, but thankfully, Dad was drinking a can of lager.

Dad looked well, considering he'd been in a psychiatric ward only a week earlier. He was clean shaven, with a fresh haircut. Even though it had been clear from his phone calls that he was back on the drink, he seemed sober enough on this day. He was sporting a new black suit and smiling. But knowing Dad as I did, I knew that the calm bravado was all front.

I couldn't help thinking Grandad was still a handsome fella. I could tell he didn't recognise us at first, but when he did, he embraced us both, one by one. I laughed when Dad embraced us and thanked us for coming. As if we weren't going to come! Christ, I would have never heard the last of it. But the truth be told, I was only here for him.

As we sat at the back and listened to the eulogy, it was like being at a stranger's funeral. It pissed me off when the priest spoke fondly about Nan's apparent love for all her grandkids, especially when me or Sarah had never had as much as a birthday card from her.

I didn't feel any emotion at all, but I could hear sobbing coming from the front. When I looked to see where it was coming from, I realised it was Dad. Whilst my aunts and uncles all appeared to be keeping their cool, Dad was inconsolable. I wished we'd been closer to console him, but Auntie Jane was doing her best.

By the time we got to the wake at Uncle Mick's local, any signs of emotion had vanished. I'd barely had a moment to speak to Dad and now he was surrounded by people that I didn't know, and I could tell he was hell-bent on getting pissed.

He bought me and Sarah a drink and we made our excuses to head out into the beer garden. I needed a fag. Most of our cousins had gathered in the backyard of the pub. We went to stand with the Irish contingency and reminisced about the time Dad had taken us over to Ireland to visit as kids.

It was weird; I hadn't seen them for years and yet I had an intuitive bond, bound by our shared DNA. The Ford blood ran through all our veins. A couple of cousins had mentioned that they knew about Dad's drinking but didn't seem to care, in fact no one had a bad word to say about him. In their eyes he was like a hero. Everyone loved Uncle Frank.

My cousin Jane reminisced about the time Dad had been over at theirs for a Christmas party a couple of years ago. Apparently, they'd come downstairs in the morning to find their living room door hanging off its hinges and Dad lying underneath, and laughed about him blaming it on the dog.

Our Coran told us about how Dad bought him his first football kit and boots and had even sponsored their local footy team. David, my other cousin, affectionately regaled us about all the times Dad had taken him on trips to Ireland. How they went rabbiting and fishing together.

It turned out Dad had gifted young Michael with a video copy of *ET*, which stung. Especially as remembered asking for a copy for myself, only to be refused.

I couldn't help thinking that they had far more happy childhood memories with Dad than me and Sarah had ever had. I laughed it off and tried to pretend that I didn't care, but I have never felt so envious. I turned to Sarah, and I could sense she was thinking the same.

It was nearly time to go. Uncle Mick came outside.

'Youze don't have to go! You can stay over at ours.' I was touched because I knew he meant it. Uncle Mick had been the only person back in Stoke who had an inkling, or who seemed to care about what we were going through at home. I couldn't help comparing him to Dad.

Uncle Mick was a great Dad. He would have never promised to pick his kids up to take them out, only to leave them in the pissing rain and never turn up. He would never have told his daughter that he had cancer when he hadn't. He would have never had rung his daughter on New Year's Eve telling her that he was going to kill himself.

I had been feeling sorry for Dad, up until this point. But I also couldn't help thinking that nothing had really changed. He'd hardly spoken to us all day. Typical Dad, the man who always seemed to have time for other people's kids, but not his own. Another stark reminder of our one-sided relationship. Me chasing him, desperate for him to reciprocate the same level of unconditional love I had for him that never came.

It was getting late, and we would risk missing the train. I went to find Dad, but he was seriously hammered, and I couldn't help feeling ashamed that he was my dad.

Uncle Mick must have picked up on my embarrassment. He sorted us with a taxi and made me promise to call him when we got back home. It had been a long day. Me and Sarah were physically and emotionally shattered. It was time to head back to Sheffield.

# 106: Count For Something

The only downside to my job was I never knew how much money I was bringing in from one week to the next. At least Paul wasn't bothered, now he had his lucrative side-line selling drugs on the weekends.

He was more obsessed with money than ever though and was becoming increasingly tighter with it. Previously, what had been mine was ours, but what was Paul's was his. He was reluctant to put his earnings back into the house or give me any form of housekeeping, but it didn't stop his designer wardrobe from expanding.

It felt degrading having to ask him for scraps of money if I was short one week. Occasionally, I could sneak a few pound coins from his trouser pockets while he slept after a night out, which always felt like a small victory. It wasn't worth arguing about, not when we had another child on the way.

I knew I wouldn't be able to work straight after the baby was born and that I would probably have to wait and get a little part-time job when he or she started nursery, so for now, I would have to bide my time.

During the week, I was at home, but I spent most of my weekends at Mum's house with Sarah. Thankfully the cheating allegations were never spoken about again, and it was like we were a proper family again, having Sunday lunch together; the only difference was that I and Sarah were no longer kids. Danielle loved our weekend visits, too. She loved nothing more than playing in the back garden, or snuggling on the settee, and watching Disney films with her uncle Mark.

Ever since I'd confided to Mum about the abortion and my failed attempt to leave Paul, our relationship had blossomed. She'd started to open up more about her own past and what it had been like living with Dad. I already knew about her having an abortion, but I hadn't known about the time we lived in a hostel, fleeing from Dad's abuse. I hadn't known that she'd suffered a mental health breakdown after trying to suffocate me as a baby because I wouldn't stop crying, or about how many times she'd had to rely on Nan to bail her out to pay her rent or with basics such as food.

She also confirmed that Dad had snapped my beloved chair and hit her with it.

Mum told me that she wished she'd had the courage to leave Dad sooner, but she was stuck in a cycle of mental and emotional abuse, which she claimed was worse than the physical abuse. He'd cheat and abuse her, then be full of remorse, telling her that he'd always loved her, then have possessive outbursts where he'd start accusing her of cheating, especially once she'd started working. He'd even begged for a second chance after she'd started dating Ada.

The more Mum shared, the more I started to understand why Nan hated Dad so much, although I still couldn't understand her disdain for me as a kid and wondered if she blamed me for Mum staying so long.

I couldn't believe that it had taken so long for me to realise that we had so much in common. We'd both experienced the shame of becoming a young Mum and the guilt we felt about letting not just ourselves down, but our parents too.

Despite being in an unhealthy relationship, she'd done everything to make it work, even at the expense of her own mental health. The only difference was that when Mum had left Dad, she'd taken us kids with her instead of walking away like I'd done. And, unlike Dad, Paul had never hit or cheated on me. That had to count for something.

# 107: Emotional Rollercoaster

It had been a couple of months since Nan's funeral, and Dad was still drinking. It didn't help that he'd started having his divvy mates back round the flat at all hours.

Both me and Sarah had been keeping home visits to a minimum since the funeral, but it didn't stop Dad calling us three to four times a day. Mostly, he was ranting but there were the odd occasions when he'd openly admit that he'd been overdoing it. At those times he sounded so remorseful and sincere, but I had to remind myself that they were just words.

He was convinced that his mental health blip over the new year had been a one-off and that he'd never get in that state again. I had tried to get him to agree to see Giz, the alcohol consultant, on numerous occasions, but he'd flatly refused.

I'd taken on the unofficial role of being Dad's mediator around the claim. He was getting more and more confused and verbally abusive with the staff, so much so, some of them refused to deal with him. I'd naively assumed that the claim would be close to being settled, but it seemed it was going to take a lot longer.

Apparently, there were still questions around Dad's PTSD, and the train company was after a second opinion. Dad was absolutely furious. He was like a man possessed and his obsession only fuelled his drinking.

At times, it was hard to sit back and watch him slowly deteriorating, I hardly recognised the man he had become. I had all the resources and the support at my fingertips, but nothing had worked. It was all so frustrating.

I had witnessed so many people who had changed, who'd been far worse off that Dad. People who had managed to pull themselves out of their own destructive, addictive hell. People who had turned their back on crime, who had swapped prison for education. People who'd pulled themselves out of being homeless and being on the streets to owning their own homes. I was surrounded by so many success stories, and I truly believed that Dad had the potential to change. It was hard not to compare. He had his very own cheerleading squad, his own place, a steady income with the prospect of a windfall at the end and the perfect woman, who adored him, and yet, in his drunken haze, he just couldn't see it.

I'd had this fairy-tale notion in my head that I could fix Dad. I imagined him being in recovery, making amends for the past and fixing what had been a fractured relationship. I'd thought that he might finally accept his faults, and we'd all live happily ever after.

I knew, deep-down, that he hated what he'd become and drank to protect himself, but he just couldn't see that the more he drank, the worse his life was getting. It was a vicious cycle. In my head, I knew his outrageous behaviour was due to the alcohol. I also I knew that, deep-down, in his fucked-up way, he loved us, but I also knew that this was just Dad.

When he'd turned up on my doorstep a couple of years ago, I'd hoped that things would be different, that we'd got a second chance. But now, instead of women and mates, the booze was his priority.

Part of me craved the life I'd had before Dad had re-entered it. Since he'd come back to Sheffield, I'd felt like I'd been on an emotional rollercoaster. I'd tried accompanying him and comforting him during all his highs and lows, but it was taking its toll. Dad had been a constant source of distraction; my work was suffering, and I certainly was as present as I should be with the kids and Pat. I had to accept that there was nothing I could do until he accepted that he needed to change. It was time to get off that rollercoaster of insanity and focus on me.

# 108: Naughty Girl

My birthday was just around the corner and, inspired by Shauna passing her driving test, I'd asked Mum to buy me my provisional driver's license. I was five months pregnant and planning a quiet birthday, but my colleagues had other ideas.

My desk was littered with cards and gifts. I'd never had so much fuss made of me. I thought nothing of it when Shauna asked me to cover the front desk for her for ten minutes whilst she popped out, but no sooner had she left, then a police officer arrived. He was smiling when he walked through the door, so I wasn't alarmed, but his face changed when he approached the desk. He explained that he was there to interview someone.

I was just about to call one of the managers, but then he said. 'I'm here to talk to Tracey Ford.'

*What an earth did he need to speak to me for?* 'Is it Paul? Has something happened?'

'Don't worry, nobody has been hurt, but I am afraid it's more serious than that.'

I thought my heart might explode from my chest. I wondered if someone had snitched about me bringing drugs in *and* they were still in my bag too. I hadn't even had the chance to give them to the sales lads.

I wracked my brains as to who might have grassed me up. My life flashed before my eyes; I envisioned myself sitting alone, heavily pregnant, in a prison cell, waiting to be charged with possession of drugs. The next thing, Shauna was walking back into the office all smiles, utterly oblivious to the severity of the situation.

'What's up?'

The officer turned to Shauna. 'It's nothing for you to worry about.'

Then he turned his attention back onto me. 'Tracey Ford. I am charging you for being a naughty girl and, on behalf of your friends, I'm here to wish you a Happy Birthday.' And with that, he started to swing his hips and unbutton his shirt.

Everyone came bursting into the reception area shouting: 'Happy Birthday Trace!'

I didn't know what to think as he gestured for me to approach him from behind the counter. All my colleagues gathered around chanting: 'Get erm off, get erm off', whilst he sat me on a chair and gyrated his ass in my face.

I was mortified, especially when he stripped his shirt off and started pouring baby oil over his chest, encouraging me to caress his chest. I couldn't concentrate. All I could think about was Paul's face and his reaction when he found out I'd been fooling about with a stripper.

The only people that seemed to be enjoying themselves were the other staff, whereas I was worrying about how I would get baby oil out of my new shirt. The whole strip lasted no longer than a couple of minutes; the whole office was buzzing. I couldn't get my head around how much trouble they'd gone to, to make sure I had the best birthday.

I joined Shauna in the kitchen, and she still couldn't stop laughing. 'Ah, Trace, your face was a picture!'

'It was *you* wasn't it? Fuck me. I wanted the earth to open and swallow me up, and look at my shirt!'

'Look, if he says owt, you can blame me, ok?' She smirked. 'Anyway, forget about him, have you had a nice birthday?'

I still couldn't wipe the smile off my face. 'Ya know what, I reckon it's been the best birthday ever. Thanks so much, Shauna.'

'You're worth it,' she said, planting a kiss on my cheek. 'Look, tell me to mind my own business, but I see behind that brave face and all the bravado that you are not always happy.'

I suddenly went from feeling happy to feeling vulnerable and exposed. 'What do you mean?'

She shrugged. 'I dunno. I sometimes think that bloke of yours takes the piss. I just don't like the thought of you being taken advantage of, that's all. I'm sorry, I know I've never met him, but I don't like him. I bet he doesn't give you a cut of the money from the drugs you are selling for him, does he?'

I didn't answer her, but she was right. He never had.

'Look, I'm sorry. All I see is him going out living the life of Riley whilst you are slogging your guts in the hope for some measly commission.'

It was like she'd been reading my mind, and she was right. Part of me wished I'd met Shauna sooner when I'd first left Paul; then, perhaps I might never have moved back, but I did, and I had.

'Look, Shauna, I know you mean well, but it's complicated.' I pointed to my swollen belly.

'Ah, Trace, I'm not suggesting you leave him. I suppose what I'm trying to say is, make sure you look after *you*, ok? Come 'ere.'

She pulled me in for a hug.

'Come 'ere and just remember this place wouldn't be the same without you, ya know that, don't ya?'

I was so happy to have my work family, but things were about to change.

# 109: The Green Stuff

Me and Sarah had a pact that neither of us would call Dad unless we absolutely had to. We knew that if he needed anything, he'd call. But three days had passed and neither of us had heard from him, which was unusual and out of character.

We agreed to drive over together and check on him. On the drive over, Sarah said that I might have to restrain her if it turned out he was wallowing in self-pity or if he'd taken the phone off the hook on purpose. But I think deep-down, we both knew that Dad would never leave the phone off the hook; either the phone had been dislodged and Dad hadn't noticed, or something more serious was afoot.

It wasn't ideal that we had Lauren and Sarah's daughter Charlotte with us, because it was the school holidays and we couldn't take them inside because we didn't know what state Dad or the flat would be in, so we left them in the car.

Arriving at his flat door, I felt a rush of adrenaline and nausea. Sarah tried the door, and it was open. We could hear the TV and headed straight for the living room. But it was empty. The only evidence that he'd been there were the usual bottles of brandy and Coke bottles on the coffee table.

My anxiety ramped up another notch.

'I wonder if he's been taken in again?'

Sarah popped her head in the kitchen. Again, there was no sign of Dad. I followed her up to Dad's bedroom. Sarah stalled at the door, and it didn't take long for me to see why.

Sprawled out on the bedroom floor was Dad's motionless body. He was lying on his left side, his arm outstretched, and head slumped, somehow wedged between his set of drawers and his wardrobe.

Dad was distinctly jaundiced in colour and this awful-looking green discharge coming out of his nose and mouth. It looked like dried up mushy pea juice, and some of it had obviously been there for a while. Dad was naked apart from a pair of boxers and his legs were heavily bruised and yellow. At first glance, we thought he was dead. I froze and Sarah took charge. She knelt down next to Dad, trying to rouse him and checking for a pulse, whilst I just stood there in disbelief.

'Trace, call an ambulance!' she shouted.

My body and hands were shaking uncontrollably whilst I desperately attempted to ring 999. Sarah was still knelt by Dad's side, calling his name, asking him to talk to her.

The operator answered.

'999, what's your emergency?' I tried explaining what had just happened, what we had just found, and she asked me for Dad's address and for the life of me, I couldn't remember it.

Taking control again, Sarah took the phone off me and proceeded to give Dad's address to the operator.

I was transfixed by the green mucus. It wasn't just on Dad's face. There were remnants of the green shit all over the place. It was on the walls, on the floor, on his bedside drawers. There was even some in his large tea mug on the side.

The operator asked Sarah if we could move him onto his back, but we were both fearful of causing more damage as he was laid precariously on the floor. The operator then suggested that we should try and clear his airways, but I froze. I just couldn't bring myself to put my hands into his mouth.

I could hear an ambulance in the distance. Dad's address was hard to find at the best of times, so this gave me the perfect excuse to go outside and get the attention of the crew. As soon as I got outside the fresh air, the fresh, crisp fresh air seemed to sober me up from the shock.

I'd completely forgotten about our Lauren and Charlotte. Those poor kids' faces. I felt torn between wanting to reassure the kids and needing to get the attention of the ambulance. Conscious of not wanting to upset the girls more than they already were, I tried to briefly explain to the kids that Grandad was very poorly.

I reassured the kids that I wouldn't be long, then beckoned for the ambulance crew to follow me to Dad's flat.

Climbing the stairs to his flat, I tried to explain to the crew how we'd found Dad. I directed the crew to Dad's bedroom. Sarah backed off, allowing them to take charge. We watched helplessly while they checked his pulse and tried to get Dad to respond or tell them his name.

I was relieved to hear him mustering the odd moan and groan, but then in true Fordy style, he suddenly shouted.

'Fuck off and leave me alone!'

*Leave him alone? Leave him alone? The ungrateful bastard.* My adrenaline really started pumping, turning any sympathy I had towards Dad into anger. Even in his disoriented state, he was still managing to insult the very people who were trying to help him.

Despite Dad's protest, the crew were able to manoeuvre Dad onto a chair-style stretcher, wrap him in a blanket and strap in him quite easily.

We followed the crew and Dad downstairs as they explained that they'd be taking Dad to the Northern General. Being mindful that the kids were in the car, and that they might see Dad, I rushed past the crew, making my way to the back seat of the car door, to reassure the kids that Grandad was going to be ok, but also to block their view. It definitely wasn't a sight that they should have been privy to.

Both me and Sarah were in a daze as we stood outside, watching the ambulance crew settle Dad in, close the doors, reactivate the siren and head off to the hospital. Sarah, in full possession of her wits, reminded me that the flat still needed to be locked.

We were like Cagney and Lacey investigating a crime scene as we walked round each room, trying to make sense of Dad's last movements. It was obvious that he'd fallen again, but his quilt was on the settee, so what the hell was he doing in the bedroom? And what was the green stuff? The stench was unbearable, and even though we were supposed to be locking up, I had to open the windows.

Sarah was investigating the large mug on his bedside cabinet when she started retching. It got so bad that she rushed to the toilet and started to be uncontrollably sick.

I don't know how long we spent walking around Dad's flat, trying to make sense of what might have taken place. But it was time to lock the place up and head up to the hospital.

# 110: Shut Down

The telesales company was being shut down. Apparently, we'd been featured on *Watchdog* and were being investigated for defrauding customers. So that was that. We were all going to be out of job. No-one was going to employ me at five months pregnant, but I was more worried about not seeing my work family again. And then one of the managers, Michelle, took me to one side.

'Look, Trace. I've only told a few people, but me and the hubby have been working on setting up our own security company. The pay might not be brilliant at first, being new and all that, but help us build it up, and there could be a promising career in it for you.'

'Who else have you asked?'

She knew I was thinking about Donna and Shauna.

'I was hoping you might speak to Donna, and I haven't had the chance to speak to Shauna yet, but I'm sure she'll come.' She slipped a piece of paper into my hand. 'Look, here is my number. Just think about it and give me a call.'

No sooner had Michelle spoken to me then one of the other managers, Shaun, wanted a word. He looked around to see if anyone was listening.

'Trace, I only live up the road from you, so I was just wondering if there was any chance you could still get me some gear?' I shook my head in disbelief. We were all losing our jobs and all he could think about was getting some speed, sad bastard.

But then I considered it for a second.

'Yeah, sure, why not?' I reasoned that we needed all the money we could get.

Unfazed by the news, Shauna was already planning a last night out for us all, but I knew already that I wouldn't be going; there was no point. It wasn't like I could get off my face like the others. Shauna promised to stay in touch, but I knew it wouldn't be long before she would be buggering off, travelling the world, doing all the things I could have only dreamed about, and the last thing that she needed was a mother of two holding her back.

Our lives were so different. I couldn't imagine why our paths would ever cross again. But in that short time, she'd helped me realise there was more to me than being a mother and a partner. She'd shown me how it was ok to let my hair down now and then and do me.

I still had loads of happy memories for the memory bank that I could tap into if I were ever feeling low. I didn't know then, just how low I could get.

# 111: The Poor Bleeding Staff

We finally arrived at the Northern General Accident & Emergency Department and headed straight for the receptionist. We naively assumed that she would have already been informed of our pending arrival and would be expecting us.

But instead, we were told to wait in the main waiting area and that we'd be called shortly by a member of staff. Still in shock, me and Sarah held hands, consoling each other in between silent sobs. After waiting for ages with still no word, not sure what was happening, Sarah went back to the receptionist to find out.

This time, the receptionist directed us to a corridor at the entrance to a ward. We'd only been there for a couple of minutes when a guy in dark blue overalls came over, asking if we were with Frank Ford? He then chaperoned us to a small private waiting area, explaining that someone would be with us shortly, who could give us a progress report on Dad.

There we were again left alone, waiting. I could feel myself almost explode with anxiety. I'd seen this scene many times before on tv. Those scenes where the medical staff would take you to a small waiting room, the type of room where they'd break bad news to the relatives.

Me and Sarah sat in silence. After another anxious wait, a doctor finally came into the room. He tried to explain that they were still trying to ascertain what was wrong with Dad, and that their main task now was to try and settle him.

The nursing staff were in the process of trying to clean him up, because he'd messed himself upon arrival. His initial diagnosis was that Dad was in fact very ill, and that they couldn't speculate what was exactly wrong with Dad until they'd managed to conduct more tests. With that, he turned and left the room. Leaving us yet again, alone and waiting once more.

Sarah turned to me. 'What does very ill mean? Do you reckon it's really serious this time?'

Sarah's calm demeanour was starting to falter, and I could tell she was getting anxious. It had been nearly two hours after finding Dad and we were still none the wiser.

Coupled with what the doctor has just told us, each of us were trying to remember whether we'd missed anything that the doctor had said or trying to find a hidden meaning behind what we'd just been told.

The doctor had left the door ajar, and we could just make out the entrance to one of the emergency wards. We strained our necks and watched as staff in different coloured uniforms came and went and tried to work out who they might be and whether they were tending to Dad.

It was now nearly three in the afternoon, and I realised that I hadn't even called in work to let them know what was happening. The door opened, and a lady popped her head around the door.

'Ooops, sorry.'

In a split second we both recognised each other.

'Oh hiya, Tracey. I do apologise. We were just looking for a spare room to have a meeting. Is everything ok?'

It was one of the nurses from the alcohol service. I was incensed. This was clearly a family room, and I wanted to scream: *'Do I fucking look ok?'*

The awkwardness was broken by the doctor, who was coming to give us an update. The nurse apologised again before sheepishly backing away. The doctor explained that they would be admitting Dad for the foreseeable future, before taking us to see him.

Dad didn't look good at all, but it was a relief to know he wasn't dying. The doctor stepped aside so that me and Sarah could get closer to Dad. We tried to talk to him, to get him to acknowledge that he knew we were there, but Dad was away with the fairies.

'Your father's quite a character. It's taken nearly an hour to calm him down.'

A wave of shame enveloped me. I could tell by his tone of voice that he wasn't impressed. The doctor continued to conduct tests whilst me and Sarah stood to one side, ready to give Dad what for if he started becoming aggressive again.

The doctor stood over Dad and opened Dad's dressing gown to reveal his chest; he then crunched his knuckles and proceeded to push down hard on the centre of Dad's ribcage. This certainly got a response from Dad.

All of a sudden Dad made the most pitiful, but painful groan, that gradually got louder and louder, the more the doctor pressed down. Me and Sarah glanced at Dad, then to each other, both of us struggling to contain ourselves. Dad bloody well deserved to be in pain after all the grief he'd given the hospital staff. Dad lay there, completely oblivious, whilst we tried to explain that Dad was a drinker and that he'd never been a good patient.

After getting some reassurance that he was going to be ok, me and Sarah went outside for some fresh air and a fag, whilst they decided what ward they would be taking him to. We returned to find an auxiliary calling for assistance.

'I can't handle this bloke on me own, I'm gonna need at least another two people to help me get him on the ward!'

Before I could blink, Sarah was at the side of the auxiliary nurse in a flash, confidently asking if the guy he was referring to was Frank Ford?

'Showing off, is he? Right, take me to him!'

I explained to the confused-looking auxiliary that we were Frank Ford's daughters and would help the staff settle Dad onto the ward if they needed. He didn't need asking twice.

He led us to the lift, where another auxiliary was struggling to restrain my dad. Me and Sarah tried our best to calm him and reassure him that he was ok and to settle down, but he was totally oblivious to our presence.

It took four of us to restrain Dad's arms and legs from thrashing around and prevent him from falling off the trolley. We finally got to the ward, and me and Sarah were asked to step aside whilst the staff manoeuvred Dad onto the bed. It was embarrassing. We'd only been on the ward a couple of minutes, and everyone knew he'd arrived.

Dad was finally in bed, but he wasn't ready to go to sleep yet. I don't know where he thought he was, but in his head, he wasn't hanging around to find out. It took a whole team to restrain him whilst the nurse inserted a drip. I took to laying over Dad's knees, whilst Sarah laid over Dad's stomach and the auxiliary was in charge of Dad's straying arms. While he was restrained, the doctor gave him the once over.

It was like being in the middle of a comic sketch, only it wasn't funny. I felt so sorry for the poor old bloke who had the misfortune to be in the bed opposite Dad. He'd probably been having a nice quiet visit with his missus until Dad arrived; with the curtain wide open, the poor old sod had a bird's eye view of Dad showing off.

I asked whether the doctor could prescribe something to calm him down, but the doctor informed me that if they were to sedate him, Dad might never recover, and that the medication could finish him off! This was the first inkling that Dad was seriously ill.

The doctor said that all they could do for now was monitor Dad's progress and that they'd know more in a day or two. It was eight o'clock in the evening before Dad finally started to calm down. The staff reassured us that he'd be ok and that we should head home. I wasn't worried about Dad so much, it was the poor bleeding staff.

# 112: It's a Girl

I was amazed at Michelle's sense of optimism; she was convinced that her new company would be the next best thing, but I wasn't as convinced. Shauna hadn't joined us and after a few weeks, me and Donna decided to throw in the towel.

The thought of being unable to work or earn my own money stung. As a consolation, Paul gifted me control of the family allowance book. It was his way of compensating for me not having my own money, but it could never have compensated for the loss of my independence I'd gained at work. The Thursday night at Roxy's had been the only time I'd felt like I could forget about the reality of living with someone who, given half the chance, would love to have controlled my every move, including on the dance floor.

The only thing that kept me going was the thought of our fresh start; moving back to the south of Sheffield, back to my old stomping ground and where I would be closer to Mum. All I had to do now was bide my time before I could get back to work and create a new work family.

I also had my crisp new provisional driver's license. Every so often, I would get it out of its envelope and imagine myself being able to drive wherever I wanted; it would also broaden my employment opportunities.

Danielle's fifth Birthday was just around the corner, and so was my due date, but I was expecting the baby to be late, so I agreed to throw Danielle a big party with all of her school friends, even though I was embarrassed to invite people back to our place. Donna had convinced me that we could host the party in the garden, and we agreed to have it from three until five on the Saturday nearest to her birthday.

On the Friday, with Paul out of the way, me and Donna cracked on with preparing jellies and party bags for the kids then sat down to watch 'You've Been Framed' which always had us in stitches. My stomach ached, only that night the aches were coming more frequently. I started count them; they were only mild, but they were definitely there.

'Donna, I think I'm having contractions.'

Donna laughed. 'You can't be. You've got another three weeks to go! Are they strong?'

'Nah, not really, just a dull faint pain, but they are definitely coming frequently.'

'It'll be Braxton Hicks. Let's time them.'

I waited for the ache to come back. They were about ten minutes apart.

'Fuck me, Donna. I can't go into labour now; it's Danielle's Party tomorrow.'

Ever pragmatic, Donna asked. 'Look, are they hurting?'

'Well, no.'

'Well then, stop flapping. I'm telling ya, it will be Braxton Hicks.'

But the baby had different ideas. Overnight, the pain intensified. My contractions were getting more painful and more frequent. I tried putting off calling the hospital for as long as I could, but it was half an hour before Danielle's friends were due to arrive, and I knew I wouldn't be able to settle unless I checked in with the hospital just to be sure. The last thing I needed was to be giving birth in the middle of a birthday party.

I called round to the corner shop to use their payphone. But Raff, the owner, insisted that I go into the back and use their landline.

When I explained my symptoms to the nurse, she said I should bring my overnight case and come straight in. I couldn't believe the timing, and I hadn't even packed an overnight bag; I started to freak out, but as always, Donna was the voice of reason.

'Trace, stop panicking. Go pack a bag, I've got this.'

Paul chimed in. 'I'll go get ready.'

I looked at him up and down, confused. 'What do you mean? You can go like that.'

'If you have this baby sooner then, I could still go out after, wet the baby's head and get rid of this gear.'

'Are you fucking kidding me?'

But I could tell by his face he was deadly serious. Just then, Sally, one of the other mums, arrived and assured me that they would make sure Danielle had the best party ever.

I thought about calling Mum to come and collect Dan, but Donna had insisted that if the worst came to the worst, Danielle could stay over at hers. I glanced over at Danielle, who was sitting and playing with her toys in the living room, completely obvious. I walked over to her to explain. I thought she might have been disappointed that I wouldn't be there for her party, but she was quite the opposite.

'Mummy, this is brilliant. Will I get to show my new sister or brother to my friends at my birthday party?'

I laughed, while trying to explain that it would be unlikely, but this didn't bother her.

So, with Danielle's blessing, I went upstairs and packed a bag. Paul was just splashing Paco Roban over his neck. I usually loved the smell of it, but at that moment, it just made me feel sick.

'I'm ready!' he grinned. 'This is so exciting, Trace.' He came over and rubbed his hand over my belly. 'I cannot believe this little baby is coming.'

I pushed him away; his aftershave was overbearing. 'Neither can I. Do you think you could get your ass round to the shop and call a fucking taxi, please?'

'I'm on it.'

I was pissed off. He could be such a selfish prick sometimes. Here I was in excruciating pain, missing out on Danielle's first proper birthday party, and all he was bothered about was getting out to sell his fucking drugs.

'Oh, and can you call Mum and let her know?'

Paul frowned. I knew what he was thinking.

'Paul, just fucking do it, will ya?'

Paul knew I had promised Mum that she could be at the birth this time, especially after missing out last time because she had to babysit Dad. And as for him, I had no intention of telling him; he was the last person I wanted to see, and I still hadn't forgiven him for turning his back on me. Anyway I couldn't see him driving all the way from his new pub in Leeds, not now he had his own family.

Paul hadn't been able to get hold of Mum, but Sarah had promised to track her down. A couple of hours had passed since I'd arrived at the hospital, and my contractions were intensifying. The nurses reckoned that, unlike Danielle, this baby would be coming soon. I'd already opted for an epidural, but I wasn't ready, so instead, I coped on gas and air. When the nurses were out of the room, Paul would ask for a go.

'This is alright this, Trace,' he grinned after taking a deep breath under the mask. I couldn't figure out who was off their nut more, him or me. All I did know was that he was really starting to get on my tits at this point.

The staff were outside getting the epidural ready when Mum came rushing through the door.

'You are not going to believe this, Trace. The Steelers match was just about to kick off when a message came over the Tannoy: *Mr and Mrs Flude, can you go to the hospital? Your daughter is in labour*. Honestly, it was unreal. The whole stadium stood and applauded us whilst we walked out. I felt like a celebrity! Anyway, enough about me, how are you?'

Right on cue, the staff returned with the doctor, who would be doing the epidural. I was instructed to sit perfectly still and bend over, whilst the staff prepped my back, ready for the epidural. Mum sat in front of me, reminding me to breathe whilst stroking my hand. They were just about to give me the epidural when I felt an overwhelming urge to push.

'Fucking hell' I screamed, arching my back.

The next thing I knew, the nursing staff were trying to prise open my legs, whilst I desperately tried to keep them clamped together.

'Tracey, the baby's heads there.' Mum shouted. It just took one more final push, and then it was over.

'It's a girl,' the nurse smiled before taking her off to be weighed.

I was still in shock; I couldn't believe how different this birth had been to Danielle's. Mum, on the other hand, was grinning from ear to ear. She squeezed my hand before planting a kiss on my forehead. 'Thank you, Tracey.'

She didn't need to thank me. She had been amazing. I was just relieved that she'd finally got to be there to witness her grandchild being born and I knew in my heart that we both would never forget this special moment we'd shared together.

Lauren Sarah Lomas was born on 12th September 1992. she weighed in a little less than Danielle had at 7lbs 8 ounces, but she was perfect; in fact, she was a carbon copy of Danielle when she'd been born, with black hair and blue eyes.

I smiled to myself because, this being my second time around, I knew that it wouldn't be long before they turned hazel brown. I also knew, unlike last time, what to expect. This time, I felt more prepared for being a Mum and was even more determined to be the best Mum ever.

# 113: At Least He Looked at Peace

The next day, Sarah and I both took the day off work and headed straight up to the hospital. Dad was fast asleep when we arrived. Apart from looking slightly more jaundiced, he looked peaceful.

I turned to Sarah. 'I'm telling ya, he's gonna get a piece of my mind when he comes round.'

Sarah laughed. 'You might have to join the queue.'

The nurse on duty explained that Dad now had both a drip and catheter inserted. The contents of the catheter bag looked more like coffee than pee.

I caught the eye of the old man who'd had a bird's eye view of the previous night's commotion. He smiled back so I took the opportunity to apologise. 'I'm sorry about last night. He was proper out of it.'

He shook his head. 'He's been reyt as rain since you left,' he said, then nodded towards a neighbouring bed. 'It's her who's a pain in the arse. She's been moaning all night! I'll tell ya summat, lass. I can't wait to get outta here, these places do me head in.' You and me, both, I thought.

It was over an hour before the doctor entered the ward, accompanied by a team of trainee doctors. When he reached Dad's bay, he acknowledged us before turning to the other staff.

'This is Frank. He's fifty-four years old. Brought in last night with extremely high concentrations of alcohol.' He turned to me and Sarah.

'Do you know when your dad had his last drink?' I felt ashamed when I explained that we hadn't seen him for over a week. We went on to explain how we'd found him the day before and how he was unresponsive and covered in slime.

I had to ask. 'What is that by the way? He was covered in it.'

'Ah, that will have been bile. Has he been eating?'

More embarrassment.

'Listen, the bile is the least of his concerns. Your dad has slipped into what's called a hepatic coma.'

I was shocked. 'What do you mean a coma? What does that mean?' I immediately associated coma with death.

He went on to explain that Dad's blood alcohol concentration levels were extremely high and all they could was monitor him and wait.

I was confused. 'But he was thrashing about last night. How can that happen?'

'It's hard to tell. His behaviour may have been linked to his alcohol levels. I'm sorry, but it is literally a waiting game. All we can do is keep monitoring his breathing and heart rate.'

The doctor continued with his rounds, leaving me and Sarah dumb-struck and trying to process what he'd just said.

Dad just looked fast asleep; we hadn't realised he was, in fact, in a coma. I was consumed with guilt. How long had he been laying like that? And where were his fucking mates?

We made some calls to relatives and to Tracey and said we'd keep them updated, and then we just sat and waited.

At the close of visiting hours, there had been no change in Dad and he was still unresponsive. At least he looked at peace. I just wished I was too.

# 114: Just What the Doctor Ordered

Donna gave birth two weeks after me, just after a new family had moved in across the road. The daughter, Holly, was around fifteen and wanted to work with kids, so she was always knocking to see if she could help. She'd indulge Danielle's imaginative games and had no problem helping out with changing Lauren's nappies.

Before too long, Donna was ready to go back out with her mates, and she invited me to join them. I'd never been able to go before because Paul didn't like me hanging out with Blades, but this time, I really wanted to go. I missed my nights out with work colleagues and needed to get out.

Paul practically choked on his drink when I mentioned it to him. 'You're fucking kidding, aren't you? What – down London Road?'

'Do I look like I'm kidding? I haven't been out for months – I could do with a night out.'

Paul smirked. 'And who's going to babysit? You know Fridays and Saturdays are my nights.'

Unbeknown to him, I'd already sorted that. 'Holly can. I trust her, and her Mum has offered to pop in during the night to check on her.'

'And how are you going to pay for it?'

I'd thought long and hard about that too. 'Well, you do know that the benefits we get are mine too, ya know and let's face it, you're earning enough for both of us.'

Paul shook his head. I knew what was coming but I wasn't about to back down.

'Look, Paul, I don't ask for anything. I cannot remember the last time I was able to buy myself something nice. Fuck me, you've got a new designer top every weekend. It's one night, for fuck's sake!'

'It's not that! I just don't like the thought of you being out down London Road around all of them fucking Blades fans. What if someone tries it on?'

'Why? Is that what you do when you go out?'

'Look, Trace, I don't go out chasing birds. The reason I'm out every weekend is to make us some money!'

'Whatever, Paul.'

Paul shook his head. 'Do what you want, but don't be expecting me and you to be meeting up at the end of the night, like Donna's bloke.'

'I wanna go out with Donna, not you!' I snapped and stormed out of the room, high on the adrenaline of standing my ground.

Donna and I spent weeks prepping for the night out. She even persuaded me to buy a striped two-piece in the sales. I'd felt good when I'd tried in on in the shop, but when I came to meet Donna's mates, I still felt nervous and out of place.

Two of her mates were skinheads with shaved heads and long fringes. I was in awe of the apparent lack of fucks they seemed to give about what other people thought. Unlike me, they did this every weekend, and they had the blessings of their other halves.

Paul had been wrong, there were no signs of any football allegiances, no red and white tops or chanting. Everyone was really friendly and normal. During the night, I occasionally thought about Paul, who was literally less than a mile away.

I briefly considered going to surprise him at the end of the night on the off chance that he might have been happy to see me. But I didn't have a clue where he hung out, and I'd promised to be home early for Holly. Instead, I left Donna with her mates before the last orders were called, jumped in a taxi and headed home.

Holly's mum was just stepping out of the back door as I arrived.

'So, have you had a good night?' she asked.

'Ya knows what? I have, Sue! It was just what the doctor ordered, thank you.'

I paid Holly before kicking my shoes off and throwing myself onto the sofa. It would be hours before Paul would be home, but I didn't care. All I cared about was that I'd stood my ground and had a fabulous night. I was determined to do it all again soon.

# 115: All We Could Do Now Was Wait

The next doctor was a consultant who took us to a small family room, like the one we'd been in earlier days, only this one was smaller. She was smiling as we sat down, but it was a sympathetic smile, and my gut told me this wasn't good news. Even we could see that there'd been no change.

'I'm afraid that it's not looking good for your dad,' she said.

I was confused. 'What do you mean?'

I half expected her to say that he might have long-term brain damage from the coma. The thought of Dad being like that was inconceivable.

'I'm afraid your dad's vital stats aren't improving. In fact, there are signs that his organs are shutting down.'

I shook my head, confused. 'I knew that his liver was bad, but I hadn't realised it was that bad.'

She went on to explain that it wasn't just Dad's liver that was the problem. She said he'd been experiencing severe acute DTs from alcohol withdrawal, which would account for his delirium. Each withdrawal could lead to more severe withdrawal symptoms, hence Dad's coma. Since Dad's admittance, they'd been treating him with lactulose and antibiotics, but his potassium and magnesium levels were dangerously low. His kidneys were also failing, a side-effect of cirrhosis of the liver.

Sarah stepped in. 'So how long has he got?'

'Well, it's hard to say. Two or three days. We don't like to predict, but I would recommend that you call his family.'

It was like someone had turned down the volume in my head. The consultant was still talking, but I couldn't take in any more information. All I could think was that I needed to put some more money on the parking meter and that I wouldn't be making my afternoon meeting after all.

I went outside and made a call to work who were great. They told me to take as long as I needed. Then I called Uncle

Mick and other family members, who promised to come over. With each call, I was met with a flurry of questions, many of which I couldn't answer. Never in a million years did I expect this to happen, not to Dad, not like this.

By the time we arrived back onto the ward, they had moved Dad into a private room. He didn't look like he was dying; he just looked like he was in a deep sleep. There was none of the high-tech equipment I'd seen on TV, just a drip and the catheter, which still seemed to be full of coffee.

Throughout the day, nurses came and went, checking pulses and writing on clipboards, but there was no change. The auxiliary staff checked in regularly, offering refreshments.

One member of staff made me chuckle when she remarked: 'Ey up, he's a handsome chap, isn't he?'

'Hear that, Dad! I can't believe that tha' still managing to pull on your deathbed!' But Dad couldn't hear anything, because apparently his brain was shutting down.

Part of me was relieved that Dad wasn't aware of what was going on around him. My head, on the other hand, was full of unanswered questions. If he'd known he would end up like this, would he have heeded the warnings?

The auxiliary might have thought him handsome, but Dad looked like he'd aged overnight and the grey stubble around his face didn't help.

I realised now just how much weight he'd lost. There was still evidence of Dad's muscular frame, but his face was gaunt, and even his skin looked thinner. Me and Sarah held a hand each and I was secretly praying that he might squeeze my hand back, but he didn't.

I couldn't help noticing that his nails were filthy. I asked the nurse if they had anything we could clean him with. The very least we could do was smarten Dad up ready for his visitors; Uncle Mick had called and said he'd been coming later. The nurse obliged and for the next hour me and Sarah worked our way round Dad, chatting to him as if he was awake. Sarah shaved Dad whilst I cleaned and trimmed his nails.

The nurse also suggested that me and Sarah could take responsibility for keeping Dad's lips moist by occasionally swabbing his mouth with cotton buds. They were just small acts, but they helped make us both feel like we were doing something.

We were half dozing when Uncle Mick arrived at ten that evening. It was a relief to see another member of the family, a reminder that we weren't on our own. He embraced me and Sarah, whilst telling us about the nightmare he'd had trying to park his thirty-tonne lorry near the hospital. I offered up my chair so he could sit beside Dad, but he declined, shaking his head whilst taking the sight of Dad before him.

'You silly fucker, Frank.' He turned to me and Sarah. 'Can you give us a minute, please?'

I saw a crack of emotion through his stoic Ford demeanour, and we left him alone with Dad. When he emerged, I could tell that he'd been crying.

'Listen, I've said what I needed to say to him.'

Part of me hoped he might expand, but it was clear it was a private matter. There was nothing more to say. All we could do now was wait.

# 116: Jaunty Avenue

Finally, after months of waiting, a semi-detached three-bedroomed house on Jaunty Avenue became vacant. It was just around the corner from Mum's.

Paul was royally pissed off with me when I told him I'd invited Mum and Ada to look around the place with us. 'For fuck's sake, can't we do owt without your family interfering?'

His attitude lately had been getting worse. This was meant to be our fresh start, and I wasn't about to let him start walking all over me again.

'Nah then, had it not been for *my* family, we would still have *fuck all*, remember that. And who do you think will be helping us to move, eh, cos it won't be your fucking family?'

Paul couldn't argue back, because he knew I was right. His own mother had recently packed all her bags and moved to Selby with a bloke she met through a dating agency.

Thankfully, Paul was on his best behaviour when we met Mum and Ada outside the house. The place was twice the size of our current house. And it wasn't just the house; there was a large front and back garden and an outside brick porch, perfect for storage.

There was a downstairs and upstairs toilet. The kitchen was nearly the same size as our current kitchen and living room. The only downside was the lack of kitchen cupboards, but Mum suggested we could recycle her old fitted kitchen cupboards, as she was due to have hers replaced. Ada even offered to fit them for us.

I saw Paul roll his eyes and I nudged him to keep his mouth shut. But his face soon lit up when Mum offered to give us her sofa because they were replacing that, too. Hers was practically new compared to the bag of shit we'd been sitting on.

Paul had negotiated compensation from the woman we were exchanging with. He'd already placed an order for a new catalogue to be delivered and had planned to have a phone installed, claiming that the old debt would stay with the old house.

He'd even found a company who would give us credit for carpeting the whole house. We hadn't even moved, and he was already spending money we didn't have.

A week after signing the keys for the house, Donna got the news that she was moving too. She'd managed to get an exchange to a place on Shoreham Street; a stone's throw away from the United football ground. It was also on my bus route, which meant we could still visit each other, which was just as well, because the new neighbours weren't very friendly.

'What do you and your husband do for a living?' asked one of the local mothers, sizing me up and finding me wanting. She couldn't wait to tell me about her husband's recent promotion, brand new car and how they were taking the kids to Disneyland, Florida, in the summer.

Thankfully Danielle loved her new school and soon made new friends whose mothers welcomed me too, even though they all seemed employed, unlike me and Paul.

Ada came around and fitted the new cupboards as promised, and soon the house was fully decorated. Paul had sourced a second-hand gas fire from his mates and bought a new hearth and a fireplace and soon we had fresh carpets too.

Mum had suggested we get a dining table for the kitchen, but Paul installed an eight-foot breakfast bar that stretched across the whole kitchen.

I knew Mum was dying to ask where the extra money was coming from to furnish the house, but she didn't pry. We could have managed until Lauren started school, but I felt suffocated and hated not having my own money, so I started looking for a new part-time job.

# 117: You Both Look Like You Need It

Three days had gone by and still there was no change. There were times when I was convinced that I'd seen his legs or hands twitching, a sign of life, but the nurses said that was normal and that it was just his body shutting down. The only thing that was moving was his chest. I watched it rise and fall, never knowing if it would be his last breath.

Eventually, the nurse forced Sarah and I to go home for a proper sleep, but I tossed and turned and couldn't settle. I got up and, sitting alone with my own thoughts, I reached for my notebook, compelled to write. Each thought that I dumped onto the page brought some relief and soon tiredness enveloped me, and I slept.

It was only a couple of hours later when the alarm woke me. I got the kids ready for school and prepared to head back to the hospital, as more visitors would be arriving. I brought the notebook with me, thinking I should get on with planning Dad's funeral.

When we arrived, there was still no change in Dad but at least he looked at peace. For a while, me and Sarah automatically took our seats on either side of the bed, but I was restless and, having paced the room for a while, I sat on the chair at the bottom of his bed and started making a list about what we would need to do for the funeral.

I thought back to Nan's funeral where they painted her as a saint and I wondered what we could say positive things we could say about Dad.

I hadn't got very far when I was interrupted by Aunty Jane and Uncle John arriving. I could tell Aunty Jane had already been crying. Uncle John looked gutted. Out of all the siblings, they had always been the closest. Unlike Uncle Mick, he couldn't hold back his tears and soon, they were both weeping.

Aunty Jane alternated between holding Dad's hands and willing him to wake up. She started reminiscing about fun childhood memories and part of me felt jealous that I didn't have the same fun memories of growing up with Dad.

Watching her and Uncle John, I realised I hadn't cried yet and wondered when the tears would hit me. Would it be as he took his last breath? Or would it be at the funeral?

A large part of me still felt numb. It was only eighteen months since Dad had returned to Sheffield. I could still see him now, getting out of Sid Vicious' car with his battered brown suitcase, showing no signs of addiction, no indication of what was to come. How long ago it seemed.

I couldn't help wondering if I had done enough. Could I have stepped in sooner? Put my foot down more? Then my attention turned to his family. Could they have done more?

Then there were those divvy mates. I wouldn't be responsible for what I would do if they came to visit. And finally, that damn claim. What a fucking waste.

Not long after Auntie Jane and Uncle John left, there was a knock at the door. A guy I hadn't seen before stood in the doorway, before sheepishly asking if he could come in.

He was wearing a black and white collar around his neck and had a Bible clasped in both his hands. He explained that he was the hospital chaplain. I looked at Sarah, who rolled her eyes. I knew she was thinking the same thing as me.

'Look, I appreciate you calling in and all that, but we don't go to church or owt like that and Dad certainly didn't.'

The guy smiled. 'That's fine. You don't have to believe. I just wanted to introduce myself and let you know that if you did need anything, like to talk, that I'm here, not just for your dad but for you too.'

I looked at Dad and then back to the priest and joked. 'Trust me mate, no confession is going to get this bloke through the pearly gates. Hell will have frozen over before Dad has finished getting through his sins.'

Smiling sympathetically, he said: 'Trust me, everyone has a place in God's heart. I'm more than happy to bless him if you are comfortable with that?'

Sarah shrugged. 'Go on, then. I mean, it can't do any more harm, can it?'

I stepped away from Dad's bed, offering my chair to the priest and watched as he lay his hands on top of Dad's and started to pray. What had seemed like a tokenistic gesture suddenly felt symbolic, an act of kindness.

Dad was ready now to pass. But not before Tracey had said her goodbyes. When she arrived, I could see that she felt she might be imposing, but I had no such qualms; I knew that Dad would have wanted her there. We left her alone with Dad and were just going for a breath of fresh air when the consultant stopped us.

'Can I have a quick word, please?'

She took us into the small room again and we sat in the very same chairs we'd sat in before.

'I have some good news,' she said.

I was confused. What could possibly be good news in these circumstances?

'It appears that your dad is showing signs of improvement.'

I stopped her in her tracks. 'What? So you are now saying he isn't dying?'

'Well, judging by his stats, it looks like that.'

I couldn't hear anything else she was saying, all I could feel was my pulse picking up speed, then I erupted. 'You are fucking joking. Please tell me you are joking!'

Judging by the look on her face, I could tell she wasn't expecting this reaction.

I had to stand. I was pacing the room. I turned on her again. 'We've just had him fucking blessed for crying out loud. Called all his family to pay their last respects, and now you are saying he'd not dying!' I was consumed with anger; this was too much to take in.

'Look, I know this is a shock,' she said.

I laughed. 'That's a fucking understatement!'

The consultant tried again, but this time she focused on Sarah. 'We are as surprised as you.'

Sarah seemed to be taking the news far better than me. 'So will there be brain damage? Will he be able to walk again? Will he need carers?'

The consultant shook her head. 'At this stage, we really don't know what the longer-term damage might be. All we can do is wait.' And with that she left the room.

I felt overwhelmed. I was still pacing the room

'Honestly Sarah, I don't think I can't do this.' The tears that I had been waiting for finally came flooding out. How the fuck were we supposed to break the news and tell everyone that Dad wasn't dying? I just wanted to crawl in a dark hole and never come out again. I wasn't sure I could take any more of this nightmare.

Sarah took me outside for some fresh air and gradually the news sunk in. There were more calls to make. After his initial shock, Uncle Mick seemed to find the news funny.

'I'm telling ya, he's got more fucking lives than a cat,' he said. But I didn't see the funny side. Then we had to return to Dad's bedside and break the news to Tracey.

Later, I'd have the kids to deal with; they gone off close to tears that morning, thinking that their Grandad was dying. And what about work? They'd think I was taking the piss.

Hours passed and there was still no change in Dad. I wondered what would happen when he came round. Would he even be able to talk again?

The best-case scenario would be that he would see the errors of his ways and never touch a drop of drink again. That he'd buy the static home he'd talked about and live happily ever after with the financial gains from his claim The worst-case scenario, him being a head on a bed, didn't bear thinking about.

Eventually, Dad started to stir. His legs moved and then there was a groan, like he was waking from a deep sleep. Me and Sarah took our places at either side of him. I moistened his lips and watched as his eyelids slowly opened.

'Where am I?'

I shot up to get the attention of one of the nurses, who came to check on Dad. Sarah and I stood back, whilst she attempted to bring Dad round. She chatted to him like a long-lost friend.

'Hello Frank, you had us all worried here.'

I could hear Dad murmuring but couldn't make out what he was saying. I still felt conflicted. Part of me wanted to steam into him and give him what for, but this wasn't the time. He was still half asleep, half awake.

'Where am I? What's happened?'

He was clearly still confused and vulnerable. He looked at me.

'Dad, you're in hospital. You've been in a coma for the past four days – you nearly didn't make it.'

The nurse returned into the room with a jug of water and a straw. 'Look, why don't you two get off home. It could take some time for him to come around. We'll take it from here. Go get some rest. You both look like you need it.'

# 118: You Must Be Tracey

I'd been searching the Job section in the Sheffield Star for weeks, when I stumbled across a small advert looking for someone to work a couple of days in a café in the Castle Markets. No experience was required. It was twenty quid a shift and they only needed someone to start immediately for a couple of days a week. It was an early start, but I'd be done by three and they were willing to give me a try.

'Who's going to take Dan to school?' asked Paul.

'Who do you think? It's not like you're working or owt.'

One minute Paul was complaining about how much he'd spent on the house, and now he was complaining that I'd be working. I couldn't win.

'I don't like the idea of you working in the markets either.'

Ah, that was more like it. He was just concerned about me being around other blokes.

'I'm not thrilled about working in the markets neither, but it's a job. I wanna start taking driving lessons, plus I can help to pay off those carpets.'

It was five in the morning when I set off. The streets were pitch black, and it was freezing. I stood patiently waiting for the bus, trying to envision what my new job might be like, praying that I liked it but, more importantly, that they liked me.

I arrived fifteen minutes early and the main entrance to the market was in darkness. But then, out of nowhere, a security guard appeared and let me in. None of the stalls had opened yet. It was like a ghost town.

Sharon's café was nestled in the far corner of the ground floor of the markets beside the stairs that led down to the fish markets. There was a guy dressed in a white catering overcoat, standing between the hatch, smoking a cigar, and engrossed in what looked like an intimate conversation with a woman I assumed to be his wife. He pulled away as soon as he saw me approaching.

‘Ah, you must be Tracey.’ He wiped his hands down on his overalls before shaking mine. The woman he’d been talking to took my arrival as a cue to leave, and John presented me with a red and white striped bib.

‘Right Chuck,’ he said, whilst rubbing his hands together, ‘There’s not much to it really. I’ve already cooked the bacon and sausage, and we’ll cook the eggs to order.’

He then pointed to some recycled butter tubs filled with precooked meats. ‘All you need to do is pop ‘em in the microwave for a couple of minutes then, Bob’s ya uncle!’ He smiled, then he turned to the toaster and breadboard. ‘The toast is really popular!’

I’d never seen so much bread in my life.

‘Hope you’re good with cutting bread, cos that’s what you’ll be mostly doing.’ He chuckled to himself whilst cutting a few slices to give me an idea of the thickness, before handing me the bread knife. ‘Here you go, it’s your turn.’

I tried to steady my nerves so as not to fuck up and was even impressed with my own first attempt.

‘Perfect,’ John exclaimed. ‘Right, now that’s out of the way, let me show you the coffee machine.’

He reached for a large mug, then a scoop of coffee, and filled it half-full with milk. He then turned to the machine and shoved the cup under one of the nozzles. ‘You’ll need to watch ya self with this,’ he warned. The machine sounded like a bomb about to explode. ‘Don’t be put off by the noise!’

As he was demonstrating how to make the coffee, when two blokes leaned over the counter, eying me up I immediately felt self-conscious.

John must have picked up on this. ‘Tom, this is Tracey, it’s her first day, so be nice.’

‘Well, hello Tracey!’ Tom reached over the counter to shake my hand. He turned to his mate. ‘This lump of meat is Wayne. Watch ya self with him. He’s single and he’s got an eye for the ladies.’

'Well, it's just as well I'm spoken for then, isn't it? Now, what you having?' I tried to hold my nerve. I suspected I would have to get used to the banter if I wanted this job.

There were lots of things I had to get used to that day, and lots of new people. Sally, who John said was the real gaffer, filled me in on who was who while I made the sandwiches.

'See her?'

I looked up to see a pretty brunette walking past the café to discard some cardboard.

'She works in the florist. She's a reyt snotty bitch, thinks she's better than everyone.'

Then, as soon as the owner of one of the butchers left the counter, she spilled the beans about him apparently having an affair with one of his staff. I was bemused by the way Sally went off. Behind the scenes, the markets were a den of iniquity.

Apparently, Sally was already in a relationship, but that didn't stop her from flirting shamelessly with any men who approached the counter, and she was incredible at remembering all their orders.

The dinner rush was just starting to tail off when Andrea, John's wife finally arrived.

'Sorry I'm late.' She seemed flustered but had a kind face. 'Hi love, you must be Tracey. John says you've done really well this morning.'

She wasn't what I'd been expecting at all, nor was she the woman John had been chatting to earlier. She was pretty and dressed like a poster girl for Laura Ashely. But she was no pushover. She hadn't been there a few minutes before she was telling me to cut the break thinner and use less cheese.

I was nervous that my trial wasn't going as well as I expected, but at the end of the day, I was taken on one side by Andrea who gave me twenty quid and told that the job was mine.

# 119: A Long Way to Go

I wasn't sure what to expect when we walked back into Dad's hospital room, but I wasn't expecting him to be sitting up in bed. His face lit up as soon as he saw me and Sarah standing there. I'd been fantasising about giving a piece of my mind, but when I saw him, I couldn't. Even though he was sitting up in bed, he still looked weak.

'Ey up,' he said.

'Ey up, ya sen. You do know that ya lucky to be alive, you are, don't ya?'

'Honestly Trace, I don't remember nowt.'

'Well, we do,' said Sarah. 'Dad, you were in a reyt tangle when we found ya.'

Dad looked confused. 'Why what happened? Was I that bad?'

I shook my head. 'Dad, you were worse than bad, you didn't have a clue where you were when they brought you in! Then ya wa' kicking off – it took me and Sarah and two members of staff to help try and restrain ya. Then the next thing we know, tha's in a coma and they've given ya three days to live!'

Dad winced, but then he smiled like he was trying to laugh it off.

'Dad, it was fucking serious! Fuck me, we've had Uncle John, Uncle Mick and Aunty Jane all up from Stoke to say their last goodbyes.' I was trembling all over. 'And Tracey! She was here yesterday too. I've been planning your fucking funeral, for crying out loud!'

Dad closed his eyes and pinched the bridge of his nose. I noticed his hands shaking. 'Honestly, I don't remember a thing.' He took a deep breath. 'Look, I'm sorry, ok?'

I could tell by his pained expression, he meant it. I'd finally got my head around the fact that Dad wasn't dying anymore, but I still wasn't quite ready to forgive him yet. And despite his apology, which seemed sincere at the time, I still wasn't convinced he was truly aware how serious the past four days had been.

Dad wasn't even humbled when the priest popped in to see him. We explained about the blessing.

'Well, that were a waste of time, weren't it? I'm telling ya, I ain't going nowhere yet, mate.'

I elbowed Dad. His arrogance pissed me off no end. 'Nah then, there's no need for that, remember we thought you were dying!'

Dad shrugged. 'Sorry mate, no offence.'

The priest nodded. 'None taken, Frank, I'm just glad you're feeling better. It was touch and go for a while.'

'I reckon the old man upstairs isn't ready for t'old Fordy yet! So, thanks for what ya did and all that, but your services won't be needed anymore.' I was so embarrassed as he made his excuses and left the room.

The conversation with the consultant was more enlightening. He explained to Dad that a seizure was the probable cause of the coma. I was taken aback and surprised when she explained that the nervous system couldn't adapt to the lack of alcohol once it was addicted.

I hadn't realised just how dangerous it could be to just stop taking alcohol. She asked Dad what and how much he'd been drinking.

I didn't want him fobbing her off. I turned to Dad. 'Look, Dad, now's the time to get honest.'

I was surprised to hear admit matter-of-factly that he'd been drinking more than a litre of brandy every day, but I was relieved that he was being honest.

She didn't mince her words about the prospect of drinking again because damage to his liver was irreversible. Dad seemed to be taking on board what she was saying.

He turned to me and Sarah. 'Look, I know I have been hitting it hard, and I know I have just put you both through hell. I promise this won't happen again.'

He sounded so confident and sincere, and I really appreciated the apology, but part of me still wasn't convinced. I knew Dad still had a long way to go.

# 120: It's A No Brainer

Paul and I weren't getting on, and I was getting tired of the petty arguments. He'd gone from being a hermit into a social butterfly. He was obsessed with his newfound status.

The more he earned, the more self-obsessed he became. He thought everyone was his mate; if I ever said that people were only using him for drugs, he would snap my head off, claiming I didn't know what I was talking about. Nothing was allowed to get in the way of his weekends, and he spent the week preparing for the nights out: sourcing the best deals, cutting and wrapping his dealer's bags.

According to him, it was essential to look the part; he wouldn't blink an eye at coughing up over a hundred quid for a top, and he wouldn't dream of missing his weekly appointment at the hairdresser to ensure his hair was on point. But I knew that no amount of flash clothes and fake smiles could hide the fact that behind closed doors, he was profoundly paranoid and insecure.

I wondered if this was what Mum must have felt like living with Dad, her being the compliant stay-at-home housewife whilst Dad went out partying every night. According to her, he didn't like parting with his money either.

Paul seemed to be happy with me having my own money, but he still didn't like me working at the markets. He would grill me every time I came back from work, about who I'd seen or who I'd spoken to. I loved my job. I could take or leave the toxic gossip that went on behind the scenes, but I enjoyed the banter with the customers, and it wasn't long before they greeted me by my first name.

It soon became apparent that for many regulars, the cafe was their lifeline. Many were pensioners, retired or widowed, and some would spend the whole day walking around the markets rather than sitting home alone, and I couldn't blame them.

There were some characters, too: the gypsy lady with her jet-black hair tied back, who told fortunes in return for a couple of quid. You could smell the guy with straggly long grey hair before you could see him walking round the market, happily chatting to himself. I had a soft spot for him and assumed he was homeless, but I soon learned that he was a patient at Middlewood Hospital, the local nut house, as the locals refereed to it, so when I heard that, I gave him a wide berth.

Then there were the shoplifters. Christ, you could get your hands on anything at half the price you'd pay in the shops. Some even took orders and would be back in ten minutes.

I was just serving a customer one day when I heard someone shout: 'Boo!'

It was Shauna and she was grinning from ear to ear. 'I didn't know you worked here!'

The café was packed, and I couldn't stand and chat, so I quickly made an excuse that I needed the toilet and beckoned Shauna to follow me. As soon as we turned the corner, we hugged each other. I hadn't realised until then just how much I'd missed her. It was like nothing had changed when, in fact, everything had. I'd moved house and had another child, and Shauna had big news of her own.

'Y never gonna guess what?' She was still grinning from ear to ear.

'You're getting married?' I joked.

'Nah, am I hell! I've just signed up for the RAF! Start me basic training in two weeks!'

'No way! Are you mad? Fuck me, Shauna, you don't even like running for the bus!'

I was laughing my head off by now.

'Look, don't get me wrong. I'm not looking forward to the physical training, but once it's done, the world is my oyster. I get to travel the world *and* get paid for it! It's a no-brainer.'

I had to get back to work, but we promised not to lose touch again and she said she'd bring me the address of the training camp as soon as she had it.

When I got home, I couldn't wait to tell Paul about bumping into Shauna and her news.

'You'll not see her again,' he mocked, shaking his head. 'She said she'd stay in touch before, and you haven't seen her.'

His words stung. He could be such a cynical bastard sometimes. But the thing was, he didn't know Shauna as I did; there was a genuineness about her and she wasn't fake, not like all his mates, and she didn't want me for anything else except my friendship. I just hoped that she would prove him wrong.

# 121: Where The Fuck Am I?

The solicitors were questioning Dad's medical records and were still looking for a second opinion because it appeared that Dad's liver had already been in a poor state before the crash.

The solicitor warned me that they might try to use this as leverage to lower the final settlement, based on Dad's reduced life expectancy. I decided not to mention to the solicitor that only days before, Dad had been given three days to live. I also decided not to tell Dad that the solicitors had been in touch when I went to visit.

Dad had been getting stronger, but when I arrived, the nurse had bad news. Dad had been coughing up blood and was being moved onto the gastro ward. He'd also managed to contract MRSA and been started on antibiotics. I was alarmed, but the medical staff reassured me that stomach problems were common with heavy drinkers and that there was no need to be too concerned about the MRSA. I could immediately tell that Dad was worried though.

I took my seat beside him and tried to stay positive.

'Oreyt?'

'Nah, I'm pissed off! Have they told you I've copped for that MRSA. Fuck knows how I've caught it. I've been in here on me own for days.' He stroked his arm. 'Look.' He was pointing to the rash that had been plaguing him for months now. 'They reckon it's got in through here.'

'Well look, at least they have caught it early, eh! And they have started ya on antibiotics.'

He didn't reply, instead he just stared at the wall in a world of his own. Then he started coughing and I saw the fear in his eyes.

I tried to make light of the situation. 'No fags for you, eh?'

But Dad wasn't on the same page.

'Honestly, Trace, I'm soooo fucked off. They were only on about letting me go yesterday, and now this! I reckon they have done this to me on purpose. Bent as fuck they are. Even our John said same today.'

I was confused. 'Uncle John? Has he been to see ya?'

But Dad just blanked me.

The nurse came and did her rounds and then Dad dozed off. He'd only been asleep for a couple of minutes before he sat up and screamed.

'Where the fuck am I?'

He was looking around the room, confused and at first, I wasn't even sure if he recognised me.

I stroked his arm, trying to calm him. 'Dad, Dad, calm down, it's me, Tracey! You're in the hospital.'

He stared at me like I'd grown two heads.

'I know I'm in hospital, ya fucking idiot!'

A minute later, he'd dozed off again. I shook my head and left the ward.

I called Uncle John to find out how Dad had been when he'd visited, but he told me he hadn't even been to see Dad, and then I called Sarah who was as frustrated and confused as me, but we both conceded that there was nothing we could do but wait to speak to the consultant tomorrow.

# 122: Job's A Good 'Un

As promised, Shauna called into the café a week later to hand me the training camp address in York, which wasn't a million miles away.

'You can drive up to see me,' she said.

'I've got to pass first!'

'Ahh, you'll smash it, Trace!'

My heart swelled. I couldn't help but love the faith she had in me. Brian, my instructor had said that I'd need around twenty-five lessons, but he also reckoned I was a natural and, so far, it was going well.

I even had my heart set on a car I'd seen in a sales lot. It was an orange three-door fiesta, the perfect size for us and the kids, and only two hundred and fifty pounds, which I could just about afford. Confident in my ability to pass my test, one day I jumped off the bus to take a closer look at the car.

The owner was like a Yorkshire version of Del Boy, and seemed like someone Dad would know.

'It's a little banger this one,' he smiled. 'Not had it in that long, and don't worry about the MOT, my lads can take care of that for ya,' he winked.

I knew the car had been there for weeks because I'd seen it, but there was something about him that I warmed to. 'Thanks, but to be honest, I haven't even passed my test yet.'

Just then, a lad not much older than me came bouncing around the corner. 'Nah then, fatha, why don't you ever pick up ya phone! I've been fucking trying to call, Jonno's here, with that stuff you ordered.' As soon as he saw me standing there, his face drained white.

'Oops, sorry love, I didn't see you there.'

I suspected that the stuff he referred to was shady, piquing my curiosity but I laughed.

'Nah, don't mind me, mate.'

His Dad then wrapped his arms around me like a protective father and reprimanded him. 'I've not answered, cos I have been dealing with this young lady. I've told her we can sort her out with a little runner when she's passed her test.'

'Aye, we can do that. Trust me, mi father, Tricky Micky will sort ya out,' his son teased.

'I haven't even started saving yet,' I confessed.

'Look, lass, once you've passed, you bring what you've saved as a down payment and leave me your licence as security, and you get to drive the car off the lot. Job's a good un.'

'You are joking, aren't you?'

'Nah, I'm not, love. I trust ya and I'm a man of me word.' He passed me a business card. 'I'm Mick, and that's my number. Be sure to give me a bell when you are ready, okay?'

A few weeks later, I'd passed my test. I couldn't believe it. It was the first time I'd passed anything, and I was so proud. I'd done it all on my own too. When I broke the news to Paul, he was buzzing.

'Ahhh, Trace, this is amazing. Well done. Listen I've already sorted a car. My mate's selling one. It's a Ford Sierra and he only wants five hundred quid for it.'

I knew he was only thinking about how he would benefit.

'I can't afford that, Paul, and anyway, Dad's already sorted it.' The truth was, I hadn't mentioned anything to Dad, but he didn't know that. I also knew there was no way that he would challenge Dad, not if he thought Mick was a mate of his.

'What do you mean, you've sorted it? I've already told my mate that if you pass, I'll have it off him; I'll even put halves too and look, you can pay me back when you've got it. Come on Trace, it's a reyt nice car an' all.'

All I could hear was me, me, me. 'Thing is, Paul, it's not your car, and you're not driving it!'

'But I've already said we'll have it!' he shouted. 'You are gonna make me look like a fucking mug.'

I was dying to say he didn't need me to make him look like a mug, but thought now was not the time. 'I'd rather mug you off than Dad. Anyway, Mick's a good guy and I trust him.'

Paul huffed. 'Well, don't be expecting me to pay for it.'

I was expecting this. Paul knew I was strapped for cash, but he didn't know about the deal I'd already struck up with Mick, and neither of us knew that Mum and Ada were also going to give me fifty quid.

I don't know who was more excited, me or her, when I told her the news.

She wrapped her arms around me and whispered, 'I'm so proud of you.'

'Honestly, Mum, I'm proud of myself.'

I wrote to Shauna to break the news. What was supposed to be a short celebratory letter turned out to be eight pages long. As well as my exciting news, I found myself opening up about Paul and how unhappy I was. Just dumping the words onto paper felt therapeutic, and for a second, I even thought about keeping a journal.

But then I thought about what Paul would say if he were ever to find it. Our relationship had become like a game of cat and mouse, with each of us trying to second-guess the other's next move. But I was going to get that car and with it, my independence.

# 123: Just Ignore Him

I had managed to pin the consultant down over the phone in the morning and he'd agreed to meet me and Sarah later that afternoon. Dad's new ward was at the other side of the hospital grounds, and it took some time to find our bearings and get a parking spot. I joked with Sarah that I was going to save all the tickets and claim the money back off Dad when he got out.

My first impressions of Mr Jackson, the consultant, were good, though he looked far too young to be a consultant. As we settled into our seats, he sat forward and started wringing his hands.

'So you're Frank's daughters, is that right? How can I help you?'

I took the lead. I had so many questions I didn't know where to start, so I started at the beginning. He sat patiently whilst I babbled on and brought him up to speed.

'So basically, he's come out of this coma and now he's coughing up blood. What does that mean?'

He cleared his throat. 'Your dad is still unwell. He's suffering from what we call post-acute alcohol withdrawal syndrome, which can create a catalogue of symptoms which can last for weeks, months and sometimes up to a year.' He took a deep breath. 'I know it sounds alarming, but it is common with patients with a decomposed liver.'

'I thought Dad had cirrhosis of the liver?'

He picked up my confusion and started to explain. It was like being in a biology lesson as he explained the different stages of liver disease. There were different types of cirrhosis – compensated or decompensated. Compensated cirrhosis, where the liver is coping and maintaining its important functions, and decompensated, when it wasn't.

He said that Dad would have had alcohol fatty liver for years and told us that this was referred to as the silent killer because it had few or no symptoms. He carefully explained how it was the liver's role is to break down alcohol, only during the process, it produced nasty toxic chemicals which, over time could damage the liver permanently by scarring it. It could also lead to alcohol hepatitis, which could cause the abdomen to become distended, due to the excessive leakage of fluid, otherwise known as ascites.

He said that the gut couldn't cope with the acid, leading to more gastric problems and internal bleeding. Hepatitis then created more scarring, slowing the flow of blood, making the liver less effective, but also circulating toxic blood to all the other organs.

As the doctor continued to explain, it was like a light bulb had been switched on in my head. All Dad's symptoms: the abdominal swelling, the yellowing of the eyes, the itchy skin and the coma all made perfect sense now. No wonder they called it the silent killer.

'So basically, decompensated liver means Dad's liver is fucked!'

The doctor cleared his throat. 'Well, you could say that.'

'So, what about the coughing up blood, what does that mean?'

He explained 'It is the rupturing of the oesophageal varices that is responsible for the vomiting of blood. Basically, individuals that have advanced cirrhosis are exceptionally prone to oesophageal varices. The priority for us now is to try to reduce his blood pressure.'

Apparently, they were currently treating Dad with beta blockers, but if he didn't improve, they would have to tie his oesophagus with a band. I mentioned Dad's weird behaviour the night before and the consultant explained that it was probably because the damaged liver was struggling to break down food and medications, leading to toxicity which could affect brain function and cause cognitive impairment, otherwise known as hepatic encephalopathy.

'I'm afraid the only way of your dad improving is if he stops drinking. That will improve his life expectancy. But I need to be honest, he's not out of the woods yet. We don't yet know the extent of the damage to his other organs and then there's the MRSA...'

He carried on talking but I'd zoned out and started to rub my temples. My mind flashed back over the past week. Dad had gone from being given three days to live, then they'd been talking about discharge and now we didn't know for sure if he would even make it home.

Down in the canteen, Sarah and I tried to process the news. The words 'silent killer' echoed in my head.

'Well, that's him not drinking again,' said Sarah.

'I know. Looks like years in the pub have finally caught up with him. The problem is convincing Dad of that.'

Sarah shook her head. 'Well he's gonna have to listen, Trace. If he picks up a drink again, he's done for.'

Part of me wished someone had sat us both down sooner and explained all this when he'd been in hospital before, perhaps we could have been firmer with Dad. But I knew that it wouldn't have mattered, there was no telling Dad, because he always knew best.

Dad was still fast asleep when we got back to his room. We quietly tiptoed in and sat either side of Dad. As Dad lay there, I imagined all the toxins being pumped around his body and his organs furiously trying to keep him alive.

We stayed for another hour, but there was no change, so I agreed to call back and visit him later; hopefully he'd be awake.

I was pleased to find him awake engrossed in a newspaper. He placed the paper on his lap when he saw me. 'Ey up, shugs.'

He seemed in good spirits which was a relief. I washed my hands and pulled a chair to the side of his bed. 'Ey up, Dad.' I reached over to give him a kiss. 'How ya feeling?'

'I'm feeling a lot better. I reckon it won't be long 'for they'll be letting me out.' He seemed so confident and cocksure.

'Well, fingers crossed, eh.'

'Can't come too soon. I'm going fucking stir crazy in here. Them nurses are like the fucking gestapo. Wouldn't even give me a fag!'

I couldn't help but laugh.

'Dad, tha coughing up blood and hooked up to antibiotics.'

'Well, I ain't coughed no blood up since they brought me down here, there's nowt stopping em wheeling me out for a fag, is there. Tight bastards! Speaking of tight bastards, where's me grapes?'

I laughed.

'Anyway, how's work and the kids?'

I welcomed the change of subject. 'Yeah, work's been mad busy, that's why I'm late.' Dad shook his head.

'You shouldn't have come, Trace, you should have gone straight home.'

'Well, I didn't want too, did I? I just wanted to check you were ok.'

Dad reached for my hand and squeezed it. 'Tha a good un, Trace. In fact, you and our Sarah have been brilliant. I honestly don't know what I would have done without ya both.'

He squeezed my hand again and looked straight into my eyes. 'Look, I know I've given you both a scare. Truth be told, I've scared me sen, but I promise when I get out of here, things will be different.' I could feel myself blushing and tears in my eyes.

'Look, let's just get ya outta here first, eh.'

Our heart to heart was interrupted by one of the nurses who'd come to take Dad's obs.

'Evening, Frank.' She smiled in my direction. 'Who's this then?'

Dad looked all proud. 'This is my eldest, Tracey. She's been a good un, I'll tell thee.'

I felt myself blushing again and turned to the nurse. 'Has he been behaving himself, then?'

She smiled as she took Dad's pulse.

'Who, Frank? He's a pussycat, aren't ya, Frank?' Dad smiled smugly.

'I am wi' you, but don't you be sending that horrible cow in again.'

I gave Dad a sharp nudge. 'Hey, pack it in.' I rolled my eyes to the nurse. 'Just ignore him.'

'Oh, I am, don't you worry,' before winking at Dad.

'Oi, you two, I am here, tha knows! Anyway, will it be you who will be giving me a bed bath, then?'

I gave him another sharp nudge, but I couldn't help but laugh.

The nurse was by the bottom of Dad's bed, writing up his notes. She laughed.

'Depends on if you are going to behave or not, Frank.' And with that, she turned and walked out of the room.

# 124: A Reyt Bag of Shit

My driver's license finally landed on the doormat. I was so proud that I was tempted to frame it, but I needed it as a security deposit for the car. I called in to see Mick straight after my shift.

He greeted me with open arms. 'Here she is, Sheffield's very own Nigel Mansell!'

After a quick bear hug, we turned our attention to the Ford Fiesta. 'It's all ready for ya. Little Micky's checked her over. There's even a half tank of petrol.'

As if on cue, little Micky came bouncing around the corner with a carrier bag, which I suspected was knock-off gear.

'Ere, Fatha, here's ya stuff you ordered off Jonno.' He spotted me. 'Oreyt love, you passed ya test finally?' He passed the bag to his dad. 'Don't need any coffee, do ya? We've got shit loads out back going cheap.'

'Nah, I'm ok, I can get it all day long working in markets, mate.'

His Dad interjected. 'She's come here to buy a car, not fucking coffee'.

The bond and banter they shared made me think of Dad. It had been a while since we'd laughed like that. Mick took me into his cabin where I exchanged the money and my licence for the keys and then I was off.

Much to my relief, the car started as soon as I turned on the ignition. It felt weird not having Brian sat at my side, and I was scared that I might have forgotten everything I'd learned, but as soon as I drove the car out of the lot, everything just slotted into place.

I wanted to get used to the car before taking it home, so I drove around some old haunts. I drove past Kenninghall Mount, the block of flats where Dad lived as a kid, and then I cut through onto East Bank Road, before heading towards the Valley. It felt weird driving through my old stomping ground;

I felt like a stranger, yet I knew the estate like the back of my hand.

I took a left off Blackstock Road onto Ironside and followed the road until I reached our old house. I laughed to myself as I recalled climbing out of the bedroom window in a pathetic attempt to run away from home. I'd have done anything to go back in time and do things differently. In a matter of five years, I had conceived three children and birthed two; I'd even failed at trying to run away from Paul.

Reluctantly, I headed home knowing he'd be pacing about waiting for me. His face was a picture when I proudly showed off my newly acquired car. He walked around the car to inspect it like he was some sort of expert.

'It's a reyt bag of shit!'

'You won't want any lifts anywhere, then?' I offered sarcastically. 'Anyway, it might be a bag of shit, but it's my bag of shit!'

'Come on then; take us all for a spin.' He grinned.

It wasn't long before I was taxiing him around all over the place, doing his jobs. At least he gave me money for petrol, which was just as well because I was skint.

# 125: Don't Mind Me, Dad

Dad was asleep when I arrived but the noise of me pulling up a chair woke him. I waved a bag of grapes in his direction.

He laughed. 'About fucking time.'

I pretended to throw them at him. He seemed in good spirits and showed no signs of confusion which was a relief; last time Sarah had spoken to him he'd been talking about visits from Chinese laundry people.

'So, I hear you had some visitors?'

Dad looked briefly confused. 'Ahh, yeah. Lawson called up wi' his missus. Said he's going to keep an eye on the flat whilst I'm in here.' He chomped away on the grapes.

'Nah then, ya supposed to share 'em, ya know!'

Dad offered me a grape then leaned in and whispered 'I went out for a fag and only got caught by that fucking nurse, that gestapo one.'

I looked at Dad laid on the bed and wondered where he'd got a fag from or how he'd even managed to walk.

'Did Lawson take ya, then?'

'Lawson?'

'Yeah, Lawson. You said he'd been up?'

Dad shook his head. 'Nah, I went out on my own.' He then went on a rant about how the hospital was like a prison. I decided to let it go and changed the subject.

'So, have the docs said owt about the MRSA?'

Dad huffed. 'I reckon it's a load of bollocks. I'm fine.'

'And what about the coughing up blood, have they said anything about that?'

'I ain't coughed owt up since getting down here. I'm telling ya, Trace, I'm ok.'

This felt the perfect time to relay mine and Sarah's conversation with the consultant a couple of days before. 'Look Dad, you aren't ok. I know there's nowt wrong with you on the outside, but the drinking has taken its toll on ya insides.'

Dad shook his head.

'Don't, be shaking ya head at me, Dad! This is serious.' I tried to cover as much detail as I could from the conversation with the consultant. 'So, basically, Dad, ya liver's fucked.'

I saw Dad's eyes roll slightly. He was about to talk, but I stopped him.

'Listen Dad, this is serious, and you need to be taking it more serious too.'

'Look I've told ya I'm sorry, haven't I? Can't we just have a nice visit?'

I was starting to get frustrated, 'Dad, you don't get it! this isn't about me and Sarah. This is about you!'

Dad tried changing the subject. 'Have you heard owt from the solicitors?'

I snapped. 'Yes, I have but if you go back to drinking again then you ain't gonna be alive to see any money from the fucking claim!'

We were getting nowhere so I excused myself and went to get some air. As I was leaving, the ward a nurse pulled me to one side and asked if she could have a word.

'It's your dad,' she said. 'We caught him smoking in his room today.'

I was confused.

'In his room? He's just mentioned something about being told off for going out for a fag...'

'Well, he didn't go outside. I can assure you of that! He set the smoke alarm off on the ward!'

'Look, I'm really sorry, I don't even know where he has got a fag from.' Then I remembered Lawson. 'Unless his mate fetched him some in?'

I made my way back to Dad's room and found him half-asleep. I tiptoed inside and whispered.

'Don't mind me, Dad! I'm just getting some boxers to take back and wash for ya.'

I headed to his cupboard, and low and behold there was a good ten-pack of Bensons and Hedges with one fag missing and a lighter on the top. I picked up the packet and lighter.

Thankfully Dad was out with the fairies and hadn't noticed.

One the drive home, I called Sarah. We knew it wasn't funny, but we couldn't help chuckling. I also made a mental note to get in touch with Lawson to give him a piece of my mind. For all I knew, he'd be bringing him in brandy next for fuck's sake.

# 126: Don't Worry About Me, Trace

Paul was still sulking about me not getting the car he wanted and that I had picked up a couple extra days to work in the café. He'd been a pain in the arse for the past couple of weeks, stomping around the house, convinced that his supplier was ripping him off. His face, however, lit up when I told him that I'd bumped into a mutual friend, Stacey, who reckoned she could get him a cheaper supplier.

I'd bumped into her after finishing my shift at work. I barely recognised her at first; she was a shadow of the girl I once knew. It soon became apparent why when she told me how she was living in a women's refuge after a guy she'd been dating had been violent towards her.

I couldn't believe my ears when she told me who it was. I had heard of this Tommy through Dad, and I knew that he had a reputation for violence. I was still getting my head around the fact she'd got involved with a guy nearly twice her age, when she asked after Paul and me. She'd known us when we were first dating. I told her about our lives and our kids and then confessed about Paul's side-line. That's when she told me about her contact.

A week later, Stacey turned up at the cafe with a speed sample for Paul. Paul was literally, and I mean literally, buzzing around the house ten minutes after sampling the speed and asked me to give Stacey a call to sort him an ounce out.

He wasn't interested in going himself and suggested I go with Stacey on his behalf, which didn't faze me; any excuse to get out of the house.

I wasn't sure what to expect when we arrived at the dealer's place, but Stacey had explained that the guy who'd got her the gear was a mate of her ex and one of the main dealers in the city, but she also reassured me that he was one of the "good guys". I'd been expecting our transaction to be a cloak and daggers affair, but when we arrived at a block of flats on the Wybourn, Pete the dealer opened the door and welcomed us both like long-lost friends.

Pete was nothing like I'd imagined. He was small and unassuming and his girlfriend, Louise, was in the living room playing with their daughter. The flat was open plan. Pete went into the kitchen area and popped the kettle on.

'Got time for a cuppa? You may as well, I'll be another ten minutes cos I've not had a chance to bag it up.' He started brewing the kettle. 'But I'll tell thee, it's worth the wait, like fucking rocket fuel!'

Soon, he was handing drugs across the table as casually as he'd made the drinks.

'Reyt, Tracey, this is yours,' he said, placing a bag of white powder on the breakfast bar. And tell your old man, I've got my hands on some pink champagne next week if he's interested.'

I didn't have a clue what pink champagne was and just slid the cash in his direction. He then pushed a smaller bag in Stacey's direction. 'Here, love, that's yours.' Giving her a knowing wink.

'Cheers, Pete, I promise I'll pay as soon as I get paid.'

Stacey looked embarrassed. She was there for some gear herself, which shocked me.

'And here, love, I've made a couple up for you,' said Pete, passing me two small wraps.

I wanted to explain that I didn't partake in drugs, but I also didn't want to come across as some Mary Whitehouse either, so I accepted them gracefully.

'Oh, and here is my number. There's more where that came from. I can get a good deal on Es too, if your old man's interested. In fact.' He rummaged in his pockets. 'Take a couple with ya. Let me know what he thinks.'

Me and Stacey left and headed to the car, while Stacey told me about how angry Tommy was and how much he wanted her back. 'Everyone is blaming me for wrecking his marriage, which isn't true.'

'He was married?' I tried not to be judgemental, but her revelation did take me by surprise. 'Fuck me, Stacey. You ain't half got thee sen into a pickle there, hun.'

'Tell me about it.' She shook her head in regret 'The worst thing I ever did was meeting Tommy. I've heard that he and the missus are back together, so I just hope it all dies down soon so I can get my life back to some sort of normality, whatever the fuck that is.'

'So, apart from Tommy, is everything else ok?'

We both knew I was talking about the drugs. 'I haven't got a problem, Trace. It just helps pick me up.'

'Hey, I'm not judging ya. I'm just concerned, that's all.'

'Don't worry about me, Trace.'

# 127: The New Norm

I had assumed that with Dad not drinking, his health would improve, but I was wrong.

He'd been moved onto the main ward, and the MRSA had cleared up but now he'd developed bed sores on his coccyx on account of being laid down for so long. Some visits were good and others not so good. He would appear to be drunk, but he wasn't intoxicated because of alcohol, it was because of the build-up of toxins. Two days were never the same. Sometimes I could have a rational conversation with him and a joke. Then other days he'd be getting himself all worked up and frustrated at not being able to go home or kicking off about the claim being dragged out.

On the days when he was confused or hallucinating, he would come out with some corkers. Like his frequent visits to the pub. According to Dad, him, and his new mate (the guy in the opposite bed to him) would sneak out to the local pub without the staff knowing. Dad loved the fact that he'd got one over on staff.

The sad part was even if it had been possible, there was no way his mate could move because he was an amputee. I'd spoken to him a few times and he'd confessed that he'd lost his legs as a result of injecting crack and heroin into his groin. It was a real shame, because I could tell that he had the potential to turn his life around. Just like I thought Dad did

One afternoon, I arrived on the ward to find Dad reading his paper with a pair of glasses I'd never seen before. He looked a sight. They were like the ones Deirdre Barlow used to wear on Corrie. When I asked where he'd got them from, he took them off his nose and waved them about.

'I dunno, but they work. I can read me paper nah!' he said smugly.

'Yeah, but Dad, they must belong to someone,' I said.

Dad turned to me wearing the glasses, which were far too feminine for him. 'Well whoever they belong to, they can't be missing 'em. Anyway, finder's keepers an' all that.' He pushed them back onto the bridge of his nose and went back to his paper.

Most of the staff were great, but others not so. Not that I could blame them; there had been many occasions when I found myself apologising on his behalf after he'd been sharp with them. But other times, he could turn on the charm and would be the perfect patient.

Being on first name terms with many of the staff, they sometimes shared their frustrations and feelings of powerlessness with me. They knew that it wouldn't be long before the very same patients would be admitted again. It made me even more determined to make sure that when Dad got released, he wouldn't be one of them.

I'd noticed there was no support information for the visitors, so I brought some leaflets in and hoped that the families would use them.

Visiting the hospital was the new norm. Sarah and I took turns to visit. Some weekends, I would take the kids to visit, or Tracey or some other family members would visit, which afforded me and Sarah a much-needed break.

Lawson became a regular visitor too; I'd forgiven him for bringing the fags in after bumping into to him on a visit. He wasn't such a bad guy after all. Unlike Dad's other so-called mates, he seemed to genuinely care about Dad. The fact that he would traipse from the other side of Sheffield on the bus to visit Dad was testament to that.

## 128: I Slept Like a Baby

I hadn't heard a word from Stacey since visiting Pete, and it wasn't until Paul had called Pete to place another order, that I found out why. It turned out she'd gone back to Tommy. I couldn't believe my ears when I heard she'd gone back to the guy who she claimed had treated her so badly.

'So, what about the gear?' I asked Paul.

'Pete is still on. I've told him you'll pop in later to collect some more.'

'What on my own, aren't you coming?

He shrugged his shoulders. 'I can't. Anyway, who is going to look after the kids?'

This time, Louise opened the door.

'Hiya love, come in – Pete's out, but he won't be long.' She ushered me into the living room where their daughter was happily playing with her toys.

Louise was easy to talk to. She was much younger than Pete and her story was pretty much the same as Stacey and Tommy's. Even though they'd been together almost three years, she'd still not been accepted by some of his friends and especially his family.

I felt sorry for her when she explained how she barely left the flat, fearing being verbally attacked or spat at. After sharing the basics about the kids and work, I found myself opening up to her about Paul and how he'd recently been doing my nut with his paranoia and controlling ways. I was surprised when she disclosed that Pete also had some of the same traits.

I was impressed when she told me how the flat was hers, how, before meeting Pete, she'd worked full-time as a nurse, and how everything had changed since giving birth. There was an undercurrent of regret, especially around her loss of independence, which made me realise how lucky I was to still be able to go out to work instead of being stuck at home. I was filling her in about Dad and how I used to work for him, when Pete came bouncing in the living room.

'Ey up, love, you two seem to be getting on ok.'

Louise got up to greet him. 'We've been having a lovely chat. That was until you came and spoilt it,' she teased. 'We were just talking about Tracey's Dad, Frank. I was just saying you would probably know him.'

'What's his surname?'

'Ford.'

'Fuck a duck. I know Franky boy. Used to drink with him in the Far Lees on the Valley. Well, I never! Fordy's Babbie, eh! Well, send him my regards when you next see him, will ya?'

'I would if I saw him,' I joked, but there was no way that I was about to tell Dad about Pete because he would go ballistic if he knew Paul was involved in drugs. He hated drugs.

'Right, give me two seconds. I've already got your old man's gear ready.'

Two minutes later, he reappeared, holding a small bag in one hand and a carrier in the other. 'You smoke, don't ya? Got me hands on some cheap fags if you want any?'

I was tempted but had no cash on me.

He must have read my mind. 'Pay me next time you come; I trust ya.'

I took a sleeve of fags off him.

'Take some more if you think you can sell some down at the market. At that price, the money you would earn would pay for yours.'

I could get used to this. This wasn't drug dealing; it was just like calling around to mates for a coffee and a chat, with the added bonus of being able to earn some cash, too. I took the fags off Pete and left them in the boot, ready to sell at the markets the following morning.

Pete and Louise soon became firm friends. Their home became like a refuge for me. As well as the drugs, Pete also had a steady stream of shoplifters who came to his door at all hours and were willing to flog their wares at less than half the retail price, and it wasn't long before I was selling on the odd bits and bobs for a little extra cash.

Eventually, I was in a financial position to make the last payment for the car. As usual, Mick greeted me with a bear hug.

'She's here, our Tracey. Come on inside, love, and I'll get you your license.'

I remembered the sleeves of fags in the car. 'Got my hands on some cheap fags, if you are interested Mick?'

'I don't smoke, but our Mick does.'

Just then, Little Mick came bouncing into the cabin, dropping a set of car keys on the table.

'Our Trace here has got her hands on some cheap fags if you're interested?' said Big Mick.

'Aye, me and the lads will have 'em off ya, love – bring 'em round the back when you've done with me fatha.'

'I can also get hold of other stuff too, Coffee, razors, meat, cheese, you name it.'

Mick handed me my precious licence. 'So, you're not just a pretty face. You're a little fencer too!'

I didn't know what a fencer was, but I went on. 'Seriously, Mick. This guy I know gets a hold of loads of stuff.'

'Well in that case, if you get owt else, be sure to give me the first dibs, ok.'

Which was fine by me, any excuse to pop in and see him.

I could tell Paul had the face on as soon as I walked in the door

'Where have you been?'

'I told ya, I went to pay off the car.' I waved my driver's licence as proof. 'Oh and Mick's offered to move some knock-off gear too.'

'Is it really worth it, Trace? I mean, you are making peanuts,' he mocked.

'Oh I'm sorry, I hadn't realised this was a competition.'

'I don't like the amount of time you're spending around at theirs.'

'Are you fucking kidding me? I only started going for gear for you, but if you want me to stop going, just say the word.'

He shook his head. 'Forget it!'

But I wasn't about to back down. 'One minute, you're complaining about me borrowing from you, then the next thing, you don't like me working, so which one is it? You were more than happy for me to work my ass off for Dad and take money off me when you had fuck all!'

'I said forget it.' Then he turned his back on me.

I paced the kitchen, trying to calm down. How fucking dare he, the cheeky bastard? I was grafting my tits off and chasing after him; I never got any time for me. Calling to see Mick and spending time with Louise was the closest to a social life I had. He didn't get it, I knew he never would.

To top it off, he had the fucking audacity to try it on when we got in bed like nothing had ever happened. I couldn't even sleep next to him. Instead, I took my pillow downstairs to sleep on the sofa. I was struggling to sleep, but I must have dozed off at some point because the next thing I remember was being woken by Paul thumping on the bedroom floor because the alarm was going off in our room.

I felt like the walking dead driving into work. I parked up and noticed the two wraps of speed that Pete had given me a week earlier. I'd completely forgotten about them. Curiosity got the better of me. I opened one of the wraps, wet my finger, dabbed a sliver of powder and wiped it on my tongue. As soon as it hit my tongue, I regretted it. I immediately started gipping, and the worst part was I didn't have a drink on hand to rinse my mouth with.

My tongue immediately started to tingle, and I thought my head might explode. I was tingling all over as I walked over to the Markets. My heart was beating so far out of my chest that I feared I might have a heart attack on the spot. My mouth felt like the Sahara Desert.

I smiled and greeted Sally, pretending it was just another normal morning, but inside, I was far from normal. By now, my body was buzzing all over, and my hands were physically shaking. I couldn't stand still, so I busied myself, getting stuck into work.

'Fuck me, Trace. You're like the Tasmanian devil,' Sally joked an hour into my shift.

But little did she know I felt like him. I couldn't stand still. It took over an hour for my heartbeat to settle back to normal, and the initial panic I'd been experiencing had been replaced with a feeling of euphoria.

It was like someone had switched a light bulb on in my head. I had never felt so alive in my life, and in that moment, I finally understood what all the fuss was about. Mundane chores like washing, drying and putting away crockery became a joy. I even offered to take the rubbish to the foul-smelling refuge, a job nobody liked.

It was lunchtime before I realised that I hadn't eaten any breakfast; I couldn't even be tempted into my usual hit of uncut bread with a lashing of butter. Instead, I drank copious mugs of tea while serving customers and cleaning the café. During the day, I'd even managed to flog all the fags that Pete had laid on.

I had managed to flog them to the guys in the markets whilst doing the mug run, and the best part was, I'd not only sold all the fags, but I'd also got orders for some more.

I was buzzing at the end of my shift, not just from the speed but from my day's achievements. I'd even found the time to call in to pay Pete after work for the fags and to get some more to sell when I was next on shift.

As suspected, Paul had got the face on because I'd been half an hour later than usual, but not even his mood could dampen my spirits. I'd just put the kids to bed when I finally felt the effects start to wear off; I wasn't that far behind them. For the first time in weeks, the sleep that had been eluding me finally caught up with me, and I slept like a baby.

# 129: A Flutter of Hope

Dad had been in hospital for over a month and finally appeared to be making some progress. He was eating well and was gaining some strength back and there was even talk of him being released and about potential adaptations that might be required for him when he went back home.

Dad's health wasn't the only thing that was improving. A month off the drink and the hallucinations were subsiding, allowing more of Dad's good side to show. If Mr Hyde was the nasty, self-entitled demanding side of him that we saw when he was drunk or hallucinating, now we were seeing more of Dr Jekyll, his more vulnerable alter ego. Dr Jekyll could acknowledge the severity of the damage that alcohol had done to his body and would frequently promise that another drop of brandy would never pass his lips and in those moments, I believed him. He was also preoccupied with making amends for the past.

One afternoon, he started to reminisce about his reaction when he'd found out Mum was pregnant.

'God, I was fucking shitting me sen, Trace. I mean, I was only a kid me sen! D'ya know what I mean?'

I laughed at the irony. 'Yeah, I do know what you mean.'

Dad reached for my hand and squeezed it affectionately. 'Oh yeah, I suppose ya do. We don't do things by halves, do we us Fords, eh? I did love her, ya know.'

I nodded. I knew he was referring to Mum.

'I was just a twat. I know I was. She didn't deserve the way I treated her, nor did you two, for that matter.'

I could hear the regret in his voice. 'Look Dad, that's in the past, innit?'

Dad shook his head. 'It's still there though. I've got loads of regrets. I know I've slagged Ada off in the past, but he's done a good job wi' your twos.'

'Look Dad, we've all made mistakes in the past. Stop beating ya sen up.'

'Pat's a good un, Trace. Tha' fell on thee feet wi him. Whereas I've fucked up, monumentally, ant I? I mean look at me, I'm fucking single, got no job and nah I'm a fucking cripple.'

I stopped him before he could go on.

'Look, Dad, you know opening up like this is just what you need to do more of. Half of the time it's guilt and shame that drives people back to drink or drugs, but you got nowt to feel ashamed or guilty about. It's in the past, innit!'

'Look, I know I've said it before, but I do really appreciate what you both have done for me.' I could see Dad's eyes welling up.

'Ahhh, come on, Dad, don't be getting upset, tha'll be starting me off soon.'

I stood up to give him a hug which he reciprocated for a couple of seconds before pushing me away. 'Come on now, Trace.' He scanned the ward. 'There are people watching.'

'Ahhh, you don't want anyone thinking big bad Fordy's getting all soft in his old age.' I laughed. 'Listen, on a serious note Dad, ya know them support groups I've mentioned?'

Dad's eyes rolled.

'No listen to me, there are loads of other people in them groups who've been through the same, and have some of the very same regrets you have, but guess what? They're doing great cos they are clean. Will you consider going to one? I'll take ya.'

Dad didn't say yes, but he didn't say no neither, which was progress. I just hoped that the seed I'd planted might start to germinate. Something had shifted in me too. After years of feeling like an inconvenience and thinking that Dad never cared, I was realising that he just didn't know how to show it.

I just hoped that when he was released that he might finally access some emotional support and rid himself of Mr Hyde for good. For the first time in ages, I felt a flutter of hope.

# 130: Stash of Cash

I'd not heard a dicky bird from Stacey since she'd gone back to her bloke, so I was surprised when she telephoned me out of the blue and asked me if I wanted to go out to meet her and Tommy and his mates down the Scottish Queen. I wasn't sure. I'd heard the Scottish Queen was rough, then there was all the stuff Stacey had told me about Tommy, but curiosity got the better of me.

'Go on then.'

Paul wasn't happy about me going out and especially to meet Tommy. 'I don't like the idea of you hanging about with the likes of them,' he said.

I laughed. 'You do know you are a drug dealer, right?' Anyway, I'm going to see Stacey, not Tommy.'

The Scottish Queen pub was nestled underneath the Park Hill flats. They reminded me of Kelvin, but on a much larger scale. Inside, the atmosphere was more like a community centre than a pub. Everyone seemed to know each other, and I couldn't help but feel out of place, but that all changed when Stacey introduced me to Tommy, who greeted me like a long-lost friend. Pete was there too.

'Eye up, Trace. I didn't know you were coming out. Let me get you a drink.'

'No need mate,' said Tommy, who was already handing me a drink. He wasn't what I'd expected. He was far more handsome for a start.

'Hey, Tommy, ya know our Trace here is Frank Ford's daughter, don't ya?'

'Fuck off!' Tommy looked as surprised as Pete had done. 'Well you must have got your looks from ya Mum! Anyway, how is the old bastard?'

I was just about to explain how Dad was living in Leeds, but we were interrupted by a young lad stepping in between us with a carrier bag full of perfume bottles.

'I'll have this, Tom, if that's ok?' said Stacey.

Tommy went into his pocket and pulled out the biggest wad of cash I'd ever seen in my life. 'And what about you Trace, seen owt you want?'

'I'm ok, thanks.' I was about to hand the bag back to the lad when Tommy interjected.

'Goo on lass, treat ya sen.'

I was embarrassed watching him barter over the perfume, but I was also touched. I couldn't remember the last time anyone had bought me anything. And it wasn't just the perfume either; Tommy refused to allow me to pay for any drinks while I was there. I felt like royalty.

Every time Tommy introduced me as Frank's daughter, I was welcomed with open arms. I always knew that Dad was involved in criminal activity and now I was standing in the centre of what felt like a criminal underworld, and I loved every minute of it. Any previous fears about feeling out of place going to the Scottish Queen had vanished and had been replaced by a warm feeling of acceptance, I felt like I'd just been accepted into an exclusive members club.

I soon became a regular. I'd call in every Wednesday night, and it wasn't long before I felt welcomed by everyone. I loved the banter; there were no airs or graces, what you saw is what you got, and I loved it.

Even though Stacey had initially invited me, I wasn't just Stacey's mate; I was also known as Frank Ford's daughter. Being the new face, a couple of the blokes had tried it on, but they soon gave up when I'd made it perfectly clear I was interested in any relationship, *and* I certainly wasn't about to be anyone's bit on the side.

'So why don't you bring your bloke down with ya?' Tommy asked one night.

The Scottish Queen wasn't his scene at all. 'He's got the kids, hasn't he? And we don't go out together, and to be honest I don't want him here.'

'You are a feisty fucker, Trace, I'll give you that,' Tommy teased.

I didn't let on that behind the bravado, Paul was just a pretty boy who didn't have the backbone to hold his own in the real world.

I'd started taking small dabs of gear daily. I would secretly refer to the speed as my 'fuck it gear', because not only did it help me be super productive, but I also started to give less fucks about what Paul thought.

Paul would have hit the roof had he known I was taking gear, let alone if he found out about the little stash hidden away in a drawer. He wouldn't have liked the fact that I was doing my own dealing, either. Sometimes if someone asked me to get some gear off Paul, I would sell them some of mine instead, which paid for mine. That's how I met Toni.

She invited me in for a cuppa when I dropped her some stuff off and she didn't need to ask twice. She was an attractive woman, and I liked her immediately. It seemed like I wasn't the only one.

In the time it took me to finish my coffee, there must have been five people who would knock and let themselves in just to call in for a quick chat and to say hello. It was like an open house, but the nice part was that she greeted everyone with the same warmth she'd greeted me with, and I knew before I left that I would also become a regular visitor.

One of the women who called had come to buy some knock-off t-shirts. Toni told me they were selling like hot cakes, and I could see why. It was hard to tell they were fake, and the best part was, they were retailing on the streets at a tenner each, but she was selling them for six quid.

'Can I take a couple, then and call you with some orders? I'm at work tomorrow. I know I could shift loads of these.'

'Yeah sure, I've got some spares in the living room, you can take a couple of samples with ya.'

Paul's eyes lit up when I got home. 'Where you got these from?'

I wasn't about to let on about my side-line-selling speed, but I could tell he was impressed with the fakes. 'Someone from the markets.'

I knew what he was thinking whilst he inspected them. ‘How much?’

‘Eight quid. She can get her hands on any make ya want: Nike, Adidas, you name it.’

‘I reckon I could sell these on for twelve or fifteen, easy.’

I could have kicked myself. Had I known that, I would have told him I was getting them for a tenner, but it still felt good, knowing that I’d finally brought home something he was interested in, and the best part was I’d be making money off him.

Toni was right. I’d managed to sell a shit load of t-shirts in just a couple of weeks. I was at Toni’s every other day with orders. She especially loved it if I brought Lauren with me, showering her with treats, claiming she hated that her own kids were growing up too fast. I knew I’d made a friend for life.

Apart from Paul being a controlling prick, life was good. I could put up with his paranoid ways, just as long as he didn’t stop me from doing my hustle and finally being able to have my own little stash of cash put aside for a rainy day.

# 131: DNR

I was having the best day. I'd taken the day off work and Danielle had just called to tell me that she'd smashed her exams. All those worries that I'd been neglecting her for Dad were put aside when she told me her results. I rushed onto the ward with Sarah, excited to tell him the news, only to find Dad's bed empty.

I went to get one of the nurses, who broke the news that the MRSA had returned. Dad had been moved because they had found traces of MRSA. I couldn't believe it; I'd walked into the hospital on cloud nine; now I felt like I was wading through treacle.

The nurse took us to Dad's new room. Dad was asleep but I could see immediately that he didn't look good. In fact, he looked terrible.

I turned to the nurse. 'How long has he been like this?'

'Well, I've not long since come on shift, but he was asleep when I arrived. His temperature's been pretty high.'

I couldn't believe how frail he looked in comparison with when I'd last seen him the day before. It was like gravity had been working overtime since I'd last seen him. His cheeks were protruding, and his eyes looked hollower.

Another nurse came into the room to do his obs and explained that they had already started Dad on a course of antibiotics, and that the best thing for him was to rest and let the antibiotics do their job. I was tempted to call back later that evening, but we had already planned to do something to celebrate Danielle's exam results.

When Sarah called in the following day, he was in and out of consciousness and hallucinating. He didn't know where he was. He hadn't touched any of his food but had insisted on her getting him a couple of ice lollies which apparently, he devoured.

It was my turn to visit Dad in the evening, and I was surprised when Danielle asked if she could come and if she could bring her friend. I warned her that I didn't know what to expect but even I was shocked when he shouted out: 'What the fuck have you brought them with you for?' There was desperation in his eyes, and I realised he must have been hallucinating.

I walked over to the bed. 'Dad, it's Danielle, and that's Emma, you've met her before.'

Dad grabbed a hold of my hand. 'You aren't listening, are ya?' He looked around the room. They are fucking killing kids!'

Now I knew he was tripping. I ushered the girls out of the room. I couldn't tell if Danielle was scared or embarrassed; she'd heard all about Dad's hallucinations, but she'd never seen it before. Before I went back in to see Dad, I tracked down one of the nurses and aired my concerns, but she reassured me that Dad appeared to be responding well to the treatment. But I wasn't convinced.

When I got back into the room, I washed my hands, then I went to sit beside him. I told him the girls were safe, but he wasn't interested. He was just shivering and mumbling.

'I'm freezing.'

I gathered the blankets and pulled them over him and rubbed his arms in an attempt to warm him up. I placed my palm on his forehead, and it was extremely warm.

Dad looked up at me. 'Have you got any ice-lollies?

It was like being asked by a five-year-old kid. He looked so innocent, but also desperate.

'No Dad, but I can get you some if you like?'

Dad didn't say a word, he just nodded. I left him sucking his Calippo and took the girls home.

I didn't sleep well at all. This was definitely worse that the last bout of MRSA.

The following day, my suspicions had been confirmed when the consultant asked to see me and Sarah. We were taken into a small room where Mr Jackson addressed us.

'So, as you are aware, we had started your dad on a course of antibiotics, but he hadn't been responding very well. This morning, we had confirmation from the laboratory that your dad has a more severe strain of MRSA, which means we are going to have to treat him with stronger antibiotics.'

I was confused. 'This is good, isn't it? I mean that you've caught it?'

The doctors smiled, but it was a regretful smile. 'It's good that we know what we're dealing with, but we can't be sure how your dad's body will respond to treatment.'

'So what are you saying?' asked Sarah. 'That he might not survive?'

The doctor cleared his throat, 'That's why I wanted to speak to you directly. With some of his internal organs now being compromised, there's already tremendous pressure on his heart. We should know within forty-eight hours if it's working or not.'

I was struggling to take the news in; it felt like déjà vu.

The doctor spoke again. 'I understand that there is a DNR on his notes.'

'What's that mean?'

Sarah responded before he could. 'It means do not resuscitate.'

'Does Dad know this is on his records?'

I found it hard to imagine that Dad sat alone contemplating his death; he'd never mentioned it to us before, but the doctor explained that he must have agreed to it.

'Just do what's right by Dad, will ya? Can we go see him?'

The doctor stood up. 'Yes, of course you can.'

I was hoping to speak to Dad about the DNR, but he was out of it. Sarah and I agreed that we'd let the family know, but there was no point in them coming over again, all we could do was wait.

## 132: They Don't Fucking Scare Me

That rainy day I'd been saving up for came about one night when Stacey invited me out for her birthday. Paul was pissed off that I was going, but I was making my own money, and I'd arranged the babysitter, so there was nothing he could do about it.

The daily dabs of speed were also doing wonders for my weight and confidence, and I'd been on a mission to look and feel a million dollars for my night out. I'd done my hair and bought a new outfit, which seemed to have done the trick.

'Fuck me, Trace, you scrub up alreyt!' Tommy teased when I walked into the Scottish Queen that night.

'Why thank you, Tommy, now get us a drink, will ya?'

The speed I'd taken just before leaving the house had started kicking in, and I felt amazing. Stacey had already sorted an itinerary for the night – she mentioned the names of all the pubs we could go to, which was wasted on me, because apart from Roxy's, I hadn't been in town for years, but I did recognise the name of the club where she was planning on meeting Tommy. It was Occasions, the same place where Paul sold his drugs. I mentioned it to Stacey.

'Fuck him, Trace! You're out with us anyway.' I knew she was right, but I didn't want or trust Paul not to make a scene and ruin my night. We'd already had a row about me going out with Tommy and he wasn't keen on me bumping into him while he was grafting.

We only stayed for a half before jumping into a taxi and heading to the first bar.

'Here, I've got us something.' Stacey was grinning like a naughty school kid. She opened her hand, revealing a clear bag with what appeared to have a small piece of paper in it

'What's that?'

'It's a trip. I thought we'd share one.'

I was already on a high from the speed. 'Fuck that, I don't fancy seeing any leprechauns tonight thanks very much.'

Stacey laughed hysterically.

'You won't, you silly mare. Come on, Trace, it's only half. Pete gave them to me for us both. We will have a real laugh, I promise.'

She took the square paper out of its wrapping, ripped it in two and took her half before holding out the other for me. I still wasn't sure.

'Ah, fuck it!' I took it off her and swallowed it.

Our next destination, Berlins, was heaving, and the atmosphere was electric. I felt an overwhelming urge to dance as the beat of the music pulsed through my body.

After getting our drinks, Stacey and I were weaving our way to find a spot in the corner of the club when a woman shoved past us. I was about to say something but then the culprit tripped and fell to the floor. Stacey and I turned to each other and grinned.

'Karma!' We chimed in unison.

Stacey started giggling. Her laugh was infectious, and it wasn't long before we were both howling uncontrollably. But the best part was we didn't even know what we were laughing at, which just made us want to laugh more.

I could see people staring, but I didn't care. It was like there was only me and Stacey in the room. Just then, Paul appeared. He looked really pissed off.

'What are you doing in here?'

Me and Stacey just looked at each other and laughed hysterically. Which made him angrier.

'What's so fucking funny?' he hissed, but I couldn't reply, because I was laughing too much.

He stepped closer, grabbed my arm and whispered in my ear. 'Seriously, Trace, you're showing yourself up.'

I yanked my arm away. 'Ah fuck off, Paul. I'm having a good time. What's your fucking problem?'

Stacey joined in.

'Yeah, what's your problem? She's not doing owt wrong. It's *you* who's showing ya sen up.'

'Just stay out of my way, will ya!' snarled Paul, then he spun around and walked off, sulking.

'What's his fucking problem, Trace? I've never seen him act like that before,' said Stacey.

I just shook my head. 'That, my friend, is what the real Paul looks like.'

I knew I wouldn't hear the last of it when I got home later, but in that moment, I didn't give a fuck. On cue, 'Girls Just Wanna Have Fun' came blasting through the speakers.

'Come on! Fuck him, Stacey!'

I grabbed her hand before pulling her through the bar in the opposite direction Paul had just headed in. Then to my surprise, I clocked our Sarah, standing with a group of girls. I went over to chat to her and was just filling her in on what had happened with Paul, when I spotted a bunch of girls talking animatedly to Stacey, and I knew instinctively that they weren't sharing makeup tips.

I was about two feet away before one of the girls lunged for Stacey. I was about to intervene and try to split them up, when one of the other girls threw in a sneaky punch.

Before she could look up, I'd chinned her in the face and continued punching her until two hands the size of spaces were dragging me from behind, out of the club. And I wasn't alone.

One of the other girls who'd started the fight was on the pavement. She looked dazed, but I didn't care, my heart was beating out of my chest and rage was pumping through my veins, so I went back for more. Before I knew it, I was fighting with two people, but neither was a match for me. Then, out of the corner of my eye, I saw my sister being pummelled to the floor, by two women. I ran over to drag them both off and delivered some more punches.

It wasn't until I looked up that I realised that our fighting had attracted quite an audience, which included Paul. He stormed over and grabbed me by the arm again.

'Fucking hell, Trace. I fucking knew it. You can't go fucking anywhere!'

Just then one of his mates chipped in. 'Fuck me, Pauly. Your lass was like Rocky Balboa.'

I laughed, but Paul tightened his grasp on my arm and hissed in my face. 'It's not fucking funny, Trace. I have to drink in here! I knew you would show me up. Come on. Let's go home.'

I yanked my arm out of his hand. 'Are you fucking kidding me? They started it! And 'I'm not going anywhere apart from to the club to meet Tommy.'

'Are you fucking kidding me?' He screeched. 'Them birds will be in the same club!'

I shook my head again. 'And they don't fucking scare me!'

Paul didn't scare me either. I was back where I belonged. And Paul could go fuck himself.

# 133: Tha's Started Me Off Nah

The next two days were intense. It was touch and go if Dad would survive, but on the third day on the antibiotics, Dad started showing improvements. His body was extremely weak though and he still had a long way to go.

It didn't help that the bed sore on his coccyx had got worse; what was once a small blister was now a hole in the base of his back. The hole needed packing with gauze to absorb the puss. It was hard to see Dad looking so vulnerable. His body was so frail, he could have easily passed as a prisoner of a war camp survivor.

Days turned into weeks, and whilst he'd gained some weight, the longer-term damage caused by Dad's drinking was becoming clearer, and he certainly wasn't going to be bouncing back to life like he had done after previous hospital episodes.

I knew Dad knew it too; I could see it in his eyes. He rarely talked about all his previous grandiose ideas he'd had about what he was going to do when he got his pay-out. He even talked about accepting the first offer from the solicitors, which was a first. It was like the fight had deserted him, along with his pride.

He would sometimes get snappy with the staff, but I knew it was more to do with his frustration at the lack of dignity of not being able to do simple acts like going to the toilet for himself. And that wasn't going to end any time soon, as there were discussion about adaptations and carers for him when he left hospital.

The main priority for us was to build up his strength and nutrition, which was hard because he would constantly complain that he wasn't hungry. It was like dealing with a baby at times. I'd still try to spoon feed him, but he'd only have a couple of mouthfuls before refusing to eat any more. The only thing that he would eat was ice lollies, which was better than nothing.

Some days he could be optimistic, pragmatic almost, but when he was low, he was really low. Alcohol was like a big elephant in the room; we rarely talked about the consequences of his drinking or about what life might look like for him once he was released.

I was trying to feed him one afternoon. I could tell he was getting impatient with me, then he took hold of my hand.

'Listen, I need to talk to ya.' His tone sounded serious, so I placed the food on the side and gave him my full attention.

'What's up?'

'Everything!' He sighed regretfully. 'Listen, you know how you have been managing my claim for me, well I wanna make it official.'

I still wasn't sure what he was asking. 'Okay?'

'As soon as I'm outta here, I want to sort my will out and I want you to have power of attorney.'

I felt a lump rise in my throat. Dad talking about death took me off guard.

He squeezed my hand. 'Look, I'm serious. I want to sort this out. I want it in writing that if owt does happen to me, that you and Sarah get whatever money is left. Please can you sort it for me?'

His tone was so matter of fact. I was speechless.

He squeezed my hand again. 'Look at me. Will you sort it out for me, please?'

Even though Dad had nearly died twice, I couldn't believe we were having this conversation. 'But Dad, I haven't got a clue. Do I need to get a solicitor or something?'

Dad huffed. 'Nah, fuck them, they have had enough outta me already! Nah, apparently ya can download 'em off internet somewhere. All we need is to get someone to witness it! In fact, Lawson can do it.'

It sounded like he'd been thinking about this for some time. I could feel myself welling up.

Dad tried to make light of it. 'Look, call it backpay for all the years of maintenance I never paid!'

'Dad, that's not funny!' But I laughed anyway.

'It's true though, innit! Listen.' His tone was serious again, 'I know I haven't been the best Dad...'

As soon as those words left his mouth. I started to cry.

'Come here.' Dad opened his arms for an embrace. I nestled my head into his neck, and silently sobbed. I wanted the embrace to last forever as Dad stroked my back, but then I could feel the awkwardness between us as Dad patted me gently, an indication that the cuddle was over.

I sat back into my seat and noticed Dad was wiping his eyes. He tried making light of our affectionate embrace.

'Tha's started me off nah!'

I laughed. 'Well, better late than never, eh?' I reached for his plate and spoon. 'Now come on let's get some more food down ya!'

Only Dad wasn't having any of it. 'It's clock cold, nah. Go and fetch us a couple of ice lollies, will ya?'

# 134: Nan Was Right

I felt invincible. The small dabs of speed had turned into speed bombs, wrapped in rizla and swallowed like tablets to disguise the taste, but it wasn't long before I was using a teaspoon to get my daily hit.

Paul was still furious with me, but for the first time in ages, I didn't care. I'd had enough of his moods. I found myself standing up to him more, and he didn't like it, but I'd stopped giving a fuck; I was sick of his possessive, controlling ways. I didn't need his money, and I no longer cared who he went out with because I had my own network of friends. The orders for the t-shirts were coming in thick and fast; I'd never been busier. When I wasn't home, I drove around the city dropping off orders.

When someone mentioned that I could make more money by buying stolen cheque books, I jumped at the chance. Using them in the Sheffield markets was too risky, so it wasn't long before I was rotating between Rotherham, Barnsley and Doncaster markets. It was so easy; I was just another mother out shopping with her kids in toe.

I knew we were both walking close to the wind regarding the law. I also knew it wasn't right, but for me, survival was more important, and I always reasoned if I ever got caught, I would probably get a slap on the hand for handling stolen goods, whereas the consequences for Paul selling drugs were far higher.

While Paul never said it outright, I knew he hated my newfound independence. He would constantly accuse others of influencing me, especially Pete. He was particularly jealous of our friendship. But I liked my new friends. They didn't put me down or act like they were better than me and they didn't try to control me like Paul did. Paul was so self-obsessed, he'd become delusional; there he was, prancing about in town thinking he was the dog's bollocks, when he was just a small-time pretty boy drug dealer.

The real people I admired were the likes of Pete, Tommy and Dad; they knew how to handle themselves in the real world. Paul couldn't fight his way out of a fucking paper bag. He'd always shied away from conflict, preferring to smooth-talk his way out of it, using his good looks and charm. But I could see right through him. He believed that the world owed him a favour, whereas I believed if you wanted anything in life, you had to go out and get it yourself.

Paul was more than happy for others to do the dirty work. He'd never been prepared to work, believing it was beneath him, something I never understood. Instead, he was happy for me to go out and graft whilst he reaped the rewards.

I felt like I was finally finding myself and was realising I didn't need Paul to make me feel whole or complete, just like when I realised that I didn't need to rely on Dad. For years, I had got by on the reputation of being Frank Ford's daughter, but I had earned my own notoriety without him being in the background.

I didn't need him or Paul to fight my battles; I could hold my own in any physical or verbal fight, and my entrepreneurial skills were on point. Thoughts about leaving him were becoming more frequent. I wanted to get out, but I didn't know how. I didn't know where to start. I knew I could turn to my friends, but I didn't want to spoil our friendship or burden them with my problems. And I couldn't turn to the Council again; they'd already offered me a place to stay, but I foolishly handed it back, thinking everything would turn out okay.

However, I'd been wrong again. Nan was right. I'd made my bed and had to lie in it. I just had to figure out how I was going to kick his sorry ass out of it.

# 135: This Looks Serious, Dad

After almost two and a half months of being in hospital, Dad was finally being released. Me and Sarah were already at the flat getting things ready; all the green gunk had gone, along with the stale smell of cigarettes and drink.

We'd already made a pact that we would take it in turns each day to visit – she'd do the morning shift before work and I'd go up afterwards, and Lawson had agreed to sit with him during the day. He'd also promised to keep Dad's other associates away, which was a huge relief. I'd started to warm to Lawson.

I could hear Dad before they'd even opened the ambulance doors.

'Tha can put that away, mate!'

I heard another voice. 'It's to help with the stairs, Frank.'

'I've already told ya, you ain't carrying me about like no fucking baby, ok!'

'Come on then, ya stubborn git, let's have ya inside!'

The ambulance doors swung open and taking an arm each, me and Sarah escorted Dad back to his flat. It took over twenty minutes and frequent rest breaks on the staircase, but finally we got him onto the sofa. Sarah sat on the floor, sorting through all Dad's tablets.

'Christ Dad, this bag is like a pharmacy. There are some that need to be taken with food, some without. I'm gonna have to get ya one of them pill boxes.'

Dad shrugged. 'I haven't got a clue what's in there, I just took what they gave me in hospital.'

Sarah pulled a bottle of tablets out and passed them to me to inspect. It was a tub of Vitamin B tablets. I handed it back. 'Tha gonna need more than vitamin B, father!' I joked.

Sarah was still rummaging in the bag.

'Ere, put them in the fridge, will ya?' She handed me a bunch of Fortisip drinks. 'Oh and I've spoken to the district nurses who will be coming every day to sort ya bed sores. And we can help you into the shower.'

Dad raised his hand.

'I'm telling ya nah, there is no friggin way I am letting you two wash me. I'll manage ok!' His tone was adamant, and he quickly changed the subject.

'Listen, I'm gonna need some new clothes getting. Would one of ya pop down to Matalan at some point for me and I'm gonna need some cash getting out of the bank too.'

The hairs on the back of my neck tingled. 'But Dad, you don't need nowt. We've stocked up the fridge...'

Dad cut me off. 'I know I don't need anything, but I hate not having an empty wallet. What if I do need summat and you two aren't here?' He could obviously see the look on my face. 'Don't worry, I won't be buying any drink!'

I could hardly argue; after all it was his money, but I was worried about the tidy sum he must have accumulated whilst being in hospital.

I noticed a pile of unopened letters and made a start on shuffling through them. A letter from the solicitors immediately caught my attention. I prayed it was a settlement letter. I passed it to Dad to read. His face lit it. *Could it be?*

'What's it say, Dad?'

Dad passed it back. 'They've set a date for us to go and meet with the defence lawyers and our solicitors to help negotiate the final settlement.'

I read the letter, I was concerned the meeting was only two weeks away, I looked up at Dad. 'Are you sure you are up for it, Dad?'

But Dad was buzzing. 'You try stopping me, in fact I'm gonna need you there too, seeing as you're me executor and all that.' He hesitated. 'You will take me, wont ya?'

I wasn't going to refuse. I'd have been willing to walk over hot coals if it meant that this damned claim would be finally sorted. 'Yes of course I will, Dad.'

I continued to go through the rest of the letters, passing Dad anything that looked official. He tossed them aside once he'd read them.

'They can fuck off! I'm not paying that!'

I picked up the letter and read the bold print:

A WARRANT HAS BEEN ISSUED FOR YOUR ARREST.

It was from the Sheffield Magistrates Court for unpaid parking fines.

'This looks serious, Dad.'

Dad wasn't concerned. 'They won't be coming for me.'

'What are the fines for anyway and when did you get em?'

Dad was dismissive. 'There were only a couple of parking tickets, from ages ago. The rest is interest, cheeky bastards. They can fuck off!'

I chuckled at his arrogance. This kind of letter would freak your average person out, but not Dad. 'So, what ya gonna do then? You've have got a meeting with solicitors coming up, tha don't wanna be in nick!'

Dad motioned for me to give the letter back. 'I'll call 'em tomorrow and sort it. What are they gonna do? Arrest a frail man who's just got out of hospital? Are they fuck!'

I'd just finished sorting through Dad's post when Lawson arrived. He was all smiles and seemed as happy as us to have Dad back home. We were just getting ready to leave when Dad started to wave his bank card in the air.

'Before ya go, will ya call in at the cash machine and draw me a couple of hundred out, shugs? Oh and can ya fetch a newspaper and some of them ice lollies?'

I hesitated for a moment.

'Or I can get Lawson to go...'

I took the card off him before he could change his mind and did as he'd asked. As soon as I'd handed Dad his cash, he was handing most of it back.

'Here, you're gonna need that for Matalan.'

I took the cash and went in to give him a hug, 'I'll call in later, ok.'

Dad raised his hand. ‘No need to call back. Lawson’s going to stay all afternoon, aren’t ya?’

I turned to Lawson, who winked. ‘Don’t worry, I’ll take care of him.’

‘Oi! I am here, tha knows! And I don’t need any of ya telling me what I can and can’t do. I’ve already said I ain’t drinking!’

I could tell Dad was getting irritable, which was the last thing I wanted on his first day back home. I surrendered both hands. ‘Ok, calm down, calm down. We’ll get off and see ya tomorrow.’

We left Lawson and Dad to catch up, but I couldn’t relax. Sarah could tell I was worried.

‘We can’t police every move he makes,’ said Sarah. ‘And he’s not stupid neither. He knows he can’t drink again and if he does, he knows what the consequences will be.’

We all knew and that was the problem.

# 136: Who Grassed Me Up?

I'd just returned from dropping Danielle at school when Paul asked me to drive him over to his mates. I wasn't impressed, as Lauren was still in her pyjamas, but he insisted. I was just about to indicate away from the street when a car pulled up beside us, blocking us in. There were two guys in the car who looked pretty menacing.

'What the actual fuck!' Paul shouted, throwing his arms in the air.

I initially thought Paul must have ripped someone off, and they were coming for retribution but then the driver got out of the car and flashed his warrant card. It was the fucking police. Paul's face went white, and then, out of nowhere, uniformed officers opened my car door and escorted us both out of the car into the house whilst other officers started to search the car.

I was absolutely mortified. There were some mums returning from dropping their kids off at school, and every car that passed slowed down for a better nosey of Paul being cuffed and marched inside. I was glad to shut the door, but then they started searching the house.

They went straight for the kitchen cupboard where Paul stored his drugs, emptying the fake baked bean tins of wraps and Es and cash while Paul protested.

'Is this really necessary? It's all for personal use.'

It appeared that the police were only interested in Paul and the drugs; they didn't even attempt to search the outside porch, where I kept a stash of stolen goods.

Then I remembered the ounce of speed I had in my own bag. A couple of police officers were busy bagging up Paul's gear into evidence bags off the kitchen side, so I swiftly reached to pick Lauren up and placed her on my lap before managing to shove a bag of speed into her nappy. She wriggled out of my arms, wanting to go back and play.

I hoped and prayed she didn't pull it out. I was consumed with guilt, but the last thing she needed was for me to be arrested and shipped off to social services, too.

They took Paul upstairs for a full body search and returned with Paul's weighing scales and announced that they'd be taking him to the station.

'What's going to happen to me?' I asked.

'We are not interested in you,' the officer replied. Relief swept over me. 'So, will you be releasing him or what?'

'That's not down to me, I'm afraid.'

Paul smiled. 'Don't worry, Trace. I'll be back soon.'

I wasn't so sure. Judging by all the paraphernalia they'd found, he had some convincing to do.

The police cleared off, leaving me and Lauren alone in the house. Paranoia kicked in as I paced the kitchen. I wanted to call someone, but then I wasn't sure who. I was tempted to call Dad; he'd know what to do, but then I couldn't tell him that Paul had been arrested for dealing drugs; he hated drugs.

Then there was Mum; how the fuck was I going to explain? I knew it wouldn't be long before she found out what had happened; the whole of the estate probably knew by now. What if it just wasn't Paul? What if they'd busted others? Pete? Tommy? I couldn't risk tipping them off, but they had to know, so I called Pete.

'The police have just been at ours!'

I was expecting him to freak out, but he was calm as a cucumber, just asking if I was ok and telling me to lay low. I knew what he was actually saying was that I couldn't be seen visiting him and Louise's, which hurt because all I did need was my mates.

'Look, I'll be in touch, ok,' Pete offered, reassuringly. Then he hung up the phone.

I decided not to risk calling to see Toni for more t-shirts and followed Pete's advice to lay low. It wasn't until I noticed that Laurens's nappy needed changing that I remembered she was still running around with an ounce of speed. I knew I shouldn't have, but as soon as I'd changed her nappy, I grabbed a teaspoon from the draw to get a hit. I stared at the teaspoon, which was overflowing with white powder. A little voice in my head said, 'Tracey, this can't go on,' but I ignored it and digested it anyway.

It was two-thirty, and there was no sign of Paul, but I had to leave the house to collect Danielle from school. I left the house. The street was empty, apart from the old lady from across the way watering her plants. Did she know? Had she called the police?

Everyone I drove past, including the mothers waiting at the school gates, were potential informants. A couple nodded and smiled like nothing had happened, but did they know? Had they all already heard? I was no stranger to keeping secrets and putting on a front, but now I felt entirely exposed; there was nowhere to hide.

I just wanted to run away, but I had nowhere to run away to. Then I thought about Danielle. How would the other kids at school treat her after knowing that her parents were drug dealers? The thought of her being ostracised by her friends cut like a dagger in my heart; I couldn't bear her going through that.

I drove us all over to Herdings Park, located in the Gleadless Valley, knowing there wouldn't be other Mums from school there. I nearly crashed the car, paranoid that the police might still be following me.

I kept taking deep breaths and telling myself that everything would be ok, but no matter how many times I tried telling myself, nothing seemed to work. Even though social services were never mentioned by the police, I couldn't help but worry about them tipping them off and them coming around to take the kids away. I needed support but I was too ashamed to face Mum.

My mind was full of unanswered questions. Should I leave him now? Where would I go? What would I tell the kids if he went to prison? What would happen to the benefits? And the tenancy?

My mind was all over the place; the only thing that seemed to help with the feelings of the unknown was the gear. Then panic kicked in. My bag would only last for a few more days. I still had some cheques left that would pay for some more, but the last thing I needed was to get caught by the police handling stolen goods. I couldn't go to Pete's. That was too risky.

I had to figure out a way of getting some more gear. I needed it to get me through.

'For fucks sake, Tracey. Sort yourself out. What will be, will be,' a voice whispered in my head. 'Go home.'

I'd just put the kids to bed when Paul walked in through the back door. Relief swept over me.

'Oh my god, what have they said? What's happening?'

'Some fuckers grassed me up, haven't they? I'm telling you, when I find out who it is...' He clenched his fist, pacing the kitchen.

'You can't know that for sure.'

'Are you fucking thick?' he screamed. 'They knew where my stash was.'

I tried to stay calm; one of us had to. 'Ok, so have they charged you?'

'Yeah, with Intent to Supply.'

'So how come they have let you out, then?'

'Why? Aren't you happy to see me?'

I didn't like his tone.

'So, what has your solicitor said?'

'I didn't ask for one.'

'Are you fucking kidding me, Paul? You never talk to the police without a brief there; everyone knows that! What did you say in the interview?'

'Well, I didn't grass anyone up if that's what you're trying to imply. I told them it was all for personal use.'

I shook my head in disbelief.

'Ahhh, fuck off, Trace! You don't know what you are talking about! Anyway, this isn't about you! It's not you who's looking at two years, is it?'

'Two years?' I was in shock.

'Class A's, aren't they?'

'I thought they were class B?'

'Nah, trips are class A, aren't they?'

I hadn't even realised he sold trips.

'How many did you have?'

'Only about 20,' he said sarcastically. 'That's what they're focusing on, but I'm more interested in who grassed me up.'

'Look, Paul, you're never going to find out who grassed you up. You may as well let it go.'

'I reckon it was that Pete who grassed me up, trying to get me outta the way to make way for himself.'

I had heard some corkers in my time, but this one topped them all.

'Pete and me? Are you kidding? Have you ever thought that you got a little too fucking cocky?'

He glared at me. 'What you trying to say'

'Well, let's face it, everyone fucking knows you deal drugs. It could have been anyone who grassed you up.'

It was getting late, and I was exhausted. Plus, I had a shift to cover the next day.

'I'm going to bed. I've got work in the morning.'

'Work, are you kidding me?'

'Well, someone has got to bring some money in, haven't they?'

# 137: More Than Happy

Our new routine was working. Sarah would call in the morning before work and the nurses would arrive shortly afterwards. According to them, his bed sore was apparently healing nicely, but it was going to take months to fully heal.

Lawson would come next, and he helped Dad in and out of the bath, which saved Dad the indignity of me and Sarah having to do it. He was a godsend, running errands, getting top-ups for gas and electric and getting his shopping. When he wasn't doing errands, he'd spend the time watching DVDs with Dad. Dad was eligible for carers allowance, but me and Sarah insisted that Lawson should have it. It was only fifty quid a week, but it helped keep him in fags and afforded him a few nights out at the local working men's club with his missus.

Despite Dad still being a little unsteady on his feet, not being able to sleep and the occasional tantrum about taking tablets, he was doing well and more importantly, a drop of alcohol hadn't passed his lips.

For the past few weeks, I'd been supporting a local youth leader and her team, who'd identified that several of the troubled young people she'd been working with had parents and siblings who misused drugs.

I'd been running education session in the evenings round the corner from Dad's and it was nice to call in to see Dad for a cuppa after. I was trying to get them to open up about the impact of addiction, but they were a tough crowd, and I was a bit out of my comfort zone but gradually, they were starting to trust me.

I'd make me and Dad a cuppa before settling in the chair opposite him and candidly offload about my day at work. The sessions were rewarding but it wasn't always easy listening to hear how some kids relied on the local youth clubs for food because their parents had prioritised drink or drugs over food. Some talked about being embarrassed of their families or of being tarred with the same brush. Our job was to reassure and remind them that they weren't.

Dad listened intently and even opened up and shared some of his teenage years. I was shocked to hear about the times he'd had to step in to defend his mum from getting a beating off his dad. Or about how he'd signed up for the army in an attempt go straight and stay out of trouble with the law, and his regrets about being forced to leave on medical grounds for having flat feet. I couldn't imagine Dad taking orders from anyone and I wondered how different Dad's life might have turned out had he still been in the army.

On the weekend, I would spend longer with him and take the kids with me, which Dad loved. I had tried, on a couple of occasions, slipping in our conversations about Dad seeking some support around his drinking or to perhaps consider some tablets to help with any cravings, but Dad refused.

According to him, he didn't need them. His priority was to get the claim sorted. His latest plan was that he was going to give me and Sarah ten grand each, then buy himself a chalet/caravan down Lincolnshire somewhere, one with a fishing lake, and not too far from Tracey. He would spend summers in the UK and go abroad during the winter.

I had my doubts, but when he talked about the future, his face lit up. To be honest it was the only thing that kept him going and whilever he wasn't drinking, I was more than happy to go along with it.

# 138: All I Could Do Was Cry

The next couple of weeks were a blur. Paul's paranoia was off the scale, and we had no end of arguments about what had happened.

What was more infuriating was his inability to accept that he wouldn't have even been in this position if he hadn't got greedy and blase with the drugs, but once again, it was everybody else's fault. If I tried to plan for the worst-case scenario, he'd speculate about how it wouldn't be long before I would start seeing someone else, which would then ignite a rage about how he would never allow another man to bring up his children.

When he wasn't on a rampage, he'd sit fretting about the future and how he might cope in prison. Occasionally, he'd claim that he'd learned his lesson and would get a proper job when he was released, but I couldn't believe him anymore. Then there was the money.

He was still going out at the weekend to prove to everyone that he was still in the game, and now he wanted in on my fencing, but I was running out of people to sell to, and I was finding it harder to get my hands on any goods to sell because of his drugs bust. The only money I made was enough to cover my gear, which he still didn't know about.

I tried my best to put on a front and pretend to the kids and the outside world that everything was ok when it was far from it. I hadn't mentioned a dicky bird to anyone at work about the bust, but that didn't stop me from feeling paranoid that they all knew.

I was still tormented by the look of disappointment on Mum and Ada's faces when I'd confessed to what had happened. Ada blew a gasket and even banned Paul from coming around to the house. But once they'd had calmed down, their attention turned to concern for me and the kids.

'It explains a lot.'

'What does?'

'The weight loss, Trace. You haven't been yourself for a while. I've got to ask, are you on drugs, Trace?'

'Absolutely not!'

Mum didn't look convinced. 'Are you sure we can get you some help, take you to the doctors? I'll go with you.'

'I don't need any help. I'm ok. I just don't know what's going to happen if they send Paul down.'

'First things first, Tracey. He needs to get your name down on that tenancy because if he does go down, you won't have a leg to stand on, do you hear?'

I knew she was right, but trying to talk to Paul about what might happen if he was sent down was out of the question.

The only person I could talk about my situation with was Pete, who'd been in and out of prison his whole life but these days, I only saw him when he dropped my gear off at the cafe and even that was about to change.

Andrea, the gaffer had been off with me for a while, and she'd recently taken on some more staff, which meant no extra shifts were coming in. I'd just finished my shift when she took me to one side holding my wage packet in her hands.

'I'm afraid I won't be needing you anymore, Tracey.'

I couldn't believe my ears. 'Are you fucking kidding me?'

She didn't say a word and bowed her head with regret.

I laid into her. 'You never fucking liked me, did you?' I snatched the wage packet off her. 'Fuck you, Andrea!' Then I turned to the café, where Sally had been standing watching.

'And fuck you too, ya fucking two-faced slag!'

I stormed off to the car. Everything was falling apart, and I didn't know what to do or where to go. I needed to speak to Pete.

In desperation, I went round to their place and headed straight for the intercom. Only there wasn't any answer. I could see the car was there so why weren't they answering?

I continued pressing the buzzer in between, pacing the pavement. Then Pete finally popped his head out of the window.

'Just go home, Tracey, will ya?' He looked worried.

'Why, what's wrong? What's happened?' I was confused. 'Are you and Louise ok?'

'Just go home, ok?' This time, his words felt a lot harder, sterner. I felt like I was being reprimanded, only I didn't know what for.

'What have I done?'

'You're not well, Tracey,' he said, then closed the window indicating that our conversation was over. But it wasn't for me. I was both incensed and hurt, he couldn't turn his back on me, not now? I walked back to the buzzer and continued pressing for what seemed like hours, but I still couldn't get a response. I walked back to the car, dejected.

In one day, I'd lost the only job that I could rely on for money and had lost the only friend I felt I had in the world. Everything was falling apart.

Paul laid into me as soon as I walked through the door. 'What have you been up to?'

'I don't know what you mean.'

"Pete! I've just had him on the phone. He says you have lost the plot, that you've been harassing them at their flat.'

I couldn't believe what I was hearing. 'It wasn't like that.'

Paul was smirking. He was enjoying this. 'Well, he doesn't want you calling around anymore.'

I could feel the tears starting to well up.

'I told ya, didn't I?' he said smugly 'I told ya that they weren't ya real friends. They were just using ya. I'm telling ya, the only person that you can rely on is me, I've been telling you that for years. You and me against the world, Trace. We don't need anyone else.'

I ran around to Mum's: it was the only safe space I could think of. Only she wasn't home.

Ada answered the door instead. 'You ok, love?'

As soon as the words passed his lips I burst into tears. He wrapped his arms around me and took me into the living room and left to make us a drink. I paced the living room desperate for answers; he returned holding two mugs of tea.

'Is everything ok? Who were you talking to?'

I was confused. 'I wasn't talking to anyone.'

He handed me my drink. 'Come on love, what's happened?'

I didn't know where to start. All I could do was cry. My social network was crumbling around me, Paul didn't care; he didn't understand. I'd felt hurt before, but nothing on this level.

The next thing, Mum was crouching in front of me. 'Trace, Trace, it's me, your mum. I'm worried, love. I think you should see a doctor.'

I was incredulous. 'Are you fucking kidding me? There's nothing wrong with me!' Hurt was now replaced with anger. Even my own Mum didn't understand!

'I am worried about you, Tracey. You're not alright.'

'Of course, I'm not fucking alright. Everyone's turning on me.'

'Ssh. Your nan's in the other room.'

'Fuck her!' I shouted. 'I've had enough. I'm done!'

I was just about to leave the living room, when two police officers walked in.

Mum was crying now. 'I'm sorry, love. I didn't know what else to do.'

'Can you leave us?' One of the officers said to Mum. I was stunned and scared. I was wracking my brains to think what I had done wrong.

'Am I being arrested?'

The officer smiled reassuringly. 'No, love – ya Mum is worried about you. Can I ask, have you taken any drugs?'

I couldn't believe my ears. I'd called around for some help, and all Mum was bothered about was if I had taken any drugs!

It was the final slap in the face. I was clearly on my own; nobody ever cared or ever understood me, but the last thing I needed right now was to get arrested. Then, all of a sudden, a sense of calm enveloped me.

'I haven't had any drugs.' I wasn't lying either. I hadn't been able to get my hands on any for a couple of days.

‘Look, I’m just having a hard time dealing with everything, that’s all.’

‘Would you consider us taking you to hospital?’

I was confused.

‘What for? I’m perfectly fine. I’m sorry. I was out of order kicking off at Mum. Look, this is all a misunderstanding, I know I shouldn’t have come around here kicking off, it’s not Mums’ fault, I was out of order, I’m sorry.’

The officer took a deep breath.

‘Look, you stay here whilst I have a chat with your mum, ok?’

I could hear them talking in low voices and the next minute, the officer was reappearing and telling me to go home and get some rest. He suggested I go to see the doctor and then left.

Mum came into the room, all concerned. ‘Look Tracey, I’m sorry, ok? I didn’t know what to do.’

Nan walked in behind her shaking her head. ‘If you were mine, I’d have put you over my knee and give you a good spanking a long time ago.’

‘Well it’s a good job I’m not yours, isn’t it! And as for you, Mum, I know where your loyalties are!’ And with that, I walked out of the house, vowing never to return.

# 139: Hope And Pray

Finally, it was D-Day: the day of the meeting with the solicitors. Dad was wearing his new clothes and a blazer that looked slightly big now for his smaller frame, but he looked really smart, just like he used to in the old days. We were early, but that was good, and we sat in silence in the reception until Dad spotted someone he knew.

'What the fuck is he doing here?'

There was a guy in a smart suit chatting to the lady on reception.

'Who is he?'

'It's Brown! He's the liver consultant from the Hallamshire.'

I could feel the tension vibrate off Dad. I tried to calm him down. 'He might not be here for you, Dad.'

'I bet you he is. Well they can fuck off! I'm telling ya, Trace, they're gonna try and blame my drinking instead of PTSD.' His knee was knocking now.

'Look, Dad, calm down. You losing your shit ain't gonna help, is it?'

Half an hour later we were called into a boardroom. All the men were dressed in smart suits and were smiling and chatting away like long-lost mates. They didn't look adversarial at all.

My heart sank though when I saw the doctor from reception sitting amongst them. I grabbed hold of Dad's hand to remind him to keep calm.

One of the solicitors broke the chatter, by standing up. 'Ahh, Frank. Nice to finally meet you. I'm Mr Oldham, we've talked the phone.' He reached out to shake Dad's hand and gestured for us to take a seat. 'And you must be Tracey.' His handshake was firm.

The men around the table introduced themselves and we waited anxiously for the liver consultant to introduce himself. We both breathed a sigh of relief when he explained that he was there to represent Dad.

Then it was Dad's turn.

'Morning, I am Frank Ford, and I was on the train the day of the crash. And can I just say I am disgusted about how long this has taken to get to this place and if anything, it has made my PTSD worse.'

Mr Oldham interjected. 'Frank, we understand your frustration. Unfortunately, these things can take a while...'

Dad interrupted him. 'It's been over five fucking years!'

This wasn't the time and place to be kicking off. I caught Dad's eye to suggest as much and then addressed the meeting.

'Apologies for Dad's swearing but he's been extremely frustrated. He has every right to feel angry. I can tell you now, he certainly isn't the same man. He's a shadow of his former self and all we want from today is a resolution.'

A debate ensued between the men, and I felt uncomfortable about them talking about Dad as if he wasn't there. No-one was disputing liability or the PTSD: the issue was establishing the potential loss of longer-term earnings. The defence argued that based on Dad's medical records, his liver and health were compromised before the crash, and this would have an impact on the settlement amount.

This is when Dad's consultant Brown weighed into the debate; he was amazing. Whilst he accepted Dad's liver was in poor health before the crash, he dismissed their argument, claiming that people with PTSD are around four times more likely to be affected by alcohol dependence than the general population, so had the crash not happened, Dad might not be where he was now.

We were so impressed, and I was starting to feel optimistic, until the defence announced that they would need more time to agree a final settlement and would be coming back with an offer at later date.

‘Are you fucking kidding me?’ Dad slammed his hand on the table ‘So, you’re telling me I’ve come here for nowt!’

The defence weighed in. ‘Look, Frank. We totally understand your frustration. We’re just trying to establish what you are rightly entitled to.’

Dad snapped. ‘Like fuck ya understand. All you lot are bothered about is giving me a little as ya can.’ He turned to his solicitor. ‘And you! You’re just bothered about getting your slice of the cake. Come on, Trace, we’re done here!’

We entered the lift in silence. I tried to hold Dad’s hand, but he pulled away.

‘I’m sorry, Trace. I don’t wanna talk about it.’

By the time we arrived at the car, instead of looking angry, he looked deflated.

‘It’s all been for nowt, Trace.’

I tried to placate him. ‘Come on, Dad. You don’t know that. You’re on the home run now. It will be sorted soon.’

The change in him was dramatic. He’d left the flat full of optimism and hope and now it was like I was driving a broken man home. It didn’t matter what I tried to say to try and lift him, nothing worked. All I could do was hope and pray that a settlement was sorted soon.

# 140: The Fire

I couldn't face going home after leaving Mum's house, so I walked the streets in search of answers. I still couldn't shake that feeling of dread that had been tormenting me for weeks. I knew that something terrible would happen. The only thing was, I didn't know when or what it was. I just knew it was dark and sinister. And it wasn't the drugs either; I hadn't had any for a couple of days.

Paul had been saying I had changed for months, but I'd always fobbed him off. But now I was wondering if he might be right. People that I thought were friends were keeping their distance, I'd managed to lose a job I loved on account of my attitude, Pete was accusing me of losing the plot, and now Mum had turned on me too.

I tried to work out where it had gone wrong. It was the drugs. Ever since Paul had started dealing, everything had gone wrong. There had been more and more reports in the news about people dying from drugs, and he was the one selling them. He was a sinner and what he was doing was wrong. But it wasn't just him. It was me, too. I had always known working the fiddle was against the law, but now I was wrapped up in buying and selling stolen goods or purchasing goods with other people's cheque books. It was all immoral, the Devil's work. It was like I was possessed.

I'd always known, deep-down that no good was going to come from taking teaspoons of gear, but I'd ignored the voice in my head telling me to quit. I didn't recognise myself anymore. Had we literally been possessed by the Devil?

In that moment, it all became clear. The so-called friendships I'd made had all been fake. Which wasn't surprising, because they were possessed too, under the illusion that what they were doing and taking was ok, when it was far from ok. It was all wrong.

It felt like the evil spell that had been cast on all of us had suddenly broken and only I could see the truth. It was suddenly clear, and it was time for me to make amends.

I headed home, enthused with a desire to cleanse the whole house. Thankfully the kids were in the back garden playing. I saw that as a sign. I had to save them first. I couldn't bear them being affected by tainted goods. I couldn't live with the thought of being in a house that contained anything obtained by deception. All the tainted goods had to go. I fetched a black sack from underneath the kitchen sink and started with the kid's room. Then I went into my bedroom. Clothes, perfume, and anything obtained illegally had to go. I was on a mission, and it felt good. Even the recent bottles of shampoo and conditioner in the bathroom that once seemed harmless had to go. Just then, Paul appeared over my shoulder, looking all alarmed.

'Trace, what are you doing?'

'Trust me, Paul. It's got to go!'

He tried taking the black sack off me, but I wrestled it back off him.

'It's going, but don't worry – everything is going to be ok.'

'You have seriously lost the plot. The kids' clothes and toys are in there. You can't throw those away!'

'I'm not throwing them.' I smiled 'I'm burning them.'

Undeterred, I did a sweep of the downstairs before dumping the contents of the black sack in the back garden. The kids were excited at the prospect of a bonfire. Paul was practically hysterical now, but I didn't care. It all had to go.

I ignored his pleas, knowing that nothing I said would make a difference because he was still possessed by the dark illusion. I could help him see the light. I barged past him, picked up some lighter fluid and poured it ceremonially over the pile of items. Then I threw a match onto them.

'Fuck me, Tracey, you've lost the plot!' he continued screaming.

I could see lips moving but couldn't hear a word. I was too consumed by the flames. The darkness and sense of dread that had been following me for weeks started to evaporate, along with the dark fumes of smoke bellowing from the fire.

I knew right there and then that it was a sign that I was doing the right thing. I couldn't walk away from the fire until I was satisfied that everything had been destroyed.

# 141: Only A Couple of Cans

It had been a few days since the meeting with the solicitors and Dad had been on a right downer ever since. He'd been insisting that I call the solicitors daily to chase them up, but I didn't want to be a burden or a pest. I knew that they'd be in touch as soon as they knew anything.

I found myself making up white lies about calling or would make an excuse that I'd been too busy. I'd stopped looking forward to my after-work visits because Dad's temper was foul and now Lawson had called me out of the blue.

'Hiya Trace. I'm sorry for calling you at work but I'm not sure what to do?'

This didn't sound good.

'It's ya Dad. He's asking me to go to the shop and fetch him some cans. I've tried telling him that he's not supposed to drink, but he's adamant.'

I'd been expecting this. Mr Hyde had been showing his face again.

'Only, he's proper kicking off nah. I tried giving him his lactulose earlier and he said if I took one step closer, I'd be wearing it. An' he says if I don't fetch it, he'll just pop his head out of flat window and offer to pay someone else.' He hesitated. 'I just don't know what to do.'

I told Lawson that I'd call Dad and took a deep intake of breath. Since his release, the thoughts of him going back to drink had never been far from my mind. I'd imagined I would be angry, but all I felt was disappointment.

Dad answered my call straight away. 'Ey up, shugs, you ok?' He sounded in a good mood.

'I am. What ya up to?'

'Nowt. Just sat here with Lawson watching TV.' I heard him turn to Lawson. 'You sneaky fucker. You've rang our Tracey, haven't ya!'

I could hear Lawson trying to appease him in the background.

'You fucking snake!' Dad roared.

I shouted down the phone to get Dad's attention. 'Dad! Dad! Look, don't be having a pop at him, he's only looking out for ya.'

Dad was still furious. 'Fuck me, Trace. I wouldn't mind but it's only a couple of cans.'

I tried my best to reason with him. 'Dad, I know, but you've not long got out and your body's still healing. Look, it's just a craving. Honestly, it will pass.'

'It's literally a couple of cans. Anyone would think I'd asked for a bottle of brandy.'

I could hear him trying to play down and rationalise his need for a drink and I knew that there was no point in arguing or fighting him. His mind had been made up.

'Look, Dad, just do what you are going to do.'

There was a pause at the end of the phone. 'Nice one, Lawson, now our Trace has fell out with me.'

'Dad, honestly, I haven't fallen out with ya. I just think it's a bad idea, that's all.'

Dad's voice softened. 'Honestly, Trace. I'll be fine, it's only a couple of cans. I love you.'

'Love you too, Dad. I'll see ya later, ok?'

When I arrived, Dad was sitting watching TV with not a drink in sight.

Dad looked at me coyly. 'Eye up, shugs. Are we ok?'

I sighed. 'Yes we are, Dad. I'm not here for a fight.'

Dad smiled. 'Thank fuck for that. I'll have a brew if tha making one.'

I was relieved to find there were still two cans nestled next to the milk. At least he hadn't hammered all four. I took the drinks to the living room and sat next to him on the sofa.

'So have you and Lawson kissed and made up?'

'Aye, we're alreyt. I wa just pissed at him callin' you behind me back – I'm not a fucking kid.'

'Look, Dad. He was only looking out for ya. Poor sod was in a no-win situation, what with you on one side and me on the other.'

Dad smiled. 'I know. I don't know who's worse, me or thee.'

'I'm gonna be honest, I'm not happy about you having a drink, but I can't stop ya neither.'

He smiled. 'Look, me havin' a couple of bevies is the only pleasure I've got! I mean, look at me, for crying out loud. I feel like a prisoner in my own home.'

He was right, but I couldn't let him get off the hook that easily. 'Dad, the reason you are like this is because of the drink!'

'Ok, I might have gone in hospital cos of the drink. I know I was hitting it hard...'

I stopped him short. 'Hitting it hard? Dad – you nearly died!' My initial intention to stay calm had vanished. 'Oh, but I'm sorry, I forgot, you won't remember that part, would ya – nah you were out of it whilst me and Sarah were sortin' out ya last rights and planning ya funeral.'

Dad went on the defensive. 'I've said sorry I don't know how many times! But if I hadn't caught fucking MRSA, I wouldn't have to be having carers round every morning to sort this back out or fucking Lawson coming to help me wesh! Do you know how embarrassing that is? I've got a good mind to sue the hospital too!'

I nearly choked on my drink. 'You are taking the piss, aren't ya?'

Dad shrugged. 'I'm not gonna, the point I'm making is I would have been out sooner had it not been for the MRSA, wouldn't I?'

'MRSA or not, the bottom-line Dad, is ya livers still fucked! Look Dad, I'm sick of fighting. I just want what's best for you.'

Dad placed his drink on the coffee table and turned to me with open arms. 'Come 'ere.'

I shuffled up beside him and let him embrace me. He kissed me on the forehead and whispered into my ear. 'I know you do, shugs, but trust me, I'll be reyt. I know what I'm doing.'

As we sat back and watched the news, his words swam in my head. I did trust Dad; it was Mr Hyde inside him that I didn't trust.

## 142: My Door Is Always Open

Paul had just come off the phone when I returned into the house.

'What have you taken, eh?' he asked accusingly.

I smiled because I had never felt calmer in my life. 'Actually, Paul, I haven't taken anything, and I don't intend on taking anything ever again, and you can't either.'

'What do you mean?' Paul had an alarmed look on his face.

'I know you can't see it yet, but trust me Paul, everything is going to be ok. But we cannot continue with this: the lies, the deceit, using and selling drugs. Paul, listen to me, I mean really listen to me.'

Paul looked bemused as I sat him down on the sofa.

'I want to start off by saying sorry. I haven't been easy to live with either, but I understand now, I see it.'

'Trace, what do you understand?' Paul was hanging onto my every word.

'All the arguments, the drug use, the drugs bust, they are all linked, don't you see?' But it's ok, it's not our fault, we have both been sucked into the dark illusion that what we have been doing is ok, but it's not, none of it has. We have to change. It has to stop.'

Paul pulled away from me. 'Have you heard yourself, Trace? You sure you haven't taken something?'

I was hurt. I thought I was getting through, but it looked like I'd failed. 'Haven't you just heard a word I just said?'

'I have, but you've got a wild look in your eyes. Something's wrong. You're fucking freaking me out!'

I didn't have the energy to argue or fight anymore. 'I can see that it's going to take you a while but that's ok. Let's just get the kids and take them to the park, like a proper family.'

'You're not taking them anywhere!' he shouted.

Still calm, I called the kids to tell them that we were going to the park.

'You're not taking them anywhere, Trace.' Paul repeated, but the kids were excited.

'Can I take my roller-skates?' Dan asked.

'Of course you can.'

I changed the kids out of their smoky clothes and started to get them ready for the park. I could hear Paul talking to someone, but I just carried on packing bags and fetching the car keys. We were going to have a lovely time. They'd missed out on so much. I could see it now.

Paul tried to wrestle the car keys out of my hand and was shouting to Danille who was wobbling about on the pavement in her roller skates.

'Quick, go fetch your nan!' But she didn't need to go anywhere because a car had pulled up alongside us and Mum and Ada were rushing towards us.

'Trace, are you ok?' Her face was etched with concern.

I couldn't understand what the problem was. 'Mum, I'm only taking the kids to the park.'

'Come on Trace, let us go inside, let's go and talk.'

'Mum, listen, you were right. I know I've not been myself, but everything's ok now.' I had thought she might understand or at least be relieved and happy.

'Come on, Trace, everything is going to be ok.'

'I know it is, Mum. I'm fine, I promise.'

Only Mum didn't seem convinced. 'Now come on, Tracey, come inside. Look, you're making a scene.'

The only people I could see making a scene were her and Paul. All I wanted to do was take my kids to the park! Indignant, I pushed past her to open the car door, adamant that not even my own mum was going to stop me from taking my own kids to the park. I shouted over to Dan whilst opening the car door.

'Come on, love, get in the car.'

'You are not going anywhere!' Paul screamed.

It felt like everyone was being so dramatic, trying to pull the kids and the keys off me.

'Tracey! You are not driving this car!' Mum was shouting now, then it clicked.

'Have you had a drink, Mum?'

She looked at me confused. 'What's that got to do with anything? I've only had one. It's my birthday.'

I hadn't realised it was her birthday, but then it all started to make sense. She too was under the influence. Her body and mind had been tainted by alcohol, only she couldn't see it. She was unpure, tainted, and I knew she wouldn't be able to understand a word I was saying until the alcohol had left her body.

Undeterred, I tried to get in the car again. Just then, Mum sprawled her body over the bonnet of the car.

'Now, who's making a scene?'

Adrian came over and took me by the arm.

'Come on, love, this is getting silly. Come home with us.'

He tried tugging me, but I wriggled free.

'I'm not going anywhere.'

Mum tried coaxing me into her car, but I wasn't having any over it, using my foot against the car door to prevent them from succeeding in taking me away.

The fighting and arguing carried on. It was like being in the twilight zone. Everyone around me had gone mad except for me. Just then, an old man appeared. His face seemed familiar, and then I realised he was a neighbour from a few doors down.

'What on earth is going on here?'

Everyone stopped in their tracks; it was like his presence had brought them to their senses.

I wriggled free from Mum's grasp and ran to him. 'Please, please help me!'

I ran into the neighbour's open arms and wept in his embrace.

'Come on, let's take this inside.'

Mum instructed Paul to take the kids home, and she and Adrian followed us into the stranger's home. I couldn't believe my eyes. There were statues of Mary and Jesus everywhere. It was a sign. This man had been sent to me by God himself.

'Come on, child, start from the beginning.'

Mum and Ada looked on as I poured my heart out to this stranger. He listened intently to every word without interrupting. He left me on the sofa and took Mum and Ada into the kitchen. I could hear them talking but couldn't understand what they were saying.

I noticed a Bible sitting open on the coffee table and I started reading about John the Baptist who had been imprisoned for speaking God's truth. I instantly related to his plight. Like me, he had been persecuted because of his beliefs.

My thoughts were interrupted when everyone returned to the living room. Then shame enveloped me when I realised I was holding the old man's book.

'I'm really sorry. I was just looking. I haven't lost your place.'

He offered me a kind smile before turning to rummage through his bookcase and handing me a small red Bible.

'It's ok, love, you can take this one. There's a lot of truth in that book, child. All you need is some faith. Everything is going to be ok, I promise.' At that moment, I believed him.

'My door is always open,' he shouted as Mum and Ada chaperoned me home to Paul.

# 143: I'd Hate It If We Ever Fell Out

Dad's legs had become swollen, and his skin was like tissue paper. The nurses suspected cellulitis and wanted Dad to go to hospital, but he point-blank refused, adamant that he was never going to step foot inside a hospital again. Uncle Mick and the rest of the family were furious, so much so Uncle John made the journey over from Stoke to Sheffield to try and talk sense to him.

I'd agreed to meet him at Dad's flat and when I arrived, I couldn't help noticing that the old smell of stale alcohol and cigarettes had returned to the flat. Dad was in the living room, nursing his new drink of choice, Jack Daniels, and Coke. I ushered Uncle John in the direction of the living room.

'He's through there,' I said.

I didn't follow him, instead I headed to the kitchen to put the kettle on. I could hear raised voices coming from the living room and decided to leave them to it whilst I made a brew.

When I entered the living room, Dad was sitting on one side of the sofa nursing his JD and Coke, whilst Uncle John sat on the other side with his head in his hands.

Uncle John took the coffee from me and shook his head in disbelief.

'What the fuck, Trace?'

I wasn't sure what to say so I just shrugged.

Uncle John turned to Dad.

'Come on, Frank, are you serious? After everything you've put these lasses through, are you really going to go there again?'

'Don't you fucking dare bring my girls into this!' Dad snarled. 'I promised my babbies that I wouldn't drink brandy ever again and I haven't, have I?' He looked to me for confirmation.

'Nah Dad, you've just swapped poison for another, that's all.'

The irony was totally lost on Dad.

'You're a fucking idiot, that's all I can say, Frank. And don't be expectin' me to shoot over 'ere when tha back in hospital again, cos tha will, tha knows.'

Dad just muttered under his breath. 'Aye, whatever.'

Uncle John turned to me. 'So how are you and Sarah bearing up?'

Again, I shrugged. 'Bottom line is, we can't stop him from drinking, can we?'

Dad jumped in. 'See, if they're alreyt with it, what's your problem!'

This time I snapped. 'Nah then, who said owt about being happy with it. All I said was that we can't stop you drinking. End of the day, it's you who's gotta face the consequences.'

Dad raised his drink in the air as if to make a toast.

'Exactly!'

Uncle John changed the subject and asked about the claim.

Dad jumped in. 'See that's all tha's come over for, innit? Well I can tell ya thee nah that none of yous are getting ya hands on a penny.'

Uncle John was hurt but there was no reasoning with Dad when he was in one of his indignant moods. Uncle John didn't stay for long afterwards. I saw him out of the door and promised to keep him updated.

After, I went back into the living room to Dad. 'You were a bit harsh, weren't ya, Dad? The last time I saw him he was broken, sat by your side at the hospital.'

'Look Trace, the last thing I need is a lecture off him about drinking. I mean he's always in fucking pub! They all are. And I'm not hurting anyone, am I?'

'Well, actually Dad you are.'

Dad looked confused.

'It's not easy to sit here watching you commit slow suicide, ya know.'

I could tell Dad was taken aback. His shoulders dropped. 'Look, Trace, in your eyes, I might have been doing well, but it's been torture since I got out of hospital. I'm bored shitless. I'm like a fucking cripple. All I've got is my thoughts! I've got fuck all.'

His last words stung. 'You have got me and Sarah, Dad. Isn't that enough?'

Dad reached for my hand, 'Or course you are and that's not what I mean. You two have got your own lives, your own families. You can't be here twenty-four seven to babysit me and I don't expect you both to be, neither!'

It was hard to argue with him because he was right. We couldn't do any more than we had already been doing and yet it didn't make it any easier.

'Look, trust me. I'm ok.' Dad took my hand. 'Are we still mates?'

His sincerity won me over. 'Of course we are, Dad.'

Dad pulled me in for a hug. 'Good, because I'd hate it if we ever fell out.'

## 144: All I Wanted to Do Was Sleep

The last thing I remembered was being guided up to bed by Mum who closed the curtains and reassured me that everything would be ok.

I clung to my red Bible, determined to read it front to back as soon as I woke. Only I couldn't sleep. My head was spinning. I could hear hushed voices from downstairs. Then everything went silent. Then, out of nowhere, I heard a whisper.

*'You can't get rid of me that easily.'* I looked around to see where the voice had come from, but nobody was there. I shook my head, willing the voice to disappear, but if anything, it was getting louder, and the familiar feeling of dread enveloped my body. I ran downstairs to find Mum, but she'd already left and there was just Paul standing in the kitchen.

'I thought you'd gone to bed?'

I nervously looked around the kitchen, clutching the red Bible the old man had just given me.

'Where are the kids?'

'They are in bed, why?'

'Just asking, are they ok?'

'What do you think? You do realise that you scared the living shit out of the kids, don't you? And what's this then?' He snatched my Bible and flicked through the pages. 'A fucking Bible,' he mocked. 'Are you kidding me?'

Just then, the voice I'd heard came back, only this time he was laughing.

*'See, I told you.'* His voice got louder and louder. I snatched the book out of Paul's hands. I could see Paul's lips moving, but I couldn't hear a word he was saying. I knew it wasn't nice though.

The voice in my head continued to get louder and louder. I tried praying to stop it, but it wasn't working; nothing seemed to work. I felt like I was physically being punched in the stomach; the emotional pain was more than I could bear.

'Please, Paul,' I pleaded. But he wasn't listening. I could tell he was on a roll and there was no stopping him. I clung to my Bible and prayed for all the noise to stop; I just wanted it all to stop.

I wanted to leave the house, but Paul was in the way. Why couldn't he see he was hurting me? Just then, I started to feel lightheaded. With nowhere to escape, I retreated to the corner of the kitchen whilst he paced the kitchen floor. I was exhausted. I couldn't stand the noise any longer and slowly slumped to the floor. I scrunched up, clinging onto my legs, rocking back and forth to stop his poisonous words from hurting me.

'Look at you!' He sneered. The hatred in his voice was evident, and at that moment, I was convinced that he was the Devil himself. I started to pray.

'Please leave me alone, please leave me alone.' Just then, a miracle happened and out of nowhere, it felt like someone had turned down the volume in my head.

Both Paul's and the Devil's voices were getting quieter and quieter until there was nothing. I felt like my body had shut down; I felt nothing; I was completely numb. I could still see Paul's lips moving, but I couldn't hear a word he was saying.

Then Paul's face changed and instead of anger, I saw concern. I remember him trying to get me to stand, but I couldn't move, and I feared that I would be trapped inside my body forever. It was like my body had given up on me. I'd given up on me.

Somehow, we found our way to Mum's house where Paul handed me over.

'I've called the hospital – they are expecting us,' said Mum, gesturing me into to the car.

'Let me know what they say, won't you? I just want to know she's ok.' I knew it was all lies. 'Everything is going to be ok, Trace,' he smiled reassuringly.

The nasty, taunting voice that I had heard in my bedroom reappeared. *'See I told you,' he* sneered, almost revelling in my pain. Then there was another voice. *'Leave her alone, be gone, ignore him, everything is going to be ok.'* Her words were comforting, protecting me from his evil.

On the drive over, Ada kept asking if I was okay. I didn't dare tell him that there were now two voices fighting in my head, both vying for my attention, a battle between good and evil.

I felt a sudden urge to jump out of the car, to escape, but then I'd come back to my senses. Mum and Ada kept smiling and looking concerned but were they just being fake?

Was this just an elaborate hoax? Was this the Devil's work? I didn't know who to trust any more.

We entered some grounds through a massive set of gates and followed a drive that seemed to go on for miles before we reached a building that looked like an old stately home. But it wasn't a stately home. I soon realised that it was a lunatic asylum, and I was about to be welcomed as one of their new patients. I didn't care where I was as long as it was as far away from Paul as possible.

We were greeted by a female nurse at the main doors who already knew my name. Was this part of the Devil's plan? But the kinder voice in my head encouraged me to follow her like a compliant sheep. The place was quiet, and I wondered if I was the only one there, but then the nurse explained that everyone was asleep.

The nurse ushered us all into a small office. I was transported back to being a teenager escorted by Mum into the headmaster's office at school to be reprimanded, only I still couldn't figure out what I had done wrong. The urge to run away was ever-present but I clasped onto my Bible like my life depended on it.

*'It's ok, everything is going to be ok.'*

There it was again, that whisper. I couldn't figure out if it was the Devil trying to trick me or if it was God himself. I was so confused. Only the old man understood me, but that was enough to convince me that I wasn't insane.

The nurse tried asking me some questions, but I couldn't think straight, not with the whispers in my head, plus I didn't possess the physical energy to talk. So, Mum stepped in and did the talking for me. Just like before, I could see their lips moving but couldn't work out what they were saying; my biggest fear was that I might be stuck in this vegetative state for the rest of my life. I'd heard rumours about people who were left alone in padded rooms. Had I just signed my life away? A feeling of panic enveloped me, but I couldn't speak. All I could feel was my tears running down my face. *What about the kids; what would happen to them?*

With their business concluded, Mum and Ada stood up and hugged me. Mum was crying but promised to return the following day with some fresh clothes and toiletries. Ada tried reassuring me that everything would be ok, but was it? *Were they going to come back?*

The nurse tried to show me round, but all I wanted was to sleep so she escorted me to a bed in a ward of lifeless bodies. The thought of waking up to complete strangers terrified me. I felt another sudden urge to run again but my body felt like a dead weight.

'Come on,' he whispered. 'Let's get you into bed, shall we?'

Just then, a young woman appeared out of nowhere. She was agitated and asking who I was. I heard the nurse explain to her, Laura, that I was now on the ward, then she sent her away and helped me climb onto the bed. She offered me some sedatives, but I was clear that I was never taking another drug in my life.

I shook my head and my voice surprised me. 'No,' I said.

'Ok, love, I will go fetch you some water then. Do you want me to take your book off you?'

There was no fucking way I was letting anyone have my Bible; I clasped it to my chest and asked the nurse to pull the curtains around me; the thought of waking up in the morning with loads of curious eyes baring down on me freaked me out.

The bed sheets were tucked in tight, and it took all my strength to loosen them so that I could get comfy enough to sleep. I could hear the young woman in the hallway having a heated discussion with the nurse, but I didn't care. The nurse could deal with her.

I had my Bible, and all I wanted to do was sleep.

# 145: Some Sort of Epiphany

Dad was in hospital again. The district nurse had found him on the floor and was concerned that he might have fractured his collarbone. I wasn't surprised; his mobility had been steadily getting worse whilst he continued to drink. By all accounts, he'd kicked off alarmingly when the ambulance crew arrived and had initially refused to go with them, but eventually, he'd agreed.

My first instinct was to jump into the car and rush to the hospital, but I telephoned instead.

Dad was still in A&E and waiting for an X Ray. I explained to the nurse that Dad was alcoholic and raised my concerns about him withdrawing. I was relieved when she explained that they were aware of Dad's condition and that they could medically manage any withdrawal should he need it.

Reassured Dad wasn't in any immediate danger, I finished the call and rang Sarah and Lawson, explaining that I'd chase the hospital up later for an update.

Only I didn't get to call the hospital back, because two hours later, I got a call from Dad who sounded in a good mood. 'Ey up, shugs, are you still coming up later?'

'Yeah, Dad, I was planning on calling up to the hospital after work. What have they said?'

Dad chuckled down the phone. 'I'm at home, ya pudding!'

To say I was shocked was an understatement.

'What do you mean, you're at home?'

'They discharged me. I'm sound, just a little bruised, that's all. They've given me a sling and some pain killers, but I'll be rest. So are you coming or not?'

'Yeah, I'll see ya later.'

When I arrived at Dad's flat, he was back in his usual spot at the end of the sofa with the bottle of JD by his foot. You wouldn't have thought he'd been anywhere had it not been for the sling.

I went over to give him a kiss before settling down in the armchair.

'So, what they said then?'

Dad reached for a cigarette and winced; his arm was clearly causing him pain.

'Not much they can do, love. Said all I've got to do is rest it and keep it in this thing.'

'So, it's not broken then?'

Dad lit his cigarette. 'Just a small fracture. I'll tell thee what though, this sling's doing me head in already.'

'So have they given you any painkillers?'

He raised his glass of JD and Coke. 'Don't need em. Got this, 'ant I?'

I shook my head in disbelief and watched him fill his glass. I no longer batted an eyelid when he poured himself a JD and Coke. It was weird because apart from repeating himself, even though he was under the influence, he was almost sober.

He wasn't the same aggressive, defensive, or manipulative drunk like he'd used to be. In fact, he was quite the opposite. For the most part, he was a pleasure to be around. There were still times when I felt conflicted and today was one of them, but I'd stopped trying to reason with him. Fighting was futile.

I knew I had choices. I knew I could give Dad an ultimatum, refuse to see him if he continued to drink, but I also knew it wouldn't be enough to stop him drinking. I also knew that if I did give Dad an ultimatum and stayed away it wouldn't stop me worrying about him.

I could have never imagined that I would be in the very same position as the families that I supported in my work, and yet here I was. I thought I knew enough about addiction from my own lived experience, but as I sat and watched Dad drink from his tumbler, I'd never felt so powerless.

I had been hoping for Dad to have some sort of epiphany, but he knew too well that his drinking was slowly killing him and there was absolutely nothing I could do about it. Now, I really understood what other people were going through.

# 146: Just One Fucking Thing

I woke disoriented to the smell of toast and the sounds of crockery. My stomach cried out angrily. I couldn't remember the last time I had eaten. But it wasn't just that; there was a faint smell of rust, and my stomach was cramping. Then I realised I had come on my period. Then I remembered where I was. I lifted the covers and my heart sank; I was covered in blood, and it wasn't just on me; it was on the white sheets, too.

I thanked God for the curtains still being drawn, which was the only thing protecting me from the outside world. Then I remembered my book. I couldn't find it at first. I feared that Laura might have stolen it from me in the middle of the night and was just about to get out of bed to hunt her down when I found it under the pillow.

The sense of relief was overwhelming; my hands were shaking uncontrollably, and I was on the verge of crying when a nurse peeped her head in between the curtains.

'Ah, you are awake,' she smiled. 'How are you feeling this morning?'

I broke down crying. I just wanted the earth to come and swallow me up; I'd never felt so embarrassed in my life.

'I've come on my period,' I whispered.

'Let's get you in the bath, shall we?'

'But I haven't got a change of clothes.'

'It's ok, love, we always have some spares on hand. Although I can't guarantee they'll be fashionable.'

'Will I be able to make a call? I needed to ring Mum.'

'Yes, love, of course. Let's get you freshened up, eh? Then we can sort you out. How does that sound? Once you are done, I can show you around and introduce you to some of the other patients.'

I felt like Count Dracula woken from the dead. When she drew the curtains, the light was blinding. The ward looked completely different in the daylight. All the beds around me were empty and had already been made and thankfully, there wasn't a soul in sight, including Laura. I was fully clothed, but I felt naked and exposed as I shuffled to the bathroom with the assistance of the nurse who left me along in the bathroom while she went to fetch some towels. She returned with a big grin on her face.

'Here, love, I've found some bubble bath.' She handed me some joggers, a T-shirt and some pants. 'Unfortunately, these are the only pads I could find.' She held out the biggest sanitary pads I'd seen in my life, but at that point, I was grateful for anything.

I locked the door behind her, ran a bath and started to strip. I caught my reflection in the mirror and was horrified; I hardly recognised the person or the body staring back at me. I was emaciated; I looked like I'd just stepped out of a prisoner-of-war movie; the blood didn't help either. But what freaked me out the most was my face and my neck.

I looked like I'd been struck by lightning. There was a rash, like a birthmark, from my cheekbone, which ran down the side of my face to my collarbone. Was this the mark of the Devil?

I sank deep into the bath, letting the warmth envelop me. The bubbles felt like a protective layer, shielding me from the harsh reality outside. I closed my eyes, and memories of happier times flooded back. Being a kid, being a mother, the smile on the kids' faces, and happy times all seemed like a distant dream.

I could have stayed there forever but the nurse came knocking and I reluctantly stepped out of the bath and wrapped myself in the towel. The though of my kids being back at home without their mother hurt. They needed me now more than ever.

The reflection in the mirror was still there; it was still the same, only I felt different. I inhaled deeply, that voice was there again.

'*Everything is going to be ok*, she whispered, and an overwhelming feeling of determination enveloped me like a comfort blanket.

The nurse had been right; the bubble bath had done me a world of good. The only problem was I had no energy at all. I felt like an old woman, not someone who was only twenty-two. The nurse escorted me to the canteen and let me sit alone to eat some toast while waiting to be called by a doctor. All the time, my Bible never left my sight.

The atmosphere was a mix of calm and busyness. Men and women of various ages were scattered around. Some sat quietly, lost in thought and one man was having animated conversations with himself, while another paced back and forth, visibly agitated. In a corner, a small group of women engaged in a craft activity reminiscent of what Danielle used to do in the nursery.

Then I noticed Laura sitting alone, meticulously arranging a puzzle, her focus unwavering.

'Tracey?' A voice called, making me jump. It was the doctor. He invited me to follow him.

I had so many questions: How long would it take to get better? When would I regain my energy? When could I go back to my family? What was the rash on my face that had appeared out of nowhere?

'I see from the records that you were brought in last night that you were chanting about the Devil.' The doctor glanced at my Bible. 'And there were concerns about suicide. Do you want to talk about that?'

I didn't know where to start. I didn't recall saying anything about suicide. I told him I was just exhausted and confused.

'Based on your symptoms and the things you've been experiencing, we believe you might be suffering from drug-induced psychosis. This condition can cause you to see or believe things that aren't real, making you feel very disconnected from reality. Does that make sense?'

‘Psychosis? What about the voices in my head? I feel like I’m losing my mind...It’s just...everything feels so heavy and dark.’

‘Can you hear the voices now?’

I had to confess I hadn’t heard anything since being admitted last night.

‘I know it’s a lot to take in. Psychosis is a temporary state and can feel extremely real and scary, especially when it’s related to substance use. You will recover with the right treatment, support, and time,’ he said.

I nodded slowly, trying to absorb the information. There was a slight sense of relief in having some answers.

‘So, none of it was real then?’

‘I’m sure it felt real. Part of your recovery will be about unravelling what you experienced and distinguishing between what was real and what was a product of the psychosis. It’s a process, and we’ll be here to help you through it. We’ll make you a treatment plan: medication to stabilize your mood and reduce psychotic symptoms, then therapy to address the underlying issues. It would also be helpful to start you on some antipsychotic treatment...’

I cut him off before he could finish. ‘Honestly, I don’t want to take any form of drug.’ He acknowledged my concerns. ‘It’s just a small dose and will help until you start feeling better again. Remember, Tracey, you’re not alone in this. We have a team of professionals here to support you.’

I just nodded and asked if I could call home. I needed to speak to Paul and Mum. He left me in his office with the phone. I tried Paul first.

He answered straight away. ‘When are you coming out? What did the doctors say?’ There was no ‘hello, how are you? Nothing. I ignored his questions.

‘How are the kids? Are they there? Can I talk to them?’

“They’re at your mum’s. So, what have they said?’

His impatience annoyed me, but I knew I needed to stay calm.

'I don't know yet. Look, I've come on my period. I need you to pack some clothes to send over with Mum later. Can you do that?'

I could hear Paul huffing down the phone. 'I just want to know what's going on, that's all.'

'I'm exhausted. They reckon I was suffering from some psychosis. I still don't fully understand. To be honest, I've not long since woken up myself.'

'So it's not schizophrenia then!'

'No, it's not fucking schizophrenia.'

'Okay, OK. Calm down. I was just asking. Have they said when you can come home, then?'

'Look, I have no idea. Just send a change of clothes and some Tampax with Mum. Are you still there, Paul? Are you ok?' I hated it when he was silent.

'No, I'm not. How am I supposed to cope without you here? What do I tell people? What do I tell the kids? I cannot believe this is happening.'

I felt sick to the pit of my stomach. 'Just send some Tampax with the clothes, please?'

'Whatever.'

It was easier talking to Mum who just wanted to know how I was.

'Are the kids there? Can I talk to them?'

'Yes, of course, love. I went to collect Dan for school this morning, but we decided it was probably best to keep her off from school just for today. Paul wasn't good, mind, so I brought them both round here to give him a break.'

I just about managed to refrain from screaming. 'Give him a fucking break? They are his kids!' How did he always manage to make everything about him?

I left the doctor's office, clutching my Bible and leaflet. I felt exhausted from all the talking and explaining. The weight of the diagnosis still pressed heavily on my shoulders.

Back in the ward, I found a quiet corner and flipped through the booklet, trying to make sense of my new reality.

A nurse approached you with a warm smile. 'How are you feeling?' she asked, her voice filled with genuine concern.

'I'm not sure,' I confessed. 'It's a lot to take in, and I'm really tired.'

She nodded understandingly. 'But you're in the right place. We're here to help you through this. If you need anything, don't hesitate to ask. Why don't you go back to bed and get some rest, eh?'

I took her advice and only woke up when Mum and Ada arrived. I was so happy to see them. The canteen was empty, so I escorted them both there.

'Paul said he'd packed everything I told him you would need. I also went out and bought you some new PJs and pants. Oh, and here, I got you some cigarettes, too.'

I thanked her, but all I wanted was the Tampax; I carried on rummaging in the bag, but I couldn't find them.

'Is everything ok, love?'

'I can't find the Tampax!'

'I'm sorry, love, that's all Paul gave me.'

'Just one fucking thing, one fucking thing!' I was pacing the kitchen area, unable to contain my anger. I lifted a chair and flung it across the floor. 'The fucking selfish bastard, the fucking bastard!' I raged.

That now familiar look of terror was etched on Mum's face 'Trace, calm down, love, what's the matter?'

One of the nurses appeared. 'Is everything ok?'

'No, it's fucking not! All I wanted was some Tampax, just one fucking thing, and he couldn't even do that!'

'It's ok, Trace. I can go fetch you some now.' Mum offered, but she didn't get it; nobody did. It wasn't just about the Tampax; it felt like a slap in the face.

'I knew he wasn't listening; I just fucking knew it.' The anger was overwhelming. I couldn't stand still. Flashbacks of all the nights of loveless sex made me feel physically sick. 'Us against the world', my arse. There had never been an us; it had always been about him.

'Mum, I'm sorry. It's not you. It's him. Thank you. I do appreciate everything you have done.'

Mum didn't look convinced. She seemed upset and hurt, and it was all because of me. Again.

An overwhelming feeling of shame enveloped me. Christ, I had put my mother through so much, and yet here she was, still there for me. I felt an overwhelming urge to hug her.

'Mum, I'm sorry. I really shouldn't have lashed out at you. It's not your fault, I'm so sorry.'

Mum hugged me back tightly. 'It's okay, everything is going to be okay,' she repeated, but I knew it wasn't okay. The past few weeks felt like a bad nightmare. All I wanted to do was wake up and for everything to return to normal; the only problem was that I didn't know what normal was anymore.

# 147: It's Your Life

It had been a week since Dad had fractured his collarbone, and the bruising had really started to show. It looked bad; the top half of his body was black.

Dad would brush off our concerns, claiming it looked worse than it was. The district nurses, Sarah, and Lawson had tried talking to him about getting a doctor or going into hospital, but he would stubbornly refuse any sort of help.

As well as his shoulder, I was becoming increasing concerned about how his body was getting weaker. Lawson still called up every day and had been rolling his fags and helping him to the toilet.

Lawson had mentioned in private how there had been a couple of times that Dad hadn't made it to the toilet, but I never mentioned it to Dad; he had enough shame to carry. Dad was deteriorating, right before our eyes. His usual litre bottle of JD was lasting two days instead of the one, on account that he was sleeping more, and I was worried that he might slip into a coma again.

One morning, the district nurses called Sarah to say that they had called an ambulance because his cellulitis was getting worse. But when the ambulance had arrived, Dad had point blank refused to go with them. According to the ambulance crew, there was nothing they could do as he appeared to have capacity and the right to refuse treatment.

Frustrated, I agreed to try and have another go at convincing him to go to hospital when I called in after work

When I arrived, Dad was in his usual spot. I caught a whiff of stale urine on him. I could see why the nurses were concerned: Dad's legs were swollen and looked red and really sore. I was surprised he could even walk.

'So, how ya doing? I hear you have had some visitors today?'

Dad snapped. 'I was ok!' I could tell he was already agitated. 'Is that all you lot do all day, eh? Talk about me behind my back?' I could detect Mr Hyde in his voice and a hint of paranoia.

'Actually, no it isn't. Trust me, Dad I have enough to keep me busy as it is. But look at your legs. They need tending to, Dad!'

'I just wish people would just stop trying to force me into doing summat that I don't wanna do for fuck's sake! You just don't get it, do ya?'

'Actually, Dad, I don't. Can you tell me?'

Dad shook his head. 'I'm not stupid, tha knows. I'm fully aware that my body is fucked! In fact, I'm fuckin' sick of hearing about it! But like I keep saying, I don't want to go to hospital! Fuck me, I don't know how many times I've got to say it!'

Dad reached for his tumbler and took a large swig from the glass. 'And you still haven't sorted that will out, neither!'

The last thing I expected us to be talking about was wills. I could tell which direction the conversation was going, and it unnerved me.

'Dad, I can sort the will out. That's not a problem. The problem is you are falling apart. You need hospital treatment. This is fuckin' self-neglect, Dad.'

'Look, I know what I'm doing, okay.'

'But do ya?'

Dad laughed a sinister laugh. 'Look, I may be drunk, but I'm not fuckin' stupid!'

'Look, Dad, will ya go? Come on, for me.' I tried my best to cajole him. 'Listen, I'll take ya now in the car? They won't keep ya in, I promise! I'll bring ya back as soon as they have had a look at your legs.'

I reached for his hand and tried to make eye contact, but Dad didn't look up. 'Come on, Dad, we'll be back in an hour.'

Dad patted my hand.

'Listen, can you just drop it?'

I had to pull away. 'I'm gonna make a cuppa.'

I headed into the kitchen. I didn't need a drink; I just needed to get out of that room, and space to get my thoughts together. I paced the kitchen like a caged animal, unsure what else I could do. I made a drink and returned to the living room.

'Are we ok?'

I shook my head in disbelief. 'No Dad. I'm not ok. You're not ok! This –' I gestured to his legs. '– is not ok! Look at you? You're covered in bruises, tha's got puss coming outta ya legs! You could be dying right now! And you expect me and everyone around you to be ok with this?'

Dad shook his head. 'To be honest, I don't care.'

That hurt and I bit. 'Then why should we? I can leave ya alone if tha wants. I don't have to come around every day to check up on ya. Trust me, Dad I've got plenty of other shit to be dealing with!'

'I didn't mean I didn't care about you or our Sarah, did I?' He shook his head again. 'You just don't get it.'

He was right. I didn't but I did want to understand.

'Come on then Dad, explain.'

Dad took a deep breath. 'So, ya know when someone gets diagnosed with cancer, right?'

I wasn't sure where he was going with it, but I listened. 'Yeah, Dad, go on.'

'Well, they get a choice, don't they?' They get a choice whether or not they want treatment, but do ya know just having that radiotherapy treatment can make 'em feel ten times worse and there are no guarantees neither that it will work.'

Dad looked at me and I gestured again for him to continue. 'Now look, I know I've not got cancer...' My mind went back to the time when he claimed he had, then flatly denied it. 'But I do know my liver's fucked. I also know that if I wanted to, I could stop drinking, but I don't wanna.' Dad took a sip of his JD and Coke, then laughed. 'Fuck me, I can't even get pissed anymore. I need this just to feel normal'

He was laughing but it wasn't funny.

'I'm being honest wi ya now, babby. I've had enough and if I'm going to go, then I wanna go here, wi me babbies around me not in some fucking hospital bed.'

I tried to process what Dad had just said.

Dad bowed his head and continued. 'I just ain't got another detox in me, I'd rather die than have to go through one of them again.'

I moved closer to him and grabbed his hand.

'Look Dad, I get it. I really do and I hear what you are saying, but you are stronger than this, you've got this, you've done it before.'

Dad laughed. 'Yeah, but what you don't know is that when I'm clean, it's still fuckin' shit. I can't sleep, I'm constantly on edge – that ain't no life, that ain't living! If I was a dog, they'd have put me down by now.'

It wasn't funny. I could tell he'd given up on himself and I wasn't sure how or what I felt. But there was nothing I could do.

'Fine, Dad. It's your body. It's your life.'

Dad smiled. He looked relieved but I felt like I'd just signed his death warrant.

# 148: Pat

The best thing about being in the hospital was that Paul couldn't reach me. It had been days since I'd last spoken to him. The staff told me he'd called, but I never returned the messages. I knew I would have to talk to him at some point, but all I cared about was the kids, who were mostly with Mum.

With each passing day, I felt myself getting stronger, but I was still very fragile. I was in no emotional or physical state to face the outside world; in fact, the mere thought terrified me.

The doctors tried several different creams to treat the rash on my face, but nothing worked. My therapist was convinced the rash had been brought on by stress and assured me it would eventually fade, but I needed it gone faster. Every time I looked at it in the mirror, it reminded me of what I'd been through.

At least the voices in my head had finally stopped. The more I talked and opened up to my therapist, the clearer it became that there was no such thing as the Devil following me. My delusional thoughts had been brought on by stress.

It was embarrassing even to imagine that I'd genuinely thought I had special powers, or that I was a Prophet from God, or even worse, a descendant of John the Baptist.

I'd tried several times to find comfort in reading my little red Bible, but none of the words resonated with me anymore. I couldn't see how fables from thousands of years ago could help me now. I couldn't understand how talking could either.

My therapist explained that the primary purpose of our sessions was to understand and establish what had been happening before the acute phase, to avoid another episode. We would talk for what sometimes felt like hours. I often had to go to sleep straight after therapy to recover because just talking left me physically and emotionally drained.

I talked a lot about my childhood, but my therapist always seemed more interested in my relationship with Paul. I had started out by saying we were childhood sweethearts, but nothing about our relationship had been sweet. I couldn't see it then, but I could now.

Paul had always been controlling and manipulative, always wanting his way. His bouts of unfounded jealousy were, at times, intolerable. But it wasn't just Paul; Dad had also played a large part in our early relationship. For years, I'd felt stuck in the middle, trying to juggle work and motherhood while feeling obligated to please both of them, which sometimes felt almost impossible.

I was starting to see how they had both taken advantage of me. Dad had just used me as cheap labour. I'd wasted much of my young adult life working for Dad in his video shop, then at the taxi firm. I'd even got on my hands and knees to clean his flat for him while he was out with other women.

The thought of how much I'd missed out on — Danielle taking her first steps or being unable to put her to bed at night — hit me hard. But not as hard as when I started to share what should have been my second child.

I realised that I'd never wanted to abort my child. All I wanted from them both was to listen to me and hear me, but all I got in return was an ultimatum from Paul to keep the baby or split, and for Dad to turn his back on me when I needed him the most.

The rejection still felt raw, but talking helped me realize that the persecution I'd been feeling had been with me all my life. I'd always felt like the odd one out, like no one had ever listened to me. In that session, my emotions started to get the better of me, and the severity of my situation came from nowhere.

I had always thought I'd made peace and come to terms with the fact that I had aborted my own child, but it turned out I hadn't. I'd been telling myself for years that I had no option at the time as a way of justification. But that wasn't true. I would have had that baby in a nanosecond had it not been for Paul and his suffocating and controlling ways, and the fact that he wasn't prepared to go out to work to provide for his own family.

The uncontrollable tears that followed the revelation scared me. Once again, I found myself rocking back and forth, trying to contain my grief, but it wasn't working. It felt like someone had opened the floodgates to a dam of emotions I had been bottling up for years.

But then it occurred to me, was this my punishment, karma for killing my unborn child. The therapist was quick to remind me that it wasn't my fault, but that did not stop the feeling of guilt and regret as I grieved for what could have been.

What hurt the most was knowing it could have all been different if Paul had been different. I recalled all the nights I spent alone with nothing to my name, sofa surfing on Auntie Dot and Uncle John's sofa. All the times Paul used Danielle, our own daughter, like a pawn in a game of chess, trying to control my every move.

All the times I scrounged for money to visit her, trying to keep up the pretence that everything was okay when it was far from it. Then, like a fool, I caved in and returned to him on the back of his false promises that everything would be different. If anything, he'd got worse. How could I have been so stupid? I thought I had experienced pain before, but nothing like this. I felt robbed and used, unsure if I could ever forgive them both for the hurt they had caused me.

It wasn't long, perhaps days after that session, when I received a very unexpected visitor. It was Pat, one of the lads who sometimes came back to ours for a bong after the nightclub to wind down. I was surprised. I didn't really know him that well, but he'd always seemed friendly enough. It was nice to see a familiar face.

'What are you doing here?'

He looked sheepish. 'I wasn't even sure if I should call in, but I'm working on the building next door. Paul said that you were in here, so I thought I would pop in and say hello.'

'Has Paul sent you to check up on me?'

He had a confused look on his face, which was also clotted in paint. 'No, no, I just thought I'd pop over on my break.' Now he seemed visibly uncomfortable, and I felt like a proper bitch for questioning him. 'Look, I can leave if you like?'

'No, no, it's ok.' I tried to break the ice. 'Well, this isn't awkward, is it? Do you like my new home?' I smiled, gesturing around the hospital canteen. 'I'm afraid there are no bongs here, but I can offer you a cuppa. Come on, what are you having?'

I'd made us drinks and we'd just sat down when Laura came over.

'That's Tracey's cup.' She glared at Pat, then at me protectively.

'It's okay, Laura, he's my friend. This is Pat. Say hi.'

'Hi,' she replied nervously before leaving us alone.

'I thought she was going to go for me then!' Pat whispered as she walked away.

'I know I felt the same when I first came in, but honestly, she is a pussycat. Just a scared child stuck in an adult's body.'

I went on to explain how, as a teenager, Laura had been involved in a canoeing incident that involved one of her best friends drowning. She'd never been the same again, according to one of the other patients. She'd been here for months.

There was Edith, a spinster who had been a full-time carer for her mum until she passed away, triggering a breakdown. In the evenings, she'd been showing me how to crochet.

Then, there was this older bloke called Bill; he reminded me a lot of Dad, with his mannerisms. He claimed to be a wealthy businessman who wasn't mentally ill. He was waiting for a trial date at court, something to do with fraud, but was using poor mental health as a defence.

Then I told him about Mary, who had been all over the news. She'd apparently been placed here during the war and had only just been moved to a nursing home after fifty years of being incarcerated.

But that wasn't going to happen to me. In fact, there had even been talk of me leaving. This wasn't a lunatic asylum anymore; it was a community mental health centre, and unlike Mary, I could walk freely on the grounds and come and go as I pleased, but I hadn't felt strong enough.

I found myself opening up to Pat about my therapy sessions. He sat and listened intently while I spewed my emotional guts all over him. I'd been chatting away when paranoia struck. *He doesn't want to hear about all your problems.*

Our conversation shifted to the outside world. Pat mentioned that some of the guys had been regularly visiting Paul. I could sense from his tone that he felt sorry for Paul, but then again, Paul had a way of making everyone feel sorry for him. Pat explained that Paul had registered with an agency for work at the post office and that he had even offered Paul some work, helping him with painting and decorating. I should have felt happy; Paul was finally doing something right, but I wasn't convinced. I think Pat sensed my cynicism.

'I reckon all this has hit him hard, Trace. He is trying.'

I shook my head. Paul might have fooled them, but he hadn't fooled me. He'd been talking about registering at the post office for weeks, but it had nothing to do with turning over a new leaf. He was a master manipulator, always playing the victim and making others feel sorry for him. I'd seen it too many times to believe that his recent actions were driven by genuine remorse or a desire to change.

Instead, I suspected his newfound interest in employment was a calculated move to gain leniency from the courts. The memories of his controlling and manipulative behaviour flooded back. His actions and the way he'd spoken to me before coming into hospital had eroded the last of my trust and hope. Rebuilding it would be a monumental task. Even when I tried to acknowledge the possibility of him attempting to change, I couldn't shake the feeling that it was too little, too late, and I wasn't ready to believe that Paul was truly capable of becoming the man he claimed to be.

# 149: He Would Just Have to Forgive Me

It had been a couple of days since my chat with Dad. He'd been sleeping a lot more and was still adamantly refusing to go into hospital. There was absolutely nothing we could do apart from respect his wishes and allow him to pass away at home. At times, we thought he might be slipping into a coma again, but we couldn't be sure. All I was sure about was that I couldn't live with myself, knowing that he passed away alone in the flat.

It was a Friday afternoon and after a brief chat over the phone Sarah and I had made a pact to both go straight to Dad's after work and stay for however long it took. Lawson left me and Sarah to take over. We gently tended to Dad, washing his face with a cloth and changing his sheets on the sofa. In-between cleaning the flat, one of us would sit with Dad and have some alone time. I used mine to talk to him, hoping he could hear me.

I found myself repeating the same goodbyes I had said months previously. I told him how much I loved him, but more importantly, how I'd forgiven him.

I so desperately wanted to make sure that when he did pass over to God knows where, that he did so without any regrets. In a sad and twisted way, we'd become closer than ever, and I was grateful he'd come back into my life.

The past voids of missed opportunities had been filled, and I'd finally got the relationship that I'd always craved. Whilst the past two years had been tough, I was glad now that he had turned up so that I could spend these most precious moments by his side.

At eleven pm, Sarah took a call from her partner. I could tell by her face it wasn't good.

'I've gotta go back, our Charlotte's not well.'

I wasn't impressed. This wasn't what we'd agreed but I couldn't stop her neither. She promised to return as early as she could the next morning.

So now it was just me and Dad. As I sat and watched his chest rising and falling, I couldn't help thinking how he looked so content and at peace, just like he'd been in hospital a few months before and I was content to sit by his bedside.

After a couple of hours though, my resolve started to wane. I realised I hadn't properly thought this through. I hadn't considered who I'd call when he did finally take his last breath. It was the weekend, so I couldn't call his doctor. Would I have to call the ambulance? But then again, why would I, what would be the point? He'd be dead already. I didn't even know where dead people's bodies went to.

Then there were the bruises. They were hard to ignore, he looked like he'd been in a car crash or tortured.

Would I get the blame for neglect? Get the blame for not making the call? What would a coroner's court say? What would the press say? And then resentment started to set in. It was ok for Dad lying there all peaceful, but what would his family say? It was bad enough before, but I wasn't sure I could go through it all again.

Would I get accused of killing their brother? I mean, was this like assisted suicide? I might get accused of killing him for his money. I agonised for what felt like hours before I came to a decision. I knew Dad would be angry with me, but I didn't care. I thought I could do it, but I couldn't. I couldn't sit there and watch him die. I couldn't risk being held responsible for his death, so I made the call.

The ambulance arrived within five minutes. I quickly explained about how Dad previously refused treatment and how he'd sent the previous ambulance crew away a few days earlier. I was expecting to be judged, to be questioned more, but instead they were really understanding.

Dad was completely obvious to the ambulance staff who lifted and strapped him into the chair. I quickly locked up the flat whilst they carried him down the flight of stairs. It was dark and bitterly cold and, apart from the streetlights and the odd house lit up, there were no signs of life.

I sat in the corner of the ambulance whilst the staff did some more tests and made sure he was secured, before we headed off to the hospital. I felt an overwhelming sense of relief listening to the siren, but also felt guilty, I'd broken my promise to honour his wishes.

The ambulance lady listened intently as I went into more detail and my fears about Dad kicking off if he ever came round. She reassured me I wouldn't have got into trouble for not calling them but that I'd done the right thing. I knew she was right, but it still didn't feel right.

It felt like a few minutes later when we finally arrived in A&E. I followed closely behind the ambulance staff as Dad was wheeled straight into an empty bay. After the handovers, the ambulance lady who'd sat and listened to me in the back of the van squeezed my shoulder reassuringly, telling me again that I'd done the right thing, which brought me some comfort.

As soon as they left, the nurse smiled in my direction, then turned her attention to Dad.

'Right then, who do we have here?' She scanned his body, but her smile turned into a frown as she touched Dad's shoulder. 'These look like old bruises...'

I started to try and explain. 'Ah, yes they are, Dad fractured his should a week or so ago...'

She didn't let me finish. 'And how long have his legs been like this?'

I felt like all my fears about being judged, or blamed were confirmed. I bit my togue as I tried to continue to explain. But I couldn't help feeling like my words were just falling on deaf ears. She started to take Dad's blood pressure. When he began to stir, her face almost lit up and she proceeded to try and rouse him.

'Frank, Frank, can you hear me? Frank, Frank?'

His eyes were still closed, but he started waving his arms as if he was trying to fight someone, but there wasn't anyone there. The nurse continued in her efforts; she tried to calm him and reassure him that he was ok.

'Frank, don't worry, you're ok.'

Dad's eyes snapped wide open. He looked from side to side, trying to figure out where he was. I knew he was going to be angry, so I stayed seated. His eyes settled on the nurse as she continued to stroke his hair.

'Where the fuck am I?' he demanded.

I stayed out of Dad's eyeshot.

'Hi Frank, my name's Liz. You are in the Northern...'

She didn't get to finish her sentence, because in a flash, Dad erupted and spat at her. Thankfully it hit her chest.

'How the fuck have I got here?' he demanded. He tried to get up, but he couldn't move. The shock on the nurse's face was a picture.

I couldn't help feeling smug, especially after how she'd treated me earlier. The nurse turned to me, but I just shrugged my shoulders.

'I did try telling ya.'

The nurse left the cubicle and by the time a doctor arrived, five minutes later, Dad was bang out again. The doctor had a far better bedside manner than the previous nurse and explained that suspected Dad might have an infection of some sort. He was sure that they would be admitting him.

It was now about four am. I sat and stared at Dad lying there motionless on the bed; I replayed everything. It had happened so fast, it all still felt surreal.

Only an hour or so earlier, I'd been sitting watching Dad peacefully lying on his sofa at home and now he was back on a hospital bed. I felt numb. I was completely physically, mentally, and emotionally exhausted. All I wanted was to go home. I didn't know what would come next and I didn't want to, neither. All I knew was that Dad would be mad, but he would just have to forgive me, just like all the times I'd forgiven him.

# 150: Nah, You Were Right

I'd been in Middlewood for a couple of weeks and had started to feel loads better. It was visible too. I had slowly started to gain weight; the rash was gradually fading. I had started to resemble the Tracey I remembered before the drugs. Even the exhaustion was lifting.

Part of my rehabilitation was slowly venturing into the real world. Mum had been to collect me on various occasions so I could spend time with the kids. I'd been nervous on my first adventure out of the hospital, especially when we drove back onto my estate on Base Green. I was paranoid that everyone would be pointing the finger, but no-one seemed to notice. We also went to visit Sarah, who looked like she'd seen a ghost when she saw us at her workplace. Mum had forgotten to warn her.

'What the fuck are you doing out?'

'That's nice, Sarah. Good to see you too.' I tried to hide my hurt with sarcasm. She got another staff member to take over the till and ushered Mum and me outside.

'I'm sorry, Trace, I was just shocked, that's all. Are you ok?' This time, her genuine concern was apparent.

'I'm feeling loads better; in fact, the hospital is looking to discharge me soon.'

'Are you and me ok then?'

I was confused. 'Of course we are. Why wouldn't we be?'

'Trace, the last time we spoke, you threatened me! You were all weird, chatting loads of stuff about God. I had to put the phone down on you. You proper freaked me out.'

The familiar feeling of shame and guilt enveloped me. I could tell that I had genuinely scared her. I apologised and explained about how I no longer believed that the Devil was real.

'Thank fuck for that, Trace!'

Paul, on the other hand, seemed genuinely pleased and relieved to see me during my first home visit and subsequent daily visits afterwards. My initial scepticism started to fade, and I wondered if there had been any truth in what Pat had conveyed about him turning over a new leaf.

I knew he didn't have the emotional capacity to comprehend what I had endured as he tiptoed around me, but I was grateful that he seemed to be trying. There were no snide digs. He didn't mention or try to initiate sex, claiming he wanted to go at my pace.

He promised me that selling drugs was in the past and that he carried regrets about getting greedy and admitted that he'd brought the pending drug conviction on himself. He shared how I'd been right all along about the mates who weren't really mates; they'd abandoned him now he'd been busted. He'd enjoyed the odd day's painting cash-in-hand for Pat and was considering doing a painting and decorating course inside if he was unfortunate to get sent down.

It was like he'd had a total personality transplant, and even though the past few weeks and months had been traumatic, it actually felt like the break had done us both the world of good, which helped confirm in my heart that it was time to go back home.

Part of me didn't want to leave the hospital. I could see how easy it could be for some people to become institutionalised. It had become my safe space, my haven. I'd grown fond of some of the patients, especially Laura, who was beyond upset when she heard I was leaving.

'Don't go, Tracey, don't leave me.'

Her pleas tugged at my heartstrings. I wished I could take her home with me, but I couldn't; I had a life and a family outside of the hospital walls that needed me. I had so many bridges to build, the first one being with my kids. The kids were ecstatic when I came home for good, and I couldn't wait to make up for the lost time and be the Mum they deserved.

Pat became a regular visitor, which I didn't mind; he was a good influence on Paul. Yeah, he liked to go for it at the weekend, but at least he paid for his own drugs out of his own pay packet instead of selling them. He even managed to talk

Paul into joining him to play footy once a week, just to help get him out of the house. He was like a breath of fresh air, genuinely wanting the best for the both of us. Nothing seemed to faze him; he was so laid-back, he was horizontal.

So, it came as no surprise when he shared the news that he was planning to travel around India, bumming it for three months with his mates. I teased him that with his shoulder-length hair, he already looked like a hippy, and that we wouldn't recognise him without being clotted in paint.

It was a sad day for us all when the day finally arrived to say our goodbyes. Pat joked about promising to write in between being off his nut, and I promised to behave myself. I would miss his sarcastic, dry banter and calming influence, but I also knew that I would be forever grateful for everything he had done for Paul and me, who had never been closer.

I'd come across a flyer in the newsagents about a psychic convention. The event was free, but you had to pay for a one-on-one reading. Every time I saw the flyer in the shop, I was drawn in and intrigued.

Despite feeling content, I still had so many unanswered questions. I'd mentioned it to Paul who had initially teased me about it all being a load of nonsense but was more than happy for me to go if it would make me happy.

The place was packed out when I arrived; most of the seats at the front where the psychic would be doing a demonstration had already been taken, so I had to take a seat at the back. I couldn't afford a one-to-one reading so I was hoping I might get picked out during the main show but there wasn't much chance of that with me at the back.

That was until the final act came on stage. He was a tall, unassuming guy, holding a crystal ball. He claimed he could read people and offer premonitions by just reading the vibrations after someone had held onto the ball. He closed his eyes, then opened them, before stepping down from the stage, walking amongst the audience for the ball to guide him to who he was meant to read.

I couldn't contain my excitement when he stood beside me and gestured for me to take the ball from him; all eyes were on me as I carefully took the ball from his hands.

'Close your eyes,' he said. I did as I was instructed. 'Now feel the ball's energy flow throughout your body. Let everything go.'

I could feel the ball getting warmer, and my hands began to sweat.

'Okay, take some deep breaths.' He paused. 'Now, slowly open your eyes.'

He wandered back to the front of the stage, closed his eyes, and clasped both hands around the ball. He started to shake his head. He looked sad.

'Wow, my child, you have certainly been through the wars recently, haven't you?'

I couldn't believe my ears; it felt like he could see straight through me.

'I can see you have been hurt and let down by someone you trusted.'

I was tempted to ask which one? There had been so many: Paul, Dad, Pete, and other people I had thought were friends disappeared into thin air when things started to go pear-shaped.

'I can feel injustice. You want justice, but I'm afraid you aren't going to get it, not the way you think you will. You need to let it go, my child, and trust that those who hurt you will get their comeuppance.' He paused again. 'Do you understand?'

I wasn't sure, but I nodded compliantly.

'I can see someone around you. He sees you, the real you, and he's never given up on you,' he said, taking another deep breath and clasping the ball. 'I can see a house move. Are you planning on moving?'

I shook my head; Paul and I hadn't discussed moving house. We'd only just got the place nice; the kids were settled, so I just shrugged. He smiled confidently and spoke again.

'Well, I'm telling you, I see a move on the cards, and it's imminent, too?'

My thoughts turned to Paul. Perhaps he was going to end up in prison.

'I can also see you are going to commit, but not yet, mind.' He closed his eyes again before opening them.

'February, that's it!' he exclaimed. 'In February, I see you committing to the man you will spend the rest of your life with. I can also see you with a briefcase?'

I couldn't help but chuckle. Me with a briefcase?

'I can see you now, walking tall and proud, proud of all you have achieved. You are destined for greatness, young lady. I can see it. I can also see you entering a church.'

He'd had my full attention until the part about the briefcase and greatness but why on earth would I be walking into a church?

I wanted him to tell me more about the move and the commitment. I had many questions: I wanted to hear more about what he'd seen when he mentioned injustice. What did he mean? Who was he talking about? What did he mean by commitment? The only problem was that I didn't have the money to pay for a one-on-one to ask him.

I left the event feeling deflated. I could just about get my head around the part about injustice and the part about letting go; I got the part about what goes around comes around, but everything else was fucking nonsense; it didn't make sense. Despite Paul's initial reservations, he couldn't wait to hear all about what had been said.

'So, come on then, did you get a reading? Did they say anything about me?'

I had enough unanswered questions without trying to answer Paul's.

'Nah, you were right, it was a load of bollocks.'

# 151: Pent Up

There were already two missed calls from Sarah when I woke up the next morning. It had been four thirty in the morning by the time I'd got home and now it was after eleven. I expected that she wasn't pleased to receive my text saying I'd called an ambulance, but I hadn't felt like I had a choice.

The previous night's events were on my mind. It felt like a bad dream, but it was real, and I'd never felt so alone and scared.

Sarah agreed to go and see Dad and give me a break. Pat and the kids were out so I had the house to myself. I could have slept some more, but the house needed a clean and there was a pile of washing that I could no longer ignore. I dragged myself out of bed, made a strong black coffee before banging on some tunes and hit the housework with gusto.

I was happily singing along with Meatloaf to *Bat out of Hell* whilst filling the washing machine with clothes when the song *I Would Do Anything for Love* came on. The lyrics about hard days and the days that never end suddenly took on a whole different meaning.

My heart started pumping and I could feel myself welling up.

*'Oh I would do anything for love...'* The song continued.

The lyrics that had once made me smile were now hurting me; it was the final line that tipped me over the edge.

It was like all the pent-up emotions I'd been carrying around had been released as I finally erupted. I collapsed onto the floor and cried until there were no tears left. I didn't know how much more I could take.

Sarah called in the afternoon to report back from the hospital. Dad had developed an infection from the cellulitis. He'd got a high temperature and was severely dehydrated.

Sarah had mentioned Dad's drinking, but as far as the hospital was concerned, they were there to treat Dad's inflection and not his alcoholism. They had bandaged Dad's legs and were treating him with antibiotics and reckoned that he'd be well enough to come home in a day or so.

Part of me couldn't believe what I was hearing. It was like he was fucking indestructible. I would have normally gone to see him the next day, but I phoned instead. The nurse said they were happy with his progress, so I decided not to visit.

I just couldn't stomach sitting by his side, waiting for him to regain consciousness, and I didn't have the energy to argue with him about the position he'd put both me and Sarah into.

Part of me felt guilty for dumping Dad on hospital staff, but they didn't care about me or all the shit we had to deal with once they released Dad back into the community, so why should I care about them?

It was time for Sarah and I to have some much-needed respite. After all, I know it wouldn't be long before he was released, and the madness would start all over again.

# 152: Nothing Changes If Nothing Changes

The old Paul was back and the cracks in our relationship were starting to show again. The court date hadn't been announced yet and I put his mood swings and sulking down to uncertainty, but it was getting worse. I could tell that he missed the nights out, being one of the lads, but the fact was we simply couldn't afford them anymore.

I was happy; I could cope with being skint, but not Paul. He was still walking around in designer clothes and ordering things from the catalogue that we couldn't afford, and even though I'd got a job as a pot-washer in an Italian restaurant, it never seemed enough.

I would try my best to reassure him but nothing I said or did seemed to appease him. He was still accusing me of wanting him to get sentenced so that I could go off with someone else. It was unfair, as I'd never cheated but the idea of living without him was starting to look more and more appealing.

But it wasn't until he declared that he was going to start selling drugs again, 'just to make ends meet?' that something snapped. As soon as the words passed his lips, I felt sick to my stomach, stupid and gullible. I tried to reason with him, but his mind was made up. The lure to go back to his old ways had won.

'I've got nothing to lose,' he claimed. 'It doesn't matter if I get caught. I'm going down anyway.'

It was like the past few weeks since coming out of the hospital had all been an elaborate lie, and I had been stupid enough to fall for it once again.

At the school gates, I'd overhead another mother confiding in her friend. 'If it weren't for the kids, I'd have left him years ago,' she'd said, and the words were stuck on a loop in my head. Did I really want to stay with Paul just for the sake of the kids? I thought of Mum and how she'd stuck with Dad for ten years before throwing in the towel, and here I was, seven years in, stuck in an intolerable relationship. I couldn't last another three days in, let alone another three years.

I berated myself for blindly hoping that things would improve and that he'd change. In fact, it was me who'd changed. Something had shifted in me during my time in hospital, and I could no longer live a lie.

'Nothing changes if nothing changes,' my therapist had said. Suddenly I was sure. I had to act now.

Instead of going home from the school, I drove myself and Lauren to the housing office in town.

A familiar feeling of déjà vu hit me while I waited patiently to be called, but instead of being a pregnant sixteen-year-old girl, I was a twenty-two-year-old mother of two. I was eventually called into a booth by a young woman who wasn't much older than me.

'So how can I help?

'I need somewhere to stay.'

'Where have you been staying?'

I briefly explained that I had been living with my partner but couldn't stay with him any longer. I kept out the part about the drugs bust because I didn't want her to judge me.

'Do you fear for your safety? Is he violent?'

I couldn't lie. 'Well, no, he hasn't been violent, but...'

She cut me off, reached for a form, and said, 'Okay, let's do a homeless assessment with you, then we can discuss your options.'

'So, you are not fleeing domestic abuse?'

Once again I couldn't lie. Paul had never laid a finger on me, and I had no bruises, just a heart full of emotional scars.

'Do you have any drugs or alcohol problems?'

Well I didn't anymore?

'Have you been in prison?'

'No.'

'Do you have any mental health conditions?'

'No.' I'd been discharged from hospital, hadn't I?

'Unfortunately, you don't meet the criteria for priority. Are you sure there isn't anywhere else you can stay?'

My heart sank. I'd not wanted to go through all the gory details about the reason I needed to get out, but I knew it was time to come clean and tell her the whole back story. I had nothing to lose, including my dignity. I went through everything, including drug use, the drug bust, and being admitted to the hospital.

'You don't understand. I can't go back. He's not violent as such, but I'm scared I'm going to lose my mind again.' I suddenly realised that my whole body was shaking.

'Now, it makes sense,' she smiled sympathetically. 'You would meet the criteria for priority under mental health grounds, Tracey, but I'm afraid the only thing we could offer you is temporary accommodation. You might have to share with other women, and it could take some time before you are offered your own place.'

I didn't care where it was so long as I didn't have to go back to him.

It didn't take them long to find somewhere. It was supported accommodation, on Daresbury Avenue, opposite where my auntie used to live.

'Can you go now?' asked the woman.

'Yes,' I said. 'Tell them I'm on my way.'

I swooped Lauren into my arms and thanked her again before heading off to my new home. I had no idea what the future had in store for me; But I did know for sure that anything would be better than living a lie. I was done. There was no going back.

## 153: You Know You Love Me

I hadn't been in to see Dad for two days and I'd benefited from the break, but it was time to go back.

On the drive to the hospital, I replayed Friday night's events over and over in my head. Despite still feeling slightly traumatised, I knew deep-down that I had done the right thing by Dad.

However, I still couldn't shake the anger I felt towards the nurse, who originally dealt with Dad when we arrived. Ever since leaving him in hospital, the disdained look on her face had haunted me. I wished I'd asserted myself more, made her understand, but I knew deep-down that any opportunity I might have had to defend or explain myself had gone and I had to let it go. I just prayed I never had to cross paths with her again.

I had no idea what mood Dad would be in when I arrived. But I was ready to face the music and was ready to stand my ground. After locating the ward, I checked in with one of the nurses to get an update and some idea of how much longer he'd be in for.

I was gutted when she said that the doctor was on about letting him out the following day. Apparently, he'd responded well to the antibiotics and the swelling on his legs had reduced. I asked if he'd been showing off, but according to her, Dad had been the perfect patient.

I made my way to the ward where Dad was busy chewing the fat with the guy in the next bed to him. His new mate saw me first.

'Ey up, Frank, I think tha's got a visitor.' He lifted his newspaper as if it blocked out the sound of our conversation.

'Ey up, shugs. I wa' just talking about you.' He was beaming like a Cheshire Cat as I took a seat by the side of his bed.

'So, how ya feeling?'

Dad was still beaming. 'They've said I can probably leave tomorrow, which is a good fuckin' job, tha knows I can't stand these places.'

'Do you remember anything about why you were brought in?'

'Nah, I don't remember fuck. All I know is I'm ready for getting outta here!'

A wave of relief washed over me, at least he wasn't mad at me,

'Anyway, have you heard owt from the solicitors. I've just been telling Mick here, how they've been taking the piss.'

Mick dropped his paper. I knew he'd been earwigging all along.

'Yeah, I've said to thee Dad he wants to fuck em off!'

I could sense he was about to give me a lecture about what he would do if he was Dad, so I cut him off before he could.

'Ey, well, it's nearly sorted nah, but thanks for the advice.' I turned back to Dad. 'No Dad, I've heard nowt. I've been mad busy at work, but I will call em for ya tomorrow.'

I turned the conversation back to his admission. I needed to talk about it. 'So, you don't remember anything?'

Dad looked at me sheepishly. 'All I remember is waking up in 'ere, wi me legs all bandaged up.'

'So you don't remember gozzing on the staff nurse?'

Dad looked shocked, 'Fuck off! No way? I didn't.'

'Aye tha did, but don't worry, she deserved it. In fact, had you not spat on her, I might have clipped her myself.'

'That bad, eh?'

'Look Dad, I know that this is the last thing you wanted, coming in here an' all that, but I didn't have a choice, I was scared.'

Dad looked surprised. 'Why?'

'You really don't remember, do you?' I reminded him of the conversations about him dying at home and about mine and Sarah's pact and how I'd bottled it.

Dad went to squeeze my hand.

'I'm sorry, shugs. Tha knows I can be a stubborn bastard at the best of times. Anyway, how's work?'

I shook my head in disbelief.

'What have I said now?'

'Nothing, I just love how you can change the subject. You're becoming the master of deflection.'

'You know you love me.' Dad smiled.

One minute he seemed to take on board the severity of his situation, then the next minute, he was completely oblivious. I couldn't help thinking that a couple of days away from the drink had done him some good too. In fact, he looked better than he had in ages.

I wished that the hospital might let him stay in a little bit longer and I even thought about having a word with the doctor, but I knew they wouldn't. As far as they were concerned Dad was responding well to the antibiotics and there wasn't any need to keep him in unnecessarily and they would probably argue that they needed the beds, which would have been a fair point.

The only problem was, I knew that it wouldn't be long before he'd be back in again, I just didn't know when or what the circumstances might be next time.

# 154: We Are Done

My new home was at the top of a cul-de-sac and sat beside the block of maisonettes that I remembered from days of knock a door run. It was surreal being back there.

As promised, a support worker was waiting for me. She introduced herself as Michelle before escorting me into one of the ground-floor flats that had been turned into an office. Another lady was in the room, busy typing away. She looked up.

'Morning, love, would you like a brew?' She then turned her attention to Lauren. 'Now then, young lady, why don't you come over here? I have got a box of toys that are desperate to be played with.'

Lauren didn't need to be asked twice. She wriggled free from my grasp and ran into the corner of the room. Michelle took my arm.

'Come on, love, let us get the paperwork out of the way and have a chat.'

We took a seat at her desk.

'So, first things first, are *you* ok?'

'I'm not sure, to be honest,' I joked nervously. 'I'm not sure I've thought this through properly.'

Michelle sat and listened without interruption while, once again, I shared about the events that led me here. Part of me felt like a fraud. It wasn't like Paul beat me or anything.

I tried my best to articulate what it was about him that made him intolerable to live with. I explained how I felt like I was being brainwashed into believing that everything in our relationship was my fault; how I could never win and how I wasn't sure I had the mental or emotional capacity to carry on and that I just needed out.

Michelle reached over the table to take hold of my hand and looked me directly in the eye.

'It's going to be ok – I promise. It sounds to me like you have made the right choice for you and your daughters. Come on, let's get the paperwork sorted and get you settled in, eh?'

It was when she started talking about benefits that suddenly I lost it. Paul was going to go mad if I took my share of benefits away from him. As she pressed on with the paperwork, the severity of what I was about to do dawned on me.

'You don't know my partner,' I spluttered. 'He doesn't even know I'm here. I only left to take my daughter to school!'

Michelle was so sympathetic, even sharing that she'd been where I was fifteen years ago and that, while it hadn't been easy, she was glad she'd made the decision.

'I promise it will get better,' she said. And something about her made me believe it. She looked so together and normal. If she could do it, why couldn't I? I looked around the room. It all felt so surreal, like I was in a dream, only I wasn't. Then it hit me: I'd done it; I'd finally left Paul, and I might not have got much, but at least I wasn't alone, and I had Michelle.

My new home was directly above the office. It was small and basic, but in my eyes, it was perfect. It had it all: a TV, a small stereo player, a cooker, a small fridge freezer, a kettle and drawers and cupboards full of pots, pans and utensils. The only thing I needed was my personal belongings from home.

Michelle handed me the keys and with them, a book. 'Read this. It's the best thing I've ever read. It's like my Bible.'

I read the title: *Feel the Fear and Do It Anyway*. I couldn't remember the last time I'd read a book.

'I'll have a read later, but I need to get the rest of my stuff from the house. Can I use your phone please? I need to call my sister.' Sarah would know what to do.

'I can't believe you have left him, Trace. About fucking time, so come on, how come you have left?'

'I don't know where to start. All I know is I cannot go back. I'm done, it's over.'

'Well, if you want my opinion...'

I didn't, but I knew she would give it to me anyway. She'd never been a fan of Paul, not since she'd accused him of cheating on me.

'It should be him leaving the house, not you.'

'The house isn't even in my name. And anyway, he can keep it. He can keep the lot. It's all material shit. I can replace that in time, but I can't replace my sanity.'

'Have you told Mum yet?'

'I haven't told anyone. Fuck me, I only decided myself this morning!' I still couldn't believe it.

'Do you want me to come with you?'

'No, I just need you to watch Lauren for me. Can you call Mum and tell her what's happening? Tell her I'll call her later.'

Now I had to do the hard part.

As predicted, Paul was pacing the kitchen when I got home.

'Where the fuck have you been? And where's Lauren?'

'She's at Sarah's.'

'Why? You said nothing about going to hers. I've been waiting and sat here like a mug, wondering where you have been.'

'I haven't just been at hers. I've been down to the housing. I'm leaving you, and I'm taking the kids with me this time.'

Paul stormed over to me. His head looked like it was about to explode. 'Over my dead fucking body, you are.' He snarled before grabbing me by the arm. 'Have you gone fucking mad again?'

I pulled away from his grasp. 'I have never felt more saner than in my life.' I smiled 'It's over, Paul. I've had enough. I can't continue like this.'

'Like what? I thought we were okay.' He genuinely looked confused.

'Yes, of course, *you* always think we are okay. That's the main problem. Look, I just need to get some clothes for me and the kids.'

He grabbed my arm again, but it was more aggressive this time. 'You can't do this, Trace. You're not leaving, not after everything I have gone through for you.'

I yanked my arm from his grasp. 'Are you fucking kidding me? You have done nothing for me, you never have. It's always about you. It always has been.'

I grabbed some black sacks and started packing.

'So what? You are moving in with your Sarah?' he scoffed.

I stood up to front him. 'Actually, I've been offered a flat, but it's only temporary until the housing finds something bigger for me and the kids.'

'Where?'

'I can't tell you.'

'What do you mean you can't tell me? They are my kids!'

'It's a refuge. Men aren't allowed.'

Paul exploded. 'A fucking refuge! I haven't laid a finger on you *ever*, you lying bitch!'

'I haven't said you have!' I screamed back. 'Now, please get out of my way.' I pushed past him again. He followed me upstairs to the kids' bedroom.

'I knew it! I knew you would leave.' He leaned against the kid's bedroom door frame while I packed the kids' clothes. 'Who is he, then?'

I ignored him. There was no point in trying to argue or reason, because he would never be able to comprehend that it was him that was the problem.

'I bet it was you who grassed me up to the police.'

'Now, who's deluded? I'm leaving *you*, Paul, not to be with anyone else. I'm leaving because I cannot continue to live a lie. This isn't love; it is control, it always has been, and I'm out, I'm done.' I shoved past him to our bedroom.

'So that's it, seven years down the pan for nothing – I'm telling you now, Trace, if you leave now, there is no coming back; I mean it!'

Satisfied I had enough clothes, I tried to leave.

'Can I pass, please?'

Paul complied and stepped to one side then followed me downstairs. 'And what about the kids?'

'What about them? I would never stop you from seeing the kids, Paul. You know that! I'm sure we can figure something out. Don't worry about Danielle; I'm on my way to collect her from school. I'll call you when we are settled in.'

He followed me out of the house and watched me load the car.

'You are making a BIG mistake, Trace. I'm telling you, if you leave now that's it; we are done!'

I slammed the car door and started the car before winding my window down.

'Yes, Paul, we are done.'

As I drove away, I caught sight of Paul in my rearview mirror. He looked like an abandoned kid, standing there all alone. It was a pathetic sight.

However, any sense of guilt or obligation towards him had evaporated. This time, leaving Paul felt different because I was different. I knew I was never going back.

# 155: Back On The JD

Dad was back on the JD, and we'd fallen back into our familiar routine. Sarah would call in the morning before work, the district nurses would soon follow and tend to Dad's legs and bed sores and I'd pop in after work and spend an hour with him, chewing the fat, mostly small talk. Every so often, Dad would get an idea in his head about getting a pub again or setting up a new business once he'd cashed in his claim, but I knew it was all pie in the sky talk. I could never see him living a fully functional life again, not unless he stopped drinking, which was highly unlikely. But I humoured him.

I was at work one afternoon when the solicitors called to explain that the defence team had finally made an offer. I was excited for Dad as the solicitor went on to explain.

'So, the defendants have offered a settlement payment of a hundred and ten grand.'

I was gobsmacked. I knew that Dad had been expecting more but I was sure he'd still be happy.

'That's brilliant,' I said.

'The thing is,' the solicitor continued to explain. 'Your dad will only receive sixty, because he's had just shy of fifty thousand in interim payments over the past three years.'

I knew Dad wouldn't be impressed and I said as much.

'The thing is, your dad could challenge it, but it would mean him going to court, which will take even longer and then there is no guarantee he'll be offered more. My advice would be to ask your dad to take the offer.'

I was relieved but also shocked. I couldn't believe that he'd already had shy of fifty grand and had nothing to show for it. In fact, he was a shadow of the man he'd once been.

I decided to break the news face to face.

He was pleased to see me. 'Ey up, shugs.'

'Ey up, Dad. I've got some news for ya.'

'Go on then,' he prompted. 'Have the solicitors been in touch?'

'I took a deep breath. They have. Hundred and ten grand.'

Dad's eyes lit up. I needed to get in quick. 'But listen, you are only gonna get sixty, because they will have to deduct the interim payments you've already had.'

'Sixty grand!' Dad yelled angrily. 'Well, you can tell 'em to shove it!'

I knew he'd react this way, but this was no time for temper tantrums. I had to be firm with him.

'Look, Dad, you can refuse and take it all the way to court, but do you really want to do that? I mean all you will be doing is dragging it out more *and* there is no guarantee that you'll get any more.'

Dad reached for his tumbler and poured himself a large shot of Jack Daniels, this time minus the Coke. His hand was shaking, and it wasn't just the drink. I could tell he was really angry.

I left him to calm down and went to make myself a cuppa, praying he'd see sense and accept the offer.

When I returned he was sat forward, clinging onto his tumbler, staring into space. He didn't even acknowledge me coming back into the room.

I could see his mind working overtime. Every so often, he would shake his head before taking another swig of his drink. I just left him until he was ready to talk. Eventually, he snapped out of his daydream and turned to me.

'What do you think I should do? It's not two hundred and fifty grand!' Dad snapped.

'It's sixty grand more than you have now! I raised my voiced 'Fuck me, Dad that's a lot of money and you have already had fifty outta them! Personally, I don't think tha has done bad.'

Dad shook his head. 'The bastards have well and truly screwed me over. Look at me. This is all their fuckin' fault!'

He was well and truly on one and I wasn't about to try and reason with him; he'd lost what common sense he might have had years ago, and I wasn't in the mood to argue or listen to his rants.

'Look Dad, I'm going to get off, are you going to be ok?' As soon as the words came out, I realised how stupid they were.

'I haven't got a fuckin' choice, have I?'

He was right. He'd run out of choices a long time ago.

'Just accept the offer, ok?'

As I drove home, my thoughts turned to the log cabin beside the fishing lake that he'd been fantasising about for years and knew that it would never come to fruition.

The day's news should have been a reason to celebrate. Instead, I knew that Dad would use it as another excuse to drown out his sorrows.

# 156: Her Mind Is Made Up

By the time I'd finished unpacking, feeding, bathing and putting the kids to bed, I was emotionally and physically exhausted. Danielle had taken the news well, considering I was turning her life upside down. Paul was her hero, and it was a lot for her to take in, but I'd promised that it was just our house that was changing; she'd still see Paul, and Nan and Grandad, and wouldn't have to change schools. Now I was sitting alone in our temporary new home, which was like a hotel compared to the shitty bedsit I'd had to live in when I'd tried leaving Paul before.

I picked up *Feel the Fear* and flicked through the pages for some inspiration before starting at the beginning. It started by asking: *what are you afraid of?* There was a list. Number two on the list caught my attention: leaving someone and being alone. But what resonated with me the most was when the author talked about how she'd changed her own life. She explained how everyone experiences fear and that it is perfectly normal, but that the only way to eliminate it is to face it and do something about it.

I was hooked. I wanted to read more, but my eyes wouldn't let me. I needed sleep, so I headed to the bedroom. The kids were sound asleep. I kissed them both gently on the forehead, careful not to wake them, before heading back into the other room to sleep.

The next morning, Michelle came to introduce herself to the kids and to check on me.

'How did it go? Are you ok?' she whispered, once the kids were out of earshot, watching TV.

'It went better than expected, to be fair, but I know Paul won't make it easy for me.'

'Well, he might well try, but you need to remember you have your own mind. What you have just done takes courage.'

'Feel the Fear and do it, eh?'

She smiled. 'You started reading it? Keep going.'

I didn't know whether she meant with the book or with my future plans. Either way, her visit gave me strength to do what I had to do next.

First, I went to see Mum. We talked for what felt like hours, and there were many tears and hugs of reassurance. Mum looked me in the eye.

'You aren't alone, Tracey. Look at me, it took me loads of attempts to finally leave your dad and I'm not saying it was easy, but I can tell you, it was well worth it.'

She was right. It wasn't easy. I had to go back for some more of our things. But it was a lot easier knowing that my family had my back and knowing that Mum was coming with me.

There was no sign of Paul when we arrived. It was also a relief because it meant me and Mum could get in and out of the house without a fuss. Mum was upstairs, and I was rummaging in the kitchen drawer for the family allowance book when Paul walked in. It looked like he'd been out all night.

'What are you doing?' he asked accusingly.

'I'm getting us some more stuff.'

'Where have you been?' I regretted asking as soon as the words passed my lips.

'None of your fucking business. Remember, you don't live here anymore,' he snapped.

'I said, what are you looking for?' he demanded.

'The family allowance book?'

'You're not taking that as well?'

"Well, it's me who has the kids?'

'You have for now,' he threatened.

Just then, Mum appeared.

'Is everything alright? She smiled.

Paul started to stutter.' Er, er hi Gill, I didn't know you were here.'

'Yeah, that's not a problem, is it?'

'Er, er no, no Gill.' Then his lip started to tremble, and his eyes started to well up. 'Can't you talk some sense into her? I love her.'

'I think her mind is made up, Paul.'

He was sobbing now; it was a pitiful sight.

'What about the kids? She can't do this, Gill, I promise I'll change, please...'

Mum had never seen this side of Paul before, and I could tell by her face that she was starting to feel sorry for him. Mum dropped her bags, I thought for one minute that she was going to comfort him, so I stopped her in her tracks.

'Mum! Don't' I warned, before turning my attention back to Paul.

'Look, Paul, I have no intention of stopping you from seeing the kids. I can drop them around this afternoon if you want?'

But Paul wasn't interested. As soon as Mum had gone to the car, he was back to his old ways. The spell had been broken and I wasn't looking back.

Any sliver of compassion or respect that I might have had for Paul soon dissipated.

After all his declarations about loving the kids and his demands to see them, he always seemed to have an excuse not to see them when I offered. He'd claim he had something on, though I was never sure what he could be so busy with, considering he did nothing apart from selling drugs and getting off his nut.

But I also knew this was just part of his MO. He'd been the same when I left him before, trying to make things as difficult as possible, using the kids as pawns or making my life financially tricky in the hope that I would change my mind and go back to him with my tail between my legs as I had done previously. But this time, it wasn't working. It finally felt like I'd removed the rose-tinted glasses I had worn for years.

The more that I read *Fear the Fear*, the more I realised that I'd been looking at things the wrong way around.

The reality was that Paul was nothing without me. He never had been. It had been me who pleaded with my family to bail him out when he was homeless. It had been my family that rallied around us and set us up in our new home. It had been my family that offered him work, which he declined because it was beneath him.

Then there were all the risks I had taken on his behalf: ferrying his drugs, turning my hand to buying and selling stolen goods, cheque book fraud to make ends meet, or being hospitalized for drug-induced psychosis hadn't been enough for him. The only sad part was that all I had to show for my efforts and dedication was exhaustion and an overwhelming feeling that I'd been used.

# 157: One Day at a Time

Another Christmas was fast approaching and whilst everyone seemed to be looking forward to the festive season, I was dreading it. The solicitors were processing Dad's settlement, which could take up to another couple of months.

Dad continued to drown his sorrows in the bottle; it was like he'd given up. I couldn't help thinking that all the effort and patience sorting out the claim had been for nothing, because none of his plans for a new life would ever come to anything unless he at the very least cut down on his drinking. Which was never going to happen. Especially since the doctors at the hospital had explained that if he suddenly stopped drinking, he was at a higher risk of dying.

This time last year, Dad had been staying with Tracey. I'd even dared to think at the time that he might turn his back on the drink once and for all, but I'd been wrong. It had been a rollercoaster year of relapses, hospital admissions and near-death experiences.

He looked nothing like the man he'd been: his body was deformed from the fractured collarbone that stood no chance of healing properly because he refused to wear the sling, and he was so malnourished that he resembled someone who'd have just walked out of a concentration camp. I was finally coming to accept the fact that Dad was never going to stop drinking. It was easier than being let down by false hope.

The uncertainty and not knowing what would come next was the hardest to cope with, along with the never-ending feeling of powerlessness.

The only time I felt like I was making a difference was in my work. Since Dad had come back into my life, my work supporting families had gone from strength to strength. Which was ironic, because while I flourished, Dad deteriorated.

The local authority had agreed to invest more funding into support services for families affected by addiction. I was co-chairing a regional family and carers support network and I'd been asked to represent families and carers on the National Treatment Agency board.

I couldn't believe it when I was asked to speak at the government's new drugs campaign, aptly called FRANK. The irony wasn't lost on me. I even joked with Dad that they had named it after him, much to his amusement. Sometimes, I found it hard to put my personal experience aside and stay professional.

I'd thought that I had learned a lot after overcoming my own stint with addiction, but nothing could have prepared me for being on the other side. Sometimes I'd get pangs of guilt about what I'd put my own Mum through. I knew she resented the fact that I was still caring for Dad, especially when he hadn't been there for me when I needed him the most, but I would have to remind myself that it was in the past. All I could do now was focus on the future and take one day at a time.

# 158: You Should Be Proud of Yourself

Four weeks after leaving Paul, Michelle came to tell me that they'd found me and the kids a place of our own. The only problem was that I was terrified. As soon as I thought about moving, my hands started sweating and began to shake, anxiety and the old familiar sense of dread enveloped my whole body. For the first time in months, I had a sudden urge to go and score. I just wasn't ready.

Michelle suggested that I talk to the doctor who was on the premises that day to see if he could prescribe me something for my anxiety. But Dr Shrieka wanted to hear my whole history and before I knew it, I was telling him all about it. I just wanted some pills and to get out of there. The more I spoke, the more I was afraid that he was going to send me back to the mental institution. He was asking enough questions about it.

'Were you offered any aftercare after leaving the hospital?'

'Well, they did say I could call if I needed anything, but they couldn't help me leave Paul, and I haven't used any drugs.'

'Were you referred to a drugs service then?'

'Nope.'

He shook his head in disbelief. 'You know what, Tracey, from what you have told me, you have done pretty amazing to get this far without any support, but you do know you don't have to do it on your own.'

'Well, I have got Michelle, but then she won't be allowed to help me when I leave...' Just then, the prospect of not having Michelle released the tears that I had been desperately trying to hold back. 'The past few weeks have been really hard. The pressure of taking care of the kids and managing everything on my own is just too much sometimes. I feel like I'm on the edge, and I don't want to go back to using drugs.'

'How would you feel about speaking to a Community Psychiatric Nurse – a CPN – for additional support? A CPN can provide you with ongoing emotional support, help you manage your anxiety, work with you on coping strategies and provide a link between you and other support services.'

'Are they part of social services? I mean what if they think I'm failing? They might take the kids off me?'

'Now, now, they aren't part of social services, and nobody is going to take your kids away from you, do you understand?'

'But I don't want to feel like I'm failing. What will people think?'

'Look, Tracey, seeking help isn't a sign of failure. It's a sign of strength and determination that you want to get better, and a CPN can offer that extra layer of care, a safety net, let's say... And I'm here?' He gestured with his hands. 'We all need someone to lean on every now and then. Think of me as that brick wall you can lean on.'

'Thank you, Doctor. I am trying, I promise, I just want to make sure I stay on the right path for myself and my kids, so what about some drugs?'

'Well, you said it yourself,' he smiled. 'You have done perfectly well so far without them. Let's see how you get on with the CPN, shall we first? Then let us revisit it. And in the meantime...' He scribbled a number on a piece of paper before handing it to me. 'Here's the number to my surgery. Call any time and tell my receptionist that you're a priority. And again, Tracey, well done. You should be proud of yourself.'

# 159: Let's Get Thee to the Pub

It was Boxing Day morning. Pat was going out to watch the football and the kids were at their dad's. My dad had given me fifty pounds for Christmas, so I headed into town for the Boxing Day sales. It was a rare treat, having some alone time to browse the rows and rows of clothes in TK Maxx.

A black Jasper Conran cardigan caught my eye; it was unique and fit beautifully and was forty-five pounds. Normally I would have never spent that amount on a top, but Dad's words spurred me on. 'Treat ya sen, ya deserve it.' I decided to call and see Dad; show him what he'd bought me for Christmas.

He was laughing with someone on the phone when I entered. It was good to see him smile. Once he'd said his goodbyes, he turned his attention to me.

'What are you doing here? I didn't think you were coming today?'

'I wasn't! But I did as ya said and treated myself to a new cardy with the money you gave me for Christmas. Look!' I stood up and gave Dad a twirl.

'About time ya treated ya sen,' Dad smiled, but there was a tinge of sadness.

'Ahh come on Dad. What's up? Tha wa' laughing and jokin' a minute ago. Who was on the phone?'

He shook his head.

'Ahh, it was Malc, Tracey's Dad. He'd just called to wish me Merry Christmas!'

It was nice that they were still in touch. Tracey's relatives had become like family to Dad while they were dating.

'Ahh bless him.'

'Him and the lads are off out for their annual Boxing Day session. He asked if I wanted to join 'em, but of course I said I couldn't.'

The look of resignation and regret was written all over his face. I felt so sorry for him; then I had an idea.

'Where are they going?'

'A pub in Dronfield, why?'

'Ring Malc back and tell him ya coming!'

'I can't go like this.'

'Of course you can't go like that, but I'll help ya get ready, spruce thee up and drive ya over. If ya want to?'

Dad's face lit up like an excited kid. 'Really?'

'Yes, really.'

I threw myself into action. I wasn't going to attempt to shower Dad, that was Lawsons job, so I went to fetch a flannel and some soap and took it back into the living room.

'Here, you clean ya sen up and I'll go fetch ya some clothes.'

I'd never seen Dad move as quick, and his enthusiasm spurred me on. I went into Dad's bedroom. I grabbed some boxers and socks before heading for the wardrobe. I shook my head in disbelief – there were still clothes hanging up that were brand-new; they still had the labels on.

I reached for a pair of Farrahs and one of the crisp white shirts. Then I noticed Dad's old tan dog-toothed blazer. I'd always admired Dad in that jacket.

I showed him the clothes I'd chosen for him.

'But that's me feyting jacket!'

I couldn't stop laughing. 'Dad, trust me, tha not gonna be doing any feyting today, mate. Anyway, it's my favourite jacket, you always look reyt smart in this, so tha wearing it.'

I placed the clothes on the sofa beside him. 'Ere, put them on, whilst I look for a brush for ya hair. Giz a shout when ya decent.'

After a few minutes, he was ready. Dad had already changed his boxer shorts and into his trousers, but he was waving a pair of socks in the air, smiling.

'Ya gonna have to help with these though.'

The socks were a standing joke between me and Dad. I'd always swore I'd never kneel down to put any man's socks on. But this was different. As I tugged the socks onto each foot, memories from the past flooded back, of Dad sitting in his bath towel while Mum styled his hair and put his socks on before he went out.

This might be the very last time that Dad would ever have the chance to dress up and go to the pub like he'd done for the whole of his life.

After putting his socks and shoes on, I helped him into his shirt, then remembered the deodorant. I ran back to the bedroom and squirted some on his pits, before buttoning up his shirt. Dad was staring at me smugly.

'What are you smiling at?'

'You!' Dad chuckled. 'You're loving this really, aren't ya?'

Dad smiled. I couldn't deny it. Just putting some clean clothes on had made a world of difference. He looked almost human again.

'Right, you, stand up. It's time to put ya feyting jacket on.'

After helping him in his jacket, I stood back to admire my handy work. Despite the fact that Dad's clothes looked too big, he still looked smart.

'Ahh. That will do! Nah come on, let's get thee to that pub!'

## 160: Nobody

After reassurance from Dr Shreika, Michelle and Mum, I finally felt ready to take the next step on my independence journey. However, when I told Paul about the area we were moving to, he completely lost it.

'Down by Byards Leap? Are you fucking kidding me? It's rough as fuck around there, you are not bringing my kids up there!' Then he went on a rant, accusing me of being a bad mother for uprooting the kids from their comfortable and familiar home.

I could deal with his tantrums, but what I did find hard to swallow was his refusal to let me take any furniture with me, not even the kids' beds. He couldn't see that he was hurting the kids, not me. But his torment didn't stop there. I'd bumped into a couple of people since I'd left him, and the rumour mill was rife about how I was still mentally unwell, that I'd lost my mind, that I was still using drugs. The best one was that I'd left Paul for another man, which was, of course, untrue.

Most days, it took everything I had not to react to his rants and ludicrous lies, because I now knew this was more about him losing control, but it was hard.

Thank God for Mum. She'd been my rock. She had even offered to come with me to view my new home, which wasn't quite what I'd been hoping for. The place had been neglected and would need some TLC to fix up – a bit like me. But, once again, Mum and Ada came up trumps, and within a week, I had moved into a house furnished by other people's cast-offs.

Michelle had helped me sort out a grant, which just stretched to buying a cooker, fridge and double bed, and she'd also managed to get her hands on an old TV and some bunk beds for the kids. She promised that her door would always be open. She even insisted I take the book *Feel the Fear*.

I'd been reluctant to hand the keys back. That little flat had been my cosy, compact, safe space compared to my new home, which felt colder due to my inability to afford carpets.

But I had to keep reminding myself that whilst I might not have had much, what I did have was mine and that Paul couldn't take anything away from me.

Money was tight; I was still waiting for the benefits to send me a new child benefits book because Paul was still cashing them in and refusing to hand them over.

Of all the tough decisions, letting go of the car was one of the hardest. It was more than just a vehicle to me; it symbolised my independence and letting it go felt like losing a part of myself.

Mum, ever the voice of reason, reminded me that no one could take my license from me and that at some point in the future, I could save for another car. I would have taken it back to Big Mick, but he'd sold up, so I took it to a garage where I used to sell gear and couldn't believe that they only offered a hundred and fifty quid for it. He offered me some cheque books to sell as compensation, but I declined.

Handing over the keys and walking away from my beloved car felt like I'd also walked away from the last bit of identity of who I once was. Giving up the drugs had been easier than walking away from the lifestyle I'd got so used to. When I was out and about fencing, at least I was someone. But now, I was a nobody, just another single mother sponging off the state.

After two bus rides, I finally got home, and a letter awaited me. It was from the CPN, inviting me to arrange an appointment with her.

# 161: A Final Act of Dignity

As I drove to the pub, I kept on glancing at Dad sitting in the passenger seat. He was gaunt but he still looked so handsome all dressed up, sitting upright, looking ahead at the road.

He had always been such a proud man and despite all his claims about not giving a fuck what others thought about him, I knew that that he secretly did, and I knew he was touched that he'd been invited out with the Andrews clan.

Dad looked deep in thought, but I didn't want to break the illusion that everything was ok by asking him what he was thinking. None of this was ok, but for now, we were making the best of it.

We finally pulled into the pub car park. Conscious that Dad was still unsteady on his feet, I parked as close to the front doors as I could, before helping him out of the car. I tucked my arm into Dad's to allow him to lean in on me for support, but he pulled away.

'I'm ok, shugs.' I could tell he was determined to walk through the pub doors unaided.

I went to get the door. 'Ready?'

'As ready as I'll ever be,' he smiled before heading inside, straight to the bar.

Malc headed straight to meet Dad at the bar and offered to get us both a drink, but Dad was firm.

'No way, I'm getting these.'

Malc tried to protest, but Dad was firm. He held his hands up. 'Look, let me get these in, it might be the last chance I get, OK!'

A lump formed in the back of my throat. 'There's no point in arguing, Malc, tha knows what he's like!'

Dad threw fifty quid on the bar. ''ere, that should cover it.'

It was far too much, but nobody questioned it.

We made our way over to the corner where the Andrews clan were seated. Everyone shook Dad's hand as if this was a normal Boxing Day. It was just like old times, watching him and his mates banter back and forth as if they only seen each other yesterday, but I could tell they were shocked by the change in Dad. Thankfully, they hid it well and didn't let on or pry, though there were some playful jibes.

'Fuck me Frank, has tha been on a diet or what?'

Dad laughed. 'Aye, it's called a liquid diet.' He raised his drink to make a toast. 'Thanks for this, lads'.

Out of nowhere it hit me that this would probably be the last time I would see my dad in a pub. The only place he ever felt at home. I tried my best to hold back my tears, but I was flushing up, so I made an excuse to go outside on the pretence of checking in on the kids.

It was bitterly cold outside, but I needed it, I felt like I was choking on all the unspoken words. I gulped down deep breaths of fresh air in an attempt to calm myself down.

One of Tracey's uncles followed me out. I didn't know him that well, but I knew he'd known Dad for years. He nodded silently, acknowledging me, and stood beside me before lighting his own fag.

'Are you ok?'

I nodded.

'I cannot believe how ill he looks, kid. I mean I'd heard he was bad, but I hadn't realised how bad he really was.'

I took a deep drag on my fag. 'I know, it's pretty sad, innit! I'd hoped him getting back with your Tracey would have helped, but it didn't.'

Her uncle pulled me in for a hug and kissed me on the head before looking me in the eye.

'Everyone knows that deep-down he's got a heart of gold, but he's one of the most stubborn bastards I've ever met. But ya know what, you bringing him here today will have made his day, made his Christmas even.'

I knew he was right. I hadn't seen Dad this happy for ages, and the last thing that Dad needed was to see was my crying. Today wasn't about me, it was about Dad. I gave my head a wobble before heading back indoors.

Dad was in his element and centre of attention. The humour and the old sense of sarcasm was back in abundance. It was nice to see him amongst real friends again instead of the leeches who used to come round to the flat.

I listened as they all shared memories from the past. Dad regaled us with memories of his many brushes with the law. One of his claims to fame was that he'd never done any jail time. But he reckoned it wasn't about luck, it was down to him being clever and always being one step ahead of the feds.

No-one asked about his health. They didn't need to, but I was just grateful that they played along and pretended along with Dad that there was nothing wrong.

Dad didn't mention the claim or his previous grandiose ideas about how his windfall would change his life, in fact, I realised he rarely talked about the future anymore. Instead, he preferred to rehash memories of the man he was before the drink took a hold.

I had heard most of his stories before but today I was more than happy to listen to them all over again and pretend that just for that afternoon, I'd got my old Dad back.

A couple of hours had passed, and I could tell Dad was getting tired.

He was obviously thinking the same. 'Let's get off after this.'

After making our excuses to leave, everyone came forward one by one to say their goodbyes. There were handshakes, hugs, and pats on the back all round. No one said it, but everyone knew that this would probably be their last meeting with Dad.

On the drive home, Dad was deep in thought and barely spoke. We were sat at a set of traffic lights when Dad reached for my hand. He didn't look at me; he just stared straight ahead. He squeezed my hand.

'Thanks for today, shugs.'

I turned to him, but he was still staring ahead.

'No problem, Dad.'

He squeezed my hand tighter. 'No, I really mean it! Thanks.'

The lights changed and I realised that I'd given him the best Christmas present that money could never have bought – a final act of dignity.

I'd never felt closer to Dad than in that moment. We didn't need words but sat in silence enveloped by a sad feeling of warmth and, something I hadn't felt for so long; a feeling of calm and peace.

Over recent months, Dad had made it very clear that he had given up and accepted his fate. Whereas I'd still been struggling to reconcile to the fact that Dad would die from his addiction.

I'd been clinging onto the hope of a miracle, but I knew and accepted in that moment that it would never come. I knew I would cherish that moment for the rest of my life.

# 162: She Believed in Me

As promised, Cathy, the CPN, knocked on my door a week later. I'd expected her to turn up wearing a nurse outfit, but she was dressed casually, with the only sign of her professionalism being the lanyard around her neck. She explained that our first session was about getting to know each other. We talked for what felt like hours. Well, truth be told, I did most of the talking while she listened intently. Her face lit up when I mentioned that I had been reading *Feel the Fear and Do It Anyway*.

'That's one of my faves too,' she smiled. 'Have you tried the affirmations?'

'I have, but I feel stupid. *I am powerful and I am loved*. I don't feel it.'

Cathy nodded sympathetically. 'It's completely normal to feel that way at first. Affirmations can feel awkward because they're challenging your old beliefs about yourself. But the more you practice them, the more you internalise those positive messages. It's about reprogramming your mind.'

I sighed. 'I guess it just feels like I'm lying to myself.'

'It's not lying,' Cathy reassured me. 'Think of it as planting seeds. They won't grow overnight, but with time and consistent effort, you'll see changes. It's all about shifting your mindset from fear to empowerment.' I looked at her, feeling a glimmer of hope.

'So, I've got to keep at it?'

'Exactly,' she said. 'Keep at it and be patient with yourself. You're doing the hard work, and that's what matters.'

I decided as soon as she left to fully embrace the affirmations, despite feeling awkward and unsure at first. Each morning, I would stand in front of my bathroom mirror, look myself directly in the eyes, and repeat the affirmations aloud: *I am powerful, and I am loved. I am powerful, and I love it.*

I also started working on my vocabulary shift, replacing "pain" words with "power" words in my daily thoughts. I even started writing them on sticky notes and placed them around my house — in the kitchen, on my bedside table as a reminder. Throughout the day, whenever I caught a negative thought creeping in, I would pause, take a deep breath, and repeat the affirmations silently to myself.

Instead of focusing on what I had lost, I tried to focus on what I already had, looking for the positives instead of focusing on the negatives all the time. 'I should' was replaced with 'I could, I can'. 'If only' became 'Next time.'

Instead of saying: 'I can't handle it,' I replaced it with 'I can handle everything' and then reminded myself about how far I had come.

In the evenings, I would take a few moments before bed to reflect on my day and repeat the affirmations. Over time, I noticed subtle changes in my mindset and how I perceived myself. But also, how I perceived others. Paul had been right, Arbourthorne did have a reputation for being rough and the majority of those who lived around me survived on benefits, but they were still decent people.

As for Paul, he'd sometimes drop by unannounced on the pretence of seeing the kids, but I knew it was to boast. I'm sure he got a kick out of seeing me on my arse. All he talked about was his nights out. He'd make innuendoes about sleeping with other women, then ask me if I was ready to come back home. He would walk around the maisonette, making snide comments about the state of the place, but I tried not to let him get to me.

Every visit from Paul was a reminder of how far I'd come, and how much further I still had to go. His snide remarks and condescending attitude only fuelled my determination to prove him wrong.

The twice-weekly visits from Cathy had been doing me a world of good. During our sessions, we would agree and set some little goals to reflect on during her next visit. As soon as she left, I always felt a renewed sense of hope and belief that change was possible and that all the steps I was taking were in the right direction.

When Cathy asked me what my dream job would be, I laughed.

'At the moment, I'd take owt,' I joked.

'I'm serious, Tracey. If you could do any job, what would it be?'

I hadn't considered it before and thought about it. 'I would love to work with young people, ya know, those who are off the rails. I reckon I could relate to them.'

'So why don't you? From what you have told me, you would be great.'

'Are you kidding? I've already told you I haven't got any qualifications and anyway, I can't work—I've got the kids.'

'I know,' she smiled. 'But you could go to college.'

'What, back to school? I hated school.'

'Yes, but you're not a kid anymore. College is completely different. Lauren could attend the creche.'

'But I wouldn't know where to start.'

'I can help with that.' She smiled. 'I'll have a look and bring you some information about your options on my next visit, if you like?'

The idea of going back to school seemed daunting, almost impossible. But there was also a flicker of excitement at the thought of a better future.

I realised that Cathy saw something in me that I had long forgotten – potential. She believed in me, and maybe it was time for me to start believing in myself, too.

## 163: It Was the Least I Could Do

News came through in February that the compensation money would be landing any day in Dad's bank account any day. I went straight to Dad's flat after work to break the news. He wasn't as pleased as I'd expected him to be, considering it was all he'd talked about for the last two years.

He raised his glass. 'About fucking time! But it's a bit too late, innit?'

'Come on, Dad, don't be like that.'

'Look, you know, and I know that I ain't gonna be around to spend none of that money. Anyway, I'm not bothered.' He took a deep breath. 'I think it's time you sorted that will out.'

I'd managed to brush Dad's previous requests about sorting out a will under the carpet for months, but this time Dad was insistent. I promised to investigate it for him the following day at work.

I only stayed for another half hour, before making an excuse to leave on the pretence that I needed to get back home to the kids. But it was a white lie. I just had to get out of there. I'd secretly hoped that the news about the claim might miraculously lead him to have a change of heart about his future, but instead he was planning his last days. It was hard to take.

I set off in the car, with no end destination in mind, but found myself heading back in the direction of Meadowhead, my thoughts in overdrive. I knew I was going to end up with money from the claim, but I didn't want it. It felt like blood money.

I reached the same traffic lights where we'd had our intimate moment on Boxing Day and suddenly I understood that when he'd said thank you, he was really saying thank you for not walking away.

Dad's drinking had nearly driven a wedge between us and there had been many times that I'd felt like giving up or walking away, but I never could. For the past two years, I'd spent more quality time with Dad than I had in my whole lifetime, enough time for him to reveal a side to him I never knew existed.

It was almost like his alcoholism had helped reveal the side of Dad I'd always hoped existed but never saw. I'd learned to see beyond the tough exterior to vulnerabilities that he'd fought so hard to hide and protect. I now knew for certain that he'd always cared about me and my sister, he'd just never learned how to show it.

I used to think that the only thing we had in common was our shared DNA, but I now realised that we had far more in common. We'd both been in dark places, our own versions of hell. The difference between us was that I'd been able to climb out. It hurt knowing that I couldn't help Dad do the same.

I'd loved getting to know this other side of Dad, but it felt like I was only just scratching the surface. I needed more time. The thought of watching Dad signing his own will made my heart ache but there was no doubt left. We were nearing the end of Dad's life, and we didn't know how or when it might end.

All I knew for certain was that I would be there to support and care for him as best as I could and that I would sort the will out like he'd asked me. It was the least I could do.

# 164: No More Tears

Cathy had suggested that I enrol for a social sciences course. She reckoned the blend of psychology and sociology would give me a good grounding for a range of careers and she'd already established that Lauren could join the creche. I was interested but also terrified.

'What if I fail?'

'What if you don't?' smiled Cathy.

I was getting used to her positive spin and even though it was a big step, I agreed to give it a go.

I wasn't the only person who needed to be brave. Taking Danielle to school without a car was getting harder and, even though I'd promised she wouldn't have to change schools, I was going to have to break my promise.

When I broke the news, she wasn't happy. She was settled at her current school, and she liked her friends and teachers. Even when I explained that it would be nearer and that she'd make new friends, she wasn't convinced.

'I'm scared, Mum.'

I thought of Cathy and the advice she'd given to me. 'I know, chuck. Change is always a bit scary. Look at me. I'm thinking of going back to school – well, college – and I'm scared too.'

Danielle looked at me with wide eyes. 'You're going back to school, and you are scared?'

I could feel a lump in my throat. 'Yes, sweetheart. I'm scared of the changes and the challenges, just like you are. But I believe that we can do this together. We can support each other and get through the tough times. How about that, eh?'

She still looked uncertain, but she squeezed my hand. 'Okay, Mum. If you're brave enough to go back to school, I can be brave enough to change schools.'

'Thank you, Dan,' I said, feeling a mix of relief and pride. We were feeling the fear and doing it anyway together.

After contacting the school, my next priority was sorting out the family allowance book. I had finally had a response from the social, who'd insisted I needed to go in person to see them after Paul's repeated refusals to hand it over.

As I got off the bus on the High Street, I noticed the Cathedral, standing there in all its glory and I had the sudden urge to go in. Though I'd walked past it many times, it was the first time I'd really noticed it.

I stood looking in awe at the architecture, the intricate designs crafted out of stone by someone's hands many years ago. Thankfully, the entrance doors were open, and I dared to walk inside. The vastness of the building was breathtaking – it felt cold, yet warm and inviting at the same time. There were rows and rows of benches in front of me, with only a couple of people sitting silently with heads bowed.

Then, all of a sudden, like being woken from a spell, I looked around and questioned why I was there. I was in two minds to turn around and walk out of the building, when something inside of me whispered: *'It's okay, just keep walking.'*

To my right, I could see a set of benches separate from those in the main hall. The silence was deafening as I walked closer and sat on one of the benches. I looked up and stared at a statue before me and thought: *'Now what?'*

I suddenly felt an overwhelming sense of sadness. My mind took me back to recent events, and I shuddered at the reminders, ashamed of how I had hurt loved ones, but also hurt and angry towards those who I felt had let me down or who had hurt me.

The memories came in waves and gradually my emotions got the better of me, and I realised I was crying silently. I was glad I had chosen this part of the church, out of the way from the others so that they couldn't see my tears.

Alone in my thoughts, I recalled each memory that had brought me pain and heartache. As the pain started to peak, I was enveloped by what felt like two big arms wrapped around my shoulders and felt reassuring whispers, like someone saying: *'It's okay, let it go.'*

One by one, the memories came, heartache bubbled, threatening to overwhelm me, but just as it reached its peak, I heard the comforting whispers again: *'It's okay, let it go.'*

As well as the comforting words, it physically felt like someone, something, was washing away the pain and hurt that I had been carrying around for who knows how long. It felt like nothing I had ever experienced.

I stayed there until there was nothing left – no more tears, but best of all, the sense of sadness that I had been carrying around with me since walking out of the gates of Middlewood was no longer there. I felt lighter somehow and calm, like a different person.

Walking out of the church doors felt like stepping into a parallel universe. The hustle and bustle of buses and people going about their day-to-day business starkly contrasted with the serene and transformative experience I had just had. But I instinctively knew that everything would be okay.

As I walked to the social, I suddenly recalled my visit to the psychic months before. *'I can see you walking into a church; I can see you moving house.'* Everything he had said that sounded ridiculous previously had come to fruition. I felt a cold shiver as it dawned on me. *Fuck me, he was right!*

# 165: The Death Rattle

It had been a couple of weeks since the paperwork for the will had been completed, and Dad was going downhill. He barely ate anymore and our pleas for him to drink his Complan shakes fell on deaf ears.

'What's the point?' he'd say. 'I can't keep owt down.'

He was becoming more and more reliant on care. He'd reluctantly agreed to start wearing incontinence pads after having one too many accidents and now Sarah and I were helping him to bed each evening.

It was a monumental achievement, because he could barely walk and what should have been a two-minute task, took ten. And, of course, there were conditions attached. After settling him in bed, we would have to fetch him his tumbler of JD and Coke.

'Just to take the edge off during the night.'

Some nights after tucking him in bed, I'd lay by his side and snuggle up against him whilst waiting for him to nod off. Dad was more tactile of late, so much so that he would allow me to stroke his head or arm, often returning the gesture.

I'm not sure who got the most comfort, me or Dad. I could have laid watching him sleeping for hours, he seemed so content.

Sometimes he was so matter of fact about his death and even his funeral. He was insisting that he wanted to be buried and even requested that we inscribe his headstone with the words: 'Here lays Frank Thomas Ford, who couldn't give a flying fuck!'

I humoured him by explaining that swearing wasn't probably allowed on headstones.

'Well, if I'm paying for it, I can have what the fuck I want.'

The hardest part was leaving him at night and the fear that we would find him dead one morning was always at the back of my mind. But each morning, we'd find him back in his usual spot on the sofa, sipping his Jack Daniels and Coke.

I could never figure out how he would manage to get his fragile skeleton frame back into the living room. I would often joke with my sister that we should install a video camera just to find out how Dad bloody managed it.

Only one morning, he hadn't even made it to the sofa.

It was a Saturday morning. The 19th of March. Me and Sarah had decided to go visit Dad together, but instead of finding him on the sofa, he was sprawled out lifeless on the living room floor. My immediate thought was that he was dead, but when we rushed to his side, we could see that he was still breathing. Apart from his boxers, he was naked. He'd also soiled himself.

I could see the shame written all over his face. His whole body looked emaciated, apart from his stomach which was always swollen. The flat was boiling but he was shivering, in fact he looked freezing.

Sarah went to fetch a blanket to cover Dad. I wrapped it around him, trying to get him warm whilst Sarah headed into the kitchen to fetch a cloth and some soapy water.

Dad didn't say anything, but I could tell just by the look in his eyes that he was grateful that we were there. He snuggled into my lap and gripped my arm.

"Sorry, shugs, what am I like eh? I bet you two are fed up with this, aren't ya?'

But in fact, it was quite the opposite. I'd stopped referring to Dad as Dr Jekyll or Mr Hyde, because he was neither of them. The argumentative or nasty drunk rarely made an appearance these days and he was just a vulnerable adult that I loved and wanted to take care of.

I noticed his breathing sounded different, almost like he'd got some phlegm lodged in his throat that wouldn't clear, Dad was making rattling, rasping noises every time he inhaled or exhaled. I just assumed it would clear once we'd got him settled and sat up right on the sofa.

Sarah returned with the soap and water. She'd previously worked in a nursing home, so had better skills and confidence around cleaning Dad than I did. I was far better at talking to

Dad, reassuring him, cracking jokes and basically distracting him from the task at hand.

I could see Sarah was concerned, frowning constantly whilst she cleaned Dad up. She then mouthed to me silently.

'Something's wrong.'

But it was hard to talk what with Dad laid between us. Thankfully, it didn't take her long to change his pad and dress him in some clean boxers and a fresh sweater.

Lifting Dad wasn't a problem, weight-wise as he'd lost so much weight, especially over the past few months. The problem was trying to lift him without hurting his already fractured collar bone.

He reached out his hand for a lift.

'Come on, help me up, I'm going for a pint,' he said.

I shook my head and burst out laughing.

'I don't think you are, Dad.' Sarah chipped in.

'Why, it's only there!' He nodded in the direction of the chimney breast. But obviously there wasn't a pub in the living room.

Still, we finally managed to settle Dad upright on the sofa and left Dad smiling smugly to himself. I don't know where he thought he was, but he wasn't fully with us.

Sarah beckoned me to the kitchen, out of Dad's earshot. 'Something's not right, Trace. I have heard that type and sound of breathing before in nursing homes. It's called the death rattle.'

I pulled back. 'What the fuck's that?'

'It's a sign that he's near the end of life.'

'Well, what are we gonna do? Cos he's gonna go mad if we call an ambulance.'

Dad started calling from the living room.

Sarah turned to me. 'You go check on him and I'll call the doctor. I'll also call the district nurse and tell her not to bother coming.'

I went back into the room to tend to Dad.

'I need a drink.'

I knew he meant his JD, but looking at his chapped lips, giving him whiskey would have been like pouring paint stripper into an open wound.

'Tha can have some water first! Ok?'

It wasn't a question; it was an order. Dad shrugged his shoulders in defeat. I shouted for Sarah to get a glass of water, whilst I propped him up more so he would take a sip more easily.

Sarah came back into the room, mouthing: 'I've called the doctors,' before handing me the glass of water, but he'd barely taken a sip before he started to choke. The small amount of fluid made the noise on his chest even worse.

I snapped.

'Dad, you're seriously not well. We need to get ya to hospital.'

Dad glared at me. I knew the look well. 'Look I've told ya, I ain't going into no fucking hospital, alreyt!' He pointed to the coffee table. 'Pass me some of that chocolate, will ya?'

I was bemused. The chocolate had been on the table unopened for weeks and it had been the first time he asked for something to eat in weeks.

Sarah shrugged her shoulders. 'Well I suppose it's better than nowt.'

She unwrapped a couple of chunks and passed it to Dad. His face resembled that of a small child who tasted chocolate for the first time; he couldn't get enough of it! He didn't have his teeth in so all he could do was suck. His lips and fingers were coated in chocolate; he was completely obvious to the mess he was making.

The intercom buzzed.

'Wow, that was fast!' said Sarah, assuming it was the doctor but it wasn't; it was Abby the district nurse. Apparently, she'd been passing anyway and decided to call in. Sarah let her in, and they headed straight to the kitchen.

They'd been chatting away for a good few minutes before I drew myself away from Dad to join them. Abby listened intently as Sarah explained about how we'd found him this morning and about his breathing. Abby said that she'd be happy to give Dad the once over whilst we waited for the doctor to arrive. We followed her back into the living room.

'Morning, Frank!'

Dad acknowledged her with a grunt as she sat beside him on the sofa.

'Frank! How ya feeling?'

Dad snapped back. 'I might look like shit, but I'm not deaf tha knows, I could hear ya in the kitchen.'

I was just about to step in and apologise for his attitude, but she held her hand up, an indication she'd got it all under control.

'Look, Frank, you're not well. We really ought to call an ambulance.'

Dad shook his head. 'I'm not going nowhere.'

His breathing seemed more laboured and the gurgling on his chest sounded louder than before, and I instantly regretted attempting to give him a drink minute earlier.

Abby took his hand. 'So what we gonna do then, Frank?'

Dad looked at her then towards me and Sarah and nodded.

'I've said already, I just wanna die at home, wi me babbies. Is that too much to ask?'

She sat patiently patting his hand for what seemed like ages.

'No, Frank it's not. Leave it with me, ok. You've made your wishes perfectly clear.'

Abby was already familiar with Dad's previous history of refusing help, but after hearing Dad's wishes with her own ears, she jumped into action. We used cushions to prop him upright to help alleviate his breathing, but nothing seemed to work.

Each breath he took sounded painful. It was hard to listen to; he sounded like he was drowning. Abby had already tried to reassure us that Dad wasn't in pain and to be fair, he didn't seem distressed but, part of me still wasn't convinced. Abby had to leave to see another patient, but promised to call back after she'd finished her rounds later that afternoon. Now we were just waiting again. And this time it felt like he might finally have run out of lives.

# 166: I Might Just Do That

It hadn't taken the Social long to sort the family allowance book. I had hoped they could offer me back pay after going weeks without the money I was entitled to, but they said they would definitely be contacting Paul about his fraudulent behaviour. Not that he would be bothered; he was on a mission, treating every day like his last day of freedom. You would have thought he'd want to spend his "last days" with the kids, but the weekends were reserved for his nights out, getting off his nut or sowing his seed with any bird he could seduce.

Still, he was never too busy to call in unannounced at mine. He always claimed it was to see the kids, but I knew he was trying to catch me with another man; he still couldn't get his thick head around the fact that I'd left because of him.

I thought that by leaving him, it might get better, but the reality was that we were bound together forever because the kids. He was like a fucking annoying itch that wouldn't go away, and there was nothing I could do about it because I didn't want to be "that mother" who stopped her kids from seeing their Dad, and I knew he knew it too.

When he called around on one of his unannounced visits and broke the news that he was moving down the road, I nearly lost my shit.

Cathy kept telling me that I needed to set boundaries, but it was hard. He had an answer for everything. Apparently, he was just coming to see the kids, and he couldn't prearrange a time because he was too busy, and I didn't have a phone I just wanted to get away from him.

'You've got to stop letting him get into your head. Paul's trying to control you by keeping you off balance. You need to reclaim your space and your peace of mind.'

'I don't know how to, Cathy. He just won't listen.'

'Get a phone installed so he has to call before coming. Make it clear that he needs to respect your space. And if he doesn't listen, you need to be firm about it.'

'I've tried being firm. He just laughs it off.'

'You need to stay consistent and not argue with him. When he shows up unannounced, remind him of the boundaries you set. If he refuses to listen, you might need to tell him you are going to get some legal advice.'

I sighed, feeling overwhelmed. 'It just feels like nothing will ever change.'

Cathy placed a hand on my shoulder. 'It will, Tracey. It takes time, but you've already made so much progress. Remember, he's losing control because you're gaining your independence. Don't give up now.'

'I know this sounds bad, but I hope he does get sent down.' As soon as the words passed my lips, I felt guilty. I cupped my head into my hands. 'I can't do this.'

'You can, Tracey, and you are. I promise it will get better.'

'You don't know him as I do.'

'No, but I know you, and you're stronger than you think. Take it one step at a time, and don't be afraid to ask for help when needed.'

Mum agreed with Cathy about being firmer with boundaries and agreed to pay to install the phone so that Paul would stop coming by unannounced.

One of the first phone calls I made was to Pat, who was finally back from his travels around India. I was worried that he might not want to hear from me knowing I'd left Paul, but I needn't have worried. If anything, he was more concerned about how I was coping. I was taken aback when he said on the phone that he had brought me something back.

'It's not a lot. It's just a silver bracelet. I brought loads back with me,' he said, playing it down. 'I could leave it round at Paul's if you want?'

That was the last thing I wanted him to do. Besides I'd missed him, our little chats and his voice of reason, and I wanted to hear all about his travels.

‘Look, I’ve got to pop into town tomorrow. Our Sarah is looking after Lauren. Could we meet up somewhere?’

‘Okay, that works for me. I’m not back at work until next week.’

‘Nice one, it’s a date then!’

As soon as I hung up the phone, I started to berate myself. Why had I said it was a date? We were just two mates meeting up. I could feel myself cringing as I replayed what I had said. I half expected him to call back to cancel and make an excuse not to meet up, but he didn’t.

Pat was already waiting for me outside the pub when I arrived, though I might not have recognised him if it had not been for his shoulder-length hair, which was much lighter because of the sun. He’d also lost weight and had a tan to die for. Pat went to get the drinks whilst I found a quiet spot in the corner of the pub to chat.

‘Here you go,’ he said, handing me a small brown envelope. ‘It’s not much, but they were so cheap.’ I opened the envelope to find a silver roped bracelet. It might not have cost him much, but it was beautiful.

‘So, come on, tell me about your adventure.’

‘Ahh, it was amazing!’ He filled me in on all the places he’d visited in India, like the Taj Mahal, and how they’d spent some of their time staying with a family who had a pig in the back yard, which was also the family’s bin and how he lived off Aloo Gobi for most of the trip.

He said that despite the poverty, the people were some of the nicest, warmest people he had ever met, and the countless days spent on the beach drinking and smoking weed. And everything sounded so cheap! It sounded like bliss.

‘Hey, I still can’t get my head around you and Paul. You were sound when I left.’

‘We were, but then something just snapped.’

I filled him in on everything that had happened. I told him about my support worker, Cathy, and about how she had talked me around to going to college. Unlike Paul, he was fully supportive; in fact, he thought it was a great idea.

'Paul's gutted that you left him, ya know?'

'Well, he's got a funny way of showing it. And anyway, I'm not being funny, and whilst I really appreciated all the support and you playing cupid before you left, I don't need it now because I am never going back.'

Pat held his hands up. 'I promise I won't.'

'He'd hate this.' I gestured to Pat and me. 'Us meeting up. He still can't understand that I didn't leave him for someone else. He's as jealous and paranoid now as he was when I was with him. Has he told you about moving?'

Pat nodded. 'Well, don't tell him, but Cathy is going to try and get me rehoused somewhere different.'

'Look, Trace, I know me and Paul are mates, but you are my mate too.'

'I know, It's just... it's been really hard. He's still trying to control everything.'

'I do know where you are coming from. You've got to be firm with him, Trace. Set those boundaries and stick to them.'

'I'm trying. Cathy and Mum both said the same thing. That's why Mum had the phone installed so he can't use that excuse anymore.'

'And the college, that sounds like a good call. It'll give you something positive to focus on.'

'Yeah, I'm excited about it. But I just wish Paul would back off.'

I could have sat and chatted away for ages; it was just like when he used to visit me in the hospital.

'Look, I've got to go.' I gave him my number. 'Don't be a stranger. I know you're gonna be back busy with work and all of that, but if you are ever in the area, ya can pop in for a coffee if tha wants.'

Pat put my number in his wallet. 'I might just do that, Trace.' And with that, we hugged and said our goodbyes.

I couldn't stop looking at the bracelet he'd given me. He'd kept on banging on about it being cheap that he'd brought loads back for his other mates, but in my eyes, it still meant a lot.

# 167: So, This Is It, Then?

Nearly two hours had passed and there was still no sign of the GP. Dad had all on keeping his eyes open. Every so often he would draw a sharp breath, then not breathe for what felt like several moments. It felt like he might die at any time.

As well as feeling scared, I was starting to get pissed off. Abby arrived again before the doctor. She was just as frustrated as us, so she called the GP again and pushed the urgency. I was just relieved to have someone who was a professional there with us, someone who knew Dad well, but more importantly, had listened to Dad's wishes.

Finally, the doctor arrived. He gave me and Sarah a comforting smile, before sitting down beside Dad.

'Hi Frank, my name is Dr Thacker. I understand you're not feeling well but don't want to go into hospital, is that right?'

Dad turned towards the doctor and nodded.

'Can you tell me why?'

Dad glared at the doctor. I could tell he was getting angry, but didn't have the energy to kick off, not like he usually would have.

'I've already told her,' Dad said breathlessly, attempting to point his finger in Abby's direction.

'Look, let me check you over and we can take it from there, does that sound ok?'

He took his stethoscope out of his bag and rubbed it to warm it up, whilst Abby lifted Dad's top, exposing his bruised, emaciated back. I couldn't understand why he needed a stethoscope; it felt like the whole of Sheffield must be able to hear him. They then carefully laid Dad back down before checking his chest.

Dr Thacker sat beside him on the sofa and placed a thermometer in Dad's mouth before clasping Dad's wrist to check his pulse.

I looked on helplessly. I was convinced that the doctor would change his mind and call an ambulance, but I was wrong. Satisfied with his checks, he leaned towards Dad and looked him straight in the eye.

'Frank, this is serious. Do you understand? You've got what looks like advanced pneumonia.'

Dad was very sleepy and barely managed a nod.

'Now look, I'm happy for you to stay at home, but your girls here are going to need some support, ok?'

He turned to me, Sarah and Abby. 'Can I have a word please?'

I went to give Dad a hug before following them into the kitchen.

'Are you sure you won't go to hospital, Dad?' but he just shook his head.

In the kitchen, the doctor was issuing orders. Abby was to call for the Intensive Home Care nurses and Sarah was to phone an ambulance so that they could help to move Dad into the bedroom. Meanwhile, he was going to write a prescription for something to help with the fluid on Dad's chest.

'So, is the breathing part of the pneumonia?' I asked.

'It's end-stage wet respirations, which basically means he is unable to swallow his own saliva.'

'I knew it!' I shouted a little too loudly. 'I shouldn't have given him a drink!'

'Look, you weren't to know, but if he gets thirsty from now on, just keep his lips moist with a sponge. I can't guarantee that the prescription will work, but it may help.'

'So, this is it then? How long has he got?' I had so many questions I was finding it hard to take it all in.

'I'm afraid it's hard to tell. On average, a person usually lives for around twenty-four hours after the death rattle starts.'

'So, he's dying then?'

'Yes, I'm afraid he is. Look, all we can do now is make him as comfortable as possible. I'm not sure how long it will take for the Intensive Home Care nursing staff to arrive, but it shouldn't be too long.'

He gave us his number and then he was gone. We were alone again.

# 168: That Means a Lot

I hadn't seen Pat for a couple of weeks, but we would still chat over the phone. It was nice to have a friend again. But I had other things to focus on, like college. My start date was around the corner.

My old key worker, Michelle, was buzzing when I called into the office unannounced to tell her my news.

'Oh my God, Tracey, that's amazing. I did something similar! Honestly, you won't regret it – I'm so proud of you,' she gushed.

Her words made me blush but also made me feel warm inside. I couldn't remember the last time anyone had said they were proud of me.

Two days and two bus rides later, I arrived at Handsworth College. Lauren couldn't wait to get stuck into her new environment; in fact, she wandered off to play without even offering a goodbye kiss.

I quickly located my new classroom, which was just like the ones they used to have at Gleadless Valley. It was a mobile unit set aside from the main school building.

There was a group of adults who appeared to be waiting to start the same course. I stood back and sized them up and down, wondering if they might like me or if I would even fit in. Just then, a woman approached us all and apologised for being late. I was tempted to turn and run in the other direction, but then she caught my eye.

'Hi, are you here for the social science course?'

Giving me no option but to follow her indoors, I weaved through the desks to sit at the back of the class, away from prying eyes.

She introduced herself as Susan and then asked us to introduce ourselves. There was an older woman called Nora, who said she'd just signed up to 'keep the grey matter ticking over and meet some new people.' Next up was Julie. She was a nurse but wanted to go into social work. She looked well-to-do and a bit too posh for me. Next was Mark, who I suspected was around the same age as me. He seemed nice enough. He'd worked in retail for five years but felt unfulfilled. He'd been volunteering and wanted to pursue a community development job.

Then there was Pauline, a single mother to three kids, a boy aged four and two teenage girls. She'd only recently moved to Sheffield from Liverpool, then she declared: 'I just decided it was time to do me!' which was greeted with some chuckles from some of the other women.

I was instantly drawn to her. I loved her accent and infectious smile and was intrigued to know what might have brought her to relocate to Sheffield.

There was another guy who was in his early forties and had recently been made redundant from his job in manufacturing. Tom saw this course as a chance to reinvent himself and explore new career paths.

I'd been so engrossed with everyone's stories that I hadn't realised it was my turn to talk. I took a deep breath and introduced myself.

'Hi, I'm Tracey. I decided to join this course to create a better future for myself and my kids.' I shrugged my shoulders. I wasn't sure what else to say, but thankfully, judging by the nods and encouraging smiles, it was enough.

The rest of the morning was spent with Susan going over the course programme. Then she handed out a recommended reading list of books to help us with the course before the first break. I was just about to check on Lauren when Pauline approached me with a friendly smile.

'Hey, Tracey, fancy going to the library this lunchtime? Give us a chance to get the first dibs on the books before they nab em?'

'Yeah, that sounds great. I'd love to. I'm just heading to the creche to check on my daughter.'

'Ooh me too,' she said.

We checked on the kids and then headed to the library. Neither of us had a clue where to start looking and we teased each other for being old and thick, then finally, after some guidance from the librarian, we walked out with our newly acquired books. I loved her self-deprecating sense of humour and how she didn't take herself too seriously, but I sensed that behind all the smiles, she, too, had a story.

She sat outside with me while I had a fag and told me how, just like me, she'd jumped into her first relationship after leaving school and went on to have two daughters with him. She said he was a lovely bloke but that they'd grown apart.

Then, she'd met the father of her youngest. He sounded a lot like Paul in his jealous, controlling, and manipulative ways, but unlike Paul, he wasn't afraid to use his fist.

I was struck by her courage and the lengths she'd gone through to leave him, which included moving to Sheffield. I admired and appreciated her honesty and surprised myself when I started to open up about my own story.

We were like two kindred spirits, both on a mission to reinvent and better ourselves. When we went back to the classroom, I moved seats to sit next to her at her request.

I couldn't believe that this woman had been a stranger before that morning, yet she already felt like that big sister I'd never had, and I knew in my gut that we would be firm friends.

My first day at college had gone better than expected, and I was just telling Dan about it whilst cooking tea, when Pat phoned to ask how my day had gone. He said he would be in the area, and wanted to take me up on my previous offer of a coffee. I rushed to get the kids to bed. I was so excited to tell him all about it.

When he arrived, he offered to take his shoes off.

'I wouldn't bother. There are no carpets to ruin,' I joked. 'Don't mind the house,' I said apologetically whilst ushering him into the living room. I wondered what he would make of it.

'I've come to see you, not the house, Trace,' he said, which helped put me at ease. Pat sat at the dining table while I made us a cuppa.

'It's big enough, innit,' he said, glancing around.

'Yeah, it's a decent size. I'm still waiting to hear back from the council about the move. I was going to decorate, but I honestly don't see the point if there's a chance I'll be moving again.'

'So, how was your first day at college?' he grinned.

'Brilliant,' I said with enthusiasm. I filled him in about Pauline, how we'd both made a pact to help each other out, and how she'd offered to pick Lauren and me up to go to hers to study while the kids played.

'Sounds like you've made a good friend there,' he commented.

'Yeah, she's great. We're like kindred spirits,' I said. 'What about you, Pat? How's work been since you got back?'

Just then the phone rang; it was Paul.

'So how has ya first day at school gone?' There was a sarcasm to his voice I didn't like.

'It gone ok actually, what do you want, Paul?'

'Can't I call to speak to you, see if you're ok?

'Come on Paul, what do you want?'

'I wanna speak to the kids,' he demanded.

'They're in bed.'

'So what, do you think you're better than me now!' He was off now, ranting about how I was a lousy mother and how he'd make sure the kids knew who the real me was.

I pulled the receiver away from my ear. Paul was utterly oblivious that Pat could hear his every word. The look on Pat's face said it all.

'Look Paul, I'm hanging up.'

He was still screaming threats down the phone until I hung up.

I turned to Pat. 'Sorry about that.'

'Wow!' He shook his head in disbelief. 'That's a side to Paul I've never seen before.'

'Welcome to my world,' I shrugged. 'Anyway, can we forget about that and change the subject? So how's work been?'

'It's been tough, to be honest,' he admitted. 'Getting back into the routine after being away for so long has been challenging, but I'm getting there.'

'Well, I'm glad you're back. I've missed our chats,' I confessed.

'Me too, Trace. It's good to catch up and see how well you're doing,' he said, smiling.

As the evening went on, the conversation flowed effortlessly. Pat's presence was comforting, and it felt like old times. It was a perfect way to end an already great day, and the best part was after Paul's phone call, his name didn't come up in our conversation once.

'I'm proud of you, Trace,' Pat said as he was about to leave.

A feeling of warmth spread through me.

'Thanks, Pat. That means a lot.'

'Anytime. And don't hesitate to call if you ever need anything,' he said with genuine sincerity. I was lucky to have a mate like him.

# 169: Can You Hurry, Please?

It had taken me and Sarah a couple of minutes to compose ourselves, before we kicked into action. She called the ambulance as instructed, then called home to tell her partner John what was happening.

I did the same with Pat, then realised I would have to call the rest of the family. A feeling of Deja vu descended on me as I made the call to Uncle Mick. As I relayed what had happened and what the doctor had said, I could feel myself starting to panic. Up until now I'd been calm, but the severity of what was happening was starting to kick in.

'Look Trace, you go take care of ya Dad and I'll let the rest of the family know. Have they said how long he's got?'

'How long's a piece of string? They said he was dying before, and he came round, didn't he? I just don't know what to think, but it's bad – his breathing is horrendous.'

I could feel my hands starting to shake; it was like a bad dream. Thankfully the ambulance crew arrived while I was talking.

'Sorry, Uncle Mick. I've got to go.'

By now, Dad was in and out of consciousness and unaware of what was happening around him, which was a relief, but it was also scary. *Was this really it?*

We'd tucked Dad into bed, propped up by pillows to ease the noise radiating from his chest. It wasn't getting any quieter; in fact, we could hear him from the living room. I'd never felt so powerless, helpless, then I remembered the prescription.

'Look, you stay with Dad and wait for the nurse, and I'll get the prescription.'

The only chemist open was the Wicker Pharmacy, which was surprisingly busy. I handed the prescription over to the first member of staff that was free.

'Can you hurry, please? It's for my dad. He's dying.'

'I'll try and get it processed as fast as I can, but as you can see, there are a few people already waiting.'

'Yeah, but they're not dying, are they?' I snapped rather a little too loudly. I could sense everyone's eyes bearing on me, and suddenly shame enveloped me as I tried my best not to break down and cry.

My emotions were nearly getting the better of me, when a guy from behind the counter shouted, 'Frank Ford.'

I rushed to the desk.

'Yes, that's for me.'

He had a confused look on his face. 'Can I confirm his date of birth?'

I couldn't remember my own, let alone Dad's 'Why?'

'Well, this is a child's dose?'

My anger started to get the better of me.

'Look, I haven't got a clue what he has sent me for. All I know is that my dad is back at home dying and I'm stood here arguing with you. Can you just process it?'

Once again, I could feel everyone's eyes boring into me, but this time I didn't give a fuck. All I was bothered about was getting the fucking prescription and getting out of there as fast as I could

# 170: I Need to Tell Him

I'd started to look forward to my college days, not just for learning but for being around different people. Pauline and I had become firm friends and, more surprisingly. we'd both done well in our first assignments, which was encouraging.

What was even more encouraging was when one of the course tutors approached me one day after class, asking me if I had ever considered counselling. At first, I thought she meant I needed counselling, but then she explained that she was about to start a new counselling course and that she thought I'd be a great counsellor, based on my past lived experience. It was a private course, but she reckoned she could get me on. I jumped at the opportunity.

For the first time, I felt things were moving in the right direction. I'd even caught up with Donna, who had a new bloke. She'd invited me round for coffee so she could tell me all about it.

'Sooo, what's Scott said?' I asked.

She shrugged her shoulders. 'He's ok with it. He's seeing someone too.'

Part of me felt envious because I knew that even if Paul were dating someone else, he'd still blow a gasket if he thought I was.

'That's what you need,' she declared.

'What?'

'A man!'

'Fuck off, that's the last thing I need.'

'What about Pat?'

'What about him?'

'Well, he seems to be visiting more.' She grinned.

She was right; Pat had called around a couple more times since his first visit, but I didn't see him in that way. Until suddenly I did.

I'd been relaying my conversation with Donna a couple of nights later with Pat when it happened.

'You know, Trace, I've always admired your strength,' he said.

'Thanks, Pat. That means a lot,' I replied, feeling a blush creep up my cheeks. Without thinking, I leaned in, and before I knew it, our lips met and for the first time in my life, it felt right.

It had felt so right that we'd ended up in bed together having sex, and though it had been wonderful at the time, the next morning, I was a ball of anxiety, worrying that he would think I was a slag and that he would never seriously be interested in me, not with all my baggage.

My fears were confirmed when he called me later that evening.

'I can't do this Trace. Look, I do like you, but I have been working with Paul, and I've been riddled with guilt all day. We can still be friends though…'

I cut him off. 'It's ok, I understand. Look, let's try and forget it happened, eh? Listen, I have got to go. I'll call ya tomorrow.'

As soon as I replaced the receiver, my heart sank. I hadn't realised how much I liked him until that moment, and the reality was that I'd just ruined one of the few friendships I had. It hurt. It wasn't long before I found myself bawling my eyes out.

It felt like I'd had a taste of something special, only to have it snatched away from me. And once again, it was all because of Paul, and the biggest irony was that he didn't even have a fucking clue.

Pat had tried insisting on the phone that we could still be friends, but how could we? Not after what had happened between us. I couldn't believe how stupid and naive I was even to think that someone like Pat would ever see anything in me.

Donna was the only person who knew about Pat. She listened as I cried my eyes out, reliving what had happened.

‘Look Trace, I know it might not feel like it now, but maybe it is for the best.’ She paused. ‘And anyhow, perhaps Pat isn’t the one for you?’

She was right. I was just another single mother with two kids and a toxic ex in tow, whereas Pat had no strings. It would never have worked. I’d just about composed myself when, a couple of hours later, the phone rang again. It was Pat.

‘It’s me, I’ve been thinking, and I’ve had a change of heart.’

I was speechless and couldn’t believe my ears.

‘Trace, are you still there?’

I was, but I didn’t want him to hear me crying.

‘I am,’ I whispered. ‘Look, you don’t have to do this. It’s ok. I get it.’

‘No, you don’t get it! I do want it. I do want to be with you, Tracey, but I can’t go on seeing you behind Paul’s back. I need to tell him.’

# 171: Let's Go Home

It was around teatime when the intensive care nurse arrived. Her name was Rosie and, unlike the other nurses who used to come to tend to his bed sores, this lady wasn't going anywhere. She would be with us until Dad took his last breath. The first thing I did was hand over the prescription, whilst explaining about what the pharmacy had said. She smiled, as she took the prescription from me.

'What's the point of antibiotics if they aren't going to recover?' I asked

'Some GPs give them to ease symptoms. Everyone's different I suppose.' She shrugged. 'Come on, why don't you introduce me to your dad?'

I was in awe of Rosie. She was a special kind of person to be able to parachute herself into a family home, with people she had never met before, to help care for someone who was dying. And she wasn't just there for Dad. Rosie listened intently as me and Sarah talked about Dad. We laughed and cried about shared memories, and she didn't flinch when we talked about the darker side of Dad.

'He sounds quite a character,' she mused, but not in a judgmental way.

Early in the evening, Dad had started to cough up the same green phlegm that he'd coughed up last time they'd told us he had days to live. Part of me wondered if Dad would recover like the last time. I asked Rosie, but the look on her face told me he wouldn't.

'Why don't you two go and get some fresh air, eh? It will do you good.'

I remembered that we were running short on milk, so we decided to head to the petrol station on City Road. It was late, and the streets were dark and tranquil as we walked. I imagined people sleeping tucked up in their own beds, whilst Dad was back at the flat about to take his last breath.

'I still cannot believe this is happening,' I said.

'I know, but I can assure you it is.'

'I know, but there is so much that I want to say...' I broke off, choking on my words.

Sarah grabbed hold of me. 'It's going to be ok, I promise.'

I felt pathetic. I was the older sister. It should have been me comforting her, but she'd always been the stronger one, especially when it came to Dad.

'Come on, it's fucking freezing,' she joked. 'Let's head back.'

I could hear Dad from the bedroom as me and Sarah walked back into the flat. He sounded like a helicopter ready to take off.

'Is that normal?' I asked Rosie.

'Honestly, it sounds worse than it feels. He won't feel a thing.'

Dad hadn't opened his eyes for hours. It all felt surreal, like a bad dream. He'd been asking us to take him to the pub earlier, and now there was nothing.

I turned to Rosie. 'I wished I'd told him I loved him while he was semi-conscious. I hate the thought of him dying thinking we didn't care.'

She smiled sympathetically. 'Well, from what you have told me, it sounds like everything you both did was out of love and look, you made sure he got his final wish to die at home.' She paused. 'It's not too late to tell him. Why don't you spend some time alone with him? I'll leave you to it.'

I walked around to the other side of bed and snuggled up beside Dad, entwining my fingers into his.

'I still can't believe this is actually happening, Dad.'

I looked at his eyes, hoping for a flicker, a sign that he might be able to hear me, but there was nothing. The only movement was from his chest that seemed rise and fall unnaturally.

'Ya know what, Dad, I reckon we have both been pains in the arse in our lifetimes, but I would never trade you. I hope you know that. I know you fretted about being a burden, but you never were. I'll always be grateful that you came back into my life, because if you hadn't, I would be able to be here with you now and I wouldn't have ever got to know you, the real you, the real Frank Ford that hid behind all bravado. We have had some laughs, though! Can you remember the time you covered your fish and chips with sugar instead of salt? I can still see ya face nah and God, how we laughed. And what about them stupid Deidre Barlow glasses that ya nicked off some poor fucker in the hospital? I think I am going to take them home with me when you have gone. I promise to stay in touch with Tracey and Malc; I know you would want that, and I promise me and Sarah will give you the send-off you deserve. None of that God stuff, and I guess you will be happy to see ya mam and dad again, eh? I can see them now, standing propping up the bar with a pint waiting for ya.'

I nestled my head into his neck and stroked his hand, hoping that he might at least feel some of the love radiating from my own. I didn't want to ever leave his side. I wanted to be there with him whilst he crossed over...

'Trace, Trace!'

It was Sarah. I must have fallen asleep and Rosie needed to clean Dad up. I'd slept through him coughing up more phlegm.

'Look, you two look shattered and I'm sure your dad wouldn't want you both to see him like this. Why don't you go home and get some sleep? I promise I'll call if there's any change.'

Sarah looked like I felt. 'Come on Trace, Rosie's right. Dad isn't going anywhere yet. Let's go home.'

# 172: Finally, Life Was Good

As expected, Paul didn't take the news well that me and Pat were an item. He managed to tell everyone who would listen that we'd been seeing each other all along, trying to elevate his victim status. But this time, I wasn't bothered because Pat and I knew the truth, and that was all that mattered.

I'd never set out to get into a relationship so soon, but Pat and I were different. We were a team. Instead of discouraging me, he encouraged me and never put me down. Our relationship was built on trust instead of constant jealousy and I felt like I could share my deepest fears without worrying that he might use them as ammunition against me later.

We didn't live in each other's pockets but when Pat wasn't working or out with his mates, he'd be round at mine. He put me on his insurance so I could use the van when he wasn't using it for work and he was more than happy to keep an eye on the kids when I got myself a part-time job, cash in hand, working at Manor Top Chippy. It wasn't much, but it felt like I was slowly gaining back some of my lost independence.

College was going great too, and I'd also started the introductory counselling course and was loving it.

I would often pinch myself to ensure it wasn't a dream; I never knew that a relationship could be so easy. But Pat just wanted what was best for me and the kids. By the time the Council had found me a new tenancy a few months later, it felt right for him to move in, which meant a fresh start for all of us.

Paul's day in court arrived, and everyone, myself included, was shocked when he was handed two and a half years in Ranby prison. I initially agreed to take the kids on prison visits to see their Dad, but before long, I had to insist that someone else took them. The emotional toll of having him profess his love as if nothing had ever happened was too much for me. It felt like I was being dragged back to a past life I had been trying so hard to move away from.

In other ways, I was moving forward though. A guy on my counselling course was the programme manager for a structured daycare centre called Kickstart for people struggling with addiction, mainly heroin. Just like Dr Shreika before, he'd been amazed by how well I had managed without the support of a drug service, and one day, he asked me if I'd like to volunteer for the project. I felt flattered at the compliment and the opportunity. But my original aspiration or goal when starting college had been to work with young offenders, not drug addicts.

'Yeah, but I know nothing about Heroin,' I said.

'Doesn't matter what you get hooked on, addiction is an addiction,' he said. 'And from what I know about you, I reckon you'd be a natural.'

'Fuck it, go on then.' I grinned.

He told me where to meet him, and I couldn't believe my eyes when I located the building. It was the exact same place I'd stood outside as a naive sixteen-year-old, fresh out of school, about to get the news that I was pregnant. Now, I was standing there six years later and six years wiser and about to start another new adventure.

I'd expected to be helping other people, not sharing my story but when I sat alongside Leigh as the group of newly detoxed individuals did their daily check-in, I was moved to join in. There were twelve people in total: two women and the rest men, plus me and another new volunteer called Mick Holmes.

Leigh asked them to share what they were there for and how long they had been clean, for the benefit of me and Mick. Some people went into more detail than others, but their honesty struck me immediately.

Then it was Mick's and my turn. Mick shared how he'd started naively using and selling Es and amphetamines before moving on to heroin. He had the flash cars and was earning plenty of money – it sounded like he'd been doing well for himself until he started dabbling with heroin. It wasn't long before he was hooked. He'd done various stints in prison before being offered a place in rehab as an alternative. He joked about how he'd accepted the placement, thinking it would be a piece of cake, but soon realised it was a life-changing experience, including following a 12-step programme. I didn't know what a 12-step programme was, but whatever it was, it seemed to have worked for him.

Then it was my turn. My past wasn't something I talked about much; if anything, it was something I'd been trying to forget. But listening to everyone else open up, it felt safe to tell my own story. I wasn't sure what I said, but I could feel myself waffling. Whatever I shared must have resonated, judging by the nods I got from others in the room.

After a quick break, everyone gathered back in the room. Leigh was leaning against a flip chart, which featured a diagram labelled *The Cycle of Change*, and I was instantly intrigued.

He explained how the Cycle of Change was a framework they referred to throughout the programme and how it described the stages people typically go through when attempting to change addictive behaviours.

As I listened to the members of the group identifying their own patterns of behaviour, I started to understand my own. I stared at the flip chart, and for the first time in my life, I could visibly see myself at various stages – the denial, hoping and praying that Paul might change, the years of flipping between contemplating and preparation, but never having the guts to take any action because I'd tried to leave him previously and failed.

My using had become, at the time, a perfect solution to what was a very toxic relationship, not just with Paul, but with myself. What resonated throughout the session were the shared stories of living a lifetime of never feeling good enough.

People openly shared that they had grown up feeling like the odd one out or that something was wrong with them. Like me, some had endured parental separation and feelings of parental rejection and got into unhealthy relationships.

I'd learned more about myself in the past few hours than I had over the last few months, and I wanted more. Kickstart wasn't just a sanctuary for people in recovery; it became my sanctuary, a safe space where I could be myself and unpick my past and all the limiting beliefs I had acquired over the years.

Week by week, I learned more about myself and my patterns. I was like a sponge; I started to uncover patterns of self-sabotage and how my low self-esteem contributed to my addictive behaviours, including people-pleasing.

I became aware of my tendency to avoid confronting my feelings and how this had impacted me in the past and present. I soon concluded that I wasn't really addicted to the drugs but to the feeling they gave me; I was using drugs to escape the emotional pain I was experiencing at that time in my life.

It wasn't long before my one day a week of volunteering turned into three days a week and eventually a job as a project worker. Helping others on their recovery journey wasn't just fulfilling; it felt like a calling. It was as if all my past experiences had led me to this point, to be here, making a difference, to help people find themselves, just like I had been trying to do.

Finally, life was good, and I was where I was meant to be.

# 173: The Last Time

The ringing of the phone woke me. It was Rosie.

'Hi lovely. I think you and Sarah should come over.'

I looked at the clock, it was 7.30am. I jumped straight out of bed, rang Sarah, got dressed and drove to hers as fast as I legally could. My mind was in a spin. I'd never seen anyone die before and I had no idea what to expect. *Would he open his eyes before taking his last breath? Would he say something?*

Sarah was already standing outside waiting for me.

As soon as she got in the car, I turned to her. 'You watch, when we get there, he'll be sat up in bed right as rain, trying to chat Rosie up!'

But he wasn't, because Rosie was standing on the balcony and waving frantically.

'Come on, girls, come quick!'

But as soon as we walked in the room, we knew he'd already gone. I couldn't believe he'd gone without me. His eyes were open, and his hands were still warm. I'd expected to start bawling like a banshee, but nothing came. I still couldn't believe that he'd only been alive the day before and now he was gone.

Part of me felt angry with Rosie. She'd promised to make sure we would be there, and she'd failed. I could tell she was as gutted as us.

'Was he ok? Did he say anything?'

She smiled softly and shook her head. 'He didn't, but I can promise you, it was a peaceful passing. He lost a lot more phlegm after you left. It wouldn't have been a nice sight for you both. I reckon he would have wanted to spare you.'

'So, what happens now?'

'I'll call the doctor for you if you like. He'll need to confirm your dad's death, then we can call the undertakers. But...' she paused, '... just so you know, I'm not going anywhere until I am satisfied that you two are both ok. You don't have to do this alone, ok?'

'Honestly, I don't know what we would have done without you,' I said, and I meant it. She'd been priceless. I turned to Dad, whose eyes were still open.

'Look at him, never wants to miss out, nosey chuff.'

Then I closed his eyelids and gave him a kiss on the forehead for the last time.

# 174: Two Years Later

I had a day off work to catch up on some housework, but I was sitting having a coffee break and contemplating life. Since I'd started my own recovery journey, self-reflection had become a big part of my life and today I was taking stock.

Pat and I had recently bought our first house, and the kids were doing great in school. And to top it all off, I'd recently got a new job. I'd loved my time working at Kickstart. I'd had my own caseload of clients and was soon facilitating groups, but I'd found myself getting frustrated by the lack of support available for families and when a job at RODA (Relatives of Drug Abusers) had come up I'd jumped at the chance and was loving it.

Some days it was still hard to comprehend just how much my life had changed. I could never have imagined in my wildest dreams that I would be where I was now. It was a lifetime away from working the fiddle, fencing stolen goods and being admitted into hospital with drug-induced psychosis. I barely recognized myself some days.

I was so proud of myself and so grateful, not just for the life I'd built, but for the people who'd help me to get there: Michelle who'd taught me to *Feel the Fear and Do It Anyway*, Dr. Shreika and Cathy who'd seen that I had more to offer, the counselling tutor, then Leigh.

And then there was Pat (or Pat the Twat, as I'd begun referring to him). He'd been my constant. He'd seen me at my worst and still stood by me, and he continued to support me and the kids every day. He was a great stepdad, just like Ada, who was still my biggest role model. And, of course, there was Mum.

My only regret in life was that Dad wasn't in it. The kids were growing fast, and he was missing out on so much. But then I had to remind myself that Dad was Dad; there was no changing him. I gave my head a wobble and I went into the kitchen. The house wasn't going to clean itself! As I washed my coffee cup, I chuckled to myself, recalling the night I'd been to see the psychic. Everything he'd said had eventually come true. It was Pat and not Paul that I'd committed to that February when Pat had returned from India. I could still remember the words that he'd said: *'I can see you now, walking tall and proud, proud of all you have achieved. You are destined for more greatness, young lady.'* He was right. I was proud. I also knew that I would never feel the need to see another psychic to predict my life going forward because, for the first time in my life, I knew that whatever life threw at me, I would be okay.

My thoughts were interrupted by the phone in the living room, I didn't recognise the number but answered it anyway.

Hiya shugs, how are you doing?'

# Epilogue

This isn't the end of the story; it's just the beginning.

With Dad now gone, all that remains are memories. One photo of us together, me perched on his shoulders, graces the cover of this book. I still have his dodgy Deidre Barlow reading glasses, his battered wallet holding a receipt for non-alcoholic lager, a memento of one of his many attempts to stray from the top shelf, and his death certificate, where the cause reads "alcohol". The doctor gave us options. Technically, it was pneumonia that finished him off. But we knew it was the alcohol that killed him.

I wrote this story because I didn't want my dad to become just another statistic. His death deserved acknowledgement, not silence. I didn't want others to suffer quietly, as we did for years. Addiction is complex. It touches everyone differently. My father's and my own lived experiences are just two among millions, some more devastating, others more invisible. But addiction isn't a competition. We all navigate trauma in our own way, with the emotional tools we have at the time.

For me, this is just another chapter in a journey that continues to unfold.

Over the years, I've been nominated for local, national, and international awards. I've travelled to Russia, Norway, Valencia, and most recently, to the United Nations in Vienna. These journeys allowed me to speak about my work, share my story, and uplift the voices of those so often unheard.

My career has grown in ways I never imagined. The impostor syndrome that once clung to me, and at times was loud and relentless, is slowly loosening its grip. I'm still far from perfect. I wrestle with self-doubt, second-guessing, and limiting beliefs that haven't yet unravelled. But I'm learning.

I've also come to understand this: I wouldn't be here if it weren't for the people who saw something in me that I couldn't see in myself. Something called potential. Their belief gave me the courage to step beyond my comfort zone, push through fear, and lean into growth; I am eternally grateful.

For years, I worked relentlessly to prove my worth to myself and the world. I rebuilt my life piece by piece. On the surface, I became the success story – the girl who had done well. And yet... inside, I still carried the labels—the doubt, the quiet voice of impostor syndrome whispering, *'You're not enough.'* Something still felt missing.

Then I found writing.

Before I began this memoir, I had no idea how transformative telling my story would be. Writing didn't just help me process my journey – it helped me own it. There's a difference between finding your voice and truly claiming it.

Through words, I discovered that I am not just the sum of my past or the labels assigned to me. I am so much more.

Writing this memoir hasn't been easy. I wanted to throw in the towel countless times over the past five years. But I'm so glad I didn't. Because this book didn't just tell my story, it steered my destiny in a new direction. And for the first time in a long time, I know I'm exactly where I'm meant to be.

For years, I lived in a space of gender neutrality, never truly considering the differences between myself and my male counterparts. Then came an invitation to contribute to an international PhD research project led by the incredibly talented Mulka Nisic. Working alongside her and a powerful circle of women in recovery cracked something open in me. I found connection, clarity, and, more importantly, purpose.

Through that work, I discovered my new vocation: helping women dig deep to uncover their own hidden talents – buried beneath shame, silence, and circumstance. I want to use my experience to help them realise they are so much more than the sum of their past or the labels imposed upon them.

I believe that we all have doors waiting to be opened. And behind those doors is a space that belongs entirely to you – a space where you can reclaim your own authentic voice. Writing can be your key.

If anything you've read resonates, or if you'd like to stay in touch and join me on the next chapter of this journey, you can find me at www.haveawordwithyourself.co.uk.

Let's keep the conversation going.

With love, Tracey.

#UnapologeticWriter

# Acknowledgements – Personal

I'm not gonna lie, writing this book hasn't been easy. There were countless moments when I wanted to give up, throw in the towel, and walk away. Truth be told, I probably would have, if not for the unwavering support of the people around me.

This wasn't just my story to tell. I'm the one who chose to dig into the past and rake through some of the mess, but others, like **Mum, Ada,** my sister **Sarah,** and my little brother Mark, who didn't make that choice, still have stories tightly interwoven with mine. They carry their own untold histories. Thank you for standing by me, reading my truth, validating my experiences, and blessing this journey with your support.

To my two amazing daughters, **Danielle** and **Lauren**—you are my heartbeat. Strong women with blended families of your own, you carry forward the love, the lessons, and the legacy. I like to think that between the three of us, we've managed to nudge generational patterns just enough to shift the story.

**Pat the Twat**, I won't say much, because you already know. Thank you for seeing me, believing in me, keeping me grounded, and teaching me to blow my own trumpet, even when I thought I'd lost the tune.

To **Uncle Mick Ford,** all Dad's siblings, and not forgetting all my cousins on the Ford side of the family. How can cousins who barely saw each other growing up be even closer as adults? I reckon it's because we all know what having a Ford as parents feels like.

To **Tracey Andrews** – thank you for seeing beyond the labels, the chaos, and the reputation. You loved my dad warts and all and, in a world, quick to judge, you chose to understand. That kind of love leaves a mark, and I'll never forget it.

To **Nicola Cherry**, who is no longer with us, though I think she's sitting with Dad right now, taking the piss out of both of us, both down here. Knowing I had the blessing and support of your twin, **Keely Cherry,** and your daughters means the world. Nic was a remarkable human, like Dad and like so many others. She lost her way. She may be gone, but she will never be forgotten.

To **Shauna Miller**, my lifetime bestie. You held the mirror up when I couldn't face it and reminded me who I was when I'd forgotten my worth. I will always love you for that.

To **Kate Mitchell,** thank you for reminding me that my story mattered and encouraging me to trust my voice, seek guidance, and keep going. Your belief gave me the courage to finish.

To **Beverley Ward**, my writing fairy godmother, and all the fantastic people I have met from Sheffield Writers Workshop.

Beverley, I knew when I heard your voice on BBC Radio Sheffield years ago that you were someone I could trust with my story. I didn't know then how our bond would deepen beyond trust. You've been my coach, my mentor, my rock, the one who's walked beside me through six long years of self-discovery and fear, all while juggling your own life, a business, your writing, and single parenthood. I tip my hat to you. You're an extraordinary human being, and I can say, hand on heart, I wouldn't be writing these words today without you.

To **Anne Grange** for helping to format and publish the book, your patience knows no bounds. Thank you for working your magic and incorporating ideas that brought this book to life.

# Acknowledgments – Editorial

This memoir has been over six years in the making. But what's moved me most isn't just seeing the pages come to life, it's the extraordinary people I've met along the way. I'm especially grateful to those who took the time to read, reflect, and offer editorial reviews. Your words didn't just shape the manuscript; they reminded me why I wrote it in the first place.

To **Professor David Best**. Your foreword honours the heart of this story. Your leadership in recovery research across the UK, US, and Australia is matched only by your humanity. I'm proud to have your voice open this book and even prouder to know you.

To **Professor Ed Day**. The government didn't appoint you for no reason. What you've done to elevate the voice of Lived Experience Recovery Organisations (LEROs), including my own, is nothing short of transformative.

To **Dr. David Patton**, your belief in the power of storytelling to disrupt, heal, and transform has helped me stay the course. Thank you for your unwavering support and for reminding me that lived experience is not a footnote.

To **Mulka Nisic** for your thoughtful editorial eye, your kind words, and above all, your friendship. You've been a quiet current beneath this work, steady and sure, believing in its truth even when I faltered. You didn't just edit, you held space.

To **Tracey McFall,** Scottish Recovery Consortium for your fierce advocacy, brilliance, and the friendship that's bloomed since our paths first crossed.

Together, you have both helped shape a conversation that refuses to be silenced – one rooted in justice, compassion, and the power of women's voices making sure gendered recovery is no longer an afterthought.

To the **World Federation Against Drugs Global Gender Committee** – thank you for raising the profile of gendered recovery in ways that actually mean something. To **Chantel Lincoln** and **Cressida de Witte**, your support and solidarity have echoed far beyond policy papers.

To **Magdalena Boo**, your support at the start of my career still means the world. You never judged, just listened, encouraged, and believed in me when I couldn't. That kind of grace doesn't come with a job title.

To **Professor Richard Velleman**, your commitment to families affected by addiction has shaped my own journey. Your review, and your work through AFINet and Sangath, are a gift to this field and to me.

To **Mike Ward**, thank you for your tireless work around ARBD and for shining a light on the realities faced by drinkers and their families. Your advocacy is vital *and* long overdue.

To **Thomas Delaney**, keep doing what you're doing, and never stop speaking your truth. Your voice matters, and the world needs more of it.

Each of you has contributed something special to this journey. I am deeply grateful for your words, your work, and your wisdom as I take this next step. Thank you for lending your voice to mine and for helping me make sure it was heard.

Finally, **Sheffield's ever-growing Recovery Community**, you are the heartbeat of this city. You are the pulse that keeps this city alive with hope and grit. Every day, you demonstrate that recovery isn't just personal but collective. It's found in shared stories, cups of tea, belly laughs, and the quiet courage of repeatedly showing up.

You've taught me that recovery isn't about perfection but connection, compassion, and refusing to give up. I hope this book carries your spirit. You might recognise some of your voices echoing through its pages.

You remind me why I do this work, why I tell these stories, why I keep pushing. You don't just inspire resilience you fucking *embody* it. Whatever comes next, I'll keep walking beside you, proud to be part of this fierce, beautiful community.

# Sources of Support/Advice

If you ever find yourself affected by addiction, my first bit of advice would be to educate yourself. That way, you can navigate the best solutions for you, and without it, it would be like trying to assemble a puzzle without the picture on the box—you fumble through the pieces, unsure of where they fit, and if you are anything like me, you don't have the time to fumble.

**Talk to Frank** (not my dad, of course!) offers valuable facts about drugs, helping you make sense of the bigger picture. You can also enter your postcode to find commissioned services available in your local area, www.talktofrank.com, which also has a helpline: 0300 1236600.

**Recovery Answers** – a useful site to understand the science behind addiction and recovery in a user-friendly way. www.recoveryanswers.org/recovery-101/

**Drugs and me** - gives details on the effects of substances (including alcohol) and how to prevent harm. www.drugsand.me/drugs/

My next advice is to also reach out to people with professional and personal experience supporting individuals in your position.

**ADFAM** – provide advice and support, whether that be children, parents, friends, partners, siblings, or grandparents affected by someone else's drinking or drug use. www.adfam.org.uk

**NACOA** Support – Providing information, advice and support for everyone affected by a parent's drinking (including adult children) www.nacoa.org.uk and offers a FREE Helpline 0800 358 3456.

**Soberistas** is a web-based community and resource that is particularly aimed at women.
https://soberistas.com/home

**Find your tribe – peer support.**
12-Step Fellowships, whatever your view of them. AA, NA, and CA websites offer many resources, and meetings provide easy ways to connect with others who can offer support. SMART Recovery https://smartrecovery.org.uk/

As I write this, a recovery movement is gathering pace across the UK, with Live Experience Recovery Organisations, known as LEROS, popping up nationwide. LEROS groups/organisations that people with lived experience have created, to find out what's in your area or if you want to create something of your own, go to www.clero.co.uk.

**Inclusive Recovery Cities** – Sheffield is actively involved in this initiative, working to create compassionate spaces for recovery. It's part of a national movement being spearheaded by Dr David Best, you can learn more about what is happening locally and nationally.
www.sheffieldrecoverydirectory.co.uk

**Alcohol Concern & Blue Light Approach** – This initiative focuses on supporting drinkers who struggle to engage with traditional treatment services. For more details, visit www.alcoholchange.org.uk.

**Alcohol Related Brain Damage (**ARBD) – is a network to raise awareness of alcohol related brain damage www.arbd.net.

Printed in Dunstable, United Kingdom

67313677R00323